CHINA'S
CHANGING
POLITICAL
LANDSCAPE

CHINA'S CHANGING POLITICAL LANDSCAPE

Prospects for Democracy

CHENG LI
editor

BROOKINGS INSTITUTION PRESS
Washington, D.C.

Library of Congress Cataloging-in-Publication data
China's changing political landscape : prospects for democracy / Cheng Li, editor.
    p.   cm.
  Includes bibliographical references and index.
  Summary: "Leading experts examine the prospects for democracy in the world's most
populous nation and break down a number of issues in Chinese domestic politics,
including changing leadership dynamics, the rise of business elites, increased demand for
the rule of law, and shifting civil-military relations"—Provided by publisher.
  ISBN 978-0-8157-5209-7 (pbk. : alk. paper)
  1. Democracy—China. 2. China—Politics and government—2002– 3. China—
Economic conditions—2000– I. Li, Cheng, 1956–
  JQ1516.C45265 2008
  320.951—dc22   2007050245

9 8 7 6 5 4 3 2 1

The paper used in this publication meets minimum requirements of the
American National Standard for Information Sciences—Permanence of Paper for
Printed Library Materials: ANSI Z39.48-1992.

Typeset in Adobe Garamond

Composition by Peter Lindeman
Arlington, Virginia

Printed by R. R. Donnelley
Harrisonburg, Virginia

Contents

Foreword   vii
John L. Thornton

Acknowledgments   xi

1   Introduction: Assessing China's Political Development   1
Cheng Li

PART I. CHINESE DISCOURSE ABOUT DEMOCRACY

2   China's Political Trajectory: What Are the Chinese Saying?   25
Andrew J. Nathan

3   Ideological Change and Incremental Democracy in   44
Reform-Era China
Yu Keping

PART II. INSTITUTIONAL DEVELOPMENT AND GENERATIONAL CHANGE

4   Institutionalization and the Changing Dynamics of   61
Chinese Leadership Politics
Alice L. Miller

5   Institutionalization of Political Succession in China: 80
Progress and Implications
Jing Huang

6   Will China's "Lost Generation" Find a Path to Democracy?   98
Cheng Li

PART III. ECONOMIC ACTORS AND ECONOMIC POLICY

7   Business Interest Groups in Chinese Politics: 121
    The Case of the Oil Companies
    Erica S. Downs

8   China's Left Tilt: Pendulum Swing or Midcourse Correction?   142
    Barry Naughton

PART IV. AGENTS OF CHANGE: MEDIA, LAW, AND CIVIL SOCIETY

9   Political Implications of China's Information Revolution: 161
    The Media, the Minders, and Their Message
    Richard Baum

10 Legalization without Democratization in China under Hu Jintao   185
    Jacques deLisle

11 Staying in Power: What Does the Chinese Communist   212
    Party Have to Do?
    Joseph Fewsmith

PART V. FORCES FOR AND AGAINST DEMOCRACY IN CHINA

12 Fighting Corruption: A Difficult Challenge for Chinese Leaders   229
    Minxin Pei

13 The Political Implications of China's Social Future: 251
    Complacency, Scorn, and the Forlorn
    Dorothy J. Solinger

14 Straining against the Yoke? Civil-Military Relations in   267
    China after the Seventeenth Party Congress
    James Mulvenon

PART VI. EXTERNAL MODELS AND CHINA'S FUTURE

15 Learning from Abroad to Reinvent Itself: External   283
    Influences on Internal CCP Reforms
    David Shambaugh

16 Taiwan and China's Democratic Future: 302
    Can the Tail Wag the Dog?
    Chu Yun-han

Contributors   323

Index   331

Foreword

Thirty years ago Deng Xiaoping launched his policy of "Reform and Opening." In time, his decision would transform China economically, socially, legally, ideologically, and politically, no less than Mao's revolution did in 1949. The changes unleashed by Deng are difficult to overstate; they did nothing less than bring China for the first time fully into the modern world. The result is the nation of today's headlines: the third largest economy in the world; a land of 200 million Internet users and 500 million cell phones; a significant actor in some of the most pressing international concerns (North Korea, Iran, Africa); and one of the keys to whether humankind succeeds in addressing the common existential challenges of environment, energy sufficiency, and global warming. For ordinary Chinese, the impact of the changes may appear more straightforward, but they are no less fundamental. As one scholar in Beijing noted to me, "Never before in our history have as many Chinese, both in relative and absolute terms, enjoyed a better life."

Three decades of unbridled growth, however, have not come without costs or consequences. Disparities and imbalances remained unaddressed for too long and now threaten to undercut important aspects of the "better life" so hard won. China's cities choke on polluted air, hundreds of rivers and lakes either are contaminated or have run dry, and a growing gap between rich and poor calls into question the social compact in a country that is still nominally Communist.

These and other challenges have triggered a serious, ongoing re-examination in China of some of the basic tenets of the country's development model.

One of the disparities that receives the greatest scrutiny in the West—by the media, human rights groups, and the U.S. Congress, among others—is the gap between economic and political reform. Democracy in China has been slower in coming than capitalism. The Chinese Communist Party (CCP) has a monopoly on power, and the country lacks freedom of speech, an independent judiciary, and other fundamental attributes of a pluralistic liberal system. The images burned into the collective memory during the Tiananmen protests of 1989 still form the prism through which most in the West view the Chinese political system.

Yet anyone who has spent time there knows that the China of 2008 is unrecognizable from the one of 1989. China is not a democracy, to be sure, but much is taking place—in the government, the CCP, the economy, and society at large—that is changing how the Chinese think about democracy and forms of government in ways that could shape the country's political future. Bookstores in Beijing, Shanghai, and other cities now have shelves dedicated to the subject of political reform, offering books on topics such as constitutionalism, human rights, nongovernmental organizations, interest groups, civil society, the media's role in anticorruption, good governance, elections, and democratic theory and practice in China and elsewhere.

Chinese leaders these days talk about democracy with increasing frequency and detail. President Hu Jintao has called democracy "the common pursuit of mankind." In a meeting in late 2006, Premier Wen Jiabao told a delegation from Brookings (of which I was a member): "We have to move toward democracy. We have many problems, but we know the direction in which we are going." Senior officials routinely call for more democratic decisionmaking within the Communist Party itself, greater supervision by the public and media of the government's work, strengthening of the rule of law, and expanded experimentation with local elections—even while continuing to insist on the CCP's right to rule the country as a whole.

There are signs that some Chinese citizens are taking their leaders at their word and testing the limits of public participation. Last May unhappy residents in the coastal city of Xiamen launched a campaign to force the city to stop construction of a large chemical plant on the outskirts of town. Their main weapon was the cell phone. In a matter of days, hundreds of thousands of text messages opposing the plant were forwarded, spreading like a virus throughout the country. Xiamen authorities, who had ignored opposition to the plant before, announced that construction would be suspended until an environmental impact study was completed. Dissatisfied with this half measure, citizens again used message networking to organize a march of some 7,000 people demanding a permanent halt to construction. Although local party newspapers blasted the protest as illegal, it was allowed to proceed without incident, marking one of the largest peaceful demonstrations in China in recent years. In December the progressive Guangdong newspaper, *Southern Weekend*, chose the citizens of Xiamen as its Persons of the Year. In January thousands of citizens in Shanghai protesting plans to build a Maglev train line through their neighborhoods cited the Xiamen demonstrators as their inspiration.

What do such events tell us? How do we square the government's seemingly enlightened reaction in such cases to others in which dissent is still suppressed, often harshly. Clearly, an updated, more precise, and fact-based understanding is needed of where exactly the process of democratization stands in China today. The purpose of this volume is to start that effort.

Cheng Li and his fellow China scholars have produced a fresh, thought-provoking study that examines the political terrain of a rapidly changing country, identifies the most salient aspects of its political life, and synthesizes our understanding to project the most likely scenarios for China's political trajectory. In the introductory chapter, Li frames the main intellectual inquiry of the volume with an overarching question: can democracy emerge in China through incremental, systematic change? Each of the fifteen essays that follow examines this crucial theme from a distinct perspective. The result is a wide-ranging conversation about the central factors in China's political evolution, including Chinese conceptions of what democracy means; the role of ideological change; the implications of political institutionalization, especially on leadership succession; the impact of generational turnover; the influence of new forces such as business elites, the media, and social movements; transformations in center-local dynamics; the promises of a better-developed legal system; the corrosive effect of corruption; changes in civil-military relations; the impact of foreign ideas; and a comparison of democratization on the mainland with the experience of Taiwan. While the backdrop is the political evolution of the past three decades, the focus of the chapters is on the period from the Sixteenth Party Congress in 2002 up to the eve of the Seventeenth Party Congress in October 2007.

Reflecting both the complexity of the issues at hand and the frank debate we intended to foster, the contributors sometimes reach sharply different conclusions about prospects for democracy in China. Some are optimistic, seeing in emerging trends and institutional developments a potential path to democratic transformation; others are more pessimistic about the likelihood of peaceful transition or believe that incremental changes may in fact strengthen one-party rule by making the Party more resilient and adaptable.

One of the authors, Yu Keping, deserves to be singled out because, unlike the other contributors, he is not analyzing the system from the outside. As the deputy director of the Central Translation and Compilation Bureau, Professor Yu reports to the Central Committee of the CCP. He created a small sensation in China last year when his essay, "Democracy Is a Good Thing," became one of the most searched and debated items on the Chinese Internet. In that essay, Yu argued: "Among all the political systems that have been invented and implemented, democracy is the one with the least number of flaws. That is to say, relatively speaking, democracy is the best political system for humankind." His chapter in the current volume elaborates his view of the road political reform in China has taken from the start of reform and opening to the present.

Beyond stimulating scholarly discourse, the assessments presented here also hold concrete implications for governments, especially Washington. Outdated views of China's political condition and misjudgments of its intentions can only result in bad policy. A China that increasingly embraces democratic values and pluralism—and is recognized by the United States as doing so—would mitigate the ideological tensions that underlie distrust of everything from military and diplomatic intentions to investment in American firms. The dynamics of the Taiwan problem would be redefined, as would China's relationships with its Asian neighbors. China's transition to democracy is not inevitable, nor would democracy alone solve all of its problems, including friction with the West. Nonetheless, as Yu Keping's essay illustrates, a genuine and consistent progress toward democracy is recognized by increasing numbers of Chinese as their country's best hope for the future. This is a development that should give the rest of us hope as well.

JOHN L. THORNTON
Chairman of the Board of Trustees

Washington, D.C.
February 2008

Acknowledgments

This book grows out of a yearlong project studying China's political, economic, social, and military developments as they relate to the Seventeenth National Congress of the Chinese Communist Party. That research culminated in a special two-day conference held at the Brookings Institution in April 2007 bringing together fifteen prominent scholars to assess the future trajectory of China's development. The chapters included here are based in large part on the presentations made at that conference.

Thanks go first and foremost to John L. Thornton, chairman of the board of the Brookings Institution, whose vision and wisdom continually help structure the institution as a whole and the John L. Thornton China Center in particular. Without John's support, this project could never have come to life, and I particularly wish to thank him for taking time out of his busy schedule to write the foreword. I am also grateful to Strobe Talbott, president of the Brookings Institution, who has offered strong support and encouragement to the efforts of the John L. Thornton China Center. Thanks to Strobe's leadership, the China Center has gained prominence in the Washington policy scene since its launch in 2006 and has also begun to build a profile in Beijing with the opening of the Brookings-Tsinghua Center for Public Policy at the Tsinghua University School of Public Policy and Management.

A special note of appreciation goes to Brookings vice president and director of Foreign Policy Studies Carlos Pascual, whose constant backing for this project helped ensure its success. Carlos's understanding of the importance of China and its future development were reflected in his opening remarks at our April conference and were quite inspirational to all those in attendance. Carlos also generously reviewed and offered detailed comments on the manuscript for this book that led to marked improvements in the accuracy and intellectual analysis of the volume.

The director of the John L. Thornton China Center, Jeffrey A. Bader, was instrumental in conceptualizing this project and arranging the participation of top-quality scholars and experts. Jeff's extraordinary contacts in the China field, insights into Chinese domestic politics, and skills as a conference organizer were all leveraged heavily throughout the unfolding of this endeavor, and much of the success of the conference is attributable to his commitment and leadership.

We could not, of course, have completed this undertaking had it not been for the contributions of the chapter authors and conference presenters. The contributions of Richard Baum, Jacques DeLisle, Erica S. Downs, Joseph Fewsmith, Jing Huang, Alice Miller, James Mulvenon, Andrew Nathan, Barry Naughton, Minxin Pei, David Shambaugh, and Dorothy Solinger allowed us to benefit from their combined wisdom and insights. Their comprehensive research and writing shaped this final product—a volume that will continue to inform our understanding of China for years to come. A special note of thanks goes to Chu Yun-han and Yu Keping, two of our chapter authors who came from overseas to present their scholarship at our conference and whose insights expanded our perspective while deepening our understanding of how experts from the other side of the Pacific see developments inside the People's Republic of China.

My colleagues at Brookings served as moderators for the conference panels, and their valuable input stimulated intellectual debate and discussion. In addition to Jeffrey Bader, individuals at Brookings, including Chu Shulong, Wing Thye Woo, and Xiao Geng, were masterful by providing comments and structure that improved the ability of our presenters to exchange views with each other and the audience in ways that shed new light on the materials under consideration. Sidney Rittenberg, a veteran China watcher who personally knew former Chinese leaders such as Mao Zedong and Zhou Enlai, and J. Stapleton Roy, former U.S. ambassador to China, 1991–95, graced us with their experience, wisdom, and humor in a pair of inspiring and riveting keynote addresses. Our conference also greatly benefited from the participation and insightful comments of many distinguished China scholars, including David Finkelstein, Harry Harding, Nicholas Lardy, Douglas Paal, Alan Romberg, and Susan Shirk.

    This project benefited greatly from the hard work, diligence, and administrative skills of the staff of the John L. Thornton China Center, including Elizabeth Brooks, Jonathan Liu, Dewardric McNeal, and Pavneet Singh. Elizabeth got the ball rolling by helping to contact all the conference participants and make logistical arrangements. Pavneet's ability to manage calendars, tasks, and deadlines was more than matched by his ability to keep everyone light and relaxed with his upbeat personality and enthusiasm. Jon's quiet, diligent approach to his tasks meant that I never had to worry about anything slipping through the cracks. Dewardric's willingness to assist at the last minute when extra hands were needed helped to ensure that everything functioned smoothly on the day of the conference. During the conference, my colleagues and I were ably assisted by staff members of the Brookings Institution's Center for Northeast Asian Policy Studies (CNAPS), including Director Richard Bush, Assistant Director Kevin Scott, Jiyoung Song, and Sarah Thompson. The help we received from the Communications Department was crucial to the completion of this project, and I want to extend to them my heartfelt thanks.

    Scott W. Harold, research analyst at the John L. Thornton China Center, was the day-to-day manager of this project and shepherded the entire undertaking from conceptualization through completion. From drawing up lists of possible contributors to drafting invitations, managing the conference, and editing the book chapters, Scott's deep knowledge of China and passion for this endeavor inspired those of us who work with him. I am particularly grateful that Scott was able to devote so much of his energy to this project while finishing his doctoral thesis at Columbia University and teaching at Georgetown University.

    I have been fortunate to work with Christopher Kelaher, Janet Walker, and their colleagues at the Brookings Institution Press, especially Larry Converse who managed typesetting and printing, Susan Woollen who handled the cover, and Vicky Macintyre who did the copyediting of the volume. Altogether, they helped make the task of bringing to print our experts' insights far easier than I could ever have imagined. Outside Brookings, I am indebted to my friends and research assistants Sally Carman, Christina Culver, Yinsheng Li, David Sands, and Jennifer Schwartz, each of whom provided valuable proofreading, editing, fact checking, and other research support during the finalizing of the manuscript. My debt to all these individuals is acknowledged only inadequately here, but my gratitude to them is profound.

CHINA'S CHANGING POLITICAL LANDSCAPE

1

Introduction: Assessing China's Political Development

CHENG LI

> China is able to change the world because it has first changed itself.
>
> LING ZHIJUN, *China's New Revolution* (2007)

One of the world's most stunning development stories of recent decades is China's market transition and economic rise. The nation's rapid and continuing economic growth, the revival of entrepreneurialism, and the ever-growing integration with the world economy all stem from the policy of "reform and opening" adopted in 1978. The magnitude of this development is evident in the miraculous changes in China's physical landscape, from its coastal cities to its vast interior regions. A great deal has been written about this drastic transformation, not only the remarkable achievements in poverty alleviation, rural-urban migration, and foreign investment, but also the attendant devastating problems such as the growing income disparities, social dislocation, and environmental degradation.[1]

This volume focuses on changes in a different landscape: China's political terrain. For the most part, China's political development in the reform era, though intriguing and potentially consequential, has been far less fundamental or systemic than changes in the economic realm. Although a new generation of leaders that is strikingly different from its predecessors is coming to the fore at the Seventeenth Party Congress and political reforms are on the agenda of the top leadership, the Chinese Communist Party (CCP) still favors a one-party monopoly of power without an independent judicial system or free media. Human rights violations, especially in the areas of religious freedom, labor rights, and public health, remain prevalent. These facts have made most stu-

I would like to thank Sally Carman, Christina Culver, Scott Harold, and Carlos Pascual for their very helpful comments on an earlier version of this chapter.

1

dents of China skeptical about Chinese political development and the nation's prospects for democracy.

Yet it is too simplistic to think that the earthshaking socioeconomic changes of the past three decades have taken place in a political vacuum, with no corresponding changes in the Chinese political system. Some Chinese scholars would argue that China's transition from a totalitarian regime under Mao to an authoritarian system under Deng and his successors amounts to a fundamental political transformation.[2] One might also ask how it was possible for a supposedly stagnant ruling party to achieve modern China's first peaceful political succession in 2002–03. Furthermore, how has this monolithic ruling elite been able to drastically and successfully alter the course of the country's socioeconomic development from a single-minded emphasis on economic growth to a broader concern for social cohesion and a fair distribution of wealth? When Chinese leaders talk about political democracy and inner-party elections, are they simply spouting rhetoric? Or have Sinologists overlooked some potentially important trends? Will China surprise the world with a fundamental political transformation in the years to come?

Politics and economics are, of course, closely interrelated. In a study of present-day China, one cannot really separate economic reform from political change. People living in China in 1978 would not recognize the degree of civic and political freedom in the country today. New social forces unleashed by China's economic reforms have been transforming the country's political landscape. The expansion of new social and economic groups alone has been spectacular. Private firms, for example, which were not allowed until the early 1980s, numbered 4.3 million by 2006, while private entrepreneurs totaled 11 million.[3] By 2002 the country had a middle class of 80 million people whereas a decade earlier such a class barely existed.[4] According to a recent study by McKinsey & Co., by 2025 China's middle class is expected to consist of about 520 million people.[5] Rural-to-urban migration, another important force for social and political change, pushed the number of migrant workers up to 119 million in 2006, and this group continues to expand.[6] Some particularly interesting changes have occurred in leadership politics, political institutionalization, commercialization of the media, legal reform, the dynamics between central and local governments, and civilian-military relations. These developments are the subject of this volume. By way of introduction, I offer some comments on the recent discourse on democracy in China, Western theories of democracy, and the Chinese agenda for political development.

The "New Wave" of Discourse on Democracy in China

Top Chinese leaders and their advisers are remarkably candid about the fact that China's political reforms have lagged behind the country's economic and social changes. Hu Angang, the head of Qinghua University's Center for China Studies, a leading think tank in the country, argued in 2003 that the Chinese authorities should shift their principal task from the "first transition"—namely, economic transformation—to the "second transition," which should center on political reform.[7] He outlined the four main areas in need of political reform: the Chinese Communist Party, the National People's Congress (NPC), the Chinese government, and the judiciary. Hu has suggested that "democratic state-building" (*minzhu de guojia zhidu jianshe*) is essential for China as it confronts various daunting social and demographic challenges.[8]

Since 2006, Chinese intellectuals and the official media have engaged in a nationwide public discussion about democracy, something David Shambaugh has called the "democracy wave" debates.[9] This "wave" began with a well-known article entitled "Democracy Is a Good Thing" by one of this volume's contributors, Yu Keping, a professor at Beijing University and deputy director of the Translation Bureau of the CCP Central Committee. The article, which was based on an interview with Yu by the Hong Kong-based *Takung Pao* in 2005, was reprinted first in *Beijing Daily* in the fall of 2006 and since then has appeared in almost all major newspapers in the country.[10] The article concisely and thoughtfully discusses the desirability, feasibility, and identity of democracy in China. While acknowledging many of the potential problems that democracy may cause, Yu argues that China could make a transition to democracy with "minimum political and social costs."[11] Calling this approach "incremental democracy" (*jianjin minzhu*), Yu suggests that China's political reforms should be incremental over time and manageable in scale. Specifically, political reforms should place priority on inner-party democracy, grassroots village elections, and legal development. Such an approach, he believes, will ultimately result in a "democratic breakthrough" when various existing political forces are ready.

China's top leaders, including most notably President Hu Jintao and Premier Wen Jiabao, recently endorsed the idea of accelerating political reforms.[12] On many occasions, both at home and abroad, Hu and Wen have highlighted the need for democracy in China. In an interview with the *Washington Post* in November 2003, for instance, Wen Jiabao acknowledged that "without the guarantee of political reform, economic reform will not be successful."[13] Hu Jintao, too, has repeatedly said, "If there is no democracy, there will be no modernization."[14] At an important meeting of ministerial and provincial leaders at the Central Party School in June 2007, he went so far as to call for broader democratic political participation for both the public and the political establishment.[15] Clearly, the political rhetoric of Chinese leaders has changed over the past decade. The question is whether this change in rhetoric translates into new policies and behavior, and whether they in turn have the potential to transform the political system in China.[16]

Understandably, most overseas observers tend to be cynical about Chinese rhetoric on democracy. The prevailing view in the West is that Chinese leaders are not thinking of a "real democracy." This may well be the case if historical circumstances and current political conditions in China are any indication. Democratic rhetoric, certainly not lacking in China's modern history—from the Nationalists' "Three People's Principles" (*sanminzhuyi*) and the Communists' "New Democracy" (*xin minzhuzhuyi*) to Mao's "Great Democracy" (*da minzhu*)—has often invoked democracy to justify political forces whose actions and values were distinctly non- or even antidemocratic.[17] For the Chinese people, the story of democracy has been a record of failures and pitfalls far more than a record of successes and progress. At present, political power in the People's Republic of China (PRC) is monopolized by the CCP, which prohibits the formation of competing political parties. The party also exercises strict control over the content of the mass media and the Internet and has even tightened censorship since Hu Jintao became secretary general of the party in 2002. In the area of religious freedom, neither Jiang Zemin nor Hu Jintao has scored very well.

In the opinion of some China watchers, however, democracy should not be the only criterion used to measure China's political progress. According to Maurice R. Greenberg, "Every country has its own culture and comes by its political system through its own history."[18] Hence "we should stop pressing China to adopt a democratic political system—this is up to the Chinese. If it is to occur, it has to be their own choice."[19] Greenberg's emphasis on "choice" is well taken because China's political structure is unlikely to develop teleologically along a direct, linear trajectory. Many see a variety of possibilities, ranging from a highly optimistic future, in which the country will become a stable liberal democracy, to a highly pessimistic one, in which China will collapse and be left in a state of prolonged civil war, domestic chaos, environmental catastrophe, and massive human exodus.[20] Somewhere in the middle is perhaps the most widely accepted (though not necessarily the most likely) scenario that there will be a market economy combined with an authoritarian one-party political system. In this view, Chinese politics will remain by and large the same in the foreseeable future as it is today—although this combination may be far more institutionalized than at present.[21]

If decisionmakers throughout the international community, especially in the United States, are to formulate better policy options for how to deal with China, it is vital for them to be well acquainted with the political scenarios that could transpire over the next fifteen years or so. China will, of course, choose its own destiny, but the choices it makes—which will determine how Chinese politics will unfold and whether the PRC can maintain social stability—will have profound implications for the United States and the world. The political future of China is undoubtedly crucial to the Sino-American relationship, arguably the most important bilateral relationship of the twenty-first century. Hence the United States must consider how to relate to a changing China. If Washington's vision is narrow, U.S. options will be inadequate. If Washington's views of China are distorted, U.S. policies will be misguided and perhaps counterproductive. Without some insight into the direction and motivations of China's leaders and people, the United States cannot expect to conduct an effective foreign policy that advances its future interests.

Democracy: Universalism and "Chinese Characteristics"

The significance of recent political developments in China and its discourse about democracy goes beyond the policy realm. The democratization of the world's most populous nation, if it occurs, will greatly enrich theoretical understanding of the essential features and varied forms of modern democracies—some of the most important and enduring subjects of the social sciences. As Sunil Khilnani has pointed out in the context of India's political evolution since 1947, democracy is in essence "the adventure of a political idea."[22] In his view, India's transition to democracy was the "third moment in the great democratic experiment launched at the end of the eighteenth century by the American and French revolutions."[23] Khilnani explains:

> Each is an historic instance of the project to resuscitate and embody the ancient ideal of democracy under vastly different conditions. . . . Each of these experiments released immense energies; each raised towering expectations; and each has suffered tragic disappointments. The India experiment is still in its early stages, and its outcome may well turn out to be most significant of them all, partly because of its sheer human scale, and partly because of its location, a substantial bridgehead of effervescent liberty on the Asian continent.[24]

Although the motivation, condition, process, and outcome in all three of these "historic instances" were quite different, notes Khilnani, they did have one striking feature in common: a high degree of unintended consequences with fortuitous outcomes, as a result of which they all "became a democracy without really knowing how, why, or what it meant to be one," yet they felt a sense of collective democratic identity and a national pride.[25]

Observations about the paradoxical nature of democratic transitions in India and elsewhere seem to be relevant to the ongoing Chinese political experiments (such as inner-party democracy). Despite the recent wave of Chinese intellectual discourse on democracy and the top leaders' promises, the general public and political elites appear unable to reach a consensus on which direction politics in China should take. Understandably, a significant number of officials at various levels of leadership are resistant to political reforms that would subject them to greater oversight by the people, as this would likely undermine their own power and interests. In a recent survey of midlevel officials at the Central Party School, 90 percent of the respondents indicated they were not enthusiastic about political reform.[26] It seems the collective mind of the Chinese people is strongly wedded to the idea that chaos and political instability may result from a transition to democracy. Their fears are stoked by the recent financial scandals surrounding President Chen Shui-bian's family in Taiwan, political deadlock in India and other democratic countries, and the phenomenal amount of money spent on political campaigns in the United States. In a country that has valued meritocracy and the *selection* of bureaucrats for many centuries, the general public may be suspicious about, and impatient with, *elected* politicians. Thus to many observers, it seems incomprehensible that China might be genuinely interested in democratic reform, even though—ironically—it is those very bureaucrats, along with the Chinese Communist Party, that have led China to embrace a market economy and capitalism.

At the same time, one cannot discount the possibility that the CCP may, in fact, be serious about pursuing political reform because circumstances are moving it in that direction. Such circumstances might include a sharp decline in the legitimacy of one-party rule, the petering out of strongman politics, or the emergence of diverse and conflicting interests within the political elite. Other forces that would seem to augur well for democratization and transparency are growing public awareness of the rights and interests of citizens, the diffusion of international norms and democratic values, rising demands for freedom of the press, and commercialization of the media. A desire to improve the country's international image, to build its national reputation and pride, and to win the hearts and minds of the Taiwanese people could also press Chinese leaders to pursue political reform and democratization.

Some would argue, however, that China's political development will be influenced mainly by cultural prerequisites and historical experiences. Proponents of this view tend to overlook the fact that Chinese leaders and public intellectuals have become increasingly interested in and willing to accept international norms in recent years. Since the mid-1990s, Chinese scholars have been exploring the general characteristics of Western democratic theories and ideas, and official publishing houses affiliated with the Central Party School, the Translation Bureau of the CCP Central Committee, and the Chinese Academy of Social

Sciences, as well as many university presses, have translated and published numerous books by Western scholars on democracy, civil society, law, media, and interest groups.[27]

Such publications on the theory and practice of liberal democracy in other states are enormously valuable to China. Yet, as has been widely observed, the enthusiasm for "democracy" displayed in certain quarters—for example, among the students and activists at Tiananmen Square in the spring of 1989—is anchored in some misconceptions about democracy in practice.[28] Some of China's dissident intellectuals define democracy in normative and utopian terms that equate it with almost all "virtues." Their perception of democracy and the desirability of a democratic transition in China is extremely "idealistic" in the sense described by the prominent theoretician Joseph Schumpeter:[29] that is, they tend to focus almost entirely on the *source* ("the will of the people") and *purpose* ("the rights of the people") of democracy, while undervaluing the importance of democratic *methods* and *procedures* (the "institutional and procedural guarantees of the people's will and rights").[30] The political demands expressed at Tiananmen Square were for the most part substantive, not structural; they were laced with emotion and delivered via petitions but made no specific mention of broad elections. Not surprisingly, constitution makers were scarce in Beijing in 1989.[31] In the past fifteen years, however, Chinese discourse on democracy has changed profoundly, and today much of it focuses on institutional and procedural matters.

If Western scholars hope to assess the prospects for democratization in China, they obviously need to understand the Chinese view of democracy, as well as the political agenda of Chinese leaders. Otherwise it may be well-nigh impossible to grasp the implications of specific political developments, or to distinguish between universal components of democratic systems and unique Chinese innovations. As Chinese scholars, practitioners, and state officials search for the lessons of democratic transition, consolidation, and good governance from around the world, their endeavors can serve as a case study in how democratic concepts translate into practice in the world's most populous country.

At this juncture, a few words are in order about those concepts. To begin with, it is important to remember that democratic political institutions vary greatly from place to place and across time. In a way, democracy is a continuous historical process and a matter of degree. It also has three distinctive traits, all interrelated.

First, a polity's institutions must offer genuine political choices, and such choices must be made available to a broadly defined electorate. In practice, this means that elections are regular and fair, that all the votes of all adult citizens are equal in weight, and that competition for political office is institutionalized through a multiparty system and real choice among candidates. According to

E. E. Schattschneider, democracy is a competitive political system in which competing leaders and organizations define public policy alternatives in such a way that the public can participate in the decisionmaking process through the ballot box.[32] As Robert Dahl observes, Western democracy evolved from a political system dominated by one coherent set of leaders to a pluralist system run by many sets of leaders, each having access to a different combination of political resources.[33] In this sense, democracy is a matter of establishing institutions and rules for mediating conflicting interests among social groups in a given society.

Second, institutions must be based on a respect for the law and an ability to administer a genuine rule-of-law system. Under such a system, rule achieved through power and privilege would be drastically reduced, and the legal system (including the courts, police, procuratorate, and penal system) revamped to ensure that the people are governed by laws, and that government itself is ruled by, and subject to, the law. This democratic principle is rooted in two basic assumptions about social order. The first is that all individuals are equal before the law. As Dahl argues, democracy is based on the consensus that human beings possess a fundamental sense of right and wrong that is not significantly stronger in some groups than in others.[34] The second assumption is that all human beings "are imperfect, all are prejudiced, and none knows the whole truth," and therefore none can be above the law.[35] For these reasons, democracy requires the rule of law.

Third, institutions must permit the kind of freedom (civil liberties, freedom of the press) that enables the public to participate in the political process. Democratic institutions should respect political diversity in terms of values and attitudes, protect the interests of minority groups, and stress institutional means of solving socioeconomic problems. Government accountability should be monitored through various nongovernmental channels. It is also crucial to set up checks and balances among branches of government and across levels of government.

By these criteria, China has a long way to go before its institutions will qualify as democratic structures. Indeed, no one should expect China to develop a multiparty system in the near future. But this should not obscure the significant changes that have taken place both in the leadership's perceptions about the desirability of democracy and in the Chinese political system itself. One important trend is that many Chinese leaders and public intellectuals now talk about democracy, rule of law, governmental transparency and accountability, and human rights as being universal values; perhaps more important, they also treat these as Chinese goals. While some Chinese leaders and scholars may still be obsessed with "Chinese characteristics," others unambiguously favor defining democracy along universal lines (*pushi jiazhi*). For example, when Yu Keping writes "democracy is a good thing," he is not referring to Western-style democracy or to Chinese democracy, but simply democracy in a universal sense.

On a number of occasions, Premier Wen Jiabao has, in fact, emphasized the universal value of democracy. In a meeting with a delegation from the Brookings Institution in Beijing in October 2006, in which he carefully explained China's objectives for political democracy, Wen's idea of democracy was much the same as the Western concept: "When we talk about democracy, we usually refer to the three most important components: elections, judicial independence, and supervision based on checks and balances."[36] These are exactly the same three conceptual components just discussed.

In explaining the current Chinese mix of direct and indirect elections, Wen noted that direct elections are used for choosing village heads and that in the past few years the number of villages implementing these elections has risen to 680,000. Direct elections have also been used to fill seats in the local people's congresses at the township and county levels. Indirect elections are the means of selecting the members of people's congresses at the city level and above, as well as government leaders at the county, city, and higher levels. In addition, indirect elections are employed to fill posts within the party leadership at various levels. The number of candidates on the ballot for both direct and indirect elections is increasing, Wen said, adding that he could foresee a day when direct elections, if shown to be successful, might gradually be expanded, "moving up the ladder from the villages to towns to counties to provinces. Indirect elections will be improved further with increased competition."

The judicial system, Wen emphasized, was also in urgent need of reform in order to "ensure its dignity, justice, and independence." The legal system, he noted, has already undergone "comprehensive" changes: the newly established death penalty review system, for example, specifies that all death penalty cases should be subject to final approval by the Supreme People's Court.

He further explained that the function of "supervision" (*jiandu*) in the Chinese system is to restrain official power through oversight by the media and other civic channels. "Absolute power without supervision corrupts absolutely," Wen said, paraphrasing a well-known Western concept to affirm a similar Chinese view of power and its possible abuse. Wen called for checks and balances within the party and said officials need to be more accountable to the people. He felt both the media and the more than 110 million Internet users in China could participate in this supervision. All in all, Wen concluded unambiguously, China has to "move toward democracy. We have many problems, but we know the direction in which we are going."

Although Wen did not offer a timetable for further developments in these areas, he clearly outlined the party's plan for future political reforms. This was no idle promise, inasmuch as China has already launched some important experiments in these areas, with potentially far-reaching implications. By way of example, village elections are being better judged, not by how many party-nominated candidates win or lose, but by their utility in serving as a democratic training ground for 69 percent of China's total population, which includes many who live in less-developed areas, most of whom have poor to nonexistent educational backgrounds. The fact that these villagers can participate in the election process should boost the national confidence in China's capacity to hold democratic elections.

This does not necessarily mean that such elections always provide rural dwellers with real, substantive choices that can affect the quality of village governance. However, grassroots elections and political competition, in the form of inner-party democracy, are by no means insignificant developments. It remains to be seen whether the CCP will introduce multicandidate elections into the selection of Politburo members—including possible successors to Hu Jintao, Wen Jiabao, and other top leaders—any time in the near future. If that does happen, the rules of Chinese elite politics will change fundamentally. The practice of inner-party democracy will likely make political lobbying more transparent, factional politics more legitimate, and elections more genuine and regular at higher levels of political power.

To complicate matters, the Chinese leadership's position on the rule of law and judicial independence has been inconsistent. On one major occasion, Hu Jintao called the constitution "the fundamental law of the country," urging all government agencies, political parties, armed forces, business firms, and social groups to safeguard the dignity of the constitution and ensure its implementation.[37] Yet on most other occasions, Hu has stated that the party has ultimate authority over the military, the selection of government officials, the judiciary, and the media.[38] In reality, China has a constitution (*xianfa*), but no real constitutionalism (*xianzheng*). Note, however, that the PRC has, in fact, tried to establish a legal system from scratch during the reform era. In the past two decades, China has issued 245 new laws, about 1,000 new administrative laws, and some 7,000 new provincial laws.[39] The number of lawyers has also increased markedly, from a total of about 40,000 in the early 1990s to 110,000 by 2002, and will probably double in the next few years.[40] China today has 620 law schools and departments that produce roughly 100,000 law students a year.[41] It remains to be seen whether the rapid growth of the Chinese legal profession will help expand the rule of law in China.

From the standpoint of civil liberties and media freedom, the Chinese authorities are finding it more and more difficult to exert control over society. One sign of this is the growing number of registered nongovernmental organizations (NGOs), which according to the Ministry of Public Affairs was close to 280,000 in 2005; other estimates put the real number at as high as 3 million.[42] Chinese NGOs have been engaged in issues touching on the environment, public health, consumer rights, and the rights of what the Chinese call "vulnerable groups," including women, children, the elderly, the disabled, migrants, gays, and other groups. Another sign is the growing presence of teahouses, Internet cafes, karaoke bars, disco clubs, fan clubs, private bookstores, art galleries, fitness centers, private salons, home churches, and private theaters all over China. If one accepts Jürgen Habermas's argument that the pubs and coffeehouses of seventeenth-century London were the real force behind the formation of British civil society, the surge in places for informal association in reform China may signify the impending emergence of Chinese civil society. Equally important, both the ongoing commercialization of the media and the telecommunication revolution have made it more difficult for the government to control the flow of information. China today has some 2,700 television and radio stations that air some 3,800 programs.[43] By 2006 the number of mobile phones had reached 438 million, a penetration rate of 32.6 percent.[44] Twenty years ago there were no mobile phone networks, and the penetration rate of fixed phones was only 0.6 percent.[45] The Chinese authorities will almost certainly continue to use their resources to engage in censorship and from time to time will continue to ban select media outlets and arrest journalists. At the same time, the public's demand for civil liberties and media freedom is undeniably on the rise.

The emergence of civic institutions is a critical factor in the creation and consolidation of a viable democracy. Yet these institutions alone cannot ensure that democratic modes of governance will take root and be preserved. Forceful and determined authoritarianism may persist and surge again even in the face of widespread popular civic mobilization. Moreover, ingrained attitudes, expectations, and behaviors in the realm of human rights can be slow to change, thus providing a reservoir of authoritarian resilience ready to undermine the prospects of democratic consolidation. Despite the current budding of civic organizations, the regime has indeed sought to keep a very tight grip on social organizations for fear that they might serve as a platform for antiparty activities that would pose a threat to its power. In particular, the CCP has been extremely ruthless about suppressing incipient religious movements such as the Falun Gong and underground Christian house churches and has crushed any attempts to organize independent labor unions.

Like all nations, China has its own history, cultural values, and socioeconomic and political landscape, and it needs to choose economic and political systems that fit the particular circumstances created by its history, geography, and tradition. Yet its people and political leaders alike are beginning to take note of and even accept certain international norms and basic universal values. The Chinese are clearly engaged in an experiment of unprecedented scale in virtually all aspects of their political life. The following chapters provide detailed analyses of the dynamics of and constraints upon their quest.

Objectives and Organization of the Volume

This volume is the product of an international conference organized by the John L. Thornton China Center of the Foreign Policy Studies Program at the Brookings Institution on April 12–13, 2007. Approximately 300 people attended the conference to hear and discuss papers presented by 15 political science, history, law, and economics specialists (13 were from the United States, 1 from the PRC, and 1 from Taiwan). Offered here are all of these papers, revised to reflect insights gained in scholarly exchanges at, and after, the conference. This introductory chapter has been added to provide an overview of the central theme.

The main objective of this book is to address the overarching question of whether democracy will emerge from incremental political change in China. Obviously, each chapter can address only one or two specific aspects of China's changing political landscape. Chapter contributors have vastly different views regarding the idea of democracy in China. Some are pessimistic about the prospect of Chinese democracy, whereas others believe that incremental political changes will eventually lead to a more fundamental democratic transition. Some find the CCP's adaptability impressive, whereas others think it simply cannot handle daunting challenges such as official corruption or impending demographic shifts. This clash of ideas makes the volume especially lively and interesting. The emphasis of this book lies not in its theoretical innovations, but in the richness of its empirical evidence, the multidimensional nature of its intellectual inquiry, the diversity of methodologies employed, and most important, in the contrasting assessments of China's political future.

Chapter 2 by Andrew J. Nathan focuses on what influential political leaders and public intellectuals in China think about the country's future, especially the possibility of making a transition toward democracy—a question that this introductory chapter touches on as well. Nathan, however, is far more pessimistic about the prospects for Chinese democracy. He adopts what some Western social scientists call the "minimal definition of democracy," which requires that top power holders in a given country be elected "through open, competitive, and periodic elections." After examining the ideas and values of four major elite groups (the current leaders, up-and-coming Fifth Generation leaders, neoconservative intellectuals, and liberals in the political establishment), he concludes that none of these prominent Chinese actors really favor the adoption of democratic elections in the near or midterm future. What Chinese elites are really interested in, Nathan observes, is improving the quality of party rule so as "to make the authoritarian system more fair, more effective, and more—not less—sustainable." Therefore ongoing Chinese political experiments should not be seen as steps toward democracy, but rather as efforts to achieve what Nathan calls "resilient authoritarianism."

Like Nathan, PRC scholar Yu Keping concentrates on the ideological aspects of China's political development during the reform era. Yu's assessment in chapter 3 of recent Chinese political discourse on democracy differs markedly from Nathan's, especially with respect to how Chinese leaders and public intellectuals envision their country's political trajectory, and whether China is in the midst of an ideological transformation. Yu argues that China's reform and opening are to some extent a process in which new ideas and old ideas collide and the new ideas win out over old ones. He explains that ideas such as human rights, private property rights, the rule of law, civil society, and societal harmony (that is, class reconciliation)—most of which were considered taboo subjects as recently as one or two decades ago—have now become mainstream values in Chinese society. Yu believes that these ideological changes have both reflected and brought forth broad political transformations in state-society relations. Like Nathan, Yu believes that "democracy, no matter what form it takes, is defined by the free election of political leaders." Yet democracy cannot, and will not, be achieved in China overnight, Yu adds, since its logical path is an "incremental one," and he gives three "road maps" for implementing it in China in the near future.

Chapter 4 by Alice L. Miller and chapter 5 by Jing Huang both examine the trend toward political institutionalization. Miller reviews the tensions early on between the paramount leader's personalized power (*renzhi*) and the CCP's institutional norms and rules for collective leadership to show how two decades of institutional development have made Chinese leadership politics more stable, regular, and "on the whole, more predictable." She sees evidence of this "deliberate," "incremental," and "dynamic" institutionalization in elite promotion, retirement regulations, policy formulation, and political succession. Offering an insightful evaluation of the newly consolidated "leadership work system," she argues that China's ongoing political institutionalization has produced an increasingly consensus-oriented collective leadership.

Huang believes that "structural and behavioral change" is behind this political institutionalization. In his judgment, China's political structure has been transformed from a system of informal, hierarchical, faction-ridden, strongman-dominant politics based on personal ties to a more formal and orderly system based on a more balanced distribution of power. This new system is "secured by institutional arrangements" such as term limits, age requirements for retirement, and norms governing bureaucratic and regional representation. These institutional developments have had a profound impact on elite behavior. Reviewing the history of political succession in the PRC, Huang argues that Chinese leadership politics has moved from the zero-sum games of the past to an emerging pattern of power sharing, compromise making, and consensus building among competing factions, regions, and social groups. He closes his discussion with some predictions about upcoming changes in China's leadership structure and civil-military relations.

Chapter 6 by Cheng Li is about the so-called Fifth Generation of leaders that is poised to emerge at the Seventeenth Party Congress in October 2007 and the Eleventh National People's Congress in March 2008. This generation is composed of the age cohort born in the 1950s. Many refer to it collectively as the "lost generation" since its members were barred from formal schooling during the Cultural Revolution. Studying 103 prominent leaders in this age cohort, Li finds that the Fifth Generation differs profoundly from preceding generations of leaders in their formative experiences, educational credentials, political socialization, administrative backgrounds, foreign contacts, and worldviews. Many of these leaders were "sent-down youth" who spent years working as manual laborers in rural areas when they were teenagers. They later made remarkable "comebacks," entering college when the higher education system resumed functioning after 1978 and rapidly rebuilding their professional careers. If the Fifth Generation's collective characteristics are any indication, says Li, its members may think it is in their best interest to pursue substantial political reform, culminating in democratic elections, sometime in the next decade or so.

In a case study focusing on China's national oil companies (NOCs), chapter 7 by Erica S. Downs examines the role of state-owned enterprises in Chinese politics and the growing power of business elites. Downs sees the NOCs as an interest group in economic policy and leadership politics whose interests "do not always coincide with those of the party-state" because of their global business portfolios and profit-driven nature. Although the party-state maintains control over these companies, they "have become more autonomous and influential under the umbrella of China's rapidly expanding, increasingly market-oriented, and internationalizing energy sector." Their sense of accountability to the stockholders (as some of their subsidiaries are listed on both domestic and foreign stock exchanges) and the professionalism of their senior executives (especially those who were trained in the West) are causing NOC interests to further diverge from those of the state energy bureaucracy. In a broader context, Downs argues, these changes may pave the way for more Chinese NOC managers to enter the national leadership in the future, perhaps creating more diverse channels to political power and a more pluralistic decisionmaking process.

Barry Naughton's central concern in chapter 8 is the economic policies under Hu Jintao and Wen Jiabao. During the past few years, observes Naughton, Hu and Wen have "presided over a systematic reorientation of economic and social policy that has, in nearly every respect, shifted Chinese policy to the left." By "left," Naughton means populist policies that help to redistribute national wealth broadly, across geographical and class divisions, but, he adds, they do not imply a "rollback" or "halt" in reform. Examining major policy areas, he demonstrates that "Hu and Wen have extended government patronage to much larger groups of people than in the recent past," when Jiang Zemin was mainly interested in representing the interests of China's elites. Naughton goes on to explore what this economic policy shift indicates about China's political system and decisionmaking process. He provides three contrasting views of the political logic of this shift and in doing so shows there is no linkage between the leftward tilt and the prospects for democracy. Nevertheless, Naughton notes, the interests of large-scale social groups—whether "elite forces" or "disadvantaged social groups"—are now "routinely brought into the decisionmaking process."

Media independence, the rule of law, and civil society—often considered important forces for democratization—are discussed in chapters 9, 10, and 11, respectively. In chapter 9, Richard Baum examines the impact of the information revolution and media commercialization on politics. Recent developments in print, broadcast, and Internet-based media, says Baum, reflect growing tension between the Chinese authorities' desire to control and the public's demand for more varied sources of information. "Beneath the surface continuity of tight media censorship, intimidation of journalists, stringent regulatory barriers, and the ubiquitous 'Great Firewall,'" observes Baum, "a quiet revolution is under way." Drawing on several recent empirical cases, Baum argues that "the media are beginning to find an independent, critical voice." Looking at the changing role of the media in the broader context of ongoing legislative pressures to strengthen private property rights and the growing public demand for greater transparency in government, Baum finds that to some extent the media have become a "natural ally" of an emerging Chinese civil society. All these "peripheral" developments, Baum concludes, "cannot help but further erode the presumptive power monopoly enjoyed by the Leninist Party-state."

Chapter 10 by Jacques deLisle makes the thought-provoking and well-documented argument that the rise of law or "legalization" in reform-era China "is not meant to advance, and has not been advancing, democracy." Instead, from the perspective of the Chinese leadership, rule by law and the growth of the legal system "have substituted for democracy and postponed effective demand for democratization." This "legalization without democratization," says deLisle, may prove sustainable for a relatively long time, given that the relationship between rule of law and democracy, "while broadly positive, is not simple or linear." In view of the tension between Hu era populism and China's legal development (including constitutionalism) in recent years, he concludes that despite the political rhetoric of the new leadership, its strategy has been to consistently emphasize the substitution effects and check the mutual reinforcing effects between legalization and democratization.

In chapter 11 Joseph Fewsmith turns to the relationship between central and local governments in the context of China's growing social demands. Because of the daunting challenges that the CCP faces, Fewsmith points out, Chinese leaders often respond quickly to social demands and are particularly effective in localizing conflicts before they get out of control. Drawing on several recent comprehensive surveys by Chinese research institutes and think tanks, Fewsmith notes that most citizens are relatively satisfied with the current conditions in the country and express a "high degree of trust in the ability of the central government to manage the problems the country faces." At the same time, local officials are clearly aware that the governing capacity of the ruling party needs improvement. Fewsmith also presents some interesting case studies illustrating the growing role of NGOs, especially chambers of commerce, along with democratic consultation meetings and grassroots elections. All these innovations in governance, Fewsmith observes, aim to make local leaders more responsive to citizens' needs.

Chapter 12 by Minxin Pei focuses on the issue of corruption. Pei cannot imagine how China "could confront its multifold economic, social, and political challenges in the decade ahead without waging a more committed and successful campaign against official corruption." Despite all the recent rhetoric and efforts by the Chinese leadership to fight official graft, says Pei, all evidence suggests that corruption has not been constrained in any significant way, and he highlights several business areas and government institutions in which it appears to be worsening. Chinese leaders may call for the establishment of a modern legal system, he adds, but the judiciary remains heavily politicized. In assessing what rampant corruption means for China's future trajectory, Pei presents two intriguing scenarios. First, the CCP's need to fight corruption could persuade its leaders to expand the role of the media and civil society, as well as the autonomy of the judiciary. Alternatively, corruption could lead to the collapse of the regime. In Pei's judgment, such a regime collapse would not usher in a new era of liberalism but would be more likely to lead to the birth of a new oligarchy.

Chapter 13 by Dorothy J. Solinger offers a pessimistic view of China's political future on the basis of some broad demographic trends in China such as aging and urbanization. Solinger looks at the social groups most affected by these trends—namely, the aged, bachelors, rural-to-urban migrants, the urban poor and the jobless, the new middle class, and wealthy entrepreneurs—and makes some preliminary assessments of their political importance as well as their likely attitudes toward democracy, if it were to develop. She argues that the regime forms an "alliance with the upper strata of the population" but tries to keep those at the base "minimally satisfied but still politically excluded." The chapter concludes that elitism, not democratization, is likely to be the dominant feature of Chinese politics in the years to come.

Civil-military relations in authoritarian regimes such as China are often among the most important variables in determining the country's political trajectory. In chapter 14, James Mulvenon acknowledges the CCP civilian leadership's firm and effective control over the Chinese military but finds a new trend developing: the military is beginning to challenge the command mechanisms and foreign policy apparatus of the party-state in new and unexpected ways, stemming largely from the growing operational capabilities of the military. The post-Mao civil-military arrangements remind him of Ellis Joffe's concept of "conditional compliance." Mulvenon employs three contending hypotheses to analyze the case of the recent antisatellite missile test for an inkling of Chinese intentions and military/foreign policy decisionmaking processes, concluding that the military is unlikely to make any fundamental changes in the way it would react to a major political crisis similar to the 1989 Tiananmen incident. Indeed, it does not seem to possess a veto on crucial issues such as political succession, major shifts in socioeconomic policy, or democratic reform.

The two final chapters of the volume focus on the linkage between external models and China's political trajectory. Chapter 15 by David Shambaugh tells, in a systemic way, the story of China's broad interest in the lessons and experiences of foreign ruling parties since the Tiananmen Square crackdown and the fall of the Soviet and East European communist regimes. Shaumbaugh believes China's internal analysis of foreign political systems can shed a great deal of light on the nature and objectives of the CCP's reforms. In exploring the backgrounds and motivations of the party's ideological innovations, political adaptability, policy changes, and institutional reforms over the past two decades, he finds that one can trace many of these political developments to the CCP's "eclectic borrowing" from a wide range of communist, former communist, and noncommunist ruling parties.

In chapter 16 Chu Yun-han sets out three ambitious objectives. First, drawing on longitudinal survey data, he analyzes the almost parallel evolutionary trajectories in political values between Taiwan beginning in the early 1980s and China since the early 1990s. Second, he compares the similar political developments of these two originally Leninist regimes in terms of ideological transformation, elite recruitment, social movements, commercialization and liberalization of the media, and the development of limited competitive elections. Third, he argues that Taiwan is a good case for comparison with the mainland not only because of its "heuristic value" but also because it can be seen as "an agent of change"—"with important implications for China's political future." Chu finds that Taiwan's formula of "democratization by installment," which was favored by the Kuomintang leadership before the fundamental democratic transformations of the 1980s, is similar to the idea of "incremental democracy" that the CCP leaders have recently proposed. Yet, as Chu emphasizes, nothing is foreordained in the development of a country's political trajectory, and there is no guarantee that China will end up democratizing.

As the chapters of this volume demonstrate, China's political landscape is rapidly changing, with a wide range of possible future scenarios emerging from empirical information and theoretical analysis. At this point, it is impossible to determine what its final shape will be, yet the assessments here provide provocative ideas for both intellectual and policy debates on a subject that merits the utmost attention. Needless to say, the ramifications of political developments in China, the world's most populous country, will extend far beyond its national borders.

Notes

1. For the problems of economic disparity, social dislocation, and environmental degradation, see Wang Shaoguang and Hu Angang, *The Political Economy of Uneven Development: The Case of China* (Armonk, N.Y.: M. E. Sharpe, 1998); Dorothy J. Solinger, *Contesting Citizenship in Urban China: Peasant Migrants, the State and the Logic of the Market* (University of California Press, 1999); and Elizabeth C. Economy, *The River Runs Black: The Environmental Challenge to China's Future* (Cornell University Press, 2004).

2. He Zengke made this point in his article "Jianjin zhengzhi gaige yu minzhu zhuangxin" (Incremental political reforms and democratic transition), *Journal of the Beijing Academy of Administration*, nos. 3–4 (2004). Quoted from Liu Jie, *Zhongguo zhengzhi fazhan jincheng 2007 nian* (China's political development, 2007) (Beijing: Shishi chubenshe, 2007), p. 306.

3. Zhang Houyi, "The Status of Private Entrepreneurs in the New Century" (www.china.com.cn/info/07shxs/txt/2007-01/17/content_7667784.htm [July 15, 2007]).

4. Li Xueyi, *Dandai Zhongguo shehuijieceng yanjiu baogao* (Research report on social strata in contemporary China) (Beijing: Shehui kexuewenxian chubanshe, 2002), pp. 254–56.

5. Quoted from *Zhongguo jingying bao* (China Business Daily), July 9, 2006, p. 1. According to this McKinsey report, the proportion of Chinese urban families with an annual income of ¥25,000 or less will drop from 77 percent in 2006 to 10 percent in 2025. For a comprehensive discussion of the definition of the middle class in China, see Zhou Xiaohong and others, *Zhongguo zhongchan jieji diaocha* (A survey of the Chinese middle class) (Beijing: Shehui wenxian chubanshe, 2005).

6. This is based on data from China's Ministry of Agriculture (cnc.nfcmag.com/ReadNews-12400.html [July 15, 2007]).

7. Hu Angang, "Dierci zhuanxing: Cong jingji jianshe wei zhongxin dao zhidu jianshe wei zhongxin" (The second transition: From economic growth-centered development to the state building-centered approach). In *Dierci zhuanxing: Guojia zhidu jianshe* (The second transition: State system building), edited by Hu Angang, Wang Shaoguang, and Zhou Jianming (Beijing: Qinghua daxue chubanshe, 2003), p. 22.

8. Hu and others, eds., *Dierci zhuanxing*, pp. 378–79.

9. David Shambaugh, "Let a Thousand Democracies Bloom," *International Herald Tribune*, July 6, 2007.

10. Yu Keping, "Minzhu shige haodongxi" (Democracy is a good thing), in *Minzhu shige haodongxi* (Democracy is a good thing), edited by Yan Jian (Beijing: Shehui kexue wenxian chubanshe, 2006).

11. For a more comprehensive discussion of Yu's ideas about the democratic transition in China, see Yu Keping, *Zengliang minzhu yu shanzhi* (Incremental democracy and good governance) (Beijing: Shehui kexue wenxian chubanshe, 2003), and *Zhongguo gongmin shehui de xingqi yu zhili de bianqian* (The emergence of civil society and its significance for governance in reform China) (Beijing: Shehui kexue wenxian chubanshe, 2002).

12. For their recent speeches on this issue, see *Dang de chuangxin lilun* (Theoretical innovation of the Chinese Communist Party), 2 vols. (Beijing: Red Flag Publishing House, 2007).

13. "Text of *Washington Post* interview," in *China Daily*'s webpage (www.chinadaily.com.cn/en/doc/2003-11/24/content_284076.htm [July 14, 2007]).

14. "President Bush Meets with President Hu of the People's Republic of China," White House Press Release, April 20, 2006 (www.whitehouse.gov/news/releases/2006/04/20060420-1.html [July 14, 2007]).

15. For excerpts of Hu's speech, see www.xinhuanet.com/politics/hjt625/index.htm (July 14, 2007).

16. I am grateful to Carlos Pascual for this point.

17. This is probably not unique to China. As E. E. Schattschneider observed in the United States, people reconcile their democratic rhetoric and their undemocratic behavior by remaining comfortably unaware of the inconsistency of theory and practice. See Schattschneider, *The Semisovereign People: A Realist's View of Democracy in America* (Hinsdale, Ill.: Dryden Press, 1960).

18. Maurice R. Greenberg made this point in "Additional and Dissenting Views," in *U.S.-China Relations: An Affirmative Agenda, A Responsible Course*, edited by Carla A. Hill and Dennis C. Blair, Independent Task Force Report 59 (New York: Council on Foreign Relations, 2007), p. 101.

19. Ibid.

20. For a detailed discussion of the contrasting scenarios of the political future of China, see Cheng Li, "China in the Year 2020: Three Political Scenarios" *Asia Policy*, no. 4 (July 2007), pp. 17–29.

21. For a work that presents largely this assessment, see James Mann, *The China Fantasy: How Our Leaders Explain Away Chinese Repression* (New York: Viking, 2007).

22. Sunil Khilnani, *The Idea of India* (New York: Farrar, Strauss and Giroux, 1997), p. 4.

23. Ibid.

24. Ibid.

25. Ibid., p. 17.

26. Qing Lianbin, "Zhongyang dangxiao diaocha: Guanyuan shouci renwei zhi'an cheng zuiyanzhong shehui wenti" (Survey at the Central Party School: Officials believe for the first

time that social stability is the most serious social problem in China), *Beijing ribao* (Beijing Daily), December 18, 2006, p. 2; also the editorial, "Zhonggong ganbu moshi zhenggai zhengshi Hu-Wen tizhi de xin yinhuan" (Neglect of the need for political reforms among CCP officials is the new hidden problem for the Hu-Wen administration), *Shijie ribao* (World Journal), December 25, 2006, p. A3.

27. For lists of published books from these presses, see www.ssap.com.cn, www.dxcbs.net/index.asp, www.cctpbook.com/apply/jianjie.asp, and www.csspw.com.cn (July 14, 2007).

28. Vera Schwarz, "Memory, Commemoration, and the Plight of China's Intellectuals," *Wilson Quarterly* (August 1989), pp. 120–29.

29. Joseph Schumpeter first drew the distinction between rationalistic and idealistic definitions of democracy, on the one hand, and descriptive and procedural definitions, on the other. He preferred the latter. Schumpeter, *Capitalism, Socialism, and Democracy*, 2nd ed. (New York: Harper, 1947), p. 269.

30. Ibid. For a further discussion of Schumpeter's distinction of two democratic concepts, see Samuel P. Huntington, *The Third Wave: Democratization in the Late Twentieth Century* (University of Oklahoma Press, 1991), pp. 6–7.

31. For a more detailed discussion of the 1989 Tiananmen movement, see Cheng Li and Lynn White, "China's Technocratic Movement and the World Economic Herald," *Modern China* 17 (July 1991): 342–88.

32. Schattschneider, *The Semisovereign People*, p. xiv.

33. Robert A. Dahl, *Who Governs? Democracy and Power in an American City* (Yale University Press, 1961), p. 86.

34. Robert A. Dahl, *Democracy and Its Critics* (Yale University Press, 1989), pp. 59–60.

35. Schattschneider, *The Semisovereign People*, p. xiv.

36. This discussion of Wen's meeting with the Brookings Institution delegation is based on John L. Thornton, "Assessing the Next Phase of a Rising China," memo, December 2006; "Riding the Dragon: Brookings Launches New Center with a Journey across China," November 2007; and my own notes.

37. Xinhua News Agency, December 5, 2002 (www.china.org.cn/english/2002/Dec/50396.htm).

38. Liu Junning, "Zhongguo zhengzhi tizhi gaige: Dangnei minzhu yihuo xianzheng minzhu" (China's political reform: Intra-party democracy or constitutional democracy?) (http://forum.chinesenewsnet.com [December 5, 2005]).

39. This is based on an interview with Jiang Enzhu, chairman of the Foreign Affairs Committee of the National People's Congress, June 25, 2007.

40. Jean-Pierre Cabestan, "Zhongguo de sifa gaige" (China's Judicial Reform) (news.bbc.co.uk/hi/chinese/china_news/newsid_2149000/21492061.stm [July 27, 2002]).

41. Jerome Cohen, "Can, and Should, the Rule of Law be Transplanted outside the West?" paper presented at the Annual Meeting of the Association of American Law Schools, Washington, D.C., January 4, 2007.

42. See www.sachina.edu.cn/htmldata/news/2005/12/656.html.

43. This is based on an interview with Tian Jin, vice minister of the State Administration of Radio, Film, and Television, June 26, 2007.

44. See the monthly statistical report of the Ministry of the Information Industry of the People's Republic of China (www.mii.gov.cn), September 21, 2006.

45. The penetration rate of 0.6 per 100 people refers to the year 1985. See Zheng Qibao, ed., *Cong longduan dao jingzheng: Dianxin hangye guizhi lilun yu shizheng yanjiu* (From monopoly to competition: Empirical study and theoretical discussion of the telecommunications industry) (Beijing: Post and Telecom Press, 2005), p. 344.

Part I

*Chinese Discourse
about Democracy*

2

China's Political Trajectory: What Are the Chinese Saying?

ANDREW J. NATHAN

China should take its own path in enhancing democracy. We never view socialism and democracy as . . . mutually exclusive.

WEN JIABAO, "Our Historical Tasks at the Primary Stage of Socialism . . ." (2007)

Scholarly debate about China's probable political trajectory has focused chiefly on social science theories about the impact of social and economic change on future regimes. The central concern has been to identify the political effects of such trends as the expansion of the middle class, increased personal mobility, diversification of social interests, the apparent increase in corruption, the intensification of environmental problems, the rising rate of land seizures, the growing income gap, the spread of the Internet, the new rights consciousness, and the emergence of registered and unregistered citizen groups. Analysts have asked whether these social and economic changes are leading the country toward collapse, democratization, or what I have called "resilient authoritarianism." A second concern of analysis has been to assess the way the regime itself is evolving. Do more institutionalized succession procedures, more assertive legislative organs, and more active courts and administrative appeal procedures point the regime toward democratization or toward continued authoritarianism? Although the situation can always change, I have argued that so far the regime has retained its grip on power, responded agilely to policy challenges, and continues to command a high level of public support, all without democratization.[1]

On the assumption that "ideas matter," this chapter opens a third, somewhat neglected line of analysis, concerning what influential actors and intellectuals in China think about the country's future. The reasoning behind this assumption is that actors act, they do so with intentions, and their acts are shaped by their intentions.[2] This does not imply that the actors can either control or foretell the future, or that the analyst must deny the contingent nature of events or the fact that surprising things happen in history. It simply means that influential Chinese are thinking intelligently about their country's future and have some insight into and influence over it—modest assumptions that justify at least a look at what they are saying.

But which actors' ideas are worth looking at? A commonsense first step is to look at the ideas of the kinds of people with the most influence and biggest audiences today. The chapter focuses on four such groups: the current leaders, up-and-coming Fifth Generation leaders, so-called neoconservative intellectuals, and liberal thinkers who are more or less "inside the system." Each group is internally diverse, but on a big subject like China's trajectory, the members exhibit some orientations in common that can be explored by looking at exemplary figures.

This focus ignores, for the time being, the ideas of dissidents who are living in prison or in exile, rights-protection (*weiquan*) activists who are struggling to be heard, and civil society activists and ordinary citizens who do not have access to large audiences. Admittedly, it also suffers from a degree of circularity: those with the most influence in the current order may be least likely to think beyond its boundaries. Yet one should not assume without investigation that all the views within the establishment are pro status quo. Indeed, Bruce Gilley and John Thornton, among others, think that some top party leaders want to democratize the regime, and in the following sections I show that the regime's supporters are sometimes critical of its performance.[3] In short, what top leaders and intellectuals think is a valid subject of analysis. Here, however, I have space to look at only a few examples in each group.

How can one discern what people think? The task is perhaps more daunting in China than elsewhere since many actors have incentives to disguise what they believe. Aspirants for leadership positions, for example, try to align themselves with current leaders, and established intellectuals often avoid crossing state-security redlines. There is no foolproof methodology for reading the minds even of people who write a lot. But close contextual reading is one of the oldest, best-established methods in the social sciences generally, and (in the form of "Pekingology") in China studies in particular. Certainly, something can be learned by attending carefully to what people say.

A final point in preface: "democracy" is a word with many meanings, none of which takes precedence over any other. In the context of the American debate over China's trajectory, it is essential to clarify how the "d" word is being used by each speaker and whether Chinese mean the same thing by it as Americans do. Whether Chinese want to *call* their regime democratic is not what the American debate over China's trajectory is about: obviously, many Chinese use the word to describe their political system today and where it is heading.[4] The issue, rather, is whether China should have, wants to have, or is going to be forced by history to have a political system in which positions of top power are obtained through open, competitive, periodic elections.

Electing top powerholders through competitive elections is the so-called minimal definition of democracy and is widely accepted as a useful definition of the term by Western social scientists.[5] It is therefore what is implied, on my reading, when Americans discuss whether or not China is going to become democratic. Adjectives commonly used to qualify this type of democracy are "liberal," "pluralist," or "Western-style," but these terms are misleading if taken to imply specific institutional configurations, so I avoid them here. The other word I will use, "authoritarianism," is generally defined in the social science literature as a political system lacking in competitive elections for the top power positions—in other words, as any political system that is not democratic. This constitutes a broad category composed of numerous subtypes ("totalitarian," "post-totalitarian," "consultative," "fragmented," "soft," and so on). To call the Chinese regime authoritarian is not to say that it has not changed, since there are many different kinds of authoritarianism. I mention these definitions to promote clarity in the analysis and not to smuggle in normative arguments, which can be pursued in other venues.

More precisely, then, this chapter explores whether influential actors and thinkers in China want their country to have periodic open elections for top positions of power in the foreseeable future. A major finding is that the political reforms being proposed for the near- and midterm futures by all four groups would undergird or strengthen authoritarian rather than democratic aspects of the Chinese political system.

What the Current Leaders Think

In an October 2006 conversation with John Thornton, China's premier, Wen Jiabao, reportedly said: "We have to move toward democracy. We have many problems, but we know the direction in which we are going."[6] Was Wen signaling a new direction in Chinese political reform? He mentioned three aspects of democracy: "elections, judicial independence, and supervision based on checks and balances." As Wen's explanation of these three concepts made clear, however, he was not thinking of democracy in the sense defined in the preceding section. The elections he envisioned, the kind already taking place at the village level, are not open to all contenders but are controlled by the Chinese Communist Party (CCP). Although Wen said elections would "gradually" move up the hierarchy to the townships, counties, and perhaps even provinces, he did not indicate they would ever take place at the central level, where ultimate decision-making power is held. Nor did he specify which township, county, and provincial offices might eventually be open to election; the village election precedent suggests that there would be universal suffrage elections for seats in people's congresses, or conceivably government administrative offices, but not for the posts of local CCP secretaries, who are the real powerholders. As for judicial independence, this is already written into the Chinese constitution and is understood in Chinese legal philosophy to be consistent with party control of the courts.[7] Wen said checks and balances would be "within the party itself," with some occurring "as appropriate" in the media and Internet in supervising the government. These are actually old CCP ideas: except during the Cultural Revolution, the party has always maintained organs for internal supervision, such as discipline inspection commissions, and has always tasked the party-controlled media with exposing wrongdoing among lower-level officials.[8]

What Wen told Thornton appears consistent with what he wrote on the subject of democracy in a subsequent *People's Daily* article that was widely interpreted as a definitive rejection of faster political reform:

> China should take its own path in enhancing democracy. We never view socialism and democracy as . . . mutually exclusive. As a matter of fact, we see a high degree of democracy and [a] well-developed legal system as the inherent requirement of socialism and a key important feature of a mature socialist system. We are fully capable of building China into a country of democracy and rule of law under socialist conditions. We should explore ways to develop democracy with Chinese characteristics in light of China's particular conditions. We should focus on efforts to promote economic development, protect lawful rights and interests of the people, fight corruption, increase public trust in government, strengthen government functions and enhance social harmony.[9]

Wen's ideas may be excellent, but they are neither new in CCP history nor do they point toward open, competitive elections for national leaders.

The same can be said of the ideas of General Secretary Hu Jintao. Although his comments on democracy usually stick to a very high level of generality, in one of his more specific elaborations, Hu cited developing democracy as one of ten tasks involved in building a harmonious society. He put it on a par with maintaining rapid economic development, protecting the environment, and ensuring social stability, among other things. The role of socialist democracy, Hu added, is to "encourage the fuller expression of the popular masses' and various sectors' activism, initiative, and creativity," and to do this one should recognize the "organic unity" of party leadership, the people's mastery, and rule by law.[10] These are classic CCP concepts of democracy, found in the thought of Mao.[11]

Another member of the Politburo Standing Committee, Luo Gan, who is in charge of China's security apparatus, remarked in a 2006 speech that much of the social protest arising from the growing pluralization of social interests is legitimate and should be respected. He described most "mass incidents" as contradictions "among the people," which the legal system should resolve in a way that is respectful of people's rights and interests: rights and freedoms should be protected, and the party should serve the people. At the same time, Luo noted, foreign and domestic enemy forces, such as the *weiquan* movement, were taking advantage of mass dissatisfaction to try to overthrow the party. To deal properly with this complex set of challenges, he said, all the organs of the law (police, procuracy, and courts) should work together under party supervision, keeping in mind the overriding need to maintain both stability and state security—in other words, to keep the regime in power.[12] Many of the same ideas are found in Hu Jintao's comments quoted earlier. Both speeches illustrate how reform ideas that are authentically progressive in the People's Republic of China (PRC) context, and to which the CCP applies the label "democratic," are nonetheless intended to consolidate the one-party system.

An authoritative statement of the collective leadership's overall views on governance appears in the "Resolution on Enhancing the Governing Capacity of the CCP" adopted by the Fourth Plenum of the Sixteenth Central Committee in September 2004.[13] The document's fifth point pertains to democracy. It stresses the importance of "maintaining the organic solidarity of the leadership of the party, the people's mastery, and rule by law, and continuously raising and developing the capacity of socialist democratic politics," of "democratic elections, democratic decisionmaking, democratic management, and democratic supervision," and of "multiparty cooperation" (*duodang hezuo*) between the CCP and the country's noncommunist democratic parties. What do these concepts mean? They must be understood in light of the resolution's opening statement: "Our party's role as ruling party is the choice of history and the choice of the people"—that is, a choice whose legitimacy is fixed by history. Although the resolution emphasizes that the party must work continuously to maintain its grip on power, it nowhere suggests that the legitimacy of party rule needs to be periodically tested. None of the democratic procedures that the resolution praises should be understood as having any such function.

Many outsiders believe the current leadership's thoughts on democracy can be detected in a much-noticed article by scholar Yu Keping titled "Democracy Is a Good Thing." Yu considers democracy good for supervising officials and promoting development, but he says that it must be implemented by "government officials who represent the interests of the people" if it is not to cause instability. Democracy, he adds, should be implemented when economic, cultural, and political conditions are ripe, and democratic systems need to be protected with laws, authority, and even violence. Drawing forth the implications of these strictures for China, he says this means creating "socialist democracy with unique Chinese characteristics" and not "import[ing] an overseas political model."[14] In short, Yu is not pointing toward competitive electoral democracy. Likewise, the reforms Yu describes in chapter 3 of this volume that would increase openness and responsiveness in the party's governing style and thus contribute to a "dynamic stability" are intended to buttress the party's effectiveness and acceptability, not subject its rule to challenge by nonparty outsiders. Such reforms, if they were implemented, would be substantial. But they would neither include nor lead toward competitive elections for top positions of power.

All the statements reviewed in this section are consistent with the views published chiefly for foreign consumption in a 2005 State Council white paper on democracy. The white paper states: "China's socialist political democracy shows distinctive Chinese characteristics. . . . China's democracy is a people's democracy under the leadership of the [Chinese Communist Party]. . . . China's democracy is a democracy guaranteed by the people's democratic dictatorship. . . . China's democracy is a democracy with democratic centralism as the basic organizational principle and mode of operation."[15] These statements make clear that China's current system of no open competition for top power positions comports with the party leadership's idea of democracy. Changes already made or contemplated, some of which are substantial, are aimed at sustaining single-party rule.

What Fifth Generation Leaders Think

What about the younger leaders coming up under Hu and Wen, who are slated to succeed to power during the two-stage transition in 2007 and 2012? They are the people best positioned to change the nature of the regime in the near future if they want to. Their ideas are the most difficult to discern because their statements must coincide with the ideas of the party leaders if these people are to remain contenders. But available evidence, albeit imperfect, should be consulted.

The people who were promoted in 2007 and are in line for further advancement in 2012 are insiders of the current regime. They have had long party and government careers in a variety of economic, regional, and party posts. In contrast to contenders in a competitive electoral system, who try to criticize the incumbent regime and present their own ideas as fresh, aspirants for promotion in China rise by demonstrating the ability to get along with and show loyalty to superiors. If they have new ideas, they tend to present them as elaborations of the ideas already in force.

Xi Jinping, promoted to the Politburo Standing Committee in 2007, is considered most likely to succeed Hu Jintao as party secretary in 2012. Born in 1953, he is the son of a party elder, Xi Zhongxun. Of all the Fifth Generation leaders, Xi has the richest experience in government, having served as a village production brigade leader, a county magistrate, the leader of a special economic zone, and a provincial governor and party secretary.[16] In all his positions, he strongly promoted private enterprise; under his rule, Zhejiang Province maintained its leading position in developing the private economy. An Internet search discloses no substantial public remarks by Xi about democracy, although it is a word he uses, as do all provincial leaders, in writing about the harmonious society and about "mass work" at the local level. If he comes to power, it is believed that he will promote more adventurous steps in economic liberalization, but without sacrificing the party's ability to maintain ultimate control over the economy and the political system.[17]

Li Keqiang is considered most likely to succeed Wen Jiabao as premier in 2012. Born in 1955, Li was trained in law and economics. He served under Hu in the Communist Youth League in the mid-1980s. He resembles his mentor as a politician who moves carefully and maintains consensus. Some of his earlier policy positions—distributing wealth, helping the peasants, and looking out for the environment—resemble those of Wen Jiabao.[18] Since 2002 he has been a conspicuous promoter of Hu Jintao's idea of a "harmonious society." His recent public speeches repeat formulas found in central documents like those quoted in the preceding section.[19] According to one informant, if Li gains a top leadership post, he might push for expanded local and intraparty elections, more judicial independence, and less party control over the media and the Internet—agenda items clustered under the heading of "democracy and rule of law."[20] But such initiatives would aim at strengthening the party's authority, not at allowing it to be challenged.

Other Fifth Generation figures who won seats in the 2007 Politburo and remain in contention for important posts in 2012 include Jiangsu party secretary Li Yuanchao, Beijing mayor Wang Qishan, Organization Department director He Guoqiang, and Minister of Commerce Bo Xilai. The only one of these figures who seems to have said much in public about democracy is Li Yuanchao, who has been more active than other provincial secretaries in promoting a system of consulting party and government cadres as an adjunct to the party organization department's decisions on cadre appointments.[21] But this does not mean that Li is more interested in democracy than the other Fifth

Generation leaders; more likely it signifies that he needed to push the center's meritocratic cadre promotion procedures harder in Jiangsu than secretaries did elsewhere because of Jiangsu's long history of contention over the dominance of appointments by cadres from the northern part of the province.

Also moving up, although belonging by age to the Fourth rather than the Fifth Generation, is Zhou Yongkang, who inherited Luo Gan's Politburo Standing Committee seat as the person in charge of security. Born in 1942 and trained at the Beijing Petroleum Institute, Zhou worked in the oil sector until the late 1990s. He became minister of public security in 2003. The word "democracy" appears in Zhou's published speeches and interviews in the context of such formulas as "democracy and rule of law" and "scientific democratic decisionmaking," but without elaboration. As a person tasked with maintaining public security, Zhou can be expected to focus any reforms that he promotes on maintaining party control of society, just as his mentor has done.

Although there is room for surprise about what future leaders really think, as well as about how they might react to crises, current evidence suggests their views on political reform do not differ markedly and are by and large in accord with those of today's leaders. Once they hold power, they are likely to work to consolidate that power rather than undermine it.

What Influential Intellectuals Think

Another influential group consists of the established intellectuals—university professors, institute researchers, and some independent writers, including some based in Hong Kong and overseas. They operate within what Wang Juntao has called "a limited independent public sphere" and shape something that Chinese refer to as public opinion, meaning a general climate of opinion, primarily among the intellectuals themselves, that has an effect on party policies and rhetoric.[22] More than the two groups reviewed so far, the intellectuals tend to say what they think, making their intentions easier to decipher. Even though they must steer away from certain forbidden topics and ideas, their debates are substantive and intense.

Since 1989, as Wang's Columbia Ph.D. dissertation demonstrates, the mainstream of intellectual discourse has turned against democracy. The dominant line of Chinese thought has been what Wang calls "neoconservatism" (some other scholars label it the "New Left").[23] This is his umbrella term for a wide range of schools and subschools under such labels as neoauthoritarianism, statism, nationalism, postmodernism, the third way, China exceptionalism, neo-Confucianism, and new leftism. Although the schools and the individual thinkers within them are diverse, they all reject democracy and prefer authoritarianism for China in the foreseeable future. They value liberty, equity, legality, and accountability. But they consider democracy, as defined in this chapter, too "radical" or too "Western," or both, for China, which they think needs a form of political development that is gradual and both culturally and institutionally Chinese.

Specific reasons for rejecting democracy vary. They include the following: China is too turbulent to be governed democratically, at least until reform and modernization are completed; a nonauthoritarian system would exacerbate the unfair distribution of economic goods, which is the chief problem Chinese society faces today; China's cultural traditions are not suited for competitive politics; the international environment is too threatening to allow for internal divisions; electoral competition benefits selfish, exploitative people; democracy promotion is a Western strategy to weaken China and keep it in a subordinate position; national pride should prevent China from modeling itself on a condescending West.[24] All in all, democracy is an inferior, fake, or dysfunctional system. Prescriptions for how China should be governed also vary, but converge around the idea of leadership by a moral and technical elite over a population engaged in cultivating virtues of harmony and cooperation, the ultimate aim being to achieve effective modernization, fair distribution, political order, and national security.

There are as many versions of these ideas as there are thinkers propounding them, but a few examples will give a sense of their range and seriousness. According to one leading neoconservative, Kang Xiaoguang, China needs a "cooperative state" (*hezuozhuyi guojia*) to deal with the potentially destabilizing problems of corruption and unfair distribution of wealth.[25] Born in 1963, Kang is affiliated with the School of Agricultural Economics and Rural Development at People's University and holds concurrent posts at Qinghua University and other institutions. In a 2002 essay, "China: Political Development and Political Stability in the Reform Era," he argued that an alliance of ruling political and economic elites is prone to abuse its powers by inordinate exactions from the masses. Political stability can be maintained only if the state distributes wealth in a fair way, even though this will hurt the interests of elites.[26] Indeed, asserts Kang, equity among classes is more important than consent of the governed. To carry out the necessary redistributive policies, China needs a regime in which community members organize functional groups that represent the various classes and negotiate with one another to make policy suggestions, to be followed by state decisions in the public interest. The advantage of such a cooperative state is that it can deny the capitalist class a dominant position over other classes in the society and thus maintain fairness. By contrast, he says, the political establishment in liberal democracies serves the interests of capitalists and cannot deliver fair treatment to other classes. Citing political scientist Samuel P. Huntington, Kang argues further that liberal democracy fosters destructive individualism, which has brought disaster to many countries involved in the third wave of democratization. The cooperative state—or even better, the ideal type of authoritarian regime, to which he applies the Confucian term "benevolent"—would instead promote harmonious values consistent with traditional Chinese culture.[27]

Another influential neoconservative is Wang Hui, who in recent years has unfurled a trenchant critique of liberalism that many Chinese find compelling.[28] Born in 1959, Wang is a research fellow at the Chinese Academy of Social Sciences and chief editor of the influential *Dushu* (Reading) magazine. In a 1997 essay, Wang leveled a devastating attack on the usefulness of the liberal ideas popular in China in the mid-1980s.[29] For all its failures, averred Wang, Maoism was at least a creative attempt to design a form of modernity suited to China. As alternatives to Maoism, both Dengism and pre-1989 Chinese liberalism were based on the naïve assumption that Western-style modernization would suit China. But the post-1989 intensification of capitalist development and globalization had shown that this was not true. Indeed, it was precisely the practice of liberalism in the realm of the economy that created the problems—the corruption, socioeconomic inequalities, and repressive collusion of the rich and the powerful—against which the 1989 pro-democracy demonstrations were directed.[30] Those problems were a reflection of the deeply rooted flaws in liberal theory. By giving priority to individual rights, liberalism blocks the development of institutional arrangements that could promote social equity across groups and remains blind to the structural unfairness of the way the current international order distributes benefits among different nations.[31]

A third influential neoconservative thinker is Cui Zhiyuan, a political science Ph.D. graduate of the University of Chicago who taught at the Massachusetts Institute of Technology before going to Qinghua University.[32] Cui argues that China should not follow Western institutional models but should innovate to solve its own challenges on the basis of its own experience. As Cui's Ph.D. adviser, Tsou Tang, remarked in his preface to Cui's first book, Cui promoted Chinese exceptionalism just as Americans had long promoted American exceptionalism.[33] Seeking institutional models suited to China, Cui considered some of the Maoist experiments rejected by Chinese liberals, such as township and village enterprises, the Dazhai model (a village of selfless peasants who under Mao allegedly transformed their harsh environment through collective physical labor), and the Angang Constitution (a Mao-era system for worker management of industrial enterprises). Far from being neotraditional, he argued, such Maoist experiments pointed toward a non-Western, alternative form of modernity suited to China. In his view, China should base its political system on public ownership and collectivism, not on private ownership, and thereby obviate the need for competition among political parties, since these exist only to promote the interests of competing factions of wealthy property owners.

A fourth neoconservative, Pan Wei, is a Beijing University scholar who published a much-noticed article in *Zhanlue yu guanli* (Strategy and Management) in 1999, which he updated for later publication in English.[34] Pan's key point is that rule of law and democracy, often viewed as inherently linked in the West, are two separate things—"one can exist without the other." China needs the rule of law but not democracy. His reasons for this—by now familiar—are that open political competition is not respected in Chinese culture, it would be polarizing in the Chinese context, and it would serve the interests of the wealthy rather than the masses. If democracy is to work well, it requires a foundation in rule of law, but this is not yet established in Chinese society and hence takes priority as a task for political development. Furthermore, if rule of law is established, it will by itself fix most of what is wrong with China's current system. It will produce honest, effective, transparent government and protect citizens' legitimate freedoms without the need for destructive competition among class-based political parties.

As is evident from these summaries, the neoconservatives offer a critique of globalization that is similar to that offered by liberals in the West, and they endorse values that Western democrats would view sympathetically. Their argument for a distinctive Chinese political model is not grounded in a culturally specific vision of the social good, but rather in the idea that China has distinctive "national conditions" (*guoqing*) of culture and social structure that shape the ways in which universal values can be realized. In this sense, the neoconservatives' support for authoritarianism implies some sharp criticisms of the current regime, for failing adequately to combat corruption, redistribute wealth, protect the disadvantaged, and defend the national interest. Even though most neoconservatives are happier with the Hu-Wen policies than with those of the preceding Jiang Zemin government, they retain the capacity to be sharply critical, which entails holding the regime's feet to the fire to deliver the goods on which it bases its claim to legitimacy. The weakness of their position lies in their inability to explain how an actual authoritarian regime as flawed as the current one can be expected to turn itself into their idealized type of authoritarian regime without the pressure of competitive elections.

Thus Chinese Marxism has gone bankrupt, as anticipated by many in the West, but with an unexpected outcome: not the victory of liberalism but reinvigorated support for authoritarianism, albeit on grounds different from those provided by the official ideology.[35] Being independent of the regime's ideology, the neoconservatives could turn against it, just as mass nationalism has sometimes swung from a regime-supporting to regime-opposing stance. But on current evidence, even if the neoconservatives defected, they would not turn toward democracy.

What Liberals Think

Although neoconservative ideas seem to dominate intellectual discourse, some liberal views are also being espoused within the (broadly defined) establishment.[36] Some thinkers of this persuasion are senior retired party figures such as Li Rui (Mao's one-time secretary), Hu Jiwei (former editor-in-chief of *People's Daily*), Zhu Houze (former director of the party propaganda department), and He Jiadong (retired editor). Others teach at Chinese universities and include Qin Hui (history, Qinghua University), He Weifang (law, Beijing University), Zhu Xueqin (history, Shanghai University), and Sheng Dewen (economics, Beijing University).

Of the four groups described in this chapter, the liberals currently have the least political influence. This is partly because many are retired, the regime gives them less room to publish and speak than it gives the neoconservatives, and the people in power—the first two groups I described—are less interested in the liberals' ideas than in the ideas of the neoconservatives.[37] However, influence can change. It is still worth asking whether the liberals advocate electoral competition for top positions of political power.

Liberals are perhaps most concerned with the abuse of power under Mao and the damage Mao did to the country. They analyze the failure to check the abuse of power as a genetic flaw of authoritarian rule. Instead of promoting distinctive Chinese institutions to solve distinctive problems, as the neoconservatives do, they therefore favor institutions that have proven universally effective to check abuses of power—institutions that they describe as liberal and democratic. Having said this, however, the liberals diverge in their specific proposals and time frames, and—what is crucial for this chapter—seldom, if ever, openly advocate competitive elections for top positions of authority. Either out of caution, realism, or conviction, they do not publicly call for the establishment of other political parties to challenge the CCP's grip on authority.

For example, Li Rui's 2002 proposal for wide-ranging political reforms, submitted to the Sixteenth Party Congress on behalf of himself and other senior retired party liberals, called for intraparty freedom of speech, competitive elections for top party posts, competitive elections for seats in the people's congresses, an end to party leadership of the courts, and other democratizing measures in both the party and the state.[38] But at no point did Li suggest that the CCP should face an electoral challenge to its status as the country's ruling party.

When interviewed by *Southern Metropolitan News,* retired *People's Daily* deputy editor Zhou Ruijin said he thought the party needed to put more trust in both government officials and nongovernmental organizations (NGOs), that county government and party chiefs could be competitively elected by the county party congresses and people's congresses, and delegates could be directly elected to county and eventually provincial people's congresses. But when asked whether the CCP should emulate the Vietnamese Communist Party's experiment with putting up two candidates to compete at the national party congress for the post of general secretary, Zhou answered, "This would not be easy."[39]

The liberals, in short, do not publicly advocate that the CCP should place its hold on power at risk. For some, the stated goal is to democratize the CCP internally—by exposing those who exercise power to the challenge of alternative views that can be expressed within the CCP. Others would like to see the CCP placed under some outside constraints, whether from the media, the courts, government agencies, or public opinion. But few advocate placing the party in a competition for power that it could lose. On this key point, their thinking agrees with that of the other three groups described earlier.

Of course, the liberals may not say everything they mean. They may be hinting at what they cannot say or may wish to advocate baby steps that will make further steps possible later. One place to look for signs of what the liberals really mean is the actions and writings of the late Zhao Ziyang, thus far the party's highest-ranking advocate of bold political reform and often portrayed as the ultra democratizer within the party. Whatever he contemplated is demonstrably within the bounds of the thinkable for party liberals. Three pieces of evidence provide an idea of his conception of political reform.

First, in 1987, at the behest of Deng Xiaoping and the Politburo, Zhao convened a political reform study group that heard briefings from people with a variety of views on political reform. The process was later described in a book by a committee staffer, which provides unusual insight into the scope of the reforms that were considered.[40] Perhaps the boldest vision was that of Beijing University professor Gong Xiangrui, who argued for "pluralistic politics under monolithic leadership," which meant allowing independent parties and groups to be active but keeping party leadership in place. During the deliberations, Zhao reportedly commented: "On the one hand we can't carry out bourgeois liberalization, we can't have a two-party system, we can't have anarchy. On the other hand, we must actively increase socialist democracy, since people demanding democracy is a trend." In the event, Zhao's proposal for political reform to the Thirteenth Party Congress, which of course was a collective product of high-level party deliberations, called for the acknowledgment of diverse interests in society and for the "separation of party and government," but not for any challenge to the party's monopoly of power.

Second, in 1989, when faced with a political crisis that tested his commitment to one-party leadership, Zhao advocated a policy of "guide and divide" in dealing with student demonstrators. That is, he proposed entering into dialogue with them on the assumption that they would listen to reason and that their basic goals were the same as the party's. Had he been allowed to talk to the students, he would have tried to persuade them to go home but, as far as the record shows, would not have allowed them to challenge the party's monopoly of power.[41]

Third, during his years under house arrest after 1989, Zhao held a series of conversations with an old colleague who was able to visit him in the role of a Chinese-exercise instructor and who described the conversations in a book published after Zhao's death. In these conversations, Zhao criticized the corrupt loss of state property to private entrepreneurs, the exchange of power for money, land seizures, and the mistreatment of the common people by the wealthy and powerful. He said he was disappointed that after the passing of strongman Deng Xiaoping, different policy factions had not emerged in the party leadership to allow more open discussion of alternatives. He described the American political system as the best in the world, adding that for China truly to modernize it would have to adopt Western values of freedom, democracy, and human rights. Yet as recounted in the third person by his old friend, Zhao expressed pessimism about China's readiness for competitive elections:

> As to how to carry out political reform, if one tries a multiparty system and does it poorly then it could upset the applecart and plunge China into chaos. For now one should implement freedom of speech and relax the ban on private newspapers under the framework of party leadership. He emphasized that freedom is more important than democracy. Hong Kong under British colonial rule did not have democracy but it had freedom. Anyone could criticize the governor. The legal system was independent of government control. Later they allowed people to form associations, and this stimulated popular wisdom and raised the people's level of democratic awareness. As to [such controversial topics as] nationalization of the military and the multiparty system, for the time being it is best not to raise them.[42]

For all his commitment to a universalistic view of democracy's value and character, Zhao was no more ready to advocate multiparty competition for today's China than were any of the other figures considered in this chapter. With Zhao as the most plainspoken among them, it remains doubtful that the establishment liberals who talk about universal democratic values intend that phrase to cover reforms that could challenge the party's hold on power.

Conclusion

Similar-sounding ideas mean different things in different institutional and intellectual contexts. When Chinese leaders talk about seeking democracy (that is, democracy in their way of thinking), they are no doubt sincere, and they have undertaken significant reforms to this end. When influential intellectuals talk about the need for freedom, equity, and transparency, they, too, are being sincere, and they have proposed some far-reaching changes in the Chinese model of government. So if the theory that China will democratize assumes Chinese actors have their own concepts of democracy and are trying to implement them, then that is precisely what I have argued. But, to reiterate, it is essential not to misconstrue these Chinese actors' views of democracy. Persons of influence in China who call for democracy are not advocating competitive elections for top posts. The governance reforms under way or proposed for the future aim to make the authoritarian system more fair, more effective, and more—not less—sustainable.

I came to similar conclusions when I studied Chinese ideas of democracy more than twenty years ago.[43] Despite changes in the international environment and in China's economy and society, and despite Chinese thinkers' greater knowledge of a wide range of Western theories than was the case back then, certain core conceptions from the past about the right kind of state-society relations for China still make sense to many Chinese. Most of the actors with influence in China today believe that while China is struggling to modernize and make itself strong, citizens must stick together and serve the common enterprise, and that the state must provide moral leadership and give care to the people. Many believe that systems based on political competition foster division and reward selfishness. I would be loath (if anyone asked me) to label this set of attitudes "culture," meaning values that are inherited and unchangeable. I prefer to think of them as core ideas that make sense and seem valid to those currently situated within China's particular historical experience and international environment, and with its social structure and language.

Whatever one calls this set of beliefs, their implication for the topic of this volume is that the Chinese actors who currently hold influence are not likely intentionally to steer their system toward what most in the West call democracy, for the simple reason that most of them do not believe in it. If democracy in the liberal, pluralistic sense is going to come to China, either the actors will have to change their minds or they will have to lose control over the process. The lesson of history may be that precisely such things are likely to happen; but to say this is merely to voice the truism that the future is unknown. What is knowable is that for the time being the wind in China blows but weakly in the sails of the democratic idea.

Notes

1. See, for example, Gordon G. Chang, *The Coming Collapse of China* (New York: Random House, 2001); Bruce Gilley, *China's Democratic Future: How It Will Happen and Where It Will Lead* (Columbia University Press, 2004); Minxin Pei, *China's Trapped Transition: The Limits of Developmental Autocracy* (Harvard University Press, 2006); Andrew J. Nathan, "China's Changing of the Guard: Authoritarian Resilience," *Journal of Democracy* 14 (January 2003): 6–17; Nathan, "Present at the Stagnation: Is China's Development Stalled?" (review essay), *Foreign Affairs* (July/August 2006), pp. 177–82; and Nathan, "Is the Chinese Communist Party's Rule Sustainable?" remarks presented at "Reframing China Policy: The Carnegie Debates, 2006–2007" (Washington: Library of Congress, October 5) (www.carnegieendowment.org/events/index.cfm?fa=eventDetail&id=916&&prog=zch).

2. This line of argument goes back to Max Weber. For a review of the theoretical issues involved, see Michael T. Gibbons, "Hermeneutics, Political Inquiry, and Practical Reason: An Evolving Challenge to Political Science," *American Political Science Review* 100 (November 2006): 563–71. For influential statements of the position in political science, see, among others, Peter A. Hall, ed., *The Political Power of Economic Ideas: Keynesianism across Nations* (Princeton University Press, 1989); and Judith Goldstein and Robert O. Keohane, eds., *Ideas and Foreign Policy: Beliefs, Institutions, and Political Change* (Cornell University Press, 1993).

3. Gilley, *China's Democratic Future*; and John Thornton, "Assessing the Next Phase of a Rising China," typescript memo circulated on the Internet, n.d. [December 2006], courtesy of John Thornton.

4. "In the course of their modern history, the Chinese people have waged unrelenting struggles and made arduous explorations in order to win their democratic rights. But only under the leadership of the Communist Party of China (CPC) did they really win the right to be masters of the state. The Chinese people dearly cherish and resolutely protect their hard-earned democratic achievements." State Council Information Office, *Building of Political Democracy in China*, October 19, 2005 (www.chinadaily.com.cn/english/doc/2005-10/19/content_486206.htm [March 29, 2007]).

5. For review and discussion, see Larry Diamond, *Developing Democracy: Toward Consolidation* (Johns Hopkins University Press, 1999), chap. 1.

6. Thornton. "Assessing the Next Phase of a Rising China."

7. Benjamin Liebman, "China's Courts: Restricted Reform," *China Quarterly* 191 (September 2007).

8. See Andrew J. Nathan, *Chinese Democracy* (New York: Alfred A. Knopf, 1985), chap. 8.

9. "Our Historical Tasks at the Primary Stage of Socialism and Several Issues Concerning China's Foreign Policy," *Renmin ribao*, February 27, 2007 (English translation at www.chinaelections.org/en/readnews.asp?newsid=%7bEA5FA2E5-AC4B-4E0B-B424-330EA336D144%7d [March 16, 2007]).

10. "Hu Jintao zai shengbuji zhuyao lingdao ganbu tigao goujian shehuizhuyi hexieshehui nengli zhuanti yantaobanshang de jianghua" (Hu Jintao's talk at the specialized seminar on increasing the capacity to construct a socialist harmonious society for provincial and ministerial-level important leading cadres), February 19, 2005 (www.zjkdj.gov.cn/shownews.asp?newsid=2144 [March 27, 2007]).

11. Nathan, *Chinese Democracy.*

12. Luo Gan, "Shenru kaizhan shehuizhuyi fazhi linian jiaoyu qieshi jiaqiang zhengfa duiwu sixiang zhengzhi jianshe" (Penetratingly carry out education in the concept of the socialist legal system and realistically strengthen the ideological and political construction of the political-legal ranks), *Qiushi zazhi,* December 2006, pp. 3–10. Luo repeated most of the same ideas in another speech published in *Qiushi,* no. 3 (2007), which was the subject of a report by Joseph Kahn, "Chinese Official Warns against Independence of Courts," *New York Times,* February 3, 2007, p. A5.

13. "Zhonggong zhongyang guanyu jiaqiang dang de zhizheng nengli jianshe de jueding" (The resolution on enhancing governing capacity of CCP), September 19, 2004 (www.news.xinhuanet.com/newscenter/2004-09/26/content_2024232.htm [March 15, 2007]).

14. Yu Keping, "Democracy Is a Good Thing," originally published in *Beijing ribao,* October 23, 2006 (English translation at www.chinaelections.org/en/readnews.asp?newsid={75091FCF-3101-4767-A71FE958265DE614}&classid=77&classname=Political%20Reform [March 27, 2007]).

15. See note 4.

16. Andrew J. Nathan and Bruce Gilley, *China's New Rulers: The Secret Files,* 2nd rev. ed. (New York Review of Books, 2003), pp. 146–51 and chap. 7.

17. See, for example, "Unremittingly Struggle to Realize the All-Round Revitalization of Liaoning's Old Industrial Base—Report at the Liaoning Provincial CCP's Tenth Representative Congress" (www.lnqg.gov.cn/Swift/jsp/db3PageAction.action?qid=4aebe99c0e8db8d6010ebfb1d84d09bb [March 27, 2007]).

18. Zong Hairen, interview.

19. Nathan and Gilley, *China's New Rulers,* pp. 137–43.

20. Zong Hairen, interview.

21. "Use Democratic Methods to Select Cadres Trusted by the People," *Xinhua ribao,* February 8, 2004 (www.jschina.com.cn/gb/jschina/2003/24/node5405/node5406/node5408/userobject1ai404174.html [March 27, 2007]). The system is called *gongtui gongxuan* (open recommendation and open promotion).

22. Juntao Wang, "Reverse Course: Political Neo-Conservatism and Regime Stability in Post-Tiananmen China," Ph.D. dissertation, Columbia University, 2006, chap. 2. For another account of the same period and many of the same thinkers, see Chaohua Wang, *One China, Many Paths* (London: Verso, 2003).

23. Wang, "Reverse Course," passim. Also see Daniel C. Lynch, "Envisioning China's Political Future: Elite Responses to Democracy as a Global Constitutive Norm," *International Studies Quarterly,* vol. 51 (2007), pp. 701–22. Another major source on post-Tiananmen neoconservatism is Joseph Fewsmith, *China since Tiananmen: The Politics of Transition* (Cambridge University Press, 2001), part 2. For a discussion of disillusionment with liberalism and democracy in post-1989 cultural criticism, see Ben Xu, *Disenchanted Democracy: Chinese Cultural Criticism after 1989* (University of Michigan Press, 2002).

24. On the theme of democracy promotion's being a Western strategy to keep China weak, see Daniel C. Lynch, *Rising China and Asian Democratization: Socialization to "Global Culture" in the Political Transformations of Thailand, China, and Taiwan* (Stanford University Press, 2006), chaps. 4 and 5.

25. My account of Kang Xiaoguang's thought is based on Wang, "Reverse Course," pp. 286–96.

26. "Zhongguo: Gaige shidai de zhengzhi fazhan yu zhengzhi wending" (China: Political development and political stability in the reform period), *Dangdai zhongguo*, no. 3 (2002) (www.usc.cuhk.edu.hk/wk_wzdetails.asp?id=1829 [March 13, 2007]).

27. "Lun hezuozhuyi guojia" (On the cooperative state), *Zhanlue yu guanli*, no. 5 (2003) (www.usc.cuhk.edu.hk/wk_wzdetails.asp?id=2724 [March 27, 2007]); "Renzheng: Wei-quanzhuyi guojia de hefaxing lilun" (Benevolent politics: A legitimacy theory for an authoritarian state), *Zhanlue yu guanli*, no. 2 (2004) (www.usc.cuhk.edu.hk/wk_wzdetails.asp?id=3026 [March 27, 2007]); "Confucianization: A Future in the Tradition," *Social Research* 73 (Spring 2006): 77–120.

28. My account of Wang Hui's ideas is based on Wang Juntao, "Reverse Course," pp. 359–66. See also Pankaj Mishra, "China's New Leftist," *New York Times Magazine*, October 15, 2006, pp. 48–53.

29. "Dangdai Zhongguo de sixiang zhuangkuang yu xiandaixing wenti" (The situation of contemporary Chinese thought and the problem of modernity), published in *Tianya* and *Xianggang shehui kexue xuebao* in 1997; used here is the English version, "Contemporary Chinese Thought and the Question of Modernity," trans. Rebecca E. Karl, *Social Text* 55 (Summer 1998): 9–44.

30. "Xin ziyouzhuyi de lishi genyuan jiqi pipan: Zai lun dangdai Zhongguo dalu de sixiang zhuangkuang he xiandaixing wenti" (Historical origins and critiques of neoliberalism: Discussing again the situation of contemporary Chinese thought and the problem of modernity in contemporary mainland China), *Taiwan shehui yanjiu jikan*, no. 42 (June 2001) (www.tecn.cn/data/detail.php?id=12659 [March 27, 2007]).

31. Wang Hui, "Chengren de zhengzhi: Wanminfa yu ziyouzhuyi de kunjing" (The politics of recognition: Universal law and the dilemma of liberalism), *Ershiyi shiji* (August 1997) (www.frchina.net/data/personArticle.php?id=2743 [March 27, 2007]).

32. My account of Cui Zhiyuan's ideas is based on Wang Juntao, "Reverse Course," pp. 382–91.

33. Cui Zhiyuan, "Zhidu chuangxin yu di'erci sixiang jiefang" (Institutional innovation and the second thought liberation), *Ershiyi shiji* (August 1994) (www.tecn.cn/data/detail.php?id=12724 [March 27, 2007]).

34. Pan Wei, "Toward a Consultative Rule of Law Regime in China," in *Debating Political Reform in China: Rule of Law vs. Democratization,* edited by Suisheng Zhao (Armonk, N.Y.: M. E. Sharpe, 2006), pp. 3–40.

35. This was not foreseen in such works as Bill Brugger and David Kelly, *Chinese Marxism in the Post-Mao Era, 1978–1984* (Stanford University Press, 1990); Ding Xueliang, *The Decline of Communism in China: Legitimacy Crisis, 1978–1989* (Cambridge University Press, 1994); and Kalpana Misra, *From Post-Maoism to Post-Marxism: The Erosion of Official Ideology in Deng's China* (New York: Routledge, 1998). All these works insightfully portray the legitimacy crisis of Marxism in post-Mao China, but they could not have been expected to foresee what would come out of this crisis. Misra discusses neoconservatism briefly at the end of her book (pp. 207–15).

36. Discussed by Fewsmith, *China since Tiananmen,* pp. 122–31.

37. And, of course, some of the most important liberals are exiled, thus falling outside the scope of this chapter.

38. Li Rui, "Guanyu woguo zhengzhi tizhi gaige de jianyi" (Suggestions for the reform of our country's political system), in *Yanhuang chunqiu,* no. 1, 2003 (www.personal.nbnet.nb.ca/stao/lirui003.htm [March 27, 2007]).

39. "Duihua Zhou Ruijin: 'Zhengfu de gui zhengfu, shehui de gui shehui'" (Dialogue with Zhou Ruijin: "Let the government manage what it should manage and let society manage what it should manage"), *Nanfang dushibao,* February 5, 2007 (www.nanfangdaily.com.cn/southnews/zt/rdzt/dxpss10/200702050074.asp [March 27, 2007]).

40. Wu Guoguang, *Zhao Ziyang yu zhengzhi gaige* (Zhao Ziyang and political reform) (Hong Kong: Taipingyang shiji yanjiusuo chubanshe, 1997).

41. Andrew J. Nathan and Perry Link, eds., *The Tiananmen Papers,* compiled by Zhang Liang (New York: PublicAffairs, 2001), pp. 148–49.

42. Zong Fengming, *Zhao Xiyang ruanjinzhong de tanhua* (Conversations with Zhao Ziyang under house arrest) (Hong Kong: Kaifang chubanshe, 2007); the quoted passage is from p. 344.

43. Nathan, *Chinese Democracy.*

3

Ideological Change and Incremental Democracy in Reform-Era China

YU KEPING

> Democracy is a major condition for emancipating the mind.
>
> DENG XIAOPING, "Emancipating the Mind, Seeking Truth from
> Facts and Unite as One in Looking to the Future" (1980)

The broad political transformation currently under way in China owes much to dynamic social and economic reform as well as the upheaval in the international environment. Equally important, however, is the change in China's political ideology, which has wide implications for its future political trajectory. As this chapter shows, the evolution of that ideology is intimately connected with the nature of politics in China, a fact often overlooked by scholars outside the country. Since changes in political ideology are usually the first sign of political reform in China, they can provide some clues to the eventual course of this reform—whether in the direction of incremental democracy or some other system.

New Political Ideas

As is well known, China has historically placed great importance on ideology, perhaps even more so under the leadership of the Chinese Communist Party (CCP). This explains why Deng Xiaoping, the chief architect of China's reforms, made "emancipating the mind" his top priority. "Our drive for the 'Four Modernizations' will get nowhere," Deng wrote, "unless rigid thinking is broken down and the minds of cadres and of the masses are completely emancipated."[1] Simply put, "emancipating the mind" means doing away with outdated doctrines and ideas, putting forward new ideas and theories that are compatible with social progress, and then using them to guide social practices. Clearly, such

44

"changes of the mind" are closely related to the social and political developments of the past two decades. To be precise, this has been a process of political progress based on the victory of new ideas over old ones. The new theories and concepts—most notably the "people-centered" principle, human rights, the rule of law, private property, civil society, harmonious society, and political civilization—have not only transcended traditional political ideology but also deeply affected Chinese social and political life, effectively pushing forward the prospect of democratic politics in China.

The "People-Centered" Principle (yi ren wei ben)

After the formal establishment of the People's Republic of China in 1949, humanitarian thought and humanism more broadly were fiercely criticized as Western-based concepts incompatible with Chinese social values and were thus held in popular disrepute. One of the negative social consequences of this ideology was that the doctrine of "class struggle" penetrated every corner of society—including families, factories, and schools. As a result, many aspects of traditional ethics were abandoned, such as kindness, amity, and trust among people. Even a show of subtle sympathy or mercy toward "class enemies" was considered a sign of a "variable class position" and would be met with serious political criticism. Intrinsic romantic tendencies were called petty bourgeois sentiment and likely to invite punishment. In due course, normal sentiments and the psychology of the common people were seriously distorted. Driven by a sense of responsibility, some Chinese intellectuals began advocating the "people-centered" principle and universal humanism in the 1980s, just as China was launching its first reforms. Unfortunately, serious political pressure was brought to bear on some advocates of humanism, and their principles failed to receive serious and sustained attention as possible contributors to Chinese political development.

Despite this political pressure, Chinese intellectuals refused to give up their inquiries into the concepts associated with the people-centered principle. By the mid-1990s, the principle had resurfaced among the Chinese intelligentsia, particularly the young cadres within the CCP, and after the turn of the century it was finally integrated into the party's mainstream ideology, having become the theoretical basis of China's reform strategy. Recognized as an important objective of political development by China's new leaders, the principle of the "all-round development of the people" has come to be seen as the basic constituent of a "scientific outlook of development" (*kexue fazhan guan*), which marks the transformation of the people-centered principle from an ideology within the intelligentsia to a policy guideline for the CCP and the government. At the beginning of 2007, President Hu Jintao further announced, "Free and comprehensive development of each person is the essence of the ideal society for human beings."[2]

Human Rights (renquan)

Much like the people-centered principle, the idea of human rights was long regarded as an outgrowth of capitalist ideology. As a result, the Chinese considered this concept politically suspect and discredited it both in theory and in practice. The most blatant example of the refusal to embrace the concept was the trampling of human rights during the ten-year-long Cultural Revolution. Even China's president and top military generals were not free from arbitrary arrest, confinement, torture, and extrajudicial execution. During this period, many ordinary people—notably teachers, intellectuals, and local leaders—were persecuted and died in jails or were subjected to political exile. In the latter half of the 1980s, however, some Chinese intellectuals began advocating on behalf of human rights following their study of Marxist theories on the subject, as well as Western theories of human rights. Initially, such efforts encountered strong opposition from conservatives, and even advocates of Marxist philosophies of human rights were charged with promoting "bourgeois liberalization."

Nonetheless, some intellectuals with a sense of social consciousness and responsibility continued their pursuit in this "forbidden academic region." By the 1990s, Marxist theories of human rights had gained prominence and were exerting influence on China's mainstream ideology. By the end of the decade, the CCP and the government had incorporated the idea of human rights into official discourse, and in late 2003 the Central Committee of the CCP formally proposed adding the principle of "protecting the human rights of the citizenry" to the constitution.[3] This proposal was approved by a large majority at the National People's Congress (NPC) in March 2004 and subsequently made a clause in the Chinese constitution.

Rule of Law (fa zhi)

China is a country that has no historical heritage of "rule of law." As the Cultural Revolution painfully demonstrated, however, China must transform this system to one that reflects the "rule of law"—meaning a legal system that is not just a tool of government for regulating citizen behavior but one that provides some constraint upon government itself and therefore affords citizen protection (see chapter 10)—now equated in China with democracy or democratic values. Initially, reform and "opening" brought increasing official recognition of "rule *by* law" (*fa zhi* or *yifa zhiguo*, meaning simply a system of regulating economic, social, and political behavior), and thus democracy and rule by law came to be thought of synonymously (*minzhu yu fa zhi*).[4] Since the early 1990s, however, some intellectuals have taken the initiative to advocate the rule *of* law instead of rule *by* law in China to ensure the protection of human rights. Although both expressions denote acting according to the law, the latter also emphasizes that no individual or group can override the law. Since the mid-1980s, some leaders of the CCP have argued that the party and its leaders should not override the law, and that as the ruling party in China, the CCP must set the example by acting within the framework of the law.[5]

In the 1990s, the concept of the rule of law began to appear in official documents and also became the long-term objective of political development in China. The Fifteenth National Congress of the CCP, held in 1997, was a turning point of historical significance in this process. The political report of this conference put forward the objective of "establishing a socialist country under the rule of law."[6] Thereafter this goal was written into the constitution, marking the transformation from a political objective of the CCP to a national political strategy. The incumbent administration further proposed "establishing a government under the rule of law," which meant the government would not only seek to build a "socialist country under the rule of law" but also take the lead in guiding the country toward that goal.

Private Property (siyou caichan)

One of the intrinsic characteristics of China's traditional socialist system was public ownership of the means of production. Hence the country's laws and policies discredited and discriminated against private property. With the establishment of the socialist market economy system, an increasing number of intellectuals attempted to argue for legalizing private ownership of property in China. Nevertheless, private ownership and private property were still "forbidden zones" of academic discussion even in the late 1980s—by which point the reform and opening-up policy had been in place for more than ten years—and some scholars advocating such ownership suffered political discrimination. Since the 1990s, the intelligentsia has viewed the private sector (referred to by the politically correct term "citizen-run economy," or *minying jingji*) in an increasingly positive light, and the CCP and the government have gradually shifted away from their previous negative views, with a growing interest in the development of the private sector of the economy. More recently, a number of intellectuals have argued that the private sector and private property should enjoy equal legal status with the public sector and public property. These comments influenced to some extent the Central Committee's 2003 recommendation to the NPC that the constitution be amended to include the principle of "protecting the legal private property of citizens."[7] In 2004 this proposal was formally written into the constitution at the First Plenary session of the Tenth National People's Congress. The "Property Law of China," finally approved on March 16, 2007, clearly stipulated that "the property rights of the state, collective, person and other rights-holders are protected by law and shall be violated by none."[8] Through this amendment, the private property of citizens achieved protection under law equal to that accorded to the properties of the state and the collective.

Political Civilization (zhengzhi wenming)

During the early implementation of the reform and opening-up policy, the CCP and the Chinese government had two basic objectives in mind: to construct a socialist civilization in both a material and spiritual sense. Some intellectuals found these two objectives incomplete because they failed to include political democracy. Subsequently, some even suggested that a socialist political civilization should become the country's third basic objective. This idea grew in popularity among Chinese intellectuals in the latter half of the 1990s and became an important strain of their discourse. In 2001 the CCP's top leader formally elaborated on the concept of "political civilization."[9] The Sixteenth National Congress of the CCP then broadened the previous Two Objectives strategy (directed at building a material and spiritual civilization) into the Three Objectives strategy (aimed at constructing a material, spiritual, *and* political civilization). Building a socialist political civilization was finally identified as a basic objective of the CCP and the Chinese government. The context from which this third objective has emerged suggests that "political civilization" boils down to democracy and the rule of law.

Civil Society (gongmin shehui)

The expression "civil society" was originally translated into Chinese using three terms: *gongmin shehui*, *shimin shehui*, and *minjian shehui* (which in English approximately translate to mean "citizen's society," "burgher's society," and "nongovernmental society," respectively). The elements of civil society are civil organizations and civic associations that act in the public sphere independently of the state. In one sense, these activities and the organizations that undertake them are derivatives of the market economy; they also form the basis for democratic politics. For a long time, China equated civil society with bourgeois society, translating it as *shimin shehui*, a term having some negative connotations. According to critics, advocating the growth of civil society amounted to promoting the growth of bourgeois society and therefore was a fundamentally antigovernment position.

With the implementation of the socialist market economy in China, however, some scholars promoted the idea of building "civil society with Chinese characteristics," a notion that triggered heated discussions, not to mention staunch political criticism. As the reforms progressed through the 1980s and 1990s and relatively independent civic organizations became more common, many people became convinced of the existence of civil society in China. As discussion of civil society continued, more and more of its critics began to recognize its significance for China's future development. As a result, both the idea and development of civil society grew more legitimate in the eyes of many Chinese intellectuals.[10] Hence in June 1998 the Ministry of Civil Affairs changed the name of the administrative organ in charge of civil organizations from the Department of Social Associations to the Bureau of Civil Organizations, thereby making the status of civil organizations legal.

Harmonious Society (hexie shehui)

At its core, traditional political ideology in pre-reform China focused on class struggle, as encapsulated in three of Chairman Mao's famous quotations: "Never forget class struggle"; "Class struggle must be held in mind every year, every month and every day"; and "Take class struggle as the guide for all work." During the Cultural Revolution, these phrases appeared in slogans scrawled everywhere across the country. Under Mao, any citizens who denied or rejected class struggle faced serious criticism or even political repression as "class enemies." Liu Shaoqi, former president of China, was politically persecuted for having advocated cooperation between capitalists and workers, which was labeled "class reconciliation" (*jieji tiaohe lun*). The first breakthrough of Deng Xiaoping's reforms was to change the focus of the CCP from class struggle to economic construction. However, the transition in emphasis from class struggle to social harmony was a long and arduous process.

Although "harmony" is an important component of traditional Chinese culture, it did not receive the support of CCP scholars until 2000 and beyond.[11] Once it was articulated at the Sixteenth National Congress in 2003, the idea quickly took root and became the basic objective of CCP. In 2004 the Fourth Plenary session of the Sixteenth Central Committee of the CCP formally put forward the strategic objective of constructing a socialist harmonious society, and in 2006 the Sixth Plenary session of the Sixteenth Central Committee passed the Resolution on Constructing a Socialist Harmonious Society.[12]

The foregoing ideas exerted a deep influence on China's political development. Other ideas and concepts have also been discussed and debated over the past two decades—such as governance (*zhili*), good governance (*shanzhi*), good government (*shanzheng*), constitutionalism (*xianzheng*), global governance (*quanqiu zhili*), legitimacy (*hefa xing*), government innovation (*zhengfu chuangxin*), incremental democracy (*zengliang minzhu*), transparent government (*touming zhengfu*), accountable government (*zeren zhengfu*), service-oriented government (*fuwu zhengfu*), and efficient government (*xiaoyi zhengfu*)—and they too have helped shape Chinese political discourse and political theory.

Ideological Innovation and Political Change

The substantial changes in political ideology just outlined have directly affected the major political developments in China, as follows.

An Emerging Civil Society

During Mao's era, the state not only overlapped with the party but also sought to occupy all of social space, leaving no room whatsoever for an independent civil society. Since the enactment of the 1978 reforms, a relatively independent civil society has slowly begun to emerge—both the numbers and categories of civic organizations have been increasing, and civil associations have grown in independence and legitimacy. Before the reforms, there were only a few "people's associations" and "mass organizations"—notably the All-China Federation of Trade Unions, the Communist Youth League, and the Women's Federation—but strictly speaking all such organizations were affiliated with and governed hierarchically by the CCP or the government and so were not independent.

China's emerging civil society is an outgrowth of the reforms that spawned a rapid expansion of civil society organizations in the late 1980s, ranging from ordinary civic organizations to a special type of "civilian-run non-enterprise units" (CRNEUs, or *minban fei qiye danwei*), which were nongovernmental and nonprofit organizations providing public services. According to preliminary statistics, the number of CRNEUs at various levels across China apparently reached 700,000 in 1998.[13] Besides CRNEUs, the number of officially registered civic organizations above county level reached over 310,000 in 2005.[14] However, this is just the number of officially registered civic organizations; a large proportion of civic organizations are unregistered while exerting influence below the county level.[15] Although no authoritative figures are available, a general estimate would put the number of such groups closer to 3 million.[16]

Gradual Deepening of "Rule of Law" and Improved National Legal System

One of the important lessons of the Cultural Revolution is that social experiments occurring outside the rule of law invite tragedy. Therefore Chinese leaders and intellectuals have paid special attention to the construction and refinement of a legal system since the beginning of the reforms. With the development of the socialist market economy, the legal system has had to be more functionally articulated and with continuing reform has advanced the prospects for greater democracy in China's political system. From 1979 to 2005, the NPC and its Standing Committee, along with the State Council and the local people's congresses and their standing committees, enacted roughly 400 laws, more than

650 administrative regulations, and over 7,500 local regulations. The Chinese government's announced aim is to establish a sound legal system by 2010.[17]

Increasing Scope of Direct Elections and Local Autonomy

At the beginning of the reforms, Chinese leaders made the development of grassroots democracy a top priority for political development. In this vein, the Electoral Law of the National People's Congress and the Local Congresses, passed in July 1979, stipulated that representatives to the people's congresses at county levels and below should be directly elected by the citizens. In addition, since the late 1990s a few provinces—Sichuan, Henan, Guangdong, and Shenzhen—have experimented with direct elections of party and government leaders at the township level. Township mayors, for example, were directly elected in Sichuan and Shenzhen in 1998 and 1999. The most striking development in aid of grassroots democracy is the nationwide implementation of village elections. According to the Law on the Organization of Village Committees passed by the Standing Committee of the NPC in December 1989, all village cadres must be freely and directly elected by the villagers. Village elections have been gradually implemented across China's rural areas. According to one source, the average turnover rate in village elections now exceeds 80 percent. By the end of 2004, China had more than 644,000 villagers' committees. Given the size of China's peasant population, estimated at more than 800 million, the implementation of village-level democracy has special significance for the overall development of democracy in China.

Enhanced Political Transparency

Since the mid-1990s the Chinese government has given increased prominence to openness and transparency in governmental affairs. This trend is reflected in the establishment of the National Leading Group on Governmental Transparency and the State Council's announcement in April 2007 of Regulations on Open Government Information, which identify "openness in governmental affairs" as the legal responsibility of every level of government. "Governmental transparency" implies that the party and government must inform the public of important policies and regulations as well as government affairs affecting citizens' interests in a timely fashion. In the main, governmental transparency consists of (a) releasing relevant information on specific regulations, policies or legislation, and official decisionmaking to relevant stakeholders in time for them to comment so that the government has an opportunity to absorb suggestions from the public; (b) regularly publicizing information on the setting up of new government organs, their functions, and operating procedures; (c) releasing important statistical data on social development strategy, national economic statistics, budget and budgetary implementation, and the like; (d) maintaining openness in judicial affairs (such as public security, census management, detention, trial, and accusations) and providing corresponding judicial supervision; (e) keeping the public informed about official appointments by releasing information on proposed candidates beforehand and listening to people's comments about them; and (f) setting up and improving the government's electronic operations at all levels through official websites, information on government affairs over the Internet, direct use of the Internet to handle public affairs, and feedback from citizens via the Internet.

"Service-Oriented Government" and Improved Public Services

China reached an important turning point in its political development when it consciously made the provision of public services the legitimate foundation of governing. In recent years, the government has taken a number of steps to transform itself into a service-oriented government. To begin with, it has simplified the administrative examination and approval system. For example, from 2002 to 2004 the State Council abolished or adjusted 1,806 items of the system, reducing the number of activities requiring administrative examination and approval by 50.1 percent.[18] Second, it has implemented a "one-stop shopping" service model in order to shorten procedure times and reduce administration costs. Third, in an effort to clarify administrative responsibilities, it has adopted a "services commitment" and "responsibility-investigating" system that refrains from buck passing and punishes delinquent officials. Fourth, an "emergency management system" capable of handling disasters is now in place. After the SARS crisis of 2003, the central government took the lead in establishing an institution for emergency management and requiring local governments at every level to do so as well. Furthermore, governments at every level have been establishing special service mechanisms that can override regular procedures to meet urgent citizen demands.

Democratizing Decisionmaking through Public Hearings and Deliberations

Since the Thirteenth National Congress of the CCP introduced the objective of "democratizing decisionmaking and making it more scientific," China has made great progress in this direction through the wide implementation of public hearings, public consultation, and public deliberation. Introduced in the 1990s, public hearings are now playing an increasingly important role in governmental decisionmaking, with policy and legislation-related hearings gaining favor at the central level. For example, numerous public hearings and six rounds of discussions preceded the NPC Standing Committee's final approval of the Property

Law of China in March 2007. Citizens exhibited unprecedented motivation and excitement about participating in the whole process.[19] The incumbent administration also encouraged ministries and commissions to hold public hearings before finalizing policies concerning citizens' crucial interests (for example, with regard to the government's decision to increase the price of public transportation, gas, and education). As a result, many local governments invited stakeholders and experts to participate in the public hearings before arriving at a decision. "Deliberative democracy," currently a hot topic in the West, is also receiving increasing attention in China, as demonstrated by the move to integrate deliberative democracy into decisionmaking in a number of local jurisdictions and by some scholarly and official attempts to combine theories of deliberative democracy with the established institution of political consultation in China.

The foregoing political developments are just a few of the basic reforms and opening-up policies being carried out in China. Interestingly, they are closely linked with the country's opening up to the outside world—without which domestic reform would have been impossible. Although many of the new political ideas and innovations originated in the experiences of foreign political systems, it is essential to recognize they represent the marriage of Chinese traditions/conditions and more universal human values such as freedom, justice, democracy, equality, and human rights, all of which serve to bolster China's political reforms. That is to say, these innovations may serve a variety of domestic purposes—such as improving administration efficiency, deterring corruption, maintaining social stability, or changing government functions—but their ultimate objective is to establish a system of modern, democratic governance across the country so that the rights of the citizenry can be fully realized and protected.

Incremental Democracy: Concept and Process

Although China's reforms have moved away from traditional political ideology and institutions, they still differ greatly from traditional Western political models. The CCP describes the distinctive political model emerging in China as "socialist democratic politics with Chinese characteristics." Its most striking feature is the use of incremental reforms to enlarge the political rights of the citizenry. I would describe the model as "incremental democracy" (*zengliang minzhu*) and believe it has six defining characteristics, all reflected in the country's recent political developments.[20]

First, democratization in China depends on "incremental" development. If the reforms to date are any indication, China's further democratic reforms will be built on the accumulated successes of the country's current economic and political reforms, which, as already mentioned, have been adapted to established socioeconomic institutions. Hence the speed and intensity of democratic reforms cannot outpace what those institutions and economic development will support. According to this theory of incremental democracy, deepening political reform requires the support of the majority of the people and the political elite and must be based on a sober analysis of the prevailing social conditions. Moreover, democratic reforms must take place within the given political and legal frameworks and must not violate the established constitution or other basic laws. At the same time, political reforms should aim at achieving not only legality but also political legitimacy. This means that democratic reforms should promote social progress and public goods to ensure they are recognized as desirable entities by the majority of the citizenry. When political legitimacy comes into conflict with the law, relevant laws should be amended through legal procedures to accommodate the needs of the reforms.

Second, democratic evolution will bring occasional "breakthroughs" in political development. According to the logic of incremental democracy, China's political development will tend to be both gradual and steady, but with some sharp punctuations here and there. Since gradual reforms may exhibit "path dependence" in that they are unable to depart entirely from their preceding historical track, China cannot expect to achieve democratization and implement political reforms overnight, but neither can it hesitate to move forward. Rather, the country should achieve breakthroughs in discrete increments. New increments are more than just quantitative increases in the "deposits" brought about by successful reforms; they are also breakthroughs in the fundamental nature of reform. Breakthroughs should be carried out when realistic conditions present themselves, but these should not amount to shock therapy; breakthroughs may trigger qualitative changes, but the process of implementing them will be gradual and long.

Third, incremental democracy will increase people's political interests as much as possible without reducing existing interests. Political reform in China will focus on adjusting the pattern of benefit allocation and on reducing the benefits gap between different social groups. In keeping with the principles of justice and equality, political and institutional reforms in China should be oriented toward helping more people—especially minority, poor, disabled, or otherwise marginalized populations—enjoy the benefits of the reforms. All political reforms should be oriented toward increasing, instead of decreasing, the existing political interests of the citizenry. In other words, incremental democratic reforms should aim at achieving Pareto optimality just as economic reforms do. Under Pareto optimality, at least one individual can be made better off without making any other individual worse off. With the amplification of the incremental interests, citizens would perceive the advantages brought about by the political reform, which would, in turn, lead them to reform outdated institutions.

Fourth, "dynamic political stability" will gradually replace "static political stability." According to the theory of incremental democracy, all political reforms should enhance social and political stability. However, the aim of incremental democracy is not to maintain traditional static stability (*jingtai wending*), which depends on "holding everything in place" (*yi du wei zhu*); rather, it is to pursue modern dynamic stability (*dongtai wending*), which depends on "channeling everything into its proper place" (*yi shu wei zhu*). In the logic of traditional static stability, social stability means everything stays still and order can only be maintained by suppressing the forces of change. By contrast, dynamic stability incorporates change, maintaining social stability (or balance) through continuous adjustment. In essence, dynamic stability is the replacement of old balances by new balances. Unlike the Cultural Revolution, which relied on repression to maintain order (yet resulted in anarchic turmoil), dynamic stability attempts to maintain order through negotiation. This is the only way to achieve the objective put forward in the report of the CCP's Fifteenth National Congress: namely, "to push forward reform and development on the basis of social and political stability, while maintaining social and political stability through reforms and developments."[21]

Fifth, political reforms will accelerate political participation by citizens and thereby promote "orderly democracy." Democracy is nothing but an array of institutions and procedures that seek to guarantee freedom, equality, and all the other human rights of citizens. The essence of democratic politics is the political participation of the citizenry. Conversely, citizen participation is the fundamental means to realize democracy. Hence, political participation of citizens should be encouraged and given high priority on China's political reform agenda. Furthermore, political participation must be legal, organized, and orderly. That is to say, the best way to stimulate incremental democracy is to spare no effort to "enlarge the orderly political participation of the citizens" and to guide the voluntary, sporadic, and disorganized political participation of citizens into a political framework led by the party and government.

Sixth, democratization and the further development of the rule of law are two sides of the same coin in China. Chinese leaders from Deng Xiaoping onward have placed equal emphasis on both of these goals. They believe that without the rule of law, democracy is not possible, dictatorship cannot be avoided, and the human rights of the citizenry cannot be guaranteed. The first step in constructing socialist democratic politics is to replace rule by man with rule of law. In this respect, the realization of the rule of law could be regarded as the realization of democracy in China. China's interest in building a democratic political system can be attributed entirely to its progress in adopting the rule of law. The CCP's ideal objective is "the organic unity of Party leadership, the people's mastering of the country, and the rule of law."[22] Democracy and the rule of law are two inseparable aspects of political development in China's future. They are also the basic components of socialist political civilization as envisioned by the CCP and the Chinese government. China will establish its preliminary socialist legal system by 2010, which will be a milestone in the history of China's democratization.

Conclusion

China's impetus for introducing incremental democracy stems from its implementation of the socialist market economy, people's increasing demands for democracy, and the impact of globalization. The CCP's transformation from a revolutionary party into a ruling party and the change in its basic objectives from seizing to maintaining power have also played a key role. A comprehensive process, this transformation touches every aspect of the party: its social foundations, organizational structure, leadership style, policies and regulations, strategy and tactics, work focus, and ideology. The Resolution on Enhancing the Governing Capacity of the CCP, passed at the Fourth Plenary Session of the Sixteenth Central Committee of the CCP, made clear to the world that the CCP's ruling position is neither inherent nor permanent.[23] Only by satisfying the increasing political, economic, and cultural demands of the citizens can the CCP retain broad support from the majority of the people. In this sense, it is in the party's long-term interest to advance incremental democracy, which is undeniably the logical end goal of China's political reforms.

China is likely to follow three "road maps" in the near future to reach this destination. The first would stimulate social democracy through inner-party democracy. As the only ruling party in China, the CCP will remain at the center of political power in contemporary China. With more than 70 million party members, the CCP has absorbed the vast majority of the country's social and political elites. In the absence of inner-party democracy, democracy in China would surely become nothing more than an empty slogan. Thus enlarging inner-party democracy will be a necessary first step toward China's overall democratization.

Second, democratization will develop from the grassroots level up. To exercise democracy in a big country like China with a long tradition of centralism, it is essential to rely on both "top-down" and "bottom-up" strategies. However, the focus and breakthrough in democratic politics today is in the grassroots arena. Some significant democratic reforms will first be tried at this level and then be pushed upward.

Third, China's democratization will be characterized by the growth of competition. Democracy, no matter what form it takes, is defined by the free election of political leaders. Hence democratization will mean enlarging the scope of people's political choices so as to move from less competition to more competition. In sum, China's citizens will gradually experience more freedom in political elections, and the election process will become more and more competitive.

Notes

1. Deng Xiaoping, "Emancipating the Mind, Seeking Truth from Facts and Unite as One in Looking to the Future," *Selected Works of Deng Xiaoping*, vol. 2 (Beijing: Foreign Languages Press, 1994), p.152.

2. Hu Jintao, "Work Hard and Earnestly to Construct a Socialist Harmonious Society and Put Forward the Great Cause of Socialism with Chinese Characteristics," *Qiushi* (Seeking Truth), no. 1 (2007), p. 4.

3. "Advice of the Central Committee of the CCP on Revamping the Constitution," *People's Daily*, October 15, 2003.

4. "The Central Committee Calls on Every Party Member to Firmly Protect the Socialist Legal System," *Selected Documents from the People's Congress* (Beijing: China Democracy and Law Press, 1992), p. 166.

5. Ibid.

6. Jiang Zemin, "Hold High the Flag of Deng Xiaoping Theory and Push Forward the Cause of Socialism with Chinese Characteristics into the 21st Century," Report to the Fifteenth National Congress of the CCP, *People's Daily*, September 12, 1997.

7. "Advice of the Central Committee of the CCP on Revamping the Constitution," *People's Daily*, October 15, 2003.

8. "The Property Law of the People's Republic of China" (Beijing: China Democracy and Law Press, 2007), p. 4.

9. Jiang Zemin, "An Address on the Occasion of Meeting of the Ministers of the National Publicity Ministry," January 10, 2001 (www.news.sina.com.cn/c/168432.html).

10. Zhu Shiqun, "Overview of Chinese Studies of Civil Society," *Sociology Studies*, no. 6 (1995), p. 54.

11. Liu Defu and Wang Chengqing, *Grand Tendencies of China* (Jinan: Shandong People's Press, 2004), p. 447.

12. "The Central Committee's Resolution on Constructing a Socialist Harmonious Society," *People's Daily*, October 18, 2006.

13. Ministry of Civil Affairs, *China Civil Affairs Yearbook, 1999* (Beijing: China Social Press, 2000), pp. 23–25.

14. Ministry of Civil Affairs, "Statistics of Civil Organizations in 2005" (www.mca.gov.cn).

15. On the political significance of the emergence of civil society in China, see Yu Keping, "The Emerging Civil Society in China and Its Significance for Governance," *Chinese Social Science Quarterly*, Hong Kong (Autumn 1999).

16. Regarding the current conditions of China's civil society and its significance to the political sphere of China, see Yu Keping and others, *Institutional Environment of China's Civil Society* (Beijing: China Social Science and Compilation Press, 2005), pp. 47–120.

17. State Council Information Office, "The Development of Democratic Politics in China," *People's Daily*, October 19, 2005.

18. Ibid.

19. Lu Ning, "The Property Law: Witness of the Social Attitudes Transformation in China" (www.business.sohu.com/20061031/n246100128.shtml).

20. Yu Keping, *Incremental Democracy and Good Governance* (Beijing: Chinese Social Science and Documentation Publishing House, 2005), pp. 137–45.

21. Jiang Zemin, "Hold High the Flag of Deng Xiaoping Theory"; and "Push Forward the Cause of Socialism with Chinese Characteristics in the 21st Century," Report to the Fifteenth National Congress of the CCP, *People's Daily*, September 12, 1997.

22. Jiang Zemin, "Building a Well-Off Society in an All-Around Way and Opening Up New Prospects for the Cause of Socialism with Chinese Characteristics," Report to the National Congress of the Chinese Communist Party, *People's Daily*, October 9, 2003.

23. "Resolution on Enhancing the Governing Capacity of the Chinese Communist Party" (passed at the Fourth Plenary session of the Sixteenth Central Committee of the Chinese Communist Party on September 19, 2004), *People's Daily*, September 26, 2004.

Part II

Institutional Development and Generational Change

4

Institutionalization and the Changing Dynamics of Chinese Leadership Politics

ALICE L. MILLER

> Even so great a man as Comrade Mao Zedong was influenced to a serious degree by certain unsound systems and institutions, which resulted in grave misfortunes for the Party, the state and himself. . . . Stalin gravely damaged socialist legality, doing things that Comrade Mao Zedong once said would have been impossible in Western countries like Britain, France and the United States. Although Comrade Mao was aware of this, he did not in practice solve the problems of our leadership system. Together with other factors, this led to the decade of catastrophe known as the "Cultural Revolution." There is a most profound lesson to be learned from this.
>
> DENG XIAOPING, "On the Reform of the System of Party and State Leadership"

Since the beginning of the Deng Xiaoping era, elite politics in China has undergone deliberate, incremental institutionalization. As institutionalized processes of leadership decisionmaking have taken hold, the dynamics of leadership competition have also been changing, in favor of an increasingly consensus-building collective leadership. Furthermore, institutionalization is revising the criteria and processes used to promote leaders to the top of the political order.

The leadership changes at the Chinese Communist Party's (CCP's) Seventeenth Congress in 2007 and the Seventeenth Central Committee's First Plenum immediately after will provide an important opportunity to gauge the impact of advancing institutionalization on elite politics in China. Some impact is already evident in the policymaking system of the top leadership and the method of appointing leaders to the Politburo, its Standing Committee, and the Secretariat as these bodies have evolved since the 1950s. This chapter draws inferences from those changes to explore what may be expected from the Seventeenth Party Congress, particularly with regard to the position and prerogatives of Hu Jintao as paramount leader and the possibility for more liberal politics under the leadership dynamic spawned by institutionalization.

61

Institutionalization in Post-Mao Politics

The impetus for institutionalization derived directly from the revision of the CCP's "general task"—its fundamental mission, to which all other priorities are to be subordinated—set down at the watershed 1978 Third Plenum of the Eleventh Central Committee. Restoring formulations that had been established at the 1956 Eighth CCP Congress, the Third Plenum communiqué shifted the focus of party work from class warfare and social transformation to modernization. The communiqué signaled an end to the "large-scale turbulent class struggles of a mass character" that had been Mao's preferred mode of politics and called for the restoration of party organizational discipline and adherence to socialist law.

Deng Xiaoping and his reform coalition favored institutionalization for three main reasons. First, routinized and predictable political and policymaking processes were deemed indispensable to the success of China's modernization. Second, since Mao's "revolutionary" politics of spontaneous mass struggle had led China into a decade of disorder and two decades of "leftist" deviation in development, the coalition sought to prevent any possible recurrence of that impulse. Third, the Deng leadership hoped to guard against the concentration of dictatorial authority that Mao Zedong had achieved and to instill collective processes within the top leadership.

Deng's agenda of institutionalizing politics became evident over the ensuing two decades. At the broadest scale, party congresses and Central Committee plenums resumed convocation as stipulated in the party's constitution. Under Mao's leadership, these bodies met only sporadically after 1959, despite stipulations issued in 1956 that congresses convene every five years and plenums convene twice a year. Under Deng, these bodies have met with metronomic regularity on the schedule prescribed by the 1982 party constitution—which calls for party congresses every five years and Central Committee plenums "at least once" every year. Annual convocation of sessions of the National People's Congress (NPC) and the Chinese People's Political Consultative Conference (CPPCC) resumed in 1979 and has continued without interruption down to the present.

Resumption of high-level party and state meetings on constitutionally prescribed schedules has instilled institutional routines in the subordinate party organs and State Council bureaucracies as well. Media accounts suggest that political reports delivered by the party general secretary to party congresses and resolutions on issues endorsed by party plenums now follow well-established routines of consultation, review, and revision by organs and constituencies down through the provincial level. Similarly, budgets presented by the minister of finance at the NPC session every spring are compiled through accounting and deliberation routines up and down the institutional hierarchy.

Institutionalization is also evident in the restoration of organizational discipline in the party, government bureaucracies, and the army, as reflected in the Central Discipline Inspection Commission created at the 1978 Third Plenum, with Chen Yun as its first secretary, and the detailed code of cadre regulations adopted in 1980. More broadly, the intensive effort to set down codes of law—launched in the late 1950s but disrupted in the escalating leadership conflict thereafter—began again in 1979 under the general direction of Peng Zhen. As the strictures of party discipline and socialist law took hold in the 1980s, "freaks and monsters" were no longer discovered lurking in the leadership, purged, and made the object of mass criticism campaigns, as had become the common exit pattern in leadership politics during the 1960s and 1970s. Instead, leaders generally retained their posts throughout their appointed terms; when they were removed, most were demoted or released without public disgrace or were subjected to legal proceedings on the basis of alleged criminality—exemplified most recently in the case of Shanghai party chief Chen Liangyu.

Leadership turnover and succession came under institutionalizing pressure as well when the constitution of the People's Republic of China (PRC) incorporated fixed term limits for top state posts in 1982 and established mandatory retirement ages for various levels within the state hierarchy. Although the CCP did not establish term limits for leadership posts in the party at that point, it did stipulate that leadership cadres "are not entitled to lifelong tenure." Since then, informal (or perhaps unpublicized) retirement regulations for positions at various levels of the party hierarchy appear to have been in force. These include the expectation, evident since 1997, that members of the Politburo who have reached the age of seventy will retire at the next party congress.

Perhaps the most dramatic indication of advancing institutionalization was the deliberate and prepared succession of Hu Jintao to the top party, state, and military posts held by Jiang Zemin. Hu's phased accession to the post of party general secretary at the Sixteenth CCP Congress in 2002, to the post of PRC president at the tenth NPC in 2003, and to the posts of party and state Central Military Commission (CMC) chairman in 2004–05 followed precedents established by Deng Xiaoping himself in his retirement from the Politburo Standing Committee in 1987, and from the CMC chairman posts in 1989–90. Hu's accession had been preceded by a ten-year course of preparation, marked by his elevation in 1992 to the Politburo Standing Committee and executive secretary of the party Secretariat, without prior service on either body, and by his appointment as PRC vice president in 1998 and as CMC vice chairman in 1999. By the time of his accession to the top party, state, and military posts, Hu had a record of ten years managing the party apparatus, five years serving as PRC vice president, and five years sitting on the CMC. Hu's orderly succession to Jiang Zemin over a three-year period stands as the only instance of successful arranged leadership change in any major communist country.

All of these steps and others indicate an incremental and deliberate institutionalization of Chinese elite politics since 1978 that resumed patterns begun in the 1950s but that broke down in the leadership conflict of the 1960s and 1970s amid the onslaught of Mao's inherently anti-institutional ideological convictions. This process has gained momentum down to the present, and it has made leadership politics more stable and, on the whole, more predictable.

Institutionalizing Collective Leadership: The 1956–58 System

The advancing institutionalization of Chinese politics has also begun to change the dynamics of leadership cooperation and competition. This is particularly evident in the party leadership's collective decisionmaking plus division of responsibility for daily tasks in specific policy sectors.

The system of collective leadership set down by Deng Xiaoping at the onset of the reform era restored the main elements of the system put in place in 1956–58, notably at the Eighth CCP Congress in September 1956 and at the Eighth Central Committee's Fifth Plenum in May 1958.[1] The most important institutional changes at the Eighth Party Congress were the creation of the Politburo Standing Committee, a powerful six-member subset of the seventeen-man Politburo appointed at the congress, and the revival of the post of general secretary (*zongshuji*) of the party Central Committee. The new Politburo Standing Committee was to take on the policymaking role formerly assumed by the party Secretariat (at the expense of the Politburo) during the Sino-Japanese and civil wars and in the early years of the PRC. The seven-man Secretariat appointed at the congress was to "attend to the daily work of the Central Committee under the direction of the Politburo and its Standing Committee." By this arrangement, the Politburo Standing Committee assumed primary responsibility for decisionmaking, while the Secretariat was more clearly responsible for coordinating implementation of Politburo Standing Committee policies.

Upon its establishment in 1921, the CCP made its top post that of general secretary but then abolished the position in 1937. In 1956 the party constitution revived the position of general secretary but made it subordinate to that of party chairman—the position created for Mao Zedong in 1943 and held by him until his death in 1976—and of party vice chairman. At the Eighth Party Congress, the post of general secretary was given to Deng Xiaoping, a man clearly marked for top positions when Mao brought him to Beijing from Sichuan in 1952. Deng was ranked sixth on the new Politburo Standing Committee, after Mao and the four vice chairmen appointed at the congress.

Reporting on the revision of the party constitution at the Eighth Congress, Deng Xiaoping explained why these structural changes were necessary: "Owing to the pressures of party and government work, existing central organs had proven inadequate." Although Deng's report did not spell out the inadequacies, they undoubtedly sprang from the effort to collectivize agriculture and nationalize industry and commerce (the tasks of "socialist transformation") and the consequent shift toward modernization ("building socialism") announced at the Eighth CCP Congress, both of which pointed to a need for clearer lines of organizational authority and more institutionalized processes.

This new collective leadership system was elaborated further with new appointments to the Politburo and Secretariat at the May 1958 Fifth Plenum and by the creation of five "small leadership groups" to coordinate policy implementation by the party apparatus throughout the political order. These small groups—for financial and economic work, political and legal work, foreign affairs, science, and culture and education—were subordinate to the Secretariat but reported to the Politburo and its Standing Committee. Under this structure, the Politburo and its Standing Committee were responsible for policy decisions and the Secretariat for "concrete arrangements" required to implement Politburo decisions.[2]

The Politburo Standing Committee was organized around Mao and the top leaders of the party and state hierarchies and thus could make balanced decisions regarding all essential policy sectors—party issues, foreign affairs, military affairs, and the economy. The Secretariat was organized around Deng Xiaoping, with party secretaries responsible for coordinating Politburo decisions in the same essential policy sectors. The respective small groups brought together the principals at the working levels of the party, government, and army related to those policy areas. Under this setup, Deng held the lowest-ranking seat on the Politburo Standing Committee but served as the critical bridge between the two bodies, one responsible for policy decisions and the other for policy coordination. At a meeting in Shanghai in 1959, Mao himself underscored Deng Xiaoping's role in this regard: "The Politburo is the 'court of political planning,' and authority is concentrated in the Politburo Standing Committee and the Secretariat. As chairman, I am the commander; as general secretary, Deng Xiaoping is deputy commander."[3] In this system, the Politburo's Standing Committee appeared to serve as the center of decisionmaking, while the Politburo—whose regular membership reflected no evident division of responsibility for specific policy sectors—served largely as a back bench to endorse decisions made by Mao and his Standing Committee.

This collective leadership system served two other important purposes. First, it clustered the "first line" of leaders—the four party vice chairmen, Liu Shaoqi,

Zhou Enlai, Zhu De, and Chen Yun—around Mao, giving them prominence and experience as he prepared to retreat to the "second line" of the leadership. By this scheme, Liu as potential successor would take over from Mao the formalities of official protocol.[4] Second, the new system laid the foundations for a higher degree of collective leadership, a priority in the broader context of Soviet bloc politics following Nikita Khrushchev's "secret speech" at the Soviet Communist Party's Twentieth Congress in February 1956, in which he attacked the cult of personality surrounding Stalin and inaugurated the de-Stalinization movement. In his report on revision of the party constitution to the Eighth CCP Congress in September of the same year, Deng stressed the need to enhance collective leadership and avoid the "cult of the individual," while gingerly avoiding any allusion to Mao in that regard.[5]

The collective leadership system established between 1956 and 1958 nevertheless failed to contain the subsequent leadership conflict or prevent the usurpation of dictatorial power by Mao. The system did not survive the Cultural Revolution. Deng Xiaoping was purged as the "No. 2 power holder in the party taking the capitalist road." The Secretariat was abolished and replaced by the Central Cultural Revolution Group around Jiang Qing, which took over much of the Standing Committee's work as well. Although the 1969 Ninth Congress again delegated some responsibilities in specific policy sectors to individual members of the Politburo, these arrangements were overshadowed by the larger politics sustaining a factional balance among a severely polarized leadership around Mao. Factional differences over policy bled easily into public view, as PRC media frequently reported high-level leaders speaking out at meetings and conferences on issues for which they had no delegated authority, often contradicting those who did have it to speak for the prevailing party line.

The Collective Leadership Work System in the Deng Period

As part of the effort in the early reform years to institutionalize Chinese elite politics, Deng Xiaoping resurrected the leadership work system installed in the 1956–58 period. At the Eleventh Central Committee's Fifth Plenum in February 1980, the Secretariat was restored and staffed with ten secretaries under the leadership of Hu Yaobang, who was given the revived post of general secretary (*zongshuji*). Hu had already been appointed secretary general (*mishuzhang*) of the Central Committee at the 1978 Third Plenum, retracing the course that Deng Xiaoping had followed in the 1954–56 period. At the Twelfth Central Committee's First Plenum, immediately following the CCP's Twelfth Congress in September 1982, a new six-member Politburo Standing Committee was appointed that, as in 1956, brought together the top leaders of the primary hierarchies of the political order—including General Secretary Hu Yaobang, NPC chairman Ye Jianying, CMC chairman Deng Xiaoping, Premier Zhao Ziyang, soon-to-be-appointed PRC president Li Xiannian, and secretary of discipline inspection Chen Yun. The broader Politburo counted nineteen regular members and three alternates. The new Secretariat included ten members under the leadership of General Secretary Hu Yaobang, each with responsibility for coordinating policy implementation in specific sectors.

Over the next few years, the restored collective leadership system apparently functioned in the manner intended for the 1956–58 system on which it was based. To judge by incomplete but still suggestive data from PRC media and by Zhao Ziyang's comments to Doak Barnett in 1984, the full Politburo, which in the late 1970s had convened regularly, became a "second-line" body and rarely met after 1982. Instead, the Politburo Standing Committee became the principal decisionmaking body and worked directly—sometimes in joint session—with the Secretariat, which coordinated the implementation of the committee's decisions.[6]

The system nevertheless was altered significantly in 1987 for two reasons. First, Hu Yaobang was forced to resign from his post as general secretary, allegedly for making policy decisions in the Secretariat that were properly the preserve of the Politburo and its Standing Committee. Although Hu's resignation was prompted by a range of charges—including tolerating the rise of "bourgeois liberalization"—his abuse of his authority as general secretary appears to have been the underlying complaint, registered in the severe reduction of the Secretariat membership at the Thirteenth CCP Congress later that year.[7]

The collective leadership system that emerged out of the October 1987 Thirteenth Party Congress departed from the one deployed in 1982. The Politburo Standing Committee continued to be the principal arena for day-to-day decisionmaking, as before. But the Politburo began meeting regularly again, following a roughly monthly schedule. The Secretariat appointed at the Thirteenth Central Committee's First Plenum, immediately after the congress, numbered only four secretaries and one alternate under the direction of Zhao Ziyang, Hu's replacement as general secretary.

The new system thus restored the authority of the Politburo as a whole. This authority was reinforced by new procedures that required the general secretary to provide the full Politburo with routine reports on the work of the Politburo Standing Committee and to report on the work of the full Politburo to the Central Committee at its successive plenums. In addition, according to former Politburo member Hu Qiaomu, the Politburo adopted new procedures for decisionmaking by consensus, effectively reducing the prerogatives of the general secretary over the Politburo's regular members and rendering him more approximately "first among equals."[8]

These steps taken in 1987 to redress the 1982 leadership system in favor of reinforced collective decisionmaking were complemented by several new departures in membership on the Politburo, reflected in appointments made at the Thirteenth Central Committee's First Plenum. For one thing, the new Politburo included no leaders serving in military positions. This was a striking departure from the 1982 Politburo, whose membership included no less than eight representatives of the People's Liberation Army (counting CMC chairman Deng Xiaoping, Vice Chairmen Ye Jianying and Xu Xiangqian, the directors of the General Staff and Political Departments, the commander of the air force, and the commanders of the Shenyang and Beijing military regions). For another, the new Politburo included four provincial party secretaries—from Shanghai, Tianjin, Beijing, and Sichuan—in the first move ever toward regional representation.[9]

These new departures appear to have served complementary purposes. First, they broadened and balanced the constituencies represented on the Politburo, which was now expected to play a more active role in policymaking. This effort reinforced collective decisionmaking and helped to inhibit the concentration of power and abuse of authority that had disrupted the 1956–58 work system under Mao Zedong and that led to Hu Yaobang's resignation as general secretary in 1987.

Second, the inclusion of regional leaders in the Politburo membership for the first time appears to have been part of a broader attempt to transform the Politburo into a body better equipped to make efficient and rational policy decisions through increased competence, expertise, and representation of significant organizational constituencies. This effort began in 1987, in the midst of the generational turnover initiated with the retirement of several high-ranking members of Deng's "Second Generation" and completed at the Fourteenth CCP Congress in 1992 with the dissolution of the Central Advisory Commission and the retirement of the last group of leaders of Deng's generation (principally, Yang Shangkun and Deng himself). In their place emerged "Third Generation" leaders whose careers marked them as both "post-liberation" leaders (in that they had little direct experience of and participation in the communist revolutionary movement before 1949) and "post-revolutionary" leaders (whose expertise rested on technocratic credentials rather than on their skills as mobilizers of mass movements aimed at "revolutionary" transformation of Chinese society).

The trend toward balanced representation of important organizational constituencies can be seen in the composition of the successive Politburos elected from the Thirteenth in 1987 to the Sixteenth in 2002, as shown in table 4-1. From 1992 to 2002, the size of the Politburo stabilized to encompass twenty-

Table 4-1. *Politburo Membership by Organizational Constituency, 1982–2002*

Constituent	Twelfth	Thirteenth	Fourteenth	Fifteenth	Sixteenth
Politburo	25 + 3	17	20 + 2	22 + 2	24 + 1
Politburo Standing Committee	6	5	7	7	9
Secretariat	9	4 + 1	5	7	7
Secs on PB[a]	4	2	4	6	5
Central Committee departments	2	1	1	1	2
SC VP/SCs[b]	2/2	3/2	4/1	4/1	4
NPC VCs[c]	2	1	2	2	1
Military	8	0	1	2	2
Regional	0	4	5	4	6
Other	12	6	8	10	11

a. Members of the Secretariat who serve concurrently on the Politburo.

b. State Council vice premiers and state councilors.

c. National People's Congress vice chairmen.

two to twenty-five members (making it larger than the seventeen-member 1987 Politburo but still smaller than the 1982 Politburo around Deng Xiaoping). One or two directors of the principal Central Committee departments—either the Propaganda or Organization Departments, or both—have routinely gained seats, augmenting the powerful bloc of four to six Politburo members who serve concurrently on the Secretariat and so represent the party apparatus. Four or five members of the State Council Executive Committee—either vice premiers or state councilors—back up the premier as a second major grouping. They are complemented by one or two vice chairmen of the NPC, bringing the combined representation of the NPC and State Council to five or six. Regional representation in the Politburo has grown from four to six provincial party secretaries. Military representation appears to have stabilized at two of the CMC vice chairmen, up from none in 1987. The two—both professional military men in the case of Chi Haotian and Zhang Wannian in the 1997 Politburo as well as Cao Gangchuan and Guo Boxiong on the 2002 body—are the only Politburo members with any meaningful military experience.

The emphasis on competence and expertise in selecting Politburo members is evident in comparisons of the educational credentials of the 1982 Twelfth Central Committee Politburo around Deng Xiaoping, the 1997 Fifteenth under Jiang Zemin, and the 2002 Sixteenth under Hu Jintao. Of the 1982 Politburo's twenty-eight members—virtually all of them professional revolutionaries who had participated in the 1935–36 Long March—none had university degrees. In contrast, seventeen of the twenty-four members of the 1997 Politburo had university degrees, as do twenty-two of the 2002 Politburo's twenty-five members. Underscoring the technical orientation of the emerging technocratic Third and Fourth Generation leaders, fourteen of the seventeen degree holders in 1997 were engineers, while seventeen of the twenty-two degree holders in the 2002 Politburo, including eight of nine on the Standing Committee, have engineering degrees.

The deliberate shaping of the Politburo over these years also shows an effort to routinize generational turnover. With the apparent adoption in 1997 of age seventy as the expected norm for retirement, the average age of newly appointed Politburo members has dropped steadily—from seventy-two in 1982 to sixty-three in 1997 and sixty in 2002—thereby allowing a normal Politburo tenure of two five-year terms before retirement.

Trends in the collective leadership system in the post-Mao period indicate a deliberate design on behalf of two overarching priorities: to keep organizational constituencies in a careful balance that will sustain collective leadership decision-making and to prevent any single bloc—or especially the party leader—from dominating or acting as its spokesman; and to appoint Politburo members on the basis of competence, expertise, and representation in order to facilitate effective and rational decisionmaking. The objective of this design since it emerged in the 1990s is to develop an oligarchic top leadership that is politically balanced, substantively competent, and best equipped to deal with the daunting challenges Beijing faces as it guides China's modernization and rise in world affairs.[10]

Generally speaking, these reinforcing trends toward collective decisionmaking in the Politburo and institutionalization of elite politics over the past two decades have produced a system in which institutional structures tend to constrain competition for power at the top and provide incentives for cooperation and compromise. The system was intended to eliminate the unbridled, free-for-all, faction-driven competition for power provoked by the anti-institutional politics of the later Mao years. The experience of that era moved Deng Xiaoping and his allies to design the new system, reinforced by the lessons of decision-making paralysis that fed into the Tiananmen crisis of April–June 1989.

To judge the success of this effort, one might note that the symptoms of vicious factional conflict prevalent in the 1970s and visible though less ferocious in the 1980s, after the reform coalition around Deng Xiaoping began to splinter over the scope and pace of reform, have evaporated from public view. Of course, some differences can still be detected in the nuances of public statements, which undoubtedly reflect deeper divisions within the leadership and a persistent competition for power. But they are dimmer, less strident, and carefully framed so as not to disturb the front of leadership consensus. Institutionalization has changed the rules of the game in Chinese leadership politics, and the premises and methods used to analyze leadership must change correspondingly.

The Short-Term Prospects: The Seventeenth Party Congress

Does the preceding analysis provide any clues to changes in leadership (see table 4-2 for its current composition) that may emerge from the Seventeenth Party Congress? A number of inferences seem plausible.

First, leadership turnover is likely to be less sweeping than it was at the Sixteenth CCP Congress in 2002.[11] If the retirement norm of age seventy continues to prevail, then, strictly speaking, only Luo Gan (aged seventy-two) will be required to retire from the Politburo Standing Committee and only Cao Gangchuan (aged seventy-two) will step down from the Politburo's regular membership. A few other leaders close to seventy may also retire. On the Politburo Standing Committee, Wu Guanzheng is sixty-nine, and Huang Ju recently died. Among the regular Politburo members, Zhang Lichang has already been replaced as Tianjin CCP secretary, and Shanghai party boss Chen Liangyu was "suspended" from his Politburo post pending a corruption investigation announced in September 2006. That investigation is likely to conclude by the time the congress opens and lead to his formal dismissal. In addition, Vice Premier Zeng Peiyan is sixty-nine and may also retire because of age. Many of the remaining members of the Politburo and its Standing Committee are not required or encouraged to retire by age seventy, however. Most of those in their mid-sixties were appointed in 2002 with the expectation that they were eligible to serve two terms before retiring at the Eighteenth Party Congress in 2012. Unless considerations of competence, performance, and calculations of power require it, there is no necessary impetus for their replacement.

By contrast, the Politburo turnover at the Sixteenth CCP Congress in 2002 marked a generational transition in leadership and so was far more sweeping. Six of seven Politburo members appointed in 1997 retired in 2002, leaving Hu Jintao as the sole holdover. Eight of the nine members of the new Politburo Standing Committee were new, all of them elevated as a bloc from their former positions as regular members of the Politburo. Of the sixteen regular members of the new Politburo, fifteen were new to that body. In addition, seven of the eight members of the 2002 Secretariat were new.

Second, new appointments to the Politburo and its Standing Committee are likely to be based on considerations of competence, representation, and personality, in addition to calculations of factional loyalty. If past trends continue, candidates will also be selected with the balance of representation among organiza-

Table 4-2. *Overview of the CCP Politburo, 2007*

Member and age	Position
Standing Committee (rank order)	
Hu Jintao (65)	General secretary, CCP; PRC president; chairman, CCP and PRC Central Military Commissions
Wu Bangguo (66)	Chairman, National People's Congress
Wen Jiabao (65)	State Council premier
Jia Qinglin (67)	Chairman, CPPCC
Zeng Qinghong (68)	Secretariat; PRC vice president; president, Central Party School
Huang Ju (69)	Vice premier (deceased, June 2007)
Wu Guanzheng (69)	Secretary, Central Discipline Inspection Commission
Li Changchun (63)	Head, Central Leading Group for Publicity and Ideological Work
Luo Gan (72)	Head, Central Committee for Comprehensive Management of Society and Security
Regular members (stroke order)[a]	
Wang Lequan (63)	Secretary, Xinjiang CCP
Wang Zhaoguo (66)	Executive vice chairman, NPC Standing Committee; president, All-China Federation of Trade Unions
Hui Liangyu (63)	Vice premier
Liu Qi (65)	Secretary, Beijing CCP
Liu Yunshan (60)	Secretariat; director; CCP Propaganda Department
Wu Yi (69)	Vice premier
Zhang Lichang (68)	(Replaced as secretary, Tianjin CCP, March 2007)
Zhang Dejiang (61)	Secretary, Guangdong CCP
Chen Liangyu (61)	("Suspended" as Politburo member and secretary, Shanghai CCP, September 2006; removed July 2007)
Zhou Yongkang (65)	Secretariat; minister of public security; state councilor
Yu Zhengsheng (62)	Secretary, Hubei CCP
He Guoqiang (64)	Secretariat; director, CCP Organization Department
Guo Boxiong (65)	Vice chairman, CMC
Cao Gangchuan (72)	Vice chairman, CMC; minister of national defense; state councilor
Zeng Peiyan (69)	Vice premier
Alternate member	
Wang Gang (65)	Secretariat; director, CCP General Office

a. Stroke order is the Chinese equivalent of alphabetical order.

tional constituencies in mind, as in the last four Politburo slates. Hence certain bureaucratic posts may carry some expectation of consideration for concurrent seating on the Politburo, and only candidates with expertise developed over an entire career may qualify for these posts. For example, Liu Yunshan worked virtually his entire political life in the party propaganda apparatus before becoming director of the Party Propaganda Department in October 2002. Insofar as the director of that department has held a seat on both the Fourteenth and Fifteenth Central Committee Politburo, Liu's selection as propaganda chief was likely made both on the basis of his career-long expertise and on the expectation that he would be appointed to the Politburo at the Sixteenth Congress a month later, apart from whatever calculations of factional allegiance may have been involved. Similarly, given the now-routine selection of provincial party secretaries to serve concurrently as Politburo members, this representational group will include new faces. In that regard, the recent appointment of former Zhejiang Party secretary Xi Jinping to replace Chen Liangyu as party chief in Shanghai assures his selection for a Politburo seat at the Seventeenth Congress. Given the priorities of the Hu-Wen leadership, moreover, there is likely to be a balance among the Politburo seats allotted to party secretaries from central and western provinces, alongside the traditional majority from the coastal provinces.

Personality is another factor likely to figure into Politburo appointments, in addition to professional competence, organization representation, and political allegiance. Given the overt emphasis on collective leadership and the incentives for elite cooperation, leaders who have demonstrated excessive ambition, combativeness, or unwillingness to compromise are likely to be weeded out even if their candidacy is backed by a great deal of factional juice. According to some recent accounts, Chen Liangyu's purported criticism of the Hu-Wen leadership in 2004 raised the hackles of more than Hu Jintao and Wen Jiabao for its apparent arrogance and abrasiveness.

Third, Hu Jintao's standing as first among equals in a collective leadership rather than as paramount leader is likely to be reaffirmed. Hu's first term as general secretary has been striking in avoiding many of the trappings extended to his predecessor, Jiang Zemin. Hu has not been described as the "core" of his leadership generation, whereas Jiang Zemin was routinely referred to as "the core of the Fifteenth Central Committee leadership collective" during his tenure as secretary. Instead, the Hu Politburo is known as "the Sixteenth Central Committee leadership collective with Comrade Hu Jintao as general secretary." Hu's first term has brought several new policy departures as well: an emphasis on "people-centered" governance, scientific development, and the concepts of a "new socialist countryside" and a "harmonious socialist society"—yet none of these efforts has been celebrated as an example of his personal initiative or innovation. Rather they are referred to as products of the entire leadership collective.

Some observers have assumed that the lack of publicity regarding Hu's top position or his ideological creativity, in contrast to the paramount role of Jiang Zemin in the years before 2002, reflects Hu's relative lack of power. Once Hu consolidates his power at the Seventeenth Congress by installing factional adherents in key positions and removing those associated with Jiang Zemin, this logic suggests, the trappings that enhanced Jiang's stature may be applied to Hu.

Given the growing emphasis on collective leadership since 1987, however, it seems more likely that Hu will continue to have a lower profile as a prime member of the leadership collective. Inasmuch as Jiang emerged as general secretary unexpectedly in the calamity of 1989, just as the new collective leadership system was being established, it may have been considered politically necessary to accent his stature in order to restore confidence in the party leadership and gain the acceptance of his leadership peers. Hu Jintao was appointed general secretary well after the 1987 work system was established and therefore must have been groomed on his way to the top to embody its ideals of consensus-building collective decisionmaking. If that is the case, then his apotheosis can hardly be expected to issue from the Seventeenth Congress, however much he consolidates his base of power.

The Seventeenth Congress may well give some thought to Hu Jintao's eventual successor, most likely to be announced at the 2012 Eighteenth CCP Congress. As discussed earlier, Hu's succession to Jiang Zemin reflected the success of a ten-year course of preparation that was a central element of Deng Xiaoping's attempt to institutionalize China's politics into predictable and stable routines. While Hu is under no explicit mandate to prepare a successor, his own process of accession serves as a significant precedent.

If he intends to groom a successor by a similar process, that individual is not likely to be explicitly named as such. Instead, Hu's successor will likely assume a cluster of leadership positions that imply this impending status, such as being named a lower-ranking member of the Politburo Standing Committee and executive secretary on the Secretariat at the Seventeenth Central Committee's First Plenum. In 2008, at the Eleventh NPC, his successor may even be appointed PRC vice president, a position that by protocol will give him an opportunity to meet visiting heads of foreign states and to travel on official state visits, and so give him international visibility. Finally, he may be named vice chairman of the party and state CMC in 2009 and 2010. These cumulative appointments would give Hu's successor five years of experience in each of these posts before assuming the top slots, assuming that Hu will step down according to the phased retirement that Deng and Jiang followed.

Although Hong Kong media and foreign observers have circulated several names in the past two years—focusing on Liaoning party chief Li Keqiang, Jiangsu party chief Li Yuanchao, and Zhejiang party chief Xi Jinping—PRC media have given no sign of who this successor might be.[12] And although Hu might even press for a candidate with long-standing ties to himself, such as Li

Yuanchao or Li Keqiang, others in the current leadership will have a predictable stake in not allowing Hu to dictate who should succeed him and thereby extend his influence beyond retirement. In all likelihood, the candidate will satisfy several essential criteria—have had previous service in the provinces and at the center, be in his fifties, and be acceptable to most of the major constituencies in the leadership. In other words, he may well not be a Hu crony.[13]

In Cheng Li's opinion, Hu's successor may emerge via different channels. The Seventeenth Congress may appoint more than one potential candidate to the Politburo and its Standing Committee, staging a competition among themselves over the next few years to succeed Hu in 2012.[14] This scenario seems less likely, however, since it would incite factionalism as each candidate would seek adherents in an effort to build a power base strong enough to win the competition and to discredit his opponents. Since the leadership work system is geared toward blunting factional competition and stressing collective leadership through balanced organizational constituencies, this competitive approach to succession would seem to run counter to the trends in leadership politics over the past two decades.

The task of choosing a candidate to succeed Hu Jintao raises another question: what to do with Zeng Qinghong, a long-time associate of Jiang Zemin. Since 2002 Zeng has been given most of the posts that Hu acquired en route to the top of the leadership in the 1990s, such as membership in the Politburo Standing Committee and executive secretary of the Secretariat, president of the Central Party School, and vice president of the PRC. The only post that Hu once held and that Zeng has not attained is vice chairman of the CMC. If this cluster of posts is to be given successively to the man picked to succeed Hu, Zeng will have to relinquish them. Zeng could retire but is not required to do so—he will be sixty-eight this year. He has also confirmed his reputation as an effective party politician in the years since 2002, apparently working collaboratively with Hu. Conceivably, he may receive a top-level post from which he may eventually retire gracefully, such as chairman of the CPPCC, which would, of course, require the removal of its current incumbent, Jia Qinglin.

Longer-Term Prospects: Systemic Change?

China's institutionalization of elite politics and establishment of the current collective leadership system in 1987 have proved effective in keeping the CCP leadership in power since then and in allowing the party to govern without experiencing a major crisis of the sort suffered in 1989. The leadership's overall effectiveness in guiding China along a path of continuing prosperity and greater strength in the international order over these eighteen years would seem to warrant the leadership's confidence in its current course. If it is on the right track, this pattern of leadership may not provoke systemic change easily or soon.

Nevertheless, things may yet evolve differently, as attested by events in the former Soviet Union, whose collective leadership placed similar emphasis on avoiding the dominance of any bloc or single leader, as well as on fielding a stable leadership effective in governance. These priorities seemed to motivate the creation of what Soviet leadership politics specialist T. H. Rigby called a self-stabilizing oligarchy in the Soviet leadership.[15] In the early 1970s, in an attempt to guard against the reemergence of a leader with dictatorial power of the kind Stalin possessed or a leader asserting dominating power as Khrushchev had attempted, Soviet leaders in the early 1970s resorted to tactics aimed at sustaining collective leadership by balancing organizational constituencies among the Politburo leadership so as to prevent any single bureaucratic bloc of Politburo seats from becoming a base of power for a single leader. In addition, for the same purpose, representation on the Politburo was expanded more routinely to include party secretaries from among the fifteen Soviet republics, as well as quasi–ex officio representation on the Politburo of some leadership posts, such as the defense minister.

As Rigby points out, stable oligarchic politics is difficult to sustain because of two contrary tendencies. Rigby describes the countervailing "dilemmas that any group of oligarchs faces" as follows:

> How do you achieve expeditious decision-making and consistent, coherent policies without a *primus inter pares* who orchestrates, guides, and adjudicates; yet, if you allow such a *primus* to emerge, how do you stop him [from] accumulating autocratic powers? If to concede some of the leadership's powers to wider elements of the polity, including perhaps some controlling assembly, might provide one avenue for countering the drift to autocracy, how do you prevent this dispersal of power from getting out of hand and threatening the security of the oligarchs individually and as a whole, and disrupting national unity?[16]

Historically, the experience of the Soviet Communist Party leadership demonstrated the difficulty of sustaining stable collective leadership against both tendencies. Despite its efforts in this regard, the Soviet Politburo failed to prevent the concentration of authority in Leonid Brezhnev's hands over the 1970s, which culminated in the political stagnation of the early 1980s. Mikhail Gorbachev's subsequent attempt to push the Politburo leadership in a more aggressive reform direction by liberalizing the political order through democratization—launched at the June 1987 Central Committee Plenum and at the 1988 Nineteenth Party Conference, followed by the creation of the Congress of People's Deputies in 1989—merely led to the unraveling of the entire Soviet Communist Party.

In the wake of both their own party's history and the Soviet political collapse under Gorbachev, the CCP's leaders certainly understand these dilemmas of oligarchy. In this sense, they have been walking a difficult tightrope since the late 1980s, attempting to ward off dictatorial authority of the sort that Mao wielded during their lifetimes while sustaining stable and effective governance through institutionalized collective leadership. So far, the pattern of Hu Jintao's leadership as first among equals suggests that they have managed to avoid a dictatorship as well as prevent the gerontocratic stagnation that the Soviet leadership suffered by the early 1980s because it failed to address the same issue.

However, the pressures of governing a rapidly changing society in the midst of explosive economic change have forced the Chinese to explore new political mechanisms and processes in order to keep the CCP in power without systemic change of the sort the Soviet Communist Party acceded to in 1990, with the abolition of Article VI of the Soviet constitution, which had identified it as the USSR's sole ruling party. The range of institutional tinkering undertaken by the Hu leadership in recent years—from increasing the frequency of party congresses at various levels to expanding voting mechanisms in intraparty processes and incorporating newly emerging political constituencies—underscores that the CCP leadership recognizes it needs to reform the political system it dominates if it is to retain power.

Exactly what pressures such liberalizing reform will bring to bear on the stability of the CCP's institutionalized collective leadership system is perhaps the most intriguing question that lies ahead. From all appearances, this system has functioned stably over the past twenty years. In turn, that record has undoubtedly helped consolidate expectations—both among the top leadership and in the broader political order—of institutionalized representation of key constituencies and institutionalized processes of decisionmaking. As the record suggests, collective leadership may function effectively as long as the major constituencies and the oligarchy of leaders representing them believe that the system's politics of compromise and balancing addresses their key interests adequately and equitably.

Circumstances may change, however, so that some constituencies and leaders no longer believe the politics of oligarchy addresses their interests fairly. They may instead choose to mobilize support for their cause from lower levels of the political order as well as outside it in the broader society. In response, the rest of the party leadership may crack down on such agitation as it did in 1989, but with unpredictable consequences for the longer-term stability and unity of the party. Alternatively, the party leadership may seek to appease the disaffected constituencies and their leaders through new attempts at reform that broaden representation and modify the institutional processes for decisionmaking by expanding intraparty voting mechanisms and other procedures. Each step in that direction inches the political order toward enhanced pluralization. In either case, whether crackdown or incremental liberalization, the prospects for democratization—perhaps through a split in the CCP as occurred in the Soviet Communist Party after 1989 with the creation of congresses of people's deputies in the Soviet state at the national level and in the fifteen republics—seem all the greater.

Notes

1. On the political background of the work system erected in this period, see Roderick MacFarquhar, *The Origins of the Cultural Revolution*, vol. 1: *Contradictions among the People 1956–1957* (Columbia University Press, 1974), pp. 99–165, and vol. 2: *The Great Leap Forward 1958–1960* (1983), pp. 58–71.

2. "Zhonggong zhongyang guanyu chengli caizheng, zhengfa, waishi, kexue, wenjiao gexiaozu de tongzhi" (Central Committee notice concerning the establishment of finance-economy, political-legal, foreign affairs, science, and culture and education small groups), June 10, 1958, in Central Committee Organization Department, Party History Research Office and Central Archives, *Zhongguo gongchandang zuzhishi ziliao* (Materials in the history of CCP organization) (Beijing: Zhonggong dangshi chubanshe, 2000), vol. 9, pp. 611–12. A prior notice of March 6, 1958, had already reported the establishment of the Foreign Affairs Small Group and listed Chen Yi as its director and a total of six members. These included the five listed in the June 10 notice plus the deputy chief of staff of the People's Liberation Army, Li Kenong. "Zhonggong zhongyang he guowuyuan guanyu zhongyang sheli waishi xiaozu he guowuyuan sheli waishi bangongshi de lianhe tongzhi" (CCP Central Committee–State Council joint notice concerning the Central Committee's establishment of the foreign affairs small group and the State Council's establishment of the Foreign Affairs Office), in *Zhongguo gongchandang zuzhishi ziliao*, vol. 9, pp. 611–13. A brief discussion of the creation of some of these groups appears in Wang Jingsong, *Zhonghua renmin gongheguo zhengfu yu zhengzhi* (Government and politics in the People's Republic of China) (Beijing: Zhonggong zhongyang dangxiao chubanshe, 1995), pp. 341–42; an incomplete list of these and other "extraordinary organs" appears on p. 378 ff.

3. "Deng Xiaoping chengwei dang de di'erdai lingdao hexin" (Deng Xiaoping's designation as the party leadership's second-generation core), in *Dang he guojia zhongda juece de licheng* (The course of important policy decisions in our party and country), vol. 8, edited by Guo Dehong, Zhang Zhanbin, and Zhang Shujun (Beijing: Hongqi chubanshe, 1997), pp. 365–66.

4. MacFarquhar, *The Origins of the Cultural Revolution*, vol. 1, pp. 105–07.

5. Deng Xiaoping, "Report on the Revision of the Constitution of the CCP," *The Eighth National Congress of the Communist Party of China*, vol. 1: *Documents* (Beijing: Foreign Languages Press, 1956), pp. 192–96.

6. A. Doak Barnett, *The Making of Foreign Policy in China: Structure and Process* (Boulder, Colo.: Westview Press, 1985), p. 9 ff.; Lu Ning, *The Dynamics of Foreign Policy Decision-Making* (Boulder, Colo.: Westview Press, 1997), pp. 9–11; and Alice Miller, "More Already on Politburo Procedures under Mao," *China Leadership Monitor*, no. 17 (Winter 2006).

7. For the political background to Hu's removal, see Richard Baum, *Burying Mao: Chinese Politics in the Age of Deng Xiaoping* (Princeton University Press, 1994), pp. 206–08.

8. These procedures, as described by Hu Qiaomu in a 1989 colloquium in Washington, D.C., are recounted in Alice Miller, "Hu Jintao and the Party Politburo," *China Leadership Monitor*, no. 9 (Winter 2004), pp. 4–6.

9. Politburo appointments at the Eighth Central Committee's Fifth Plenum in May 1958 had included two provincial party secretaries: Ke Qingshi from Shanghai and Li Jingquan from Sichuan. The routine addition of provincial party secretaries to the Politburo may have been intended as a feature of the 1956–58 work system, and the addition of four provincial party secretaries in 1987 may have been based on that precedent. In the three decades between 1958 and 1987, no provincial party secretaries served on the Politburo, including that of 1982.

10. A similar work system appears to operate at the provincial party committee level.

11. Cheng Li projects a significantly higher turnover—upward of 50 percent of the Politburo and its Standing Committee. See Cheng Li, "Anticipating Chinese Leadership Changes at the 17th Party Congress," *China Brief* 7 (March 21, 2007): 5–8.

12. The recent appointment of Xi Jinping as Shanghai party secretary ensures his appointment to the Politburo at the Seventeenth Congress, but it also suggests that he will not gain appointment to the Standing Committee as Hu's successor. On the lack of PRC media indications as to who Hu's successor may be, see Alice Miller, "The Problem of Hu Jintao's Successor," *China Leadership Monitor*, no. 19 (Fall 2006).

13. I say "he" because it appears unlikely that Hu's successor will be a woman.

14. Li, "Anticipating Chinese Leadership Changes at the 17th Party Congress," pp. 6–7.

15. T. H. Rigby, "The Soviet Leadership: Towards a Self-Stabilizing Oligarchy?" *Soviet Studies* 22 (October 1970): 167–91. On the following discussion, see also T. H. Rigby, "The Soviet Political Executive, 1917–1986," in *Political Leadership in the Soviet Union*, edited by Archie Brown (Indiana University Press, 1989), pp. 4–53; John Lowenhardt, James R. Ozinga, and Erik van Ree, *The Rise and Fall of the Soviet Politburo* (New York: St. Martin's Press, 1992), chaps. 5 and 7; Jerry Hough, *How the Soviet Union Is Governed* (Harvard University Press, 1979), pp. 466–73; and Richard Sakwa, *Soviet Politics in Perspective*, 2nd ed. (New York: Routledge, 1998), pp. 94–95.

16. Rigby, "The Soviet Leadership," p. 170.

5

Institutionalization of Political Succession in China: Progress and Implications

JING HUANG

> It is true that errors we made in the past were partly attributable to the way of thinking and style of work of some leaders. But they were even more attributable to the problems in our organizational and working systems.
>
> DENG XIAOPING, "On the Reform of the System of Party and State Leadership" (1980)

Few leadership transitions in the history of communist politics have been more elaborately predesigned and skillfully executed than the one from Jiang Zemin to Hu Jintao, which started with Hu's taking over of the party leadership at the Sixteenth Party Congress in November 2002 and ended with Jiang's retirement from and Hu's accession to the chairmanship of the Central Military Commission (CMC) in March 2005. More significant is the apparent, albeit poised, erosion of Jiang's influence in policymaking since his retirement. Owing to the still largely pyramid-like structure of political power as well as the blurry boundary between formal and informal politics in China, the Jiang-Hu transition has rekindled strong interest not only in the shifting patterns of elite alignment among China's new leadership but also in the effect of such shifts on the country's further development, especially leadership succession in the future.[1] How does this leadership transition differ from previous ones in Chinese politics? What are the underlying realities that give rise to those differences? And what impact will this transition and its aftermath have on future leadership formation and leadership relations in the policymaking process?

As this chapter illustrates, the Jiang-Hu transition reflects a new norm in China's political processes: the "hierarchical game" of life and death struggles dominated by Mao Zedong and Deng Xiaoping has been transformed into a more formal "game of competitive coexistence," with the emphasis on compromise making and consensus building. Increasingly, formal rules and compliant procedures have prevailed over factional politics based on informal personal relations among the political elites of the Chinese Communist Party (CCP). The smoothness of the Jiang-Hu transition is the result of the growing institutionalization of the political process, which explains why Jiang's political clout has substantially eroded since his retirement. A large question on many minds is whether these new "rules of the game" have any implications for political pluralism in China.

Leadership Transition: From Informality to Formality

In retrospect, few issues have cast a longer shadow over Chinese politics than that of leadership succession. Before the Jiang-Hu succession, only two power transitions had taken place at the top since the establishment of the People's Republic of China (PRC) in 1949: the transition from Mao Zedong to Hua Guofeng in 1976, and from Deng Xiaoping to Jiang Zemin in 1989.[2] Despite their distinctive historical contexts, these two leadership successions are actually more alike than different. First and foremost, both had been preceded by fierce intraparty strife, resulting in two inordinately hasty power transitions carried out in Machiavellian fashion. Moreover, both successions had caused considerable policy inconsistencies. Before finally settling on Hua in the last months of his life, Mao made two abortive selections of heirs apparent in Liu Shaoqi and Lin Biao, both of whom were toppled unceremoniously during the Cultural Revolution. After Mao's death, Hua's efforts to preserve Mao's legacy by insisting on the "two whatevers" collided with Deng's efforts to "seek truth from facts," and Hua, hardly a match for Deng in the ideological and policy arenas, eventually yielded his leadership.[3]

The passing of the baton from Deng to Jiang occurred in similar, if less disruptive, circumstances. Throughout the decade preceding the Tiananmen tragedy in 1989, fierce ideological and policy disputes raged between reformers and conservatives within the CCP leadership, a reflection of the deep-seated frictions between those who favored "reform and opening" and the advocates of a Leninist party-state in both a political and economic sense. For all his advocacy of economic reform, Deng was by no means willing to let go of the CCP's—not to mention his own—political dominance. Both Hu Yaobang and Zhao Ziyang, Deng's hand-picked successors, were deposed in 1987 and 1989, respectively, when Deng grew increasingly suspicious of them as being too "soft" on "bourgeois liberalization."[4] And, on the eve of the Tiananmen crackdown, the political compromise between Deng and other veteran leaders installing Jiang as the new CCP general secretary was reached in such a clandestine manner that it came as a surprise even to Jiang himself. Despite Deng's apparent command in the crisis of 1989, the crackdown actually played into the hands of his conservative rivals, who managed to roll back the reform policy to such an extent that Deng would not regain the upper hand until his southern tour in the spring of 1992, when he virtually "shamed" Jiang and his colleagues into reactivating "reform and opening," which constituted Deng's most important legacy.[5]

In marked contrast, the transfer of power from Jiang Zemin to Hu Jintao was not only elaborately preplanned but also methodically accomplished, even though it involved the three top positions in the CCP party-state: CCP general secretary, PRC president, and CMC chairman. Indeed, ever since Deng elevated him to the Politburo Standing Committee (PBSC) at the Fourteenth Party Congress in 1992, Hu Jintao had been regarded as the "first among equals" of those in the Fourth Generation destined to play a critical role in Chinese politics. The eleven years from 1992 to 2003 witnessed Hu's gradual, step-by-step takeover of the top leadership posts, which was a crucial part of the prerogative as well as apprenticeship of a would-be heir apparent.[6]

Moreover, the Jiang-Hu succession has brought about remarkably little, if any, repercussions in the policymaking process. The entire power transition has been shrouded in an uneventful atmosphere, void of ideological disputes or any visible disturbances in policymaking. Only after Hu fully established his leadership in March 2005 was policy reoriented toward "building up a harmonious society" and "scientific development" (see the next section). The pivotal difference, however, is the gradual but significant change in the essential dynamic of CCP politics: from informal factional politics based on personal ties to a more formal process secured by institutional arrangements, although these arrangements were largely ad hoc measures designed to maintain stability in leadership relations and policy consistency in the post-1989 period.

The fierce factional strife of the Mao and Deng periods and the resulting instability in both leadership relations and policy outcomes were the result of informal politics, characterized by highly personalized authorities, deficient institutionalization of the political process, and uncertain rules for decisionmaking. Under the faction-ridden, hierarchical leadership structure, the relationship between a supreme leader with absolute command (such as Mao or Deng) and his chosen successor could turn sour at any point. If the successor attempted to expand his power base or exhibit independence of mind, the supreme leader would undoubtedly grow deeply suspicious of his erstwhile protégé, and a deadly succession struggle would ensue in which neither would feel secure until his opponent was politically eliminated. The violent downfalls of Liu Shaoqi and Lin Biao under Mao, and Hu Yaobang and Zhao Ziyang under Deng, were all but unavoidable in this regard.[7]

By turning power into a paramount objective in the political process, factional strife was also bound to transform a policy dispute (however legitimate it might be) into a ruthless struggle for power in which the strong would prevail at the expense of the weak. Consequently, seemingly rational policy choices did not always prevail over "irrational" ones, for the reason that "policy" was often used to secure power. Given the importance of ideology in attaining legitimacy in a totalitarian system, rival CCP factions were constantly engaged in struggles for the ideological high ground. Ironically, these struggles jeopardized the ideological consensus that held the ruling elite together, thus imperiling both the long-term prospects of CCP rule and also the policy consistency and rationality necessary for continuous development.

In other words, the jarring power transitions, with brutal purges and radical policy changes, of the Mao and Deng eras were by no means flukes but the outward symptoms of the deep, structural malaise of factionalism that had haunted CCP politics ever since its founding. Although their supreme position enabled Mao and Deng to maintain exclusive control of various factional networks in both the party and military systems, political dominance was no guarantee that leadership successions would be smooth. Because of the faction-ridden realities, both leaders were *structurally predetermined* to make their final choice of heir apparent at the eleventh hour—driven by the need for expediency as much as self-interest. Because such hastily chosen successors were often too weak to stand on their own, such last-minute succession arrangements inevitably led to yet another round of factional strife, which went hand in hand with further ideological conflict. Not surprisingly, all this served to undermine both leadership stability and policy consistency.

What, then, saved Jiang Zemin from the same fate as Hua Guofeng (which some pundits predicted), and also secured a smooth leadership transition from Jiang to Hu? The answer lies in the fundamental changes in post-1989 CCP politics, especially after the Fourteenth Party Congress in 1992.

First, by 1992 virtually all the "revolutionary veterans" had become physically, and hence politically, incapacitated.[8] With their departure, a key underpinning of the old-time factional networks disappeared. This overbearing "gerontocracy" had been bound by strong relationships forged in the fires of war prior to seizing state power in 1949, whereas the new generation of leaders came to power as bureaucrats who barely knew each other before being promoted to the center of power. Although some of these new leaders had solid support from the institutions or localities in which they rose to power (such as Jiang in Shanghai and Hu in the Chinese Communist Youth League), hardly anyone had developed a power base penetrating the entire system. As a result, none of the new generation of leaders could realistically aspire to such control. Unlike Mao and Deng, who had established firm control of *both* the party and military machineries *before* coming to power, Jiang and Hu had to work hard to consolidate their power in the party before trying to establish their authority over the People's Liberation Army (PLA) *after* coming to power.[9] Unable to achieve the kind of patriarchal and *personal* authority over the military that Mao and Deng had enjoyed, Jiang, and later Hu, sought to consolidate the *institutional arrangements* designed to secure the party's command of the armed forces.

All this has led to two fundamental changes in Chinese elite politics. First of all, unlike Mao and Deng, who were veritable "godfathers" in political life, Jiang and Hu are merely first among equals and do not enjoy absolute political authority. Thus, as already mentioned, the political game no longer follows rules imposed by *hierarchical* factional connections, which can override institutional arrangements and procedures, subject the "losers" to brutal purges, and invite instability through drastic policy changes. Nowadays, interactions among the ruling elites are more like *collegial games* in which the leaders seek compromises with, rather than dominance over, their opponents in a policy dispute or political conflict. Such rules tend to strengthen the existing consensus among the political elites and hence contribute to policy consistency instead of disrupting it. Top leaders also behave differently in political conflicts, no longer engaging in "life-or-death" struggles adhering strictly to the "godfather's line." More often than not, their disputes end with moderation and compromise, while graceful "retirements," usually justified by age or term limits (established by Deng and carried on by Jiang and Hu), have replaced the purges for those who lose out in political or policy conflicts.

Second, although the new generation of leaders usually has solid support from the institutions and localities that were stepping-stones to power, relations among its members are ultimately determined by common interests or policy preferences, or both, generated through formal institutional arrangements in the policy process, rather than by the personal ties and private informal deals, as before. Factionalism, though still present, tends to be tamped down by the ongoing "institutionalization," leaving factions to compete more or less on a basis of equality since they are no longer in a position to plunder or destroy others.[10]

Indeed, of all the developments that have helped the CCP leadership maintain political stability since the 1989 crisis, probably the most important is the growing institutionalization of the political process, which has given rise to a certain "code of civility" in Chinese elite politics.[11] This not only enabled Jiang to maintain power for over a decade but also helped smooth the Jiang-Hu succession. More important, this institutionalization appears likely to continue, with a long-lasting impact on Chinese politics, especially on leadership stability and policy consistency.

Consolidation of Jiang's Leadership:
Institutionalization of the Political Process

When Jiang Zemin assumed CCP leadership in 1989, his position was very vulnerable. Without a strong power base in either the party or the military system, he could easily have experienced the same fate as Hua Guofeng and been muscled out by a veteran leader like Yang Shangkun, a revolutionary of Deng's generation who was then the PRC president and executive vice chairman of the CMC. In addition, Jiang's appearance of being weak could provoke a fierce power struggle among the CCP ruling elites, thus undermining both political stability and economic development. Recognizing Jiang's vulnerability and its wider implications for China, Deng forced Yang and his brother, General Yang Baibing, to retire from the CMC in October 1992. Meanwhile, Deng made an arrangement unprecedented in the history of the PRC: he crowned Jiang CCP general secretary, PRC president, and CMC chairman—the three top positions in Chinese politics—in order to provide Jiang with political legitimacy as well as topmost leadership in the most powerful institutions in China.[12]

Seeing that this three-in-one arrangement could also help Jiang concentrate too much power in his hands, Deng explicitly designed and reinforced a system of "collective leadership," with "Comrade Jiang Zemin as its core." Under this system, all important decisions were to be made collectively through a process of discussion, consultation, debate, and vote (if necessary) among the ruling elites. In order to prevent deadlock in policymaking, the PBSC, China's highest decisionmaking organ, was to be composed of an odd number of members—seven in Jiang's period and nine in Hu's. Hence collective leadership was a crucial aspect of the institutionalization of the CCP political process in preventing the "overconcentration" of power in individual leaders as well as in securing leadership stability and policy consistency.[13]

This remarkable effort to institutionalize the CCP political process, especially at the elite level, was an essential part of Deng's political legacy. In addition, Deng established age and term limits in the promotion and retirement system for CCP cadres. The 1982 PRC constitution stipulates that all the supreme offices of the state—the presidency and the chairmanships of the National People's Congress (NPC) and the Chinese People's Political Consultative Conference (CPPCC) Standing Committees—can be held by the same person for only two consecutive five-year terms. The 1982 constitution further states that "the Party's cadres at all levels, whether democratically elected or appointed by the leading organs, do not enjoy life tenure and their job positions can be changed or removed." Since the party constitution does not precisely mention term limits but does indicate CCP members should abide by state laws, all levels of authority have adhered to the term limits spelled out in the state constitution.[14]

Deng himself took the first step toward breaking the traditions of life tenure for high-level party cadres by retiring from all his official positions in November 1989. Although Deng did remain the most powerful person in China until the final days of his life, the precedent he set helped institutionalize age and term limits. At the Fifteenth Party Congress in 1997, Jiang forced his potential opponents to retire by citing those limits and, ironically, had to step down for similar reasons himself at the Sixteenth Party Congress in November 2002.[15]

These ad hoc normative innovations and rearrangements of the rules of the game, adopted by Deng and reinforced by Jiang and Hu, have contributed tremendously to the CCP's political institutionalization. This increasing formality has in turn exerted a far-reaching impact on China's political development, especially on leadership transition and the policymaking process. By definition, a formal political process entails a set of institutional arrangements including "formal rules, compliant procedures, and standard operating practices that structure the relationship between individuals in various units of the polity."[16] As game theory postulates, increasing political formality has effectively checked factional politics caused by informal personal interactions in the policymaking process and therefore secured leadership stability and policy consistency.[17] Furthermore, "while keeping the system essentially intact, formal institutional arrangements can provide plural channels for the expression of diverse interests in the policy process; compliant procedures can override personal ties, or *guanxi*, in decisionmaking; and standard operating practices can make it difficult to abuse one's power in political affairs."[18]

Indeed, the formal process strengthens the authority of institutions while curtailing the arbitrary power of individual leaders. By subjecting *all* individual leaders to a set of prescribed rules and abiding by procedures in decisionmaking, it renders the position of a "supreme leader" a superfluity, if not an utter nuisance. Whereas personalized authority becomes not just an object of envy but a potential threat to leadership stability (especially at the time of the supreme leader's departure), institutionalized power, since it is attached to the position, not the individual who wields it, cannot be altered by personal interactions in political affairs and so promotes stable leadership relations over the long term.

In this light, it is easy to understand why any attempts at institutionalization in the Mao period met with no success. Supreme leaders like Mao must be *the* master, rather than a "cog" (albeit a bejeweled one) of the system, with veto power over any and all established rules and decisionmaking procedures. This also explains why informal politics could prevail so easily over formal politics earlier in the CCP's history. In the absence of a full-fledged formal process, personal ties with powerful leaders count much more than any institutional arrangements in achieving one's desired outcomes.

In contrast, Jiang Zemin, the first top leader in the post-Deng period, rose to power as a party bureaucrat without a dominant power base penetrating the entire political system. Thus he could hardly afford to do away with the formal process (as Mao did) or make a mockery of it (as Deng did). Rather, precisely because he is by no means a "political strongman" in his own right, he has no choice but to strengthen the existing institutional arrangements if he wishes to (a) consolidate his primacy in the decisionmaking structures, (b) coordinate interests and policy preferences among the political elites, and (c) stabilize leadership relations in the policymaking process. In retrospect, it was by strengthening the existing institutional arrangements, with Deng's blessing, that Jiang consolidated his leadership. In practice, Jiang pushed institutionalization forward on three principal fronts: by securing authority over the military establishment, curtailing localism, and imposing age and term limits on the political elite.

Securing the Party's "Command of the Gun"

In the pre-Jiang era, the military's involvement in politics had a major impact on leadership stability and policymaking. When Jiang succeeded Deng as the new CMC chairman in November 1989, his control of the PLA was more symbolic than real. It was not until Deng removed Yang Shangkun and Yang Baibing (then the CMC secretary general) from the CMC that Jiang set out to establish his own authority within the PLA. With neither military experience nor a substantial power base in the armed forces, Jiang took full advantage of the institutional legitimacy and power his leading positions conferred on him in his effort to institutionalize the party's—and his—command of the gun. While pushing further the professionalization campaign in the PLA (started by Deng in the mid-1980s), Jiang set out to reorganize the entire armed forces as well as the command system. The consequence, with a far-reaching significance, is that the party's command of the gun has been transformed from *subjective* control, based on the military's ideological obligation and the officer corps' loyalty toward the top leader (that is, Mao and Deng), to *objective* control secured by formal institutional arrangements.[19]

Jiang's programs concentrated on (a) promoting a younger and better-educated officer corps on the objective basis of their professional expertise, rather than on superior officers' subjective assessment of subordinate officers' political loyalty (which was the key to old-time factional associations); (b) rotating top military personnel in major military regions frequently, so as to prevent senior officers from developing personal power bases; and (c) establishing a more effective and capable People's Armed Police (PAP) to take over all

duties in civilian affairs from the PLA, so as to disconnect the PLA commanders from local authorities. Moreover, starting with the Fifteenth Party Congress
in 1997, the PLA as a political institution was deprived of its seats in the
PBSC, the supreme organ in policymaking. This was not merely a further sign
of the military's waning influence over CCP politics in general but also a move
that established, for the first time since 1949, a formal precedent aimed at
ensuring the party's institutional superiority over the military. As a result,
Jiang's authority over the military was no longer secured by his power bases in
the military, which were nonexistent for Jiang at the time of his official elevation (as in the case with Hu later). Rather, the command over the PLA by the
top leader, namely Jiang and now Hu, has been legitimized by and enforced
through his leadership of the party.

Ironically, this institutionalization of the party's command over the armed
forces enabled Jiang (and now Hu) to keep the military under control *more*
effectively than their more personally powerful predecessors could. Indeed,
when Jiang ordered the PLA in late 1998 to relinquish its business enterprises—
a task perhaps even Deng could not have accomplished—the order was carried
out (under Hu's supervision) with surprising thoroughness, despite prior speculation about possible "systematic resistance" from the military.[20] The PLA com-
plied not because it was compensated with larger defense budgets (which began
growing in 1991), but because formal institutional arrangements had disen-
gaged the PLA from all civilian affairs in general, and these arrangements had
deprived the generals of their once privileged access to top decisionmaking circles. As a result, they were far less capable of projecting their complaints onto
the center's policymaking agenda.

Curtailing Localism in the Policymaking Process

One significant consequence of reform has been the decentralization of policymaking power, especially in the economic sphere. Localism, though hardly a
new phenomenon in Chinese history, grew dramatically in the mid-1990s, causing some concern about regional fragmentation of the national economy and
political debilitation of the state.[21] To keep such tendencies within acceptable
limits, the Third Generation leadership, headed by Jiang Zemin, endeavored to
reassert its authority in certain crucial policy areas. Major policy initiatives
launched to this end included regular rotations of provincial leaders and the reg-
ularization of frequent cadre turnovers up to the provincial-leader level, as
embodied in a directive from the CCP Organization Department in June
1999.[22] Since 1994 the central government, principally under Zhu Rongji's
leadership, has launched important economic and fiscal reforms to rein in the
trend toward fiscal decentralization and to take a lion's share of the revenue

through tax reforms, with some success in regaining control over financial resources from local authorities.[23]

The most substantial and far-reaching achievement of Jiang and Zhu's efforts to tame localism, though less successful than expected, was that it set forth a process of institutionalization of the central-local relationship, a process that the Fourth Generation leadership headed by Hu Jintao has conveniently assumed in its continuous effort to curb localism in political affairs. Unlike Mao and Deng, who sought to tame defiant provincial leaders by forming a coalition with some of them and then attacking those who opposed their plans, Hu Jintao (and Jiang before him) can rely on the formal institutional arrangements in central-local relations to secure their dominance in policymaking. These arrangements have bestowed legitimacy and unchallengeable power onto the "party center," with which all local leaders must align in policymaking as well as implementation.[24]

Formalizing the Cadre Promotion and Retirement System

Before the Jiang regime standardized the promotion and retirement systems for CCP cadres, the four principal criteria for cadre promotion were political loyalty (to the CCP), educational accomplishment, professional competence, and youth. Although "political loyalty" is still emphasized, there has been a conspicuous tendency since 1992 to stress education, technical expertise, professional competence, and age as more "objective" criteria for cadre promotion. Furthermore, the introduction of tentative electoral competition at various levels of party congresses has exerted a modicum of institutional restraints on the blatant abuses of favoritism and nepotism.[25] Meanwhile, senior cadres no longer enjoy lifelong tenure, and mandatory retirement is enforced more strictly than ever. Upon Qiao Shi's retirement from the PBSC at the Fifteenth Party Congress in 1997 at age seventy-three, it was tacitly established that the age limit for retirement should be seventy for ordinary Politburo members and seventy-five for PBSC members. This explains why, when Jiang Zemin, then seventy-six, remained the sole exception to retirement among his erstwhile Politburo colleagues after the Sixteenth Party Congress in 2002, he was widely criticized within the CCP for violating this "objective" age limit, which he himself had set up.[26] Again, the reform's significance lies not so much in the "objectiveness" of cadre selections (as some have suggested), but in the formal procedures and operational standards that are now integral to cadre promotions and retirements, especially among high-ranking cadres.

Political Changes under Institutionalization

As mentioned earlier, political power has been effectively institutionalized, or depersonalized. A leader wields power only as long as he occupies his institutional position; once he leaves it, he no longer enjoys the powers attached to that post. This is unquestionably a positive development in terms of political stability, especially for the leadership transition. Unlike Jiang, who had been under Deng's shadow for nearly eight years before he eventually established his full-fledged leadership after Deng's death in 1997, Hu took merely two years (2003–05) to stand fully on his own as the head of the Fourth Generation leaders. The indictment of Chen Liangyu, the Shanghai party secretary, in September 2006 was a testimony to Hu's undisputable leading role in political affairs. The essential reason was not necessarily that the alleged "Shanghai faction" had caved in, or at least compromised its interests, in a zero-sum political struggle with the "Youth League faction," led by Hu. Rather, it was because the institutionalization of power, which Deng initiated and Jiang reinforced, gave Hu the political legitimacy and authority to accomplish this task as Hu has now succeeded Jiang in all the three top leadership positions.

Formal rules and procedures have also had an impact on policymaking, particularly in resolving policy disputes. Unlike the Mao and Deng periods, when policy issues were decided by the whims of supreme leaders, nowadays policymaking consists of a lengthy process of deliberation and consultation among the policy elites; and final outcomes depend heavily on established rules and procedures rather than the preferences of "dominant leaders." All this has resulted in consistency and stability in the policymaking process, reinforcing consensus among political elites who seek compromises in an increasingly formalized "collegial game" rather than engaging in a "life-and-death" struggle in an informal but brutal "hierarchical game."

In addition, there is an increasing tendency toward formalizing the "division of labor" among the ruling elites. In the past, policymaking took place in what seemed a wild jungle where the strong (if not necessarily the wise) invariably prevailed. Policymaking is now a more orderly process, with each functionary's sphere of power and activity demarcated, with "overextension" prohibited by formal rules and procedures. Hence the process has become increasingly complicated, consensus-oriented, and pragmatic. Moreover, because power is no longer linked directly to individual personalities, policy disputes are usually considered the result of conflicting interests that need to be addressed through bargaining and compromise rather than confrontations underlined by political and ideological differences that have to be clarified through a "struggle of line." Since the policy consensus that grows out of such bargaining and compromise is easier to maintain and harder to achieve, policy consistency has become the norm rather than a rarity in CCP politics. At the same time, stability in leadership relations is no longer an aberration (as in the Mao and pre-1989 Deng periods) but a regular feature of political life.

The striking progress toward institutionalization in CCP politics explains why Jiang Zemin's political clout, instead of lingering as some pundits had predicted, eroded rapidly after he stepped down from his leadership posts. Once they leave office, no individual leaders, no matter how exalted they may once have been, can expect to retain a viable say in decisionmaking. Evidently, even Jiang Zemin cannot be exempt from this rule. After all, unlike Mao and Deng, whose absolute authority grew out of their personal authority rather than their official positions, Jiang's power was based essentially upon the offices he held, and without which he was ultimately powerless. And his former protégés in the new PBSC cannot serve as watchdogs for him in the policymaking process either, even if they share a special interest in continuing the policy that favors coastal development (all of Jiang's alleged proxies rose from coastal and metropolitan areas). The fact is, their political well-being has little to do with the blessing of their erstwhile patron. Indeed, Jiang's alleged protégés do not need him to remain politically powerful. Rather, it is Jiang himself who must count on their continuous support if he wishes to extend his relevance in policymaking. What really matters to Jiang's former protégés is how, and by what means, they can strike a bargain with the current "Big Brother" in charge, Hu Jintao. Hence the indictment of Chen Liangyu and a number of other high-ranking cadres in Shanghai cannot be considered the result of a zero-sum power struggle between Hu and the alleged "Shanghai faction." Rather, it reflects a compromise resulting from a wider and deeper policy confrontation between those who wished to continue the policy favoring the coastal and metropolitan areas and the preferences of the Hu-Wen leadership, which is determined to shift policy priorities toward the hinterland and rural areas.[27]

Notably, this compromise, as well as Xi Jinping's takeover of the Shanghai leadership, was achieved through a formal process in which virtually all the Politburo members participated according to their designated roles in decisionmaking. In the case of Xi, the party leadership took over half a year to select him from a field of four candidates and reached its final decision through a formal vote by all the sitting Politburo members.[28] Since the prevailing consensus among the elites is that the legitimacy of CCP rule today lies largely in its ability to maintain political stability and economic growth, it is in the best interests of Jiang's former protégés to work together with Hu toward that end. The formal political processes now in place have enabled the ruling elites not only to reach compromises over policy disputes but also to make sure that these disputes will not spill over and trigger broader conflicts in a society that is undergoing an unprecedented transition.[29] Faced with the task of carving out their own collective political destinies, today's Chinese leaders certainly have far weightier concerns on their minds than catering to the preferences of a retired Jiang Zemin.

Future Leadership Transition: Toward Elite Democracy?

Hu Jintao and his colleagues faced an enormous task at the Seventeenth Party Congress: they had to not only put together a new leading body for the party, with quite a few new faces replacing those who will step down, but also to develop a blueprint for the next generation of leaders that will come up at the Eighteenth Party Congress in 2012. It is not yet clear how they will fulfill this task. After all, despite tremendous differences between Jiang and Hu in terms of personality, work style, and pathway to power, the two did share an important trait: both were hand-picked and groomed by Deng Xiaoping. Nowadays, it is unlikely that either Jiang or Hu can bring up a "successor" the way Mao and Deng did, because the system of "collective leadership" makes it impossible for any individual leader to make a decision on leadership succession on his own. According to Li Junru, vice president of the CCP Central Party School, "A democratic mechanism [to produce the next generation of leadership] has been established in the Party, so there no longer exists the problem of appointing a successor."[30]

What is the "democratic mechanism" Li mentioned? How does it work? And what are the exact rules and procedures for the selection of the next generation of leaders? While the answers to these questions are at present unclear, they are likely to emerge within the next five years. In view of the stability in leadership relations and consistency in policymaking imposed by political institutionalization, future political outcomes are certain to be less unpredictable than they were in the Mao and pre-1989 Deng periods of informal politics.

Moreover, the current leaders' personal preferences and patronage are unlikely to play a significant role in the selection of the next generation of leaders. Given the well-established system of collective leadership and the maturing of formal processes in decisionmaking, a candidate's age, professional competence, personal qualities, political skills, and record of performance will weigh decisively in the selection process. If anything, a potential candidate will not want to be perceived as being too close to a particular leader. Next-generation leaders might well look to the example of "Big Brother Hu," who survived for more than ten years as the number two in CCP politics before ascending to the top position by carefully avoiding forming any kind of close relationship with any of the third generation leaders, on the one hand, and being dutifully obedient to the party center as an *institution* and effectively carrying out whatever decisions were handed down to him, on the other.

As for the role of the military in the leadership transition and in political affairs more broadly, it will continue to diminish. In part, this is due to increasing professionalism in the armed forces, which has helped make the

PLA more apolitical.[31] At the same time, the institutional arrangements reached under Jiang's leadership have deprived the PLA of its role in leadership transition, as noted earlier. It is true that the next CCP leader still has to assume the CMC chairmanship to secure the party's command of the armed forces. But the PLA may well passively accept the new CCP leader as its commander-in-chief at the next leadership transition instead of being actively involved in the process, as it was in previous leadership transitions. Given the absolute necessity of military support in sustaining the CCP's rule in China, however, the military will still hold at least some measure of "veto power" in the selection of the next leaders.

Last but not least, there is bound to be broader participation in the process of leadership succession because of prolonged consultations and compromises among the ruling elites at both the center and at the ministerial and provincial levels, where most of the Fifth Generation leaders will be incubated over the next few years. More significantly, for the first time in the PRC's history, political groups and factions among the CCP leaders will likely be based on common interests rather than on personal ties. For example, it would not be surprising to see leaders from the hinterland teaming up with each other to square off against leaders from the coastal and metropolitan areas, given the fundamentally different interests of these regions owing to their ever-widening economic and developmental gaps of the past two decades. This new phenomenon of leaders from similar areas forming coalitions over policy could exert a profound impact not only on the upcoming leadership succession but also on all of Chinese politics in years to come. With collective leadership well established and the next generation of leaders enjoying relatively equal status in the power distribution, broader participation by increasingly distinguishable interest groups at central and provincial levels could definitely deepen China's political institutionalization. At a minimum, this would help promote elite democracy, or "intraparty democracy," as claimed by CCP leaders in recent years.

Conclusion

The transition of leadership from Jiang to Hu was the most orderly and smooth transition in the history of the People's Republic. It was achieved largely through increasing political institutionalization since the Fourteenth Party Congress in 1992, especially in terms of leadership relations and the distribution of power in policymaking. Both Deng Xiaoping and Jiang Zemin were compelled to embark on institutionalizing the political process, but for different reasons. Whereas Deng correctly saw it as an effective way both to prevent overconcentration of power and to help Jiang establish his leadership, Jiang had to rely on formal institutional arrangements to consolidate his leadership in the absence of a dominant figure in CCP politics in the post-Deng period.

Institutionalization has brought gradual and irrevocable changes in both the structure and dynamics of Chinese politics. Gone are the brutal purges, unstable and unpredictable leadership relations, and drastic policy shifts of the Mao and Deng periods. In their place, compromises in decisionmaking, stable and largely predictable leadership relations, and policy consistency have become the norms. To be sure, this is not because the CCP ruling elite has become nicer, gentler, or wiser in political affairs, but because the growth and consolidation of formal institutional arrangements has depersonalized the nature of political power. The effect has been to constrain Chinese elites from radical and irrational behavior and to promote compromise despite different policy preferences and conflicting interests. These changes are all positive steps in China's development toward a more open and pluralistic political system.

Still, few would predict the emergence of a democratic China in the foreseeable future if democracy is defined as a political system in which multiple parties compete peacefully for public office, officials are mostly produced by open and public elections, and citizens enjoy the freedom of political participation, expression, and assembly. In terms of the political process, however, all types of mature democracies share a critical feature, namely, full *institutionalization* of the political process in three salient but closely related respects:

—*Institutionalization of power*, under the principle that "power stays with offices" rather than individual leaders, with clearly defined arenas of authority and separation of power in decisionmaking, and with the constitution as the ultimate authority in political affairs.

—*Institutionalization of the policymaking process*, in which formal arrangements, with abiding rules, compliant procedures, and standard operating practices, embody a system of checks and balances and ensure transparency in policymaking.

—*Institutionalization of political participation*, which guarantees the legitimacy of freedom of expression and assembly in a vibrant but stable civic society.

Clearly, in most of these respects China still has a very long way to go. Nonetheless, the ever-deepening institutionalization of the political process is encouraging. As shown in the Jiang-Hu leadership transition, institutionalization has not only brought about stability in leadership relations and the policymaking process but has also begun to incubate a system of checks and balances while broadening political participation (at least) among the CCP elite members. In fairness, these developments are by nature evolutionary and functional, rather than revolutionary and fundamental. It is true that a *revolution* can bring about fundamental changes via violent destruction; but an *evolution* can reach the same goal through gradual but irrevocable development. In this sense, China is undergoing an unprecedented evolution.

Notes

1. See, among others, Lucian Pye, "Factions and the Politics of Guanxi: Paradoxes in Chinese Administrative and Political Behavior," *China Journal*, no. 34 (July 1995): 35–53; Lowell Dittmer, "Chinese Informal Politics," *China Journal*, no. 34 (July 1995): 1–34; Joseph Fewsmith, *Elite Politics in Contemporary China* (Armonk, N.Y.: M. E. Sharpe, 2001); Cheng Li, *China's Leaders: The New Generation* (Lanham, Md.: Rowman and Littlefield, 2001); Jonathan Unger, ed., *The Nature of Chinese Politics: From Mao to Jiang* (Armonk, N.Y.: M. E. Sharpe, 2002); and Gang Lin and Xiaobo Hu, eds., *China after Jiang* (Washington: Woodrow Wilson Center, 2003).

2. Deng's takeover from Hua in 1977–79 was essentially part of the aftermath of the Mao-Hua leadership transition. See Jing Huang, *Factionalism in Chinese Communist Politics* (Cambridge University Press, 2000), pp. 354–64. Although Jiang became the CCP's general secretary in 1989, the leadership transition from Deng to Jiang was not really completed until late 1992, when Jiang took full charge of the CMC after Deng forced the Yang brothers to step down. Still, some may reasonably argue that Deng remained virtually the most powerful man in China until his death in early 1997.

3. The "two whatevers" refer to Hua's insistence that "we shall resolutely uphold *whatever* policy Chairman Mao decided upon, and steadfastly abide by *whatever* decisions Chairman Mao made." See ibid., p. 351.

4. Ibid., pp. 396–410.

5. For a detailed account of the circumstances surrounding Jiang's unexpected elevation to the top in 1989 and the subsequent stagnation of reform in China until 1992, see Robert L. Kuhn, *The Man Who Changed China: The Life and Legacy of Jiang Zemin* (New York: Crown, 2005), pp. 147–230; and Bruce Gilley, *Tiger on the Brink: Jiang Zemin and China's New Elite* (University of California Press, 1998), pp. 113–90.

6. In 1993 Hu was appointed the head of the Central Party School, which is in charge of the advanced training of elite party cadres at both the local and central levels. In 1998 he was elected vice president of the PRC (with Jiang as president). In 1999 he assumed the CMC vice chairmanship. Through these appointments, Hu had already been put in the position of the second-in-command in the Chinese leadership.

7. See Huang, *Factionalism in Chinese Communist Politics*, passim.

8. One of the reasons for the abolition of the Central Advisory Committee at the Party's Fourteenth Congress in 1992 was that all its members were over seventy. By the mid- and late 1990s, virtually all "revolutionary veterans" of Deng's generation had either passed away or simply become too senile to intervene in political life. Because of his deteriorating health after 1994, between then and his death in 1997, Deng ceased to play a substantial role in political affairs.

9. Huang, *Factionalism in Chinese Communist Politics,* passim.

10. See also Cheng Li, "The New Bipartisanship within the Chinese Communist Party," *Orbis* (Summer 2005), pp. 387–400.

11. This phrase was initially adopted by Andrew Nathan to describe the restrained nature of factional politics. What he failed to note, however, is that such a "code" could emerge only

out of a relatively balanced power distribution among factions. See Nathan, "A Factional Model for CCP Politics," *China Quarterly*, no. 53 (January/March 1973): 34–66.

12. When Mao passed the baton to Hua Guofeng in 1976, he also crowned Hua with three top positions in the CCP political system: both the CCP and CMC chairmanships and the premiership. Yet Mao failed to reduce the power of veteran leaders like Marshall Ye Jianying, chairman of the National People's Congress, and Li Xiannian, vice premier, both of whom played a critical role in "smashing the Gang of Four" in 1976 and later in helping Deng achieve political dominance. The PRC presidency was officially abolished by the 1975 PRC constitution. The 1978 constitution, drafted under Hua's leadership, relegated the power and responsibility of the PRC president to the NPC chairman, Ye Jianying. This provided Ye with legitimacy and an institutional base to balance out Hua's power, especially in military, foreign, and legal affairs. See Huang, *Factionalism in Chinese Communist Politics*, pp. 350–54.

13. Deng held that "overconcentration of power" in Mao's hands was the "most important factor" leading to the catastrophic Cultural Revolution in 1966–76. See Deng, "On Reform of the Leading Institutions of Our Party and State," in *Selected Works of Deng Xiaoping*, vol. 2 (Beijing: People's Press, 1993), pp. 321, 341.

14. See http://news.sina.com.cn/c/2006-08-20/03389795074s.shtml.

15. Intriguingly, although the retirement system based on term and age limits has been in place for more than fifteen years, it was not officially adopted in the CCP's guidelines on cadres' age and term limits until August 2006. See http://news.xinhuanet.com/politics/2006-08/06/content_4926300.htm.

16. Peter Hall, *Governing the Economy: The Politics of State Intervention in Britain and France* (Oxford University Press, 1986), p. 19.

17. Game theory provides two critical insights into the political process. First, once a formal process is established, the rules and procedures are what determine the final outcomes in policymaking. See Peter Ordeshook, *Game Theory and Political Theory: An Introduction* (Cambridge University Press, 1986), p. 257. Second, the stability of policymaking is induced by the structure of institutional arrangements. See, among others, Kenneth A. Shepsle and Barry Weingast, "Structure-Induced Equilibrium and Legislative Choice," *Public Choice*, no. 37 (1981), pp. 503–19.

18. Huang, *Factionalism in Chinese Communist Politics*, p. 7.

19. Jing Huang, "Civil-Military Relations in China," in *Armed Forces and International Security: Global Trends and Issues*, edited by Jean M. Callahan and Franz Kernic (Edison, N.J.: Transaction Publishers), p. 2003.

20. Li, *China's Leaders*, p. 69.

21. See, for example, Wang Shaoguang and Hu Angang, *Zhongguo guojia nengli baogao* (A report on the capacity of the Chinese state) (Oxford University Press, 1994); and Jing Huang, "Increase in Regional Differences and Its Impact on China's Political Stability," *Gaige* (Reform), Development Research Center of the PRC State Council Report 5 (August 1996), pp. 34–49.

22. The directive stipulates that (1) county and municipal top leaders should not be selected from the same region, (2) those who head a county and city for more than ten years should be transferred to another place, and (3) provincial leaders should be transferred more frequently to another province or the central government. See Li, *China's Leaders*, p. 66; also *China News Analysis*, July 1–15, 1998, p. 15.

23. For a survey of these reforms, see Le-Yin Zhang, "Chinese Central-Provincial Fiscal Relationships, Budgetary Decline and the Impact of the 1994 Fiscal Reform: An Evaluation," *China Quarterly*, no. 157 (March 1999): 115–41.

24. Roderick MacFarquhar, *The Origins of the Cultural Revolution*, 3 vols. (Columbia University Press, 1974, 1983, and 1997), has captured well the strategy of forming a coalition with some provincial leaders and then attacking those who opposed central plans, used frequently by Mao whenever an intraparty conflict arose. Deng used the same tatic to overcome intraparty resistance. See also Huang, *Factionalism in Chinese Communist Politics*, passim.

25. See Li, *China's Leaders*, pp. 164–68; Lin and Hu, *China after Jiang*, pp. 57–60.

26. Although Jiang stepped down from the party leadership at the Sixteenth Party Congress in 2002 and from the PRC presidency in March 2003, he held on to the CMC chairmanship until March 2005.

27. In general, the Hu-Wen leadership readjusted economic policies soon after they assumed office in March 2005. Their new policy orientations, "the Hu-Wen New Deal," can be summarized as "four shifts." That is, the priorities in economic development have shifted from (1) the quantity (rate of growth) to the quality of growth; (2) coastal areas to the hinterland, and to agriculture; (3) export-led industries to the internal market; and (4) the creation of wealth to the distribution of wealth. See Wen Jiabao, "Report on the Work of the Government" (http://english.people.com.cn/docs/2007_gov_work.pdf).

28. According to a report in *Cheng Ming Monthly*, no. 354 (April 2007), the four candidates for the position of Shanghai party secretary were Wang Gang (general secretary of the Central Office of the CCP Central Committee), He Yong (executive vice director of the CCP Central Disciplinary Committee, Xi Jinping (party secretary of Zhejiang Province), and Li Yuanchao (party secretary of Jiangsu Province). In the final round of voting, Xi won sixteen of twenty-four votes, with four abstentions. Only two (Jia Qinglin and He Guoqiang) voted against Xi's appointment. This report is consistent with information I obtained through two interviews in Beijing on March 2 and 3, 2007. For a more detailed report, see http://peacehall.com/news/gb/china/2007/04/200704092311.shtml.

29. Cheng Li, "The New Bipartisanship within the Chinese Communist Party," argues compellingly that, despite substantial differences among them on major policy issues, Fourth Generation leaders have to cooperate with each other in policymaking in order to maintain political stability and economic development (both important matters for the regime's survival).

30. *The China Review News*, a pro-Beijing newspaper in Hong Kong (http://chinareviewnews.com/doc/1003/3/3/0/100333016.html?coluid=59&kindid=0&docid=100333016.

31. This is the theme Samuel Huntington raised half a century ago but it still holds true. See his *The Soldier and the State: The Theory and Politics of Civil-Military Relations* (Cambridge, Mass.: Belknap Press, 1957).

6

Will China's "Lost Generation" Find a Path to Democracy?

CHENG LI

> When the river gets warmer, the ducks know that spring is just around the corner.
>
> CHINESE PROVERB

Every generation has its defining characteristics, nurtured during its members' formative years. The upcoming generation of Chinese leaders, known as the Fifth Generation, is composed mainly of the age cohort born in the 1950s and reared amid the political turmoil of the Cultural Revolution (1966–76).[1] As a result, it lost its opportunity for formal schooling and was referred to as the "lost generation."[2] Many became "sent-down youths," who were forced to move from cities to rural areas and work as farmers. Some, however, made remarkable "comebacks" by entering colleges when the higher-education system reopened after 1977 and were able to transcend their earlier experiences and put their professional and political careers back on track.

The Fifth Generation's coming of age today coincides with China's emergence as an economic powerhouse in the world. Three decades of market reforms have not only spawned a growing Chinese middle class but have also fomented an interest in political and cultural pluralism. At the same time, China faces many daunting socioeconomic challenges, particularly economic disparity, employment pressure, environmental degradation, and the lack of a social safety net. It is also plagued by rampant official corruption, ideological incoherence, bureaucratic inertia, and other problems common to a Leninist-type authoritarian regime. Not surprisingly, China's political system is ill equipped to deal with the complicated, sometimes contradictory, needs of the modern economy and society.

I am indebted to Yinsheng Li and Xiaobo Ma for their research assistance and thank Sally Carman, Christina Culver, and Scott Harold for suggesting ways to clarify this analysis.

Will this generation of leaders have a better understanding of their fellow citizens' needs than preceding generations did? Will they be interested in making the regime more accountable to its people and thus contribute to, rather than oppose, democratic change? Will this unique lost generation of leaders, who experienced drastic changes in their own lives, secure a brighter future for their country? And will that future lie in the realm of democracy? These questions are best explored by examining the collective characteristics and the intragenerational diversity of the Fifth Generation, their experiments with so-called inner-party democracy, and the implications of the new political dynamics for China and the world.

Defining Characteristics of China's Fifth Generation

This study focuses on the 103 highest-ranking Chinese leaders born between 1950 and 1959. The group includes all the civilian full and alternate members of the current Central Committee (CC) and all civilian members of the current Central Commission for Discipline Inspection (CCDI) of the Chinese Communist Party (CCP) in this age cohort. In addition, it includes all provincial chiefs (party secretaries and governors), ministers of the State Council, and heads of the central departments of the CCP in this age cohort but not on the CC or CCDI.

The individuals in this group are the most important political leaders in the Fifth Generation; some are leading candidates for the new Politburo (including its Standing Committee) and the Secretariat to be formed at the Seventeenth Party Congress in the fall of 2007. They include Li Keqiang (Liaoning party secretary), Li Yuanchao (Jiangsu party secretary), Wang Yang (Chongqing party secretary), Xi Jinping (Shanghai party secretary), Zhao Leji (Shaanxi party secretary), Zhang Chunxian (Hunan party secretary), Han Zheng (mayor of Shanghai), Wu Aiying (minister of justice), Wang Huning (director of the CCP Central Policy Research Center), Ling Jihua (director of the CCP General Office), and Lou Jiwei (deputy general secretary of the State Council). Largely because of the current Chinese obsession with age in elite recruitment, Hu Jintao's heir apparent is *unlikely* to be chosen from among the members of the Sixteenth Politburo.[3] The CCP's norm of promoting leaders in batches based on age brackets suggests that Hu's designated successor will most likely be chosen from the Fifth Generation. These rising stars—especially Li Keqiang, Li Yuanchao, Wang Yang, and Xi Jinping—will be in line for succession to the top posts in the party and the state in 2012 and 2013.

Of course, not all new members of the next Politburo will be Fifth Generation leaders. Some who were born in the late 1940s may also obtain seats on the

Politburo. The leading candidates include Ma Kai (sixty-one, National Development and Reform Commission minister), Wang Qishan (fifty-nine, Beijing mayor), Liu Yandong (sixty-two, director of the CCP United Front Work Department), Du Qinglin (sixty, Sichuan party secretary), Zhang Gaoli (sixty-one, Tianjin party secretary), Meng Jianzhu (sixty, Jiangxi party secretary), Zhou Xiaochuan (fifty-nine, governor of the People's Bank), and Bo Xilai (fifty-eight, commerce minister). Because they are close in age, their life experiences are quite similar to those of the leaders in this study.

The study pool includes twenty-two provincial chiefs (party secretaries and governors) and twenty-nine deputy provincial chiefs in their fifties; these individuals constitute about 50 percent of the leaders in this study. During the past decade, these provincial leadership posts have become major stepping-stones to positions of national leadership. For example, the proportion of Sixteenth Politburo members with previous experience as top provincial leaders (deputy party secretaries, vice governors, or higher) rose from 55 percent in 1992 to 68 percent in 1997, skyrocketing to 83 percent by 2002.[4] The study pool also includes several ministers in the State Council, for example, Minister of Foreign Affairs Yang Jiechi and Minister of Railways Liu Zhijun.

Using principally official information recently made available to the public in print and on the Internet, I have constructed biographies of these 103 Fifth Generation leaders.[5] Each biography contains forty-six entries indexed in seven major categories: (1) basic biographical information, (2) membership status in the CC or CCDI and other positions, (3) early work experience (especially during the Cultural Revolution), (4) career and promotion patterns, (5) educational background, (6) foreign experience, and (7) political association and networks. An analysis of these data reveals some of the important collective characteristics of the Fifth Generation.

"Sent-Down Youths": Hardship Experiences during Their Adolescent Years

The members of the Fifth Generation were between seven and sixteen years old when the Cultural Revolution took place, and between seventeen and twenty-six when it ended. China's school system—its elementary schools, middle schools, and colleges—was by and large paralyzed throughout the ten years of the Cultural Revolution. Students were engaged in political campaigns and ideological indoctrination rather than academic studies. The Cultural Revolution was a catastrophe for the entire nation, but the age cohort most affected by it consists of those who were in elementary and middle schools when the movement began in 1966. All the Fifth Generation leaders in this study characteristically belong to this "lost generation."

Table 6-1. *Work Experience of Fifth Generation Leaders during Their Adolescent Years*

Work	Number	Percent
"Sent-down youth"	54	52.4
Born into a farmer's family or began career as a farmer	8	7.8
Coal miner	2	1.9
Construction worker or stevedore	3	2.9
Railway worker	2	1.9
Factory worker	16	15.5
Soldier	8	7.8
Teacher	2	1.9
Office clerk	3	2.9
Unknown	5	4.9
Total	103	100.0

This age cohort not only lacked formal schooling but also experienced extraordinary hardships during their adolescent years as many of them were moved to the countryside to labor on farms for years. Between 1966 and 1978, a total of 16.6 million youngsters from urban areas were sent "up to the mountains and down to the villages."[6] These "sent-down youths" (*chadui zhishi qingnian*) accounted for about 10 percent of the total urban population of China at that time.

As table 6-1 shows, an overwhelming majority of the Fifth Generation leaders had humbling life experiences as adolescents. Fifty-four of them (52.4 percent) were "sent-down youths." These include rising stars of the generation such as Li Keqiang, Li Yuanchao, and Xi Jinping. Some were sent to remote areas. For example, Jiang Jianqing (chairman of the Industrial and Commercial Bank of China) was in Jiangxi for seven years, and Lu Zhangong (Fujian party secretary) was in Heilongjiang for thirteen years. The hardships in the countryside were so extreme that they had a lasting impact on the collective memory of the generation. As a result, the Cultural Revolution generation developed a better understanding of the poor in rural China and of harsh peasant life. Eight leaders (7.8 percent), including Wu Aiying, were born into peasant families and began their careers as farmers.

Most other leaders began their careers as manual laborers in construction or factories. Shanxi party secretary Zhang Baoshun worked as a stevedore in Hebei's Qinhuangdao for many years. Both Beijing University party secretary Min Weifang and vice chairman of the China Federation of Supply and Sales Wang Jun worked as coal miners. Qinghai governor Song Xiuyan, the only woman governor in China today, was a railway signal worker for five years. Cao

Jianming, executive vice president of the Supreme People's Court, spent three years as a waiter in a small restaurant in Shanghai.

These humbling and arduous experiences endowed the generation's future leaders with valuable traits such as endurance, adaptability, and humility. Lu Zhangong, for one, considered himself "merely one of the thousands of 'sent-down youths.' There was not much difference between my fellow 'sent-down youths' and me. The only difference is that I was lucky enough to seize the opportunity given me."[7] To a great extent, their interest in knowledge and their sound judgment during a difficult time helped them make the best of any opportunity that came their way. Ma Kai, for example, formed a study group with his high school classmates at a labor camp near Beijing in 1973. Together, they drafted an ambitious study plan entitled "Era, Mission, and Readiness."[8] Such dynamic efforts reflected the foresight of some in the Fifth Generation about the major changes that would shortly sweep the country.[9]

The Famous and Diverse "Class of 1982"

In 1977, as a result of Deng Xiaoping's policy initiatives, China resumed the use of college entrance examinations. A total of 11.6 million people, ranging in age from their late teens to their early thirties, registered for the exams, and about 401,000 (only 3 percent) were admitted.[10] In March and October of 1978, two classes were enrolled in several hundred universities in China. These were the students of the famous "Class of 1982." They were outstanding not only because they had passed the college entrance exams, which *Washington Post* reporter John Pomfret has described as "the most intense it ever had been and ever would be in Communist China's history," but also because, as Chinese dissident intellectual Wang Juntao has argued, "this unique group would most likely produce the country's most talented scientists, writers, philosophers, educators, and artists as well as statesmen in the future."[11]

Since college admission was no longer based on political loyalty, ideological purity, or a revolutionary or proletarian class background, the class of 1982 was a diverse group, with different family backgrounds. In addition, with the opening up of China following the Cultural Revolution, many young people were eager to learn more about Western liberal ideas. Beijing mayor Wang Qishan, for instance, became deeply absorbed in reading Western history and philosophy while a researcher in the late 1970s and early 1980s.[12] Thirty leaders (29 percent) in this study were members of this Class of 1982, including Li Keqiang (Beijing University), Li Yuanchao (Fudan University), Shenzhen party secretary Li Hongzhong (Jilin University), Min Weifang (Beijing Normal University), Lou Jiwei (Qinghua University), acting Shandong governor Jiang Daming (Heilongjiang University), and chairman of the Securities Regulatory Commission

Table 6-2. *Academic Fields of Fifth Generation Leaders*[a]

Field	Number	Percent
Engineering and science	17	16.5
Engineering	12	11.7
Agronomy/forestry	1	0.9
Biology/genetics	1	0.9
Chemistry	1	0.9
Computer science	1	0.9
Mathematics	1	0.9
Economics and management	35	34.0
Management	17	16.5
Economics	14	13.6
Finance	2	1.9
MBA	2	1.9
Social science and law	36	35.0
Political science and politics	22	21.4
Law	13	12.6
Journalism	1	0.9
Humanities	14	13.6
Philosophy	7	6.8
Chinese	4	3.9
History	2	1.9
Education	1	0.9
Unknown	1	0.9
Total	103	100

a. For those who majored in more than two academic fields, only the degree most recently obtained is coded.

Shang Fulin (Beijing Institute of Trade). Like others in the group, the future Fifth Generation leaders just mentioned pursued a wide range of academic disciplines: law, mathematics, history, education, economics, philosophy, and finance, respectively.

Popular Fields of Study and Postgraduate Degrees

For the 103 Fifth Generation leaders in this study, the four most popular academic fields were politics, management, economics, and law, followed by engineering (table 6-2). By contrast, the Fourth Generation of Chinese leaders was dominated by technocrats. Of the 24 full members of the Sixteenth Politburo (including the recently purged former Shanghai party secretary Chen Liangyu), 18 (75 percent) majored in engineering, and *all* 9 members of the Sixteenth Politburo Standing Committee are engineers by training. The Chinese political

Figure 6-1. *Technocrats in Ministerial/Provincial Leadership, 1982–97*

Percent

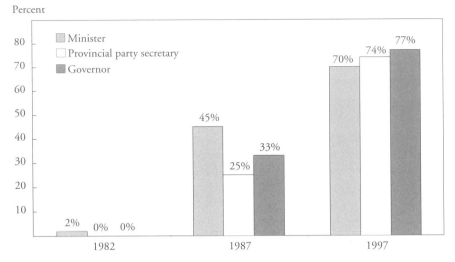

Sources: Hong Yung Lee, *From Revolutionary Cadres to Party Technocrats: The Changing Cadre System in Socialist China* (University of California Press, 1991), p. 268; Kenneth Lieberthal, *Governing China: From Revolution through Reform* (New York: W. W. Norton, 1995), p. 236; Li Cheng and Lynn White, "The Fifteenth Central Committee of the Chinese Communist Party," *Asian Survey,* 38 (March 1998): 251; and www.xinhuanet.com (December 31, 2002).

elite at all levels underwent a profound occupational change during the 1980s and 1990s with a rapid rise in the number of technocrats (see figure 6-1).

The technocrats' dominance of the Chinese leadership is now coming to an end. Of the current 62 provincial chiefs (party secretaries and governors), for example, only 18 (29 percent) specialized in engineering and natural sciences, while 32 (52 percent) studied social sciences and economics, and 12 provincial chiefs (19 percent) majored in the humanities. In the upcoming generation, 35 of the 103 most prominent leaders (34 percent) majored in politics and law, 31 (30 percent) specialized in management and economics, and only 17 (16.5 percent) majored in engineering and natural sciences. In the past decade, a degree in law or politics has become a valuable credential for aspiring political leaders.

Furthermore, all but one of the Fifth Generation leaders in this sample received a college education (table 6-3). Approximately 80 percent received postgraduate degrees; the 16.5 percent who hold Ph.D. degrees include rising stars such as Li Keqiang, Li Yuanchao, Xi Jinping, Wang Min (Jilin party secretary), and Yuan Chunqing (Shaanxi governor). By contrast, no one in the current Sixteenth Central Committee Politburo has a Ph.D. This will most likely

Table 6-3. *Educational Levels of Fifth Generation Leaders*

Highest degree obtained	Number	Percent
Ph.D.	17	16.5
Master's	65	63.1
Bachelor's	19	18.4
Junior college	1	1.0
High school	1	1.0
Total	103	100.0

change when the Fifth Generation leaders take over a large number of seats on the new Politburo following the Seventeenth Party Congress.

Most Fifth Generation leaders with postgraduate degrees earned their credentials through part-time or correspondence programs in recent years, many at the Central Party School (CPS): twenty-three (36.5 percent) of the sixty-three with a master's degree received their degrees at this institution. Although the Chinese public tends to criticize these part-time and correspondence programs for mainly helping political officials "become gilded" (*dujin*) rather than offering substantial academic training, more of this generation's high officials hold advanced degrees than any previous leaders in the CCP's history.

One who did not participate in a part-time program is Jilin party secretary Wang Min: he earned his Ph.D. at the Nanjing University of Aeronautics and Astronautics from 1983 to 1986 and also taught at the same university for many years. Another is vice president of China's Academy of Sciences Bai Chunli, who was a full-time chemistry student at the Chinese Academy of Sciences between 1981 and 1985. Both Wang and Bai also studied abroad: Wang did research at the Hong Kong University of Science and Technology from 1987 to 1989, and Bai was a visiting professor at the California Institute of Technology from 1985 to 1987, and then at Northeastern University in Japan from 1991 to 1992. Two leaders in this study received their Ph.D. degrees overseas: Zhai Huqu (president of the China Academy of Agriculture) received his Ph.D. in genetics from the University of Birmingham in 1987, and Min Weifang received his degree in education from Stanford University in 1987.

Growing Number of Leaders with Educational Experience in the West

On the Sixteenth Politburo, only two leaders of the Third Generation, Luo Gan and Cao Gangchuan, studied abroad, both in the former Soviet Union. Most Fourth Generation leaders attended universities in China, with the exception of Zhang Dejiang, who studied in North Korea. This is not surprising because China sent hardly any students to the West in the 1960s and 1970s. Only after

1978, when Deng Xiaoping began the educational open door policy, did a large number of Chinese students and scholars pursue their studies in the West.

Of the Fifth Generation group, seventeen leaders (16.5 percent) had undertaken foreign study, many as year-long visiting scholars in the United States, Japan, and other Western countries. Some Fourth Generation leaders were also visiting scholars, three notable examples being Chen Zhili (state councilor), Xu Guanhua (minister of science and technology), and Xu Kuangdi (president of the Chinese Academy of Engineering), all of whom spent time studying engineering and sciences in the early 1980s. Fifth Generation leaders, however, usually spent their time abroad studying economics, social science, and law. Yang Jiechi, for one, studied international relations at Bath University and the London School of Economics and Political Science from 1973 to 1975; Wang Huning was a visiting scholar at the Department of Political Science at the University of Iowa from 1988 to 1989; Cao Jianming studied at law schools in San Francisco and Belgium from 1988 to 1991; Bater (deputy party secretary of Inner Mongolia) studied management in Tokyo from 1989 to 1990; Jiang Jianqing and Feng Jianshen (vice governor of Gansu) both studied finance at Columbia University in the late 1990s; and Li Hongzhong and Li Yuanchao both studied public administration at Harvard's Kennedy School in 1999 and 2002, respectively. Of course, it remains to be seen whether their foreign studies in the fields of social science and law will have an impact on their views about China's political reforms and democracy as they move into some of the most important positions in China in the years to come.

The Decline of Technocrats and Rise of Lawyers

Arguably the most important difference between the Fourth and Fifth Generation leadership is that the former was dominated by technocrats while the latter has more diverse educational and occupational backgrounds. Particularly striking is the growing number of Fifth Generation leaders with training in law and politics, which may account for their greater emphasis on strengthening the country's legal system. The work report for the 2002 Party Congress, for example, called for a new Chinese-style legal system by 2010, and several of Hu Jintao's recent speeches have stressed the rule of law.

The number of registered lawyers and law school students has increased sharply since the early 1980s, when China had only 3,000 lawyers despite a population of more than 1 billion. By 2004, it had a total of 11,691 registered law firms and some 114,000 lawyers.[13] The explosive growth in the study of law can also be seen in the number of full and part-time students enrolled at the Law School of Beijing University in 2004, which equaled the *total* number of law students trained at the school over the preceding fifty years.[14]

In the past ten years, a large number of students at Beijing University's law school have regularly participated in the legal aid program, which provides various forms of legal assistance to poor and vulnerable citizens and is part of an important new phenomenon in China today: many Chinese lawyers and legal professionals now devote their careers to protecting the interests of various social groups. A new Chinese term, "lawyers for the protection of human rights" (*weiquan lushi*), was recently coined to describe this emerging group. Despite government harassment and even occasional arrests, these lawyers travel across the country to support each other and help the underprivileged take legal action against the rich and powerful. Their courageous actions have greatly enhanced public awareness of the rights and interests of citizens. Lawyers may well become an even more important political force in the years to come. Some will continue to work outside the political establishment to challenge abuses of power, but others may themselves become political leaders, as this study of Fifth Generation leaders suggests.[15]

An important theoretical proposition in Western academic circles is that the occupational character of the ruling class in a given country has strong implications for—and sometimes a determining effect on—the nature of the political system.[16] Political elites often want to leave their leadership legacy in the area in which they have a personal or professional interest. Technocrats, for example, tend to focus on economic growth and technological development because of their own backgrounds in these subjects. It is not unreasonable to expect the growing number of lawyers and students of politics in the upcoming Fifth Generation to want to have an impact on the fields of political and legal reform, as they appear to be more interested in these subjects than the generations of communist ideologues, revolutionary veterans, and economic technocrats who preceded them.

How Far Can China's "Inner-Party Democracy" Go?

Perhaps even more important than the growing diversity in educational and work experiences of China's politicians is the trend toward checks and balances among the top leadership. This chapter argues that this change in China's political landscape marks the emergence of "bipartisanship" in the CCP. That is, the leadership is now structured around two informal and almost equally powerful coalitions or factions held in place by checks and balances, which might be referred to as a "one-party, two-factions" system.

Chinese-Style "Bipartisanship" in the Making?

Two factors are contributing to this political trend. First, for the first time in the history of the People's Republic of China (PRC), the ruling party is no longer led principally by a strongman such as Mao Zedong or Deng Xiaoping. Moreover, under current circumstances, no such leader is likely to ever emerge again. Consequently, political leaders and factions are constantly engaged in negotiation, compromise, coalition building, and deal cutting, as described in chapters 4 and 5 of this volume. Second, relationships between central and local arenas have changed profoundly over the past two decades in the wake of emerging local interests and increasing regional disparity between the rich coastal region and poorer inland regions (see chapter 8).

Local leaders (mainly provincial and municipal leaders) thus tend to side with the top national leaders who will protect or advance their local interests, thereby forming two political coalitions that can best be characterized as a "populist" and an "elitist" coalition. These coalitions differ not only in their leaders' distinct personal careers, political associations, and networks but also in the socioeconomic groups and geographical regions they represent. On the whole, the "populist coalition"—led by China's current president and party general secretary Hu Jintao and Premier Wen Jiabao—represents the interests of the inland regions (China's "red states"), more traditional economic sectors, and less-privileged social groups such as farmers and migrant workers. The core group of this coalition consists of the leaders who advanced their careers through the Chinese Communist Youth League (CCYL), known as the *tuanpai*. In contrast, the elitist coalition—led by former president and party chief Jiang Zemin and current vice president Zeng Qinghong—represents the interests of the coastal regions (China's "blue states"), including the new economic sectors, entrepreneurs, the emerging middle class, and foreign-educated returnees, known as the *haiguipai*. The core group of this coalition used to be the "Shanghai gang" but is now apparently composed of the "princelings," or children of former high-ranking officials.

This bipartisanship in the CCP emerged in the post-Deng era and then became more evident in the political succession from Jiang Zemin to Hu Jintao. It is expected to become more dynamic under Fifth Generation leadership. For one thing, Fifth Generation leaders seem to follow two distinct career paths, which will further enhance this bipartisanship. For another, current top Chinese leaders have begun using the term "inner-party democracy" (*dangnei minzhu*) to endorse the idea that the party should institutionalize checks and balances within its leadership.

The Tuanpai*'s Turn: Strengths and Weaknesses*

Patron-client ties and factionalism have played important roles in the career advancement of Fifth Generation leaders. Their rise to national positions of prominence and their dynamic interactions will consolidate the factions or coalitions to which they belong. Their factional competition is also likely to provide policy options for both the political establishment and the public from which they seek support. It has widely been recognized that in the Sixteenth Politburo Hu Jintao is surrounded by Jiang Zemin's protégés; six of the nine members of the Standing Committee owe their allegiance to Jiang rather than Hu. The balance of power, however, will likely shift in Hu's favor as a result of changes at the Seventeenth Party Congress.

Of the 103 prominent members examined here, 50 (48.5 percent) have advanced their careers primarily through the CCYL. Most of them can be characterized as *tuanpai* leaders—those who served in the CCYL's national or provincial leadership in the early 1980s, when Hu Jintao was in charge of that organization. Table 6-4 identifies the 15 most prominent *tuanpai* leaders in this study. All of them began working closely with Hu more than two decades ago, and all have been linked to him in one way or another throughout their careers. Li Keqiang, Li Yuanchao, Zhang Baoshun, Zhang Qingli, Yuan Chunqing, and Han Changfu worked directly under Hu's leadership at the CCYL Secretariat or Central Committee in the early 1980s; Ling Jihua was Hu's personal secretary (*mishu*).

Hu Jintao also provided many Fifth Generation leaders with opportunities to broaden their leadership experiences. For example, Liu Qibao served as deputy editor-in-chief of the *People's Daily* in 1993, and then deputy secretary general in the State Council between 1994 and 2000; Zhang Baoshun served as deputy director of the Xinhua News Agency; Wang Yang served as executive deputy secretary general of the State Council; and Yuan Chunqing served as chief-of-staff of the Central Commission of Discipline Inspection of the CCP. Three other *tuanpai* leaders, Wu Aiying, Shen Yueyue, and Song Xiuyan, are among the most powerful female leaders in China today. Because they are relatively young and hold important posts, they are all candidates for further promotion. Some of them will be front-runners for seats on the next Politburo. And because they have similar backgrounds, they will likely stand ready to carry out Hu's concept of a "harmonious society," which pays more attention to social fairness, balanced regional development, and environmental protection than to the pace of economic growth.

An analysis of the career paths of *tuanpai* leaders also shows that they have had work experience in rural areas rather than urban industries. Furthermore, they are familiar with propaganda and party organizational work, but few have had any substantial experience in foreign trade, finance, or banking (see table 6-5). A majority have educational backgrounds in politics or law rather than engineering or natural sciences.

All these traits differ significantly from those of the technocrats who dominated the Chinese leadership in the Jiang era, especially the members of the so-

Table 6-4. *Top Fifth Generation Leaders with* Tuanpai *(CCYL) Backgrounds*

Leader	Year born	Current position (as of July 2007)	Factional ties and defining experience in CCYL
Li Keqiang	1955	Party secretary, Liaoning	CCYL Secretariat, 1982–98
Li Yuanchao	1950	Party secretary, Jiangsu	CCYL Secretariat, 1982–90
Wang Yang	1955	Party secretary, Chongqing	CCYL Anhui Committee, 1982–84 (department secretary, 1983–84)
Wu Aiying	1951	Minister of justice	CCYL Shandong department secretary, 1982–89
Shen Yueyue	1957	Vice director, CCP Organization Department	CCYL Ningbo department secretary and Zhejiang secretary, 1983–93
Ling Jihua	1956	Vice director, CCP Central Office	CCYL Central Committee, 1979–95 (Hu's mishu, 1982–85)
Zhang Qingli	1951	Party secretary, Tibet	CCYL Central Committee, 1979–86
Zhang Baoshun	1950	Party secretary, Shanxi	CCYL Central Committee, 1978–93 (Secretariat, 1982–93)
Liu Qibao	1953	Party secretary, Guangxi	CCYL Anhui secretary, 1982–83; CCYL Secretariat, 1985–93
Song Xiuyan	1955	Governor, Qinghai	CCYL Qinghai department secretary and secretary, 1983–88
Yuan Chunqing	1952	Governor, Shaanxi	CCYL Central Committee, 1980–97 (Secretariat, 1992–97)
Qin Guangrong	1950	Governor, Yunnan	CCYL Hunan department secretary, 1984–87
Luo Baoming	1952	Governor, Hainan	CCYL Tianjin department secretary, and secretary, 1984–92
Han Changfu	1954	Governor, Jilin	CCYL Central Committee, 1982–91
Jiang Daming	1953	Acting governor, Shandong	CCYL Organization Department, division head, 1984–86

called Shanghai Gang, whose younger members (for example, Han Zheng, Lou Jiwei, and Jiang Jianqing) will likely continue to play an important role in the formation of China's economic and financial policies. In the next five years at least, princelings such as Ma Kai, Wang Qishan, Bo Xilai, Zhou Xiaochuan, Xi Jinping, and Lou Jiwei will dominate the economic and financial leadership in the country.

The diverging career paths and substantive "division of labor" between *tuanpai* and princeling factions will have two important ramifications. First, the career experiences and political backgrounds of *tuanpai* officials are arguably the

Table 6-5. *Other Leadership Experience of* Tuanpai *Officials*

Official	Foreign trade	Banking and finance	Industrial	Rural	CCP organization	Propaganda	Legal and disciplinary affairs	United front
Li Keqiang			X					
Li Yuanchao						X		X
Wang Yang			X			X		
Wu Aiying			X				X	X
Shen Yueyue					X			
Ling Jihua			X			X		
Zhang Qingli			X			X		
Zhang Baoshun						X		X
Liu Qibao						X		
Song Xiuyan			X	X				X
Yuan Chunqing							X	
Qin Guangrong			X	X		X		
Luo Baoming						X		
Han Changfu	X		X			X		
Jiang Daming			X	X		X		

best credentials that Hu, Wen, and their successors need to handle China's new challenges, such as rural poverty, social fairness, and political instability. Second, their weak credentials in economics, especially in foreign trade and finance, constitute a distinct shortcoming indicating that these officials will have to cooperate—and thus share power—with other elite groups having expertise in these areas. This may also help prevent Hu and his faction from wielding excessive power or achieving social fairness at the expense of economic efficiency.

The Sociological Context of Emerging Bipartisanship

Both the populist coalition and the elitist coalition have broad sociological bases of support. Hu Jintao and his *tuanpai* protégés often present themselves as leaders who represent the interests and rights of vulnerable social groups such as peasants, migrant workers, the urban poor, and the elderly. Their "people-centered" policy agenda includes an agricultural tax waiver for peasants, leasing restrictions on commercial and industrial land in both rural and urban areas, the abolition of some discriminatory regulations against migrant workers, and ongoing concerted efforts to establish a social safety net.

The elitist coalition, by contrast, has been supported by a number of powerful forces in the country, both old and new, that control tremendous economic resources. Managers involved with foreign enterprises and foreign-educated returnees, members of the upper and middle classes, entrepreneurs, cultural elites, and liberal economists have all tended to support the elitist coalition. To a great extent, the composition of the CCP, including its leadership, has profoundly changed over the past decade or so. An official 2004 study found that 34 percent of the owners of private enterprises were CCP members.[17] Perhaps even more astonishing, a recent study showed that 35 percent of the 500 richest people in China in 2006—all of them multimillionaires or even billionaires— are CCP members.[18] Yet another study, conducted by several leading Chinese research institutions, showed that of the top leaders in firms specializing in finance, foreign trade, property development, large construction, or stock trading, 85–90 percent are princelings.[19]

China's ongoing socioeconomic transformation and the new developments in elite politics are not taking place in an ideological vacuum. Intellectuals representing various parts of the ideological spectrum have been engaged in a heated debate about the future direction of political development in China. Pan Wei, a Berkeley-educated political science professor at Beijing University, favors legalist political reforms rather than democratic elections and is more interested in a Singaporean-style rule of law rather than Western- or Taiwanese-style democracy. He bluntly criticizes the "democracy worship and election obsession" of his Chinese colleagues, arguing that in a country without the rule of law, such as China, it would be a disaster to move toward democratic elections. In his words, "the CCP will split if the Party adopts elections; and the PRC will disintegrate if the country adopts elections."[20]

Pan Wei's view reflects the persistent reservations of some in the political establishment about bold political reforms. According to a recent survey of Chinese local officials conducted by the Central Party School, 90 percent of these individuals are not willing to pursue large-scale political reforms.[21] For many Chinese political and intellectual elites, any serious effort to move toward political democracy in China may release long-restrained social tensions and quickly undermine the CCP's capacity to allocate social and economic resources. Such reforms may also cause the PRC to lose its growing international influence. As Chu Yun-han has observed, democracy is not appealing to many people in China perhaps because they see new democracies in Asia struggling with overwhelming governing challenges such as "inconclusive or disputed electoral outcomes, endless partisan gridlock and bickering, recurring scandals, widespread corruption, slower growth and foggy economic outlooks."[22]

At the same time, some other prominent Chinese intellectuals offer a spirited defense of democracy, with comprehensive critiques of the negative view of democracy exemplified by scholars such as Pan Wei. Xie Tao, former vice president of the People's University, has argued that the assessment of a political system is not a theoretical exercise, but a practical one. In an article widely circulated in the Chinese media, Xie asked pointedly: "How is it possible that China's political system is a good one, when it could not prevent the labeling and persecuting of 500,000 'Rightists,' could not prevent the national madness of the Great Leap Forward and the Cultural Revolution, and could not protect basic human rights?"[23] And Zhou Ruijin, former deputy editor of the *People's Daily*, has reportedly remarked that although democracy cannot and should not be achieved overnight, only the enactment of democratic reforms will be capable of coping with the country's sociopolitical problems and demographic challenges.[24]

Some Chinese scholars have in addition rejected the view that China's transition to democracy may make the country less competitive. Zhang Nianchi, director of the Shanghai Institute of East Asian Studies, believes that if Ma Ying-Jeou of the Nationalist Party wins the 2008 election in Taiwan, the focus of cross-Strait relations may shift from disputes over unification and independence to comparability of political systems.[25] In some circles, this consideration has become an incentive for China's democratic development. A number of scholars with strong nationalistic views also favor power sharing and inner-party democracy. According to Yan Xuetong, a professor at Qinghua University, "If China can avoid domestic in-fighting and vicious power struggles in the leadership, it will continue its rapid rise for a long time."[26] A documentary series that aired on Chinese national television in recent months, "The Rise of Great Powers," expressed the same sentiment, noting that unless China establishes a democratic political system, the country cannot stand as a major power on the world stage.[27]

In a widely read article, "Democracy Is a Good Thing," Yu Keping argued that "incremental democracy" should and will ultimately result in a "democratic breakthrough," as various existing social forces and the political leadership are ready for it to occur.[28] Yet neither Yu nor current top leaders have a timetable for when the democratic breakthrough will happen. Although Hu Jintao has said "without democracy there will be no modernization in China," he and other Fourth Generation leaders have been extremely cautious about expanding the freedom of the media, the independence of the judiciary, the transparency of the decisionmaking process in elite recruitment, and the legitimacy of political lobbying.[29]

However, it may not be too much to expect Fifth Generation leaders, in view of their previous experiences and political skills, to be bold enough to pursue a real "democratic breakthrough." Jiangsu party secretary Li Yuanchao, one of the most promising politicians of this generation, seems to understand the need for such a breakthrough, as indicated by his recent criticism of some leaders who are "obsessed with stability" (*taiping guan*) and who refuse to try new political experiments.[30] Li believes that this mentality, though seemingly safe, is, in fact, dangerous because it may lead China to lose an excellent opportunity to prevent more serious crises. In Li's view, Chinese leaders do not lack wisdom or ideas but need more courage and "guts" to pursue bolder reforms. Only time will tell what Li will accomplish through his "bolder reforms" and whether he will have a chance to play a larger role in the national leadership.

Conclusion

In the history of the PRC, each generation of leaders has had its own mandate and its own policy priorities, often designed to fix the problems created or exacerbated by preceding generations, as in the transition from Jiang's Third Generation to Hu's Fourth Generation of leadership. To a great extent, generational characteristics of likely future leaders are important—and sometimes quite reliable—predictors of China's future political trajectory.

In the case of China's Fifth Generation leaders, their extraordinary life experiences, particularly the hardships of their formative years, endowed them with humility, resourcefulness, and other valuable characteristics for leadership. Their striking comeback to college after the Cultural Revolution reflects their foresight and open-mindedness. Their exposure to Western ideas during their college years and the foreign experiences of some members of the generation have broadened their perspectives. Their common academic fields in politics and law suggest that they differ from the technocrats, their Fourth Generation predecessors, in terms of leadership skills and political values. Most important, the intra-generational differences in family backgrounds, political socialization, and policy preferences have contributed to the emerging bipartisanship within the Chinese Communist Party. At the same time, the fact that neither the populist coalition nor the elitist coalition is sufficiently powerful to dominate the other tends to make them observe rules and take turns in the exercise of power.

Inner-party democracy, though it is not true democracy, may pave the way for a more fundamental change in the Chinese political system. The democratic transition of the world's most populous nation, if it does occur, will certainly be no easy task. At present, political power in China is monopolized by the CCP, which prohibits the formation of competing political parties or an independent judiciary. In the absence of a broadly based and well-organized political opposition in the PRC, the country is unlikely to develop a multiparty political system in the near future. This actually makes the ongoing experiments with inner-party bipartisanship even more important.

Clearly, inner-party bipartisanship will not remain stagnant and in its characteristically dynamic fashion may make political lobbying somewhat more transparent, factional politics more legitimate, and elections more genuine and acceptable at higher levels of political power in the not-too-distant future.[31] Thus it is not difficult to imagine the CCP's splitting along the lines of an elitist coalition and a populist coalition after ten to fifteen more years of this inner-party bipartisanship. Because of the incremental nature of this institutional development, such a split could be achieved in a nonviolent way, and elections and competition within the CCP might one day be extended to general elections in the country.

For the next decade or so, however, Fifth Generation leaders will likely be the main players in China's changing political landscape. If the legacy of Jiang's Third Generation was rapid economic growth, and if the mandate of Hu's Fourth Generation is social harmony and social fairness, the self-perceived mission of the Fifth Generation may very well be China's political transformation.

Notes

1. China's official media seldom use the term "Fifth Generation" but instead call these leaders the "generation of the republic" (*gongheguo yidai*) since they were all born after the founding of the People's Republic of China (PRC). Cheng Ying, "Zhongguo jinru xinde zhuanzheqi" (China enters a new era of transition), *Liaowang dongfang zhoukan* (Oriental Outlook Weekly), October 9, 2005, pp. 12–18. The concept and definition of elite generations can be highly political. As some scholars have observed, it is rather arbitrary to define "where one generation begins and another ends." See Ruth Cherrington, "Generational Issues in China: A Case Study of the 1980s Generation of Young Intellectuals," *British Journal of Sociology* 48 (June 1997): 304. See also Karl Mannheim, "Consciousness of Class and Consciousness of Generation," in *Essays on Sociology of Knowledge,* edited by Mannheim (London: RKP, 1952); and Pat McNeill, "The Changing Generation Gap," *New Statesman and Society,* September 23, 1988, p. 30.

2. The prominent Chinese scholar Hu Angang, for example, defines those who were born between 1949 and 1959 as the members of the Cultural Revolution (CR) generation. Yu Zeyuan, "Guoqing wenti zhuanjia Hu Angang: Zhongguo jueqi you sanda wenti" (China expert Hu Angang on the three major problems in China's rise), *Lianhe zaobao* (United Morning News), January 15, 2007, p. 14. In a previous study, I defined the CR generation as those who were born between 1941 and 1956. They were ten to twenty-five years old when the CR began in 1966. According to this definition, the so-called Fourth and Fifth Generations both belong to the CR generation. To a great extent, subdivision of the CR generation serves to extend the rule of this political elite generation in China. See Cheng Li, *China's Leaders: The New Generation* (Lanham, Md.: Rowman and Littlefield, 2001).

3. The youngest member of the Politburo Standing Committee of the Sixteenth Central Committee, Li Changchun, is only two years younger than Hu Jintao, and the youngest current Politburo member, Liu Yunshan, is only five years younger than Hu.

4. For a detailed discussion of the growing importance of provincial leaders over the past decade, see Cheng Li, "A Landslide Victory for Provincial Leaders," *China Leadership Monitor*, no. 5 (Winter 2003).

5. For printed materials, see the CCP Organization Department and Research Office of the History of the Chinese Communist Party, *Zhongguo gongchandang lijie zhongyang weiyuan dacidian, 1921–2003* (Who's who of the members of the Central Committees of the Chinese Communist Party 1921–2003) (Beijing: Zhonggong dangshi chubanshe, 2004). For online sources, see www.xinhuanet.com.

6. The total number of sent-down youth is based on www.chinesenewsnet.com (February 17, 2007). For more discussion of the sent-down youth movement, see Deng Peng, *Wusheng de qunluo* (The silent community) (Chongqing: Chongqing chubanshe, 2006).

7. Tan Ailing and Zhang Yue, "Shengbuji gaoguan gexing shizheng" (The idiosyncratic leadership style of ministerial and provincial leaders), *Liaowang dongfang zhoukan*, June 26, 2005, p. 8.

8. Chen Lei, "Ma Kai," *Renwu zhoukan* (Southern People Weekly), October 19, 2005, p. 20.

9. Ibid.

10. "Zhongguo huifu gaokao sanshinian: chengwei qianbaiwanren mingyun de zhuanzhedian" (The 30th anniversary of the reinstallation of the college entrance examination in China: The turning point of the fate of millions of people), *Zhongguo shibao* (China Times), May 15, 2006, p. 4. See also www.chinesenewsnet.com (May 15, 2006).

11. John Pomfret, *Chinese Lessons: Five Classmates and the Story of the New China* (New York: Henry Holt, 2006), p. 10; and Wang Juntao, "Beida fengyun jiuyou dianping" (Comments about a few distinguished alumni of Beijing University) (www.blogchina.com [December 25, 2005]).

12. Wang was born in 1948 and thus was not included in this study, but his experience is exemplary. See Qiu Ping, *Zhonggong diwudai* (The Fifth Generation of the CCP Leadership) (Hong Kong: Xiafeier, 2005), pp. 129–30.

13. Ji Shuoming and Wang Jianming, "Zhongguo weiquan lushi fazhixianfeng" (China's lawyers for human rights protection: Vanguards of the rule of law), *Yazhou zhoukan* (Asia Week), December 19, 2005.

14. In 2004, 217 Ph.D. candidates, 1,128 master's degree students, and 704 undergraduates were enrolled in Beijing University's law school. In addition, the school had 1,200 part-time graduate students and 17,044 part-time undergraduates. Su Ning and Zhang Tao, "Beida faxueyuan: Bainian dili zhengnianqing" (Beijing University's Law School: The vitality after a century's ups and downs), *Renmin ribao*, May 19, 2004, p. 15.

15. In 2005, two law professors at the East China Political Science and Law University, Hao Tiechuan and Sun Chao, were appointed to serve as heads of two districts in Shanghai. "Zhongguo dangdai faxuejia canzheng de xianshi mailuo" (The road to power of China's contemporary legal scholars), *Renwu zhoukan*, August 5, 2005, pp. 2–5.

16. For more discussion of the elite theory, see Vilfredo Pareto, *The Rise and Fall of the Elites: An Application of Theoretical Sociology* (Totowa, N.J.: Bedminster, 1968); and Robert D. Putnam, *The Comparative Study of Political Elites* (Englewood Cliffs, N.J.: Prentice-Hall, 1976).

17. "Woguo 1/3 siqi laoban shi dangyuan" (One-third of owners of the private firms in China are CCP members), *Nanfang dushi bao* (Southern Metropolitan Daily), February 13, 2005, p. 1.

18. See "Hu Run's List of the 500 Richest People in China in 2006" (www.news.xinhuanet.com [October 11, 2006]).

19. Quoted from "Zhongguo yiwan fuhao jiucheng yishang shi gaogan zinü" (About 90 percent of the billionaires in China are children of high-ranking officials), *Xingdao ribao*, October 19, 2006, p. 1; see also *Shijie ribao* (World Journal), October 19, 2006, p. A12.

20. The quotation is from www.chinesenewsnet.com (April 25, 2006). For further discussion of Wei's criticism of democratic worship and election obsession, see Pan Wei, "Toward a Consultative Rule of Law Regime in China," *Journal of Contemporary China* 12 (February 2003): 3–43; also Suisheng Zhao, ed., *Debating Political Reform in China: Rule of Law vs. Democratization* (New York: M. E. Sharpe, 2006).

21. "Zhonggong zhongyang dangxiao diaocha: Jiucheng ganbu dui zhenggai meireqing" (Survey of the Central Party School: About 90 percent of officials are not enthusiastic about political reform), *Shijie ribao*, December 25, 2006, p. A3. Reprinted from *Beijing ribao* (Beijing Daily), December 18, 2006.

22. Chu Yun-han, "Third-Wave Democratization in East Asia: Challenges and Prospects," *ASIEN* 100 (July 2006): 13.

23. See www.chinesenewsnet.com (February 21, 2007).

24. Wang Jilu, "Zhou Ruijin: Gaige kaifang dao jintian, buzhenglun shi buxingle" (Zhou Ruijin: Debates are necessary as reforms and opening are accelerating today), *Nanfang dushi bao*, February 5, 2007, p. 1.

25. "Zhang Nianchi: Liang'an jiangshi zhiduzhizheng" (Zhang Nianchi: The cross-Strait dispute will be the dispute of political system), *Shijie ribao*, January 1, 2006, p. A4. Ma Ying-Jeou has said that unification depends, first and foremost, on whether Mainland China is moving toward democracy: "There will be no possibility for unification if China does not move in that direction" (www.chinesenewsnet.com, [July 16, 2005]).

26. See www.chinesenewsnet.com (December 12, 2006).

27. Zheng Yongnian made this point in his interview in the series. Zheng has also written substantially on the subject of China's political reforms and incremental democracy. See Zheng Yongnian, *Will China Become Democratic? Elite, Class and Regime Transition* (Singapore: Times Academic Press, 2004); and Zheng, "China's Incremental Political Reform: Lessons and Experiences," in *China: Two Decades of Reform and Change*, edited by Gungwu Wang and John Wong (Singapore: World Scientific, 1999), pp. 11–40.

28. Yu Keping, "Minzhu shige haodongxi" (Democracy Is a Good Thing), in *Minzhu shige haodongxi* (Democracy Is a Good Thing), edited by Yan Jian (Beijing: Shehui kexue wenxian chubanshe, 2006).

29. For Hu Jintao's remarks, see Dejin Su, "Hu Jintao's U.S. Visit Highlights China's Rising Influence," *Washington Observer Weekly*, no. 174, April 26, 2006. See also www.washingtonobserver.org/en/document.cfm?documentid=47&charid=3 (July 14, 2007).

30. See www.xinhuanct.com (August 11, 2005).

31. As Andrew J. Nathan observes, incremental adaptations may "actually change the nature of the regime." Nathan, "Present at the Stagnation," *Foreign Affairs* 85 (July/August 2006): 177–82.

Part III

Economic Actors and
Economic Policy

7

Business Interest Groups in Chinese Politics: The Case of the Oil Companies

ERICA S. DOWNS

> Monopolies and powerful industrial groups such as telecommunications, oil, electric power and automobiles recently have started to become special interest groups and have all begun to exert an obvious impact on the formulation of public policy.
>
> SUN LIPING, in *Zhongguo xinwen zhoukan* (2006)

Throughout the history of the People's Republic of China (PRC), the oil industry has been a powerful interest group. As a strategic sector of the economy, the industry has had access to the top leadership and made its voice heard in the policymaking process. It has produced successive generations of leaders who used their accomplishments in the oil sector to advance their political careers—especially in the 1950s and 1960s when the discovery of the Daqing oil field and the achievement of self-sufficiency in oil was one of the country's few success stories. Historically, the most prominent national leaders from the oil industry were Vice Premier Yu Qiuli and several of his associates from the State Planning Commission. Viewed as a "petroleum faction," this group had a large impact on economic policy, especially in the 1970s.[1]

In recent years, the industry has continued to influence decisionmaking and elite politics, but the relationship between the national oil companies (NOCs) and the party-state has changed.[2] Although still subject to party-state control, the companies have become more autonomous and influential under the umbrella of China's rapidly expanding, increasingly market-oriented, and internationalizing energy sector. Now that they have subsidiaries listed on foreign stock exchanges,

I thank Scott Harold, Cheng Li, and Xiaoting Li for helpful conversations about and comments on earlier versions of this chapter.

121

global business portfolios, and an eye on the pursuit of profits, their domestic and international interests do not always coincide with those of the party-state. Moreover, they are often able to advance these interests not only because of their substantial financial, human, and political resources but also because of the unanticipated surge in China's oil demand and imports since 2002, which has increased the value of China's NOCs to Beijing. Some of the executives of these companies have become competitive candidates for top political posts because the managerial skills developed at the helm of some of China's most profitable and internationally competitive state-owned enterprises (SOEs) are transferable to the government of a country integrating into the global economy.

Marketization and globalization have had an impact on the relationship between the party-state and SOEs in other sectors as well, notably telecommunications, automobiles, and steel.[3] As a result of their growing economic might, these firms are also helping to intensify the diffusion of power in Chinese politics. This aspect of China's changing political landscape and its implications for the state's policies and leadership, as exemplified by the growing influence of the NOCs, is the subject of this chapter.

Relationship between the Party-State and the NOCs

China's three major NOCs—China National Petroleum Corporation (CNPC), China Petrochemical Corporation (Sinopec), and China National Offshore Oil Corporation (CNOOC)—were all created from government ministries in the 1980s. CNPC, formed in 1988 from the upstream (exploration and production) assets of the Ministry of Petroleum Industry (MPI), is the largest oil producer in China and the eighth largest in the world.[4] Sinopec, established in 1983 from the downstream (refining and marketing) assets of MPI and the Ministry of Chemical Industry, has the largest refining capacity in China and the fifth largest in the world.[5] CNOOC, formed in 1982 as a corporation under the MPI and modeled after the international oil companies, was established to form joint ventures with foreign firms to operate in China's territorial waters and is primarily an upstream company that dominates China's offshore oil industry. CNPC and Sinopec are both ministry-level companies, a bureaucratic rank that they fought hard to keep so as to maintain a privileged position when dealing with the state.[6] CNOOC has the lower status of a general bureau. The current general managers of all three companies—Fu Chengyu (CNOOC), Jiang Jiemin (CNPC), and Su Shulin (Sinopec)—all hold the rank of vice minister.

Each company has a subsidiary listed on the Hong Kong and New York stock exchanges, which holds its best assets except for CNPC's investments in Sudan and Sinopec's overseas projects. The parent companies are the majority share-

Table 7-1. *Internationally Listed Subsidiaries of China's National Oil Companies, 2006*

Listed	Parent	Shares owned by parent (%)
PetroChina	CNPC	88.21
Sinopec Corp.	Sinopec	75.84
CNOOC Ltd.	CNOOC	66.41

Sources: PetroChina, *Annual Report 2006*; Sinopec Corp., *Annual Report 2006*; CNOOC Ltd., *Annual Report 2006*.

holders of the listed companies (see table 7-1). Other shareholders include individual and institutional investors.

Ownership does not always equal control, of course, and this is true for the party-state: its control over the NOCs derives not from ownership but rather from other sources of influence in the party and government. The State Asset Supervision and Administration Commission (SASAC) is the government body charged with exercising formal authority over China's largest SOEs, including the NOCs. SASAC has been a passive authority, however, because it neither harvests their profits (the NOCs and other large SOEs currently are not required to pay dividends to the Chinese government, only taxes) nor appoints their top leaders (although it does choose their high-level managers).[7] The most powerful lever of party-state influence over the NOCs is the nomenklatura system.

Nomenklatura System

The party-state's primary instrument of control over the management of China's institutions, including all major SOEs directly under the central government, is the nomenklatura system—a hierarchical system of appointing personnel.[8] All top-level appointments, promotions, and dismissals at these firms rest with the Chinese Communist Party's (CCP's) Organization Department and the Ministry of Personnel (MOP), which functions largely as an arm of the Organizational Department, with many of its officials concurrently occupying positions in the department.[9] The ultimate authority over the top positions in the NOCs lies with the Organization Department, whose decisions are ratified by the Politburo Standing Committee and implemented by the MOP. This authority extends, indirectly, to the firms' internationally listed subsidiaries. The individuals appointed general managers of the parent companies usually concurrently serve as chairmen of the boards of their respective listed companies.

Under the nomenklatura system, NOC managers must learn to balance corporate and party-state interests if they want to advance their political careers. They are evaluated not only on their general performance but also on their commitment to party-state interests. In other words, the secret to success is to demonstrate managerial prowess while not causing problems for the CCP—as illustrated by the fortunes of Li Yizhong and Ma Fucai in the Sixteenth Party Congress Central Committee elections of November 2002.[10]

The congress elected Li Yizhong (a former general manager of Sinopec and chairman of its subsidiary Sinopec Corp.) a full member and named Ma Fucai (a former general manager of CNPC and chairman of its subsidiary PetroChina) an alternate, partly because Li had done a better job handling a sizable worker protest. Workers at China's two largest oil fields, Daqing and Shengli, had risen up when PetroChina and Sinopec Corp. cut staff to make their stock listings in New York and Hong Kong more attractive to investors. In March 2002, tens of thousands of laid-off workers from PetroChina's Daqing oil field launched demonstrations to demand better severance packages than the one-off payments they had received.[11] Then in June 2002, about 1,000 workers laid off from Sinopec Corp.'s Shengli oil field also held protests in an attempt to secure better deals.[12] Whereas Ma refused to give in to the demands of the Daqing protestors, arguing that they had signed binding contracts, Li made concessions to the Shengli protestors.[13] The perception was that Ma, unlike Li, had not been responsive enough to the party-state's concerns about social unrest.[14]

Investment Approval System and Other Forms of Party-State Control

China also controls NOCs through its investment approval system. Domestic investments require the approval of the State Council for projects small or large: these range from oil fields producing 1 million tons a year (20,000 barrels a day), natural gas fields producing 2 billion cubic meters a year, and refineries with an annual capacity of 200,000 tons (4,000 barrels a day) to national crude oil storage facilities and liquefied natural gas receiving terminals.[15] Foreign energy investments in excess of US$30 million require the approval of the National Development and Reform Commission (NDRC), and those in excess of US$200 million have to be reviewed by the NDRC and then submitted to the State Council for approval.[16] Although in theory the government is supposed to authorize NOC investments, anecdotal information indicates that the NOCs have struck some deals abroad and informed the NDRC and State Council after the fact.[17]

Another means of control is CCP involvement in day-to-day decisionmaking. The CCP has representatives at all levels of the NOCs whose approval may be required for even relatively minor decisions. According to an international consultant whose firm conducted a study for a division of one NOC, the division's managers needed the permission of the division's party secretary to hire and pay the consultancy.[18]

Further leverage is achieved through credit from China's state-owned banks, especially the three policy banks in charge of state-directed lending: the China Export-Import Bank, the China Development Bank, and the Agricultural Bank. Although the NOCs are not as dependent on government funds as they were in the past because of their strong cash flows, loans from the state-owned banks, especially on concessionary terms, still function as carrots and sticks that the party-state can wield over the NOCs.

NOCs' Growing Independence and Power

As mentioned earlier, NOCs are becoming more autonomous and less influenced by the party-state—to the concern of Chinese officials, academics, and the media alike. Some in these quarters view the NOCs as a "monopolistic interest group" that prioritizes profits over social welfare, with a subsequent impact on public policy.[19] They have come to be considered an interest group for a number of reasons: their subsidiaries are listed on foreign stock exchanges, their profits are growing, senior management is becoming internationalized, and their role in securing oil imports and their relative strength vis-à-vis the central government's energy bureaucracy are increasing.

Internationally Listed Subsidiaries

When CNPC, Sinopec, and CNOOC listed their subsidiaries on the New York and Hong Kong stock exchanges in 2000–01, they became exposed to the influence of actors other than the party-state—not only the stock exchanges themselves but also entities such as the U.S. Securities and Exchange Commission, international auditing and engineering firms, independent shareholders, and members of the companies' boards of directors. As the following example illustrates, a decision by independent shareholders may now compel these companies to take actions that run counter to their interests.

In December 2005, the independent shareholders of CNOOC Ltd., a subsidiary of CNOOC, vetoed an agreement between CNOOC Ltd. and CNOOC that would have granted CNOOC the right to acquire oil and natural gas assets and given CNOOC Ltd. the option of subsequently purchasing these assets.[20] Before it was listed on the international markets, CNOOC Ltd. moved to increase its attractiveness to foreign investors by securing from CNOOC the exclusive right to engage in exploration and production.[21] However, CNOOC Ltd. decided to reconsider this noncompete agreement after it failed in its bid for Unocal (in part because of weak political support from the Chinese government) whereas unlisted CNPC succeeded in its bid for PetroKazakhstan (allegedly because of Beijing's involvement and CNPC's ability to conduct negotiations without pressure to disclose information to shareholders).[22] Although the proposed amendment to the agreement would have benefited CNOOC Ltd. by transferring acquisition risk from the shareholders to the parent company and enabling its parent to take advantage of greater political support from Beijing, the independent shareholders voted it down for fear that CNOOC and CNOOC Ltd. might engage in transactions that benefited CNOOC at their expense.[23]

Rising Profits

The profits of PetroChina, Sinopec Corp., and CNOOC Ltd. have increased substantially in recent years largely because of the rise in the price of oil, from $12.00 a barrel in 1998 to $67.00 a barrel in 2006.[24] During this period, their combined net income increased nearly fourteenfold, from ¥16 billion to ¥237 billion.[25] In 2005 the companies' pretax profits were equal to 1.6 percent of gross domestic product (GDP).[26] Higher profits have meant larger contributions to the government. Between 1998 and 2006, the total amount of taxes remitted by the three companies grew nearly eightfold, from ¥10.2 billion to ¥86.5 billion.[27] Their tax payments accounted for 15.9 percent of all the corporate taxes collected in 2005.[28]

To many Chinese observers, it seems only logical that this financial growth has made the government more responsive to NOC interests. After all, some point out, the leadership is under mounting pressure to spend more money on social projects such as education, health care, and pensions, and the NOCs are helping to provide the necessary additional revenue.[29] Although it is difficult to determine exactly how and to what extent higher profits and taxes translate into greater political influence, it seems that the companies' contributions to the government's coffers have bolstered their ability to shape government decisions.[30]

Internationalization of Senior Management

With overseas expansion, China's NOCs are reassessing the kind of personnel needed for senior management posts if the firms are to compete successfully in the global business environment. Thus the rising generation of senior managers will differ substantially from their predecessors in their educational credentials, worldviews, business practices, and international experience. As the number of executives who have worked and studied abroad increases—especially in the fields of business, law, and accounting—these companies will become more and more autonomous and exert their influence on the party-state (because the skills they possess are in short supply in Chinese industry and government).

The current senior managers of PetroChina and Sinopec Corp. closely resemble their predecessors in their backgrounds (primarily engineering or geology), career tracks (spent almost entirely with their respective companies), and lack of

Table 7-2. *CNOOC Ltd. Senior Management Team, 2006*

Name	Year joined	Current position	Year of birth	Education	Foreign study
Fu Chengyu	1982	CEO	1951	MS	University of Southern California
Zhou Shouwei	1982	President	1950	PhD	. . .
Wu Guangqi	1982	Compliance officer	1957	MBA	. . .
Yang Hua	1982	Executive vice president; CFO	1961	MBA	MIT
Victor Zhikao Gao	2000	Senior vice president, general counsel	1962	MA/JD	Yale University
Liu Jian	1982	Executive vice president	1963	MBA	. . .
Chen Wei	1984	Senior vice president	1958	MBA	. . .
Zhang Guohua	1982	Senior vice president	1960	BS	University of Alberta
Li Ning	1983	Senior vice president	1963	MBA	. . .
Chen Bi	1982	Vice president	1961	MS/MBA	Edinburgh Heriot-Watt University
Zhu Weilin	1982	Vice president	1956	PhD	. . .
Zhu Mingcai	1985	Vice president	1956	MBA	Lancaster University
Fang Zhi	1982	Vice president	1962	MBA	University of Birmingham

Source: CNOOC Ltd., *Annual Report 2006.*

experience studying or working abroad. At CNOOC Ltd., by contrast, the majority of senior managers were educated abroad and hold MBA degrees (table 7-2), while also including some engineers and geologists who joined the company at its creation in 1982. This may reflect CNOOC's substantially longer experience interacting with international companies and its efforts to distinguish itself from its larger and politically powerful peers through innovative managerial practices.

The rising generation of senior managers in China's NOCs will undoubtedly have more international experience than its predecessors.[31] In 1999 CNPC—the company with the most extensive experience abroad—decided to improve its global competitiveness by paying for mid- and high-level managers to earn MBAs in the United States and Canada. As of early 2004, the company had sent sixty students abroad (thirty of whom returned) and subsequently posted some abroad. The company recognized that to continue its foreign expansion it needed to diversify its senior management away from engineers who spent their careers in China and seldom interacted with the outside world and instead seek more individuals with business degrees from world-class universities who could easily build relationships with their counterparts in foreign companies.

Increasing Oil Imports

China's oil profile has changed dramatically since the establishment of the PRC. A net exporter until 1993, China became the world's second largest oil consumer in 2003, after the United States, and the world's third largest importer in 2004, behind the United States and Japan. In the past five years, demand and imports have both soared, demand rising 44 percent (from 5 million barrels a day to 7.2 million barrels a day), and imports 119 percent (from 1.6 million barrels a day to 3.5 million barrels a day). In 2006 imports accounted for 49 percent of the country's total oil consumption and now are projected to jump to as much as 80 percent of consumption by 2020.[32] These statistics have rekindled old fears that a growing reliance on foreign oil could undermine China's economic development and national security.

With the growing dependence on imported oil, China has encouraged its NOCs to acquire exploration and production assets abroad. Senior leaders such as Jiang Zemin and Hu Jintao have promoted overseas investment on the assumption that oil supplies obtained through China's foreign assets will be more secure and less expensive than what the international market can provide.[33] However, oil produced abroad by Chinese companies is likely to face the same transportation risks as oil purchased on the spot market or through long-term contracts. Furthermore, the host country is likely to value it at the prevailing world price to determine royalties and taxes (it will also be subject to a variety of host country risks such as nationalization and war). Nonetheless, Chinese oil executives pay lip service to this idea to demonstrate that they value the interests of the party-state and to gain support for their foreign investments, which advance their corporate interests in reserve replacement (essential for their survival) and profits.

Weakening of the Energy Bureaucracy

As pointed out earlier, NOC autonomy and power have advanced as the government's authority over the energy sector has waned. This situation has provided the companies with more opportunities to influence policies and projects. The decline in state control began in the 1980s with the transformation of energy ministries into companies. In 1988 the State Council formed companies from the Ministries of Petroleum Industry, Coal Industry, and Nuclear Industry and transferred their administrative functions, along with the power sector of the Ministry of Water Resources and Electric Power, to the newly formed Ministry of Energy (MOE). The MOE failed to govern effectively, however. Its authority overlapped with that of the State Planning Commission, and its influence was confined to the electric power sector because the other industries, some of which had vigorously opposed the establishment of the MOE, refused to coordinate their planning and investment.[34]

After the MOE was abolished in 1993, government authority over the energy sector became more fractured, and for the next ten years the State Development Planning Commission (SDPC) and the State Economic and Trade Commission (SETC) vied for primary responsibility over the sector. In 2003 the State Council dissolved the SETC and established the NDRC Energy Bureau, giving it broad responsibilities: it was to coordinate the energy plans, policies, and projects of its multiple departments and of the dozen other ministries involved in energy policymaking and energy SOEs but had neither the authority nor the resources necessary to do so. In 2005 China established the Energy Leading Group, headed by Premier Wen Jiabao, and its secretariat, the State Energy Office (SEO), adding yet another cook to the kitchen.

With a staff well-versed in energy issues and high position in the bureaucracy, the NOCs were poised to take advantage of the energy leadership vacuum. By lending employees to the government's understaffed energy bodies, they were able to influence decisionmaking to advance their own interests. Sinopec employees, for example, became involved in drafting the country's strategic oil reserve law because their company has the greatest expertise in this area.[35] And oil industry veterans Ma Fucai and Xu Dingming became deputy directors of the SEO: Ma had spent more than thirty years in the industry, and Xu, a former head of the NDRC Energy Bureau, worked for both CNOOC and CNPC. Another factor in the NOCs' favor is the small size of the Energy Bureau's staff, which has been so overwhelmed by the vast number of projects requiring approval that it has had little time to devote to forging an energy strategy. Consequently, the projects tend to shape energy policies instead of depending on such policies to guide project approvals.[36]

Being in the high bureaucratic ranks, the NOCs are able to ignore lower-ranking government departments. In most instances, the companies can bypass the Energy Bureau and press their interests directly with China's leadership. Support from a top leader for a proposed NOC project is likely to ease any opposition from the Energy Bureau.[37]

Impact on National Policies and Projects

The NOCs have influenced national policies and projects in and beyond the energy sector. Their impact within the sector can be seen in China's oil pricing and West-East Pipeline. Outside the sector, their overseas investments have created diplomatic challenges for Beijing.

Oil Pricing

The pressure from China's NOCs on the central government to liberalize domestic prices for diesel and gasoline has grown along with the country's oil imports. For the sake of social stability, the NDRC sets prices for diesel and gasoline to shield consumers, especially farmers and taxi drivers, from the full impact of international price increases. Although domestic fuel prices are linked to prices in the benchmark Singapore, Rotterdam, and New York Harbor markets, they are adjusted only occasionally and generally do not fully reflect the extent of price changes internationally.[38] Consequently, China's NOCs have lost billions of dollars in their refining and marketing sectors in recent years because of state-set prices and rising crude oil import costs.[39]

CNPC and Sinopec, which account for 90 percent of China's refining capacity, have had an effect on the Chinese government's pricing policies for diesel and gasoline through their efforts to maintain profitability in their refining and marketing operations. In response to the widening disconnect between domestic and international prices, CNPC and Sinopec decided to place corporate profitability ahead of social stability. In 2005, when international crude prices rose by 50 percent while China's state-set diesel and gasoline prices increased by only 20 percent, refiners chose to export products rather than sell them in the domestic market.[40] Widespread shortages ensued, especially in southern China, causing long lines at some service stations and forcing others to close. Ironically, the price controls were harming the very consumers they were intended to protect.

The domestic supply cutbacks, combined with the NOCs' lobbying of government officials to liberalize prices, won the companies some concessions. In March 2006 the NDRC raised prices by 3–5 percent and in May by 10–11 percent.[41] Ever intent on balancing profitability against social stability, however, the NDRC subsequently reduced the price of gasoline by 4 percent in January 2007 when crude prices dropped.[42] In addition, Sinopec received subsidies of US$1.2 billion in 2005 and US$640 million in 2006 to partly cover its losses. As long as Beijing maintains control over diesel and gasoline prices, CNPC and Sinopec will remind officials that corporate interests must be balanced against those of consumers.

West-East Pipeline

The West-East Pipeline, which delivers natural gas from Xinjiang to Shanghai, is another example of corporate interests influencing national ones. Premier Zhu Rongji championed the pipeline since it could serve a variety of objectives: help develop Western China, combat air pollution, give him the upper hand in his struggle with Li Peng for control of China's energy sector, and demonstrate

China's openness to foreign investment.[43] Although the pipeline was initially CNPC's idea, proposed in the late 1990s as a means of using resources from the West to support the economy in the East, the company soured on the project when Zhu insisted on foreign involvement.[44] CNPC's subsidiary, PetroChina, was opposed to granting foreign companies access to China's natural gas reserves and in any case considered foreign capital and expertise unnecessary.[45] Under pressure from Zhu, the company reluctantly issued a tender for foreign participation and signed nonbinding agreements with Shell, ExxonMobil, and Gazprom, but subsequently Ma Fucai, then company chairman, reportedly demonstrated little interest and flexibility in addressing the concerns of the foreign companies, especially about the project's rate of return.[46]

Although compelled to undertake a project it opposed, PetroChina was able to influence the development of the West-East Pipeline to its advantage.[47] First, the firm successfully lobbied the NDRC to set the city gate price for natural gas from the pipeline at a level that would allow the company to fully recover the costs of transport and its investment in the project even though these prices were higher than what electric power generators were willing to accept because of restrictions on their tariff structure. As a result, the pipeline has failed to reduce the use of coal in the electric power sector, as originally planned. Second, PetroChina eventually squeezed out the foreign participants. Not only did the company stick to a pricing scheme that did not provide the international companies with an acceptable rate of return, but it also built the pipeline by itself while negotiating with its foreign partners. After Zhu retired in 2003, no one in the Hu-Wen administration put similar pressure on PetroChina to involve foreign companies, and PetroChina terminated the joint venture negotiations.

Foreign Policy

The overseas activities of China's NOCs are challenging a principle at the core of Chinese foreign policy since the founding of the PRC: noninterference in the internal affairs of other countries. NOC investments in states divided by internal conflicts have embroiled the companies in domestic political disputes because they are invariably perceived as supporting one party or another. In January 2007, for example, CNPC employees in Nigeria were kidnapped after the Movement to Emancipate the Niger Delta had warned China's NOCs not to come to the region.[48] Three months later, nine employees of a Sinopec subsidiary were killed in an attack on an oil exploration site in Ethiopia's Ogaden Basin by the Ogaden National Liberation Front, a separatist rebel group that had also warned foreign companies against operating in their territory.[49]

CNPC's operations in Sudan, begun eight years before the violence in Darfur erupted in 2003, have prompted China to move away from the noninterference principle.[50] The company's substantial investments in Sudan (CNPC's second largest source of foreign oil production just behind Kazakhstan) have been a factor behind Beijing's reluctance to pressure the Sudanese government to stop the atrocities in Darfur. Its earlier attitude, summarized in 2004 by then deputy foreign minister Zhou Wenzhong, was that "business is business. We try to separate politics from business."[51] Three years later, Beijing appears to be singing a slightly different refrain. Concerns about China's international reputation (tarnished by the perception that Beijing is turning a blind eye toward the killing of Darfur rebels and civilians to protect CNPC's oil interests) and the realization that China could not stop Western governments from increasing their efforts to solve the Darfur crisis, combined with mounting pressure from those governments to use whatever influence it has—through CNPC's dominance of the Sudanese oil sector and China's permanent seat on the UN Security Council—to persuade Khartoum to change its stance toward Darfur have prompted Beijing to play a more constructive role. In 2007 China helped persuade Khartoum to allow a hybrid peacekeeping force of UN and African Union troops into Darfur and promised to contribute military engineers to that force, winning praise from the United Nations and foreign governments.

Impact on China's Leadership

The oil industry remains a pathway to China's political elite. Ten full and alternate members of the Sixteenth Central Committee of the Communist Party spent parts of their career in the oil industry (see table 7-3). Four Politburo members—Zeng Qinghong (vice president), He Guoqiang (minister of the Party Organization Department), Zhou Yongkang (minister of public security), and Wu Yi (vice premier)—come from the oil sector. Some current provincial officials also worked for China's oil industry, for example, Zhang Gaoli (Tianjin party secretary), Wang Anshun (Beijing deputy party secretary), and Wei Liucheng (governor of Hainan Province). Su Shulin, a former executive at CNPC and PetroChina, was the director general of the Liaoning Province Organization Department until his appointments as general manager of Sinopec and chairman of Sinopec Corp. in 2007. Sheng Huaren, vice chairman and secretary general of the Standing Committee of the National People's Congress, was a member of the Fifteenth Central Committee (1997–2002) and minister of the SETC (1998–2001). Some high-level leaders became ministers after serving as general managers of CNPC or Sinopec; a good example is Li Yizhong, who served as vice chairman of SASAC before becoming chairman of the General Administration of Work Safety in 2005.

Table 7-3. *High-Ranking Political Elites from the Oil Industry*

Name	Current position(s)	Company/ministry[a]
Zeng Qinghong	Politburo Standing Committee; vice president PRC	CNOOC/MPI
Wu Yi	Sixteenth CCP Central Committee (member); vice premier PRC	Sinopec/MPI
He Guoqiang	Sixteenth CCP Central Committee (member); director, CCP Organization Department	MCI
Zhou Yongkang	Sixteenth CCP Central Committee (member); state councilor; minister of public security	CNPC/MPI
Zhang Gaoli	Sixteenth CCP Central Committee (member); party secretary, Tianjin Municipality	Sinopec/MPI
Wang Anshun	Deputy party secretary, Beijing Municipality	MGMR
Sheng Huaren	Vice chair and secretary general, National People's Congress Standing Committee	Sinopec/MCI
Li Yizhong	Sixteenth CCP Central Committee (member); chairman, General Administration of Work Safety	Sinopec
Wei Liucheng	Sixteenth CCP Central Committee (alternate); party secretary, Hainan Province	CNOOC/MPI
Su Shulin	Sixteenth CCP Central Committee (alternate); general manager, Sinopec	Sinopec/CNPC/MPI
Ma Fucai	Sixteenth CCP Central Committee (alternate); deputy director, State Energy Office	CNPC/MPI
Wang Tianpu	Sixteenth CCP Central Committee (alternate); president, Sinopec Corp.	Sinopec

a. MCI = Ministry of Chemical Industry; MGMR = Ministry of Geology and Mineral Resources; and MPI = Ministry of Petroleum Industry.

Is There a "New Petroleum Faction?"

Some observers have suggested that individuals from the petroleum industry at the apex of the party-state constitute a "new petroleum faction," as distinct from the original faction whose rise to power began in the 1950s and peaked in the early 1980s.[52] Members of the original faction included Yu Qiuli (vice premier), Kang Shi'en (vice premier), Gu Mu (chairman of the State Capital Construction Commission and Foreign Investment Control Commission), Gao Yangwen (minister of coal), Tang Ke (minister of metallurgy), Song Zhenming (minister of petroleum), Sun Jingwen (minister of chemical industries), Zhang Zhen (minister of the Fifth Ministry of Machine Building), and Lin Hujia (mayor of Beijing).[53]

The current oil faction differs from the original in several ways. First, the group has far fewer shared experiences. Although five members attended the

Beijing Institute of Petroleum (Wu Yi, class of 1962; Zhou Yongkang and Li Yizhong, class of 1966; and Wei Liucheng and Ma Fucai, class of 1970), they were enrolled in different periods, and although they also worked for MPI and the NOCs, it was at different times and in different locations. Petroleum politicians with the closest ties are probably those from CNPC who worked at the Shengli oil field before it was transferred to Sinopec in 1998, especially in the years 1988–96, when Zhou Yongkang was party secretary and director general of the Shengli Petroleum Administration. According to one oil industry insider, a "rule of thumb" is that anyone above the director level at CNPC who worked at Shengli was promoted by Zhou, including Ma Fucai and current CNPC president Jiang Jiemin.[54] Other ties were formed during the development of the Daqing oil field or at the "small" State Planning Commission (SPC) headed by Yu Qiuli from 1964 to 1966.[55]

Second, unlike the original petroleum faction, today's elite politicians from the oil industry do not form a coherent group promoting a common worldview and related policy prescriptions. (Western and Chinese observers alike tend to treat Yu Qiuli and his associates from MPI and the "small" State Planning Commission as a faction, although there is no evidence that these individuals consider themselves a coherent unit.)[56] By contrast, the original faction uniformly advocated centralized planning, deficit spending, and an economic strategy of petroleum-based export-led development. Its main impact on policymaking, which directly contributed to its demise, was the importation of turn-key plants on credit that were paid for with Chinese crude oil exports and thus led to the rapid growth of China's external debt.[57]

Patron-client relationships between petroleum politicians persist, however. Yu Qiuli helped to accelerate the political career of Zeng Qinghong, who played a key role in advancing that of Zhou Yongkang, whose protégés include Ma Fucai and Jiang Jiemin. In 1979, Yu—then the chair of the SPC—hired Zeng as his *mishu* (secretary), and when Yu moved to the State Energy Commission in 1981, he brought Zeng with him as his deputy chief of staff. Yu subsequently helped Zeng secure a series of successively higher positions in China's oil industry, where Zeng met Zhou while accompanying Yu on an inspection of the Liaohe oil field in the early 1980s.[58] Zeng helped secure Zhou's appointments as minister of land and resources (1998), Sichuan party secretary (1999), minister of public security (2002), and member of the Politburo and Secretariat of the Sixteenth CCP Central Committee (2002).[59] When Ma Fucai was fighting to remain general manager of CNPC after a gas well explosion at one of the company's fields in Chongqing killed 243 people in December 2003, Zhou lobbied on his behalf.[60]

Changing Profile of Elite Politicians from the Oil Industry

Although the oil industry has remained a pathway to national leadership, the elite politicians arising from it are more cosmopolitan and have more diverse educational backgrounds than their predecessors. Furthermore, some of the country's oil executives have also held high-level positions in provincial governments.

The globalization of China's economy has created a need for political leaders with experience operating in the international marketplace. China's oil executives can easily meet this criterion, having worked at the helm of firms that rank among China's most profitable and globally competitive businesses. The recent general managers of CNPC, Sinopec, and CNOOC have run companies that have a global presence, with subsidiaries on foreign stock exchanges, and thus have had to operate under the laws of other countries and international standards of corporate governance. In addition, many of the current and rising generations of senior managers have educational backgrounds compatible with China's growing involvement in the global economy; some have studied abroad, while others have earned graduate degrees in business administration in China.

The advancement of oil executives to the political elite is actually part of a broader trend of enterprise managers entering the national leadership, as reflected in the election of seventeen corporate leaders—including four from the oil industry—to the Sixteenth Central Committee, two as full members and fifteen as alternates. Although these individuals constitute a small percentage of this 356-member body (198 are full members and 158 alternates), their membership is an indication that the party-state recognizes the value and transferability of their managerial skills.[61] Many senior managers in other Chinese flagship firms are also well positioned to enter the political leadership ranks because of their youth, educational credentials, and international experience.[62]

The political advancement of Wei Liucheng, a former general manager of CNOOC and chairman of CNOOC Ltd., illustrates the growing importance of managerial skills and of exposure to the global economy. The Sixteenth Party Congress elected Wei as an alternate member of the Central Committee in November 2002, and in October 2003 the Organization Department appointed him governor and deputy party secretary of Hainan Province.[63] A deputy director of the Organization Department told the Chinese media that Wei's accomplishments at CNOOC, including the successful listing of CNOOC Ltd. on foreign stock exchanges and CNOOC's transformation into an internationally competitive energy company, were the main reason for his promotion.[64] One innovation that received the department's special praise was Wei's decision to fill certain vacant director-level positions through an internal bidding process open to all employees.[65]

Su Shulin, the current general manager of Sinopec and chairman of Sinopec Corp. (and a former executive at CNPC and PetroChina) also impressed the CCP with his business acumen. He advocated reducing oil production at Daqing to extend the life of the field and thus gain additional time to develop alternate industries in the area. In 1999 Daqing's output fell while profits increased. Three years later, the CCP elected the forty-year-old Su an alternate member of the Sixteenth Central Committee.[66]

As already mentioned, some oil executives are competitive candidates for high political positions because of their experience in both industry and provincial government. Although the provinces are the primary channel for elite recruitment, very few provincial leaders have worked for China's flagship enterprises. In contrast, senior managers from China's NOCs—including Zhou Yongkang (Sichuan party secretary), Jiang Jiemin (Qinghai vice governor), former Sinopec and Sinopec Corp. executive Chen Tonghai (Ningbo mayor), and others in table 7-3—have had local and provincial experience. One provincial leader who moved to an NOC is Yunnan vice governor Li Xinhua, whom SASAC appointed deputy general manager of CNPC in 2007, perhaps because of his experience in the natural gas industry.[67]

If the government's increased concern about energy security is any indication, the energy expertise of NOC executives may well have opened the door to some provincial leadership positions. Some analysts maintain that one reason the Organization Department appointed Wei Liucheng governor of Hainan Province is Beijing's plan to develop oil and gas resources in the South China Sea.[68] Similarly, one factor behind Zhou Yongkang's appointment as party secretary of natural gas–rich Sichuan Province may have been his oil industry credentials.

Rising stars to watch at the Seventeenth Party Congress and beyond are Zhou Yongkang, Su Shulin, Wang Tianpu, Wang Anshun, and Jiang Jiemin. Zhou, with his ministerial posts, provincial experience, and Zeng Qinghong as patron, is poised for promotion to the Politburo Standing Committee.[69] Zhang Gaoli and Wang Anshun are also likely to advance. Zhang is currently the party secretary of Tianjin, a post that has often been a stepping-stone to a seat on the Politburo.[70] Wang, who recently became the deputy party secretary of Beijing after serving as deputy party secretary of Shanghai and director general of the CCP Organization Department in Gansu, is only forty-nine and well positioned for future promotions. Su and Wang Tianpu may also have bright political futures because of their youth (both turned forty-five in 2007) and their alternate memberships in the Sixteenth Central Committee. Jiang, the current general manager of CNPC and chairman of PetroChina, is a capable and innovative executive whose managerial skills might help him advance, provided he remains sensitive to party-state concerns.[71]

Conclusion

China's NOCs are a traditional interest group with a new role in policymaking and politics supported by marketization and globalization. These forces have heightened the divergence between corporate and national interests and increased the competitiveness of oil executives for national leadership positions. These developments are helping to pluralize the policymaking process and diversify the channels of political elite recruitment.

Indeed, policymaking overall has been moving toward greater pluralization over the past decade, as reflected in the expansion of the number of parties at the bargaining table (see chapter 8) and increased strength of traditionally influential industries. As a result, more voices are being heard, but that means decisionmaking is becoming more contentious and protracted. China's top leaders are not only less able to bend the NOCs to their will but must also balance the companies' demands with those of an increasing number of other interest groups. Furthermore, the NOCs regularly vie for markets and projects and hence rarely function as a coherent unit, leaving the government to devote more resources to managing their competition.

China's leadership faces some of its greatest new challenges in the energy sector partly because the projects pursued by the energy SOEs tend to shape the country's energy policies rather than vice versa. With the energy SOEs—especially the NOCs—becoming more dominant in this regard, the idea of creating another MOE has gained momentum; proponents maintain that simply having a government agency equal in rank to the energy companies will help ensure that other interests, such as environmental protection, are given equal weight in policy debates.[72] In short, the growing relative power of the NOCs and other SOEs may be a catalyst for further pluralization of the policymaking process.

Likewise, the continued advancement of senior managers from the NOCs—and other flagship firms—to national leadership positions may help to diffuse the channels of elite recruitment. The election of business leaders to the Sixteenth Central Committee suggests that large firms have begun to translate their economic might into political power. The experience of Taiwan's Kuomintang (KMT) Party with incorporating business groups into politics (see chapter 16) provides a model for how this process might unfold on the mainland. Just as in Taiwan, the contributions of China's flagship firms to the government's efforts to create globally competitive firms and to fill its coffers may prompt the CCP to promote more business elites to the national leadership. NOC executives are likely to be part of any such expansion because of their companies' international experience, economic clout, and role in supplying China with a strategic commodity.

Notes

1. For more on the petroleum faction, see Richard Baum, *Burying Mao: Chinese Politics in the Age of Deng Xiaoping* (Princeton University Press, 1994), pp. 54–56, 104–05; David M. Lampton, *Paths to Power: Elite Mobility in Contemporary China* (University of Michigan Press, 1989), pp. 150–99; and Kenneth Lieberthal and Michel Oksenberg, *Policy Making in China: Leaders, Structures and Processes* (Princeton University Press, 1988), pp. 46–47, 60–61, 252–54.

2. This chapter treats China's NOCs as a single interest group in order to explain the changing relationship between the oil industry as a whole and the party-state. However, the NOCs do not always function as a coherent unit. They have distinct interests and compete for projects and for market share.

3. Cheng Li, "China's Telecom Industry on the Move: Domestic Competition, Global Ambition and Leadership Transition," *China Leadership Monitor*, no. 19 (Fall 2006); "Zhongguo xinwen zhoukan: Zhongguo jinru liyi boyi de shidai" (China Newsweek: China enters the era of interest bargaining), January 5, 2006 (http://news.sina.com.cn/c/2006-01-05/15598782720.shtml [October 10, 2007]); and Scott Kennedy, *The Business of Lobbying in China* (Harvard University Press, 2005).

4. "Top 50 Rankings Based on Six Operational Criteria," *Petroleum Intelligence Weekly*, Supplement, December 18, 2006.

5. Ibid.

6. Susan Shirk, *The Political Logic of Economic Reform in China* (University of California Press, 1993), p. 94.

7. Barry Naughton, "Claiming Profit for the State: SASAC and the Capital Management Budget," *China Leadership Monitor*, no. 18 (Spring 2006), p. 3. In May 2007, the Chinese government decided to have state-owned enterprises begin paying dividends. See Barry Naughton, "Strengthening the Center and Premier Wen Jiabao," *China Leadership Monitor*, no. 21 (Summer 2007), pp. 1–3.

8. Hon S. Chan, "Cadre Personnel Management in China: The Nomenklatura System, 1990–1998," *China Quarterly*, no. 179 (September 2004): 703–34; and John P. Burns, "Strengthening Central CCP Control of Leadership Selection: The 1990 Nomenklatura," *China Quarterly*, no. 138 (June 1994): 458–91.

9. E-mail correspondence with an expert on Chinese elite politics, March 28, 2007.

10. Interview with industry insider, Beijing, April 6, 2006.

11. "PetroChina Unit, after Job Cuts, Is Besieged by Protestors," *Wall Street Journal*, March 14, 2002, p. A9; and "PetroChina—Daqing Protests Stem from Misunderstanding of Severance Deal," *AFX—Asia*, March 14, 2002.

12. "Group: Laid-off Workers Protest at China's Second Largest Oil Field," Associated Press, June 20, 2002.

13. Interview with industry insiders, Beijing, April 6, 2006, and April 20, 2007; Winnie Lee, "Daqing Oil Output Normal," *Platts Oilgram News*, March 22, 2002, p. 4; and Anthony Kuhn, "Ex-Workers Face Off with China Oil Firm," *Los Angeles Times*, March 19, 2002, p. 4.

14. Interview with industry insiders, Beijing, China, April 6, 2006, and April 20, 2007; and Richard McGregor and James Kynge, "CNPC under Pressure to Sack Leader after Gas Leak," *Financial Times*, January 15, 2004.

15. "Decision of the State Council on Reform of the Investment System," State Council Document 20, July 16, 2004 (www.ndrc.gov.cn/policyrelease/t20060207_58851.htm [April 2, 2007]).

16. National Development and Reform Commission, "Jingwai touzi xiangmu hezhun zanxing guanli banfa" (Provisional measures on the administration of approval of overseas investment projects), October 9, 2004 (http://www.ndrc.gov.cn/zcfb/zcfbl/zcfbl2004/t20051010_44801.htm [June 4, 2007]).

17. Interviews with industry insiders, Beijing, April 11, 2006, and March 13, 2003.

18. Telephone interview, March 30, 2007.

19. "Zhongshiyou wei shenme gan 'zuo gei lianghui kan'?" (Why did CNPC make a gesture of deference to the Two Sessions?), Xinhua News Agency, March 12, 2007 (news.xinhuanet.com/legal/2007-03/12/content_5833290.htm [May 15, 2007]); and "Zhengxieweiyuan fansi qunian 'youhuang'" (A CPPCC member reflects on last year's "oil shortage"), *Jinghua shibao* (Beijing Times), March 13, 2007, p. A4.

20. CNOOC is a passive owner of CNOOC Ltd. CNOOC representatives do not attend shareholder meetings or vote on resolutions.

21. Enid Tsui, "CNOOC in Strategy Shift after Failed Bid," *Financial Times*, December 12, 2005, p. 26.

22. He Qing and Yang Juan, "'Buchong xieyi' de beihou: Zhonghaiyou qianghua guojia celue" (Behind the "supplementary agreement": CNOOC tries to increase the role of the state) *21shiji jingji daobao* (21st Century Business Herald), December 26, 2005; and Tsui, "CNOOC in Strategy Shift," p. 26.

23. Wendy Lim and Tony Munroe, "Update 2—CNOOC Shareholders Reject Proposals on Acquisitions," Reuters, January 2, 2006.

24. *BP Statistical Review of World Energy 2007* (London: British Petroleum, June 2007), p. 16.

25. PetroChina, Form 20-Fs for 2002–06; Sinopec Corp., Form 20-Fs for 2002–06; and CNOOC Ltd., Annual Reports for 2002–06.

26. See note 25; also, National Bureau of Statistics (NBS), *China Statistical Yearbook 2006* (Beijing: China Statistics Press, 2006), p. 57.

27. See note 25.

28. See note 25; and NBS, *China Statistical Yearbook 2006*, p. 282.

29. Interview, Beijing, April 25, 2007.

30. Wu Jingna, "Nengyuan ju shengge: 'Zhi jian qiye bu jian guojia' zhuangtai zhongjie" (The elevation of the Energy Bureau: The situation of "corporate interests trumping national interests comes to an end"), *Zhongguo jingying bao* (China Business), no. 1603 (May 9, 2005); and Wang Yichao, "Nengyuanju zhi ju: Hui shi yige manchang guodupin ma?" (The Case of the Energy Bureau: Will it be a transitional product long in the making?), *Caijing*, no. 8 (April 20, 2003).

31. This paragraph is based on Guo Fei, *Qijian chuhai: Zhongguo shiyou haiwai MBA zhi lu* (The flagship sets sail: CNPC's overseas MBAs) (Beijing: Petroleum Industry Press, 2004); "Zhongshiyou: MBA haiwai zhizao" (CNPC: Earning MBAs abroad), *Jingji guancha bao* (Economic Observer), March 1, 2004; and Xia Changyong, "Zhongshiyou: Rencai tuidong guoji julun" (CNPC: Talented personnel promote internationalization), *Renmin ribao* (People's Daily), December 25, 2003, p. 10.

32. International Energy Agency (IEA), *Monthly Oil Market Report (MOMR)*, April 12, 2007, p. 45; and Erica S. Downs, "The Brookings Foreign Policy Studies Energy Security Series: China," December 2006, pp. 10–11.

33. Tong Xiaoguang, "Shishi 'zou chu qu' zhanlue chongfen liyong guowai youqi ziyuan" [Implement the "going out" strategy to fully utilize oil and gas resources abroad], *Guotu*

ziyuan [Land and resources] no. 2 (2004), p. 7 (China Academic Journals, Tsinghua Tongfan Optical Disc Co./Eastview Publications); and James Irwin, "China: Beijing Dictates Expansion," *Energy Compass*, January 22, 2004.

34. Zheng Min and Chu Fujun, "Nengyuanbu hu zhi chi yu" (Is the Ministry of Energy almost here?), *Zhongguo shiyou shihua* (China PetroChem), no. 1 (2005), p. 28; and Yang Fuqiang and others, "A Review of China's Energy Policy" (Berkeley, Calif.: Lawrence Berkeley National Laboratory, 1995), p. 9.

35. Interview with industry insider, Washington, October 25, 2005; and Yang and others, "A Review of China's Energy Policy," p. 9.

36. Chen Xinhua, "Nengyuan anquan yao zhongshi neibu yinsu" (Energy security must attach importance to internal factors), *Zhongguo nengyuan* (Energy of China), no. 5 (2003).

37. Interview with energy expert, Beijing, April 24, 2007.

38. IEA, *MOMR*, March 14, 2006, p. 11. For a detailed explanation of how prices are set, see IEA, *MOMR*, November 10, 2006, p. 13.

39. Daniel H. Rosen and Trevor Houser, "China Energy: A Guide for the Perplexed" (Washington: Peterson Institute for International Economics, May 2007), p. 21.

40. IEA, *MOMR*, April 12, 2006, p. 10.

41. IEA, *MOMR*, June 13, 2006, p. 12.

42. IEA, *MOMR*, January 18, 2007, p. 10.

43. "Premier Zhu Says Cross-Country Pipeline Symbol of China's Opening Up," *BBC Monitoring Asia Pacific—Political,* July 5, 2002; and "Power in the West-East Pipeline," *South China Morning Post*, September 25, 2001.

44. Interview with oil industry insider, Beijing, April 28, 2007.

45. Interview with industry insider, Beijing, April 11, 2006; and Charlie Zhu and Wendy Lim, "Pipeline JV Fails as China Reluctant to Share Fuel," Reuters, August 4, 2004.

46. Interview with industry insider, Beijing, April 11, 2006; and Carlos Hoyos, Uchenna Izundu, and Richard McGregor, "Pipeline Pullout Embarrasses PetroChina: The Withdrawal of Foreign Groups Comes as No Surprise after Talks Failed for Financial and Political Reasons," *Financial Times*, August 4, 2004, p. 8.

47. This paragraph is based on e-mails from an expert on China's natural gas sector, October 31, 2006, and June 4, 2007.

48. "China's CNPC Mum on Reports of Missing Oil Employees in Nigeria," *Platts Commodity News*, January 26, 2007.

49. Matthew Green, Richard McGregor, and William Wallis, "Nine China Oil Workers Killed in Attack at Ethiopian Oil Exploration Site," *Financial Times*, April 25, 2007, p. 1.

50. This paragraph is based on Erica S. Downs, "The Fact and Fiction of Sino-African Energy Relations," *China Security* 3 (Summer 2007): 58–62. For an excellent discussion of how the principle of noninterference is increasingly at odds with Beijing's growing need to influence policies in countries with which China has substantial energy and natural resource trade and investment relations, see Linda Jakobson, "The Burden of 'Non-Interference,'" *China Economic Quarterly*, Quarter 2 (2007), pp. 14–18.

51. Howard W. French, "China in Africa: All Trade, with No Political Baggage," *New York Times*, August 8, 2004, p. 4.

52. "Te gao: Su Shulin kongjiang Liaoning, shiyou beihou shaozhuang pai guanyuan zhan lu tou jia" (Su Shulin arrives in Liaoning, a star from the oil industry rises), *Sing Tao ribao* (Sing Tao Daily), November 29, 2006; Zheng and Chu, "Nengyuanbu hu zhi chi yu," p. 28; and Guo Dapeng, "Shiyouxi gaoguan yaolan?" (Is the oil industry a cradle for high-level offi-

cials?), *Zhongguo qiyejia* (China Entrepreneur), no. 1 (2005), pp. 56–58. For petroleum faction references, see Cheng Li and Lynn White, "The Sixteenth Central Committee of the CCP: Hu Gets What?" *Asian Survey* 43 (July–August 2003): 591; Joseph Fewsmith, "China's Response to SARS," *China Leadership Monitor*, no. 7 (Spring 2003), p. 4; and Nicolas Becquelin, "Zhu Rongji's Oil Men: A New Faction in the Cabinet?" *China Perspectives*, no. 16 (March–April 1998), p. 9.

53. Lieberthal and Oksenberg, *Policy Making in China*, p. 46.

54. Interview, Beijing, April 20, 2007.

55. Lieberthal and Oksenberg, *Policy Making in China*, p. 46.

56. Ibid.

57. For more on the demise of the petroleum faction, see Baum, *Burying Mao*, pp. 55, 104–05.

58. Andrew J. Nathan and Bruce Gilley, *China's New Rulers: The Secret Files* (New York Review of Books, 2002), pp. 84–85; and Cheng Li, *China's Leaders: The New Generation* (Lanham, Md.: Rowman and Littlefield, 2001), pp. 161–62.

59. "Chinese Analyst Zong Hairen on Politics of Sichuan Leadership Change," *BBC Monitoring Asia Pacific*, February 3, 2003.

60. Interview, Beijing, April 20, 2007.

61. Li and White, "The Sixteenth Central Committee," pp. 583–84.

62. Cheng Li, "The Rise of China's Yuppie Corps: Top CEOs to Watch," *China Leadership Monitor*, no. 14 (Spring 2005).

63. Mure Dickie, "CNOOC Chief Quits to Take Up Hainan Post," *Financial Times*, October 8, 2003.

64. See the remarks of Sun Xiaoqun in "Wei Liucheng ren Zhonggong Hainan sheng wei fu shuji" (Wei Liucheng is appointed deputy secretary of the CCP Hainan Provincial Committee), Xinhua News Agency, October 9, 2003 (news.xinhuanet.com/zhengfu/2003-10/09/content_1114810.htm [April 2007]).

65. Interview, Beijing, April 20, 2007.

66. Li Lin, "Zhongshiyou zhangmen xuannian" (Suspense over who will be the next leader of CNPC), *Quanqiu qiyejia* (Global Entrepreneur), March 2004.

67. "Guoziwei renming Yunnan fushengzhang Li Xinhua jie Zhong shiyou fuzong" (SASAC appoints Yunnan vice governor Li Xinhua deputy general manager of CNPC), *Sing Tao Net*, May 14, 2007 (www.singtaonet.com/china/200705/t20070514_536696.html [6 June 2007]).

68. Chen Ting, "Guesswork on China's New Energy Policy in Light of Wei Liucheng's New Post in Hainan," *21st Century Business Herald*, October 9, 2003, in Foreign Broadcast Information Service, Document CPP20031014000058, October 14, 2003.

69. "HK Paper on How Chinese President, Premier 'Smash' Said Corrupt Factions," *BBC Monitoring International Reports*, April 29, 2007.

70. I thank Cheng Li for this point.

71. Interview, Beijing, April 20, 2007.

71. E-mail correspondence from expert on China's energy sector, May 30, 2007.

8

China's Left Tilt: Pendulum Swing or Midcourse Correction?

BARRY NAUGHTON

> China's revolution is glorious, but the distance to travel *after* the revolution is longer, more arduous, and more glorious.
>
> MAO ZEDONG (March 1949)

> In the past twenty-plus years . . . our achievements in reform and socialist construction have attracted world-wide attention. . . . But we have only taken the first step on a long road, and if we are to fulfill our historical responsibility of building China into a rich, strong, democratic, and cultured socialist country, we still have a long way to go.
>
> HU JINTAO, speech in Xibaipo (2002)

Back in December 2002, only one month after being selected China's new leader, Hu Jintao led the entire Secretariat of the Central Committee of the Chinese Communist Party (CCP) to the Hebei village of Xibaipo. Xibaipo was a place with some resonance, having been the Communist Party's headquarters in the very last phase of China's civil war and the site of a well-known speech delivered by Mao Zedong in March 1949 as the party was on the brink of victory and preparing to move into Beijing to assume power. Mao had enjoined the party leadership to maintain its tradition of "plain living and hard struggle," to resist the corruption of privilege and status, and to continue to strive to serve the people. Invoking these words, Hu Jintao created a perfect analogy: on the brink of success in the struggle to dismantle the planned economy, the CCP was now poised to lead China in the construction of a "moderately well-off society" (*xiaokang shehui*). Therefore it was urgent and appropriate for the party to recommit to the values of plain living and honest management.

It was a nice flourish, and in style and emphasis it drew a clear dividing line between the new Hu Jintao–Wen Jiabao administration and the previous Jiang

Zemin–Zhu Rongji administration. There was an implicit rebuke to the style of Jiang Zemin, with his unrestrained celebration of elites, wealth, and fame. Moreover, the speech marked the beginning of the distinctive emphasis that Hu Jintao would subsequently put on the development of a "harmonious society." For all that, the speech was just rhetoric, easily seen as cheap lip service to a set of outdated slogans. Each top leader has to put a personal stamp on his administration, and such branding does not necessarily correspond to substantive changes in policy.

The surprise, then, has been that in the nearly five years since Hu Jintao assumed the top job, he has presided over a systematic reorientation of economic and social policy to the left in nearly every respect. As the Hu Jintao–Wen Jiabao leadership has gradually consolidated control, a shift that was initially rhetorical has increasingly been reflected in policies with bite, backed by actual changes in resource allocation. Policy has moved away from growth at all costs toward regional redistribution, less urban bias, and rural development. As of 2007, it is still too early to say exactly what the long-term significance of this policy shift will be. In certain respects, it should be characterized as a moderate and overdue effort to address problems that emerged in the course of rapid economic growth and reform. However, there is also implicit tension between some of the new policies and the pro-growth policies of the past decade. Although these tensions are currently modest, they will likely become more acute when some of these policies fail, as they surely will. In particular, current new policies of environmental protection, restructuring of the ownership system for state enterprises, and centralizing control of urban land allocation will not succeed in their current incarnation. After an initial round of implementation, the leadership will have to make a decision: Are we serious about these policies or not? Do we reformulate and intensify, or back down?

How China answers those questions will have great bearing on the future shape of its political system. Despite the extremely slow progress in democratization, some signs of "ordinary" politics with recognizable interest groups are visible. Most of the economic issues in play are similar to those in developed democratic market economies, and China's interest groups cluster around the policy issues in a way similar to interest groups in a democracy.[1] At the same time, interest group contention remains very much behind the scenes, and the legitimacy of the process is not established. Instead, policymaking is still concentrated in the hands of a group of long-serving elite technocrats in Beijing. These technocrats, through their experience and personal inclination, have thus far proven extremely skillful at balancing the conflicting demands of economic growth and redistribution. However, they have already served for over a decade, and their political skills will not be available indefinitely.

Before examining the new tilt, I need to clarify my use of the term "left," which can refer to a bundle of different and potentially conflicting political positions. This sense of a jumble of different policies, united by a common impulse, however vague, is exactly what I want to convey. "Left" policies are those that are more redistributive (geographically and by social strata), invest more in social insurance and protections (especially for labor), tend to support some kinds of protectionism in favor of national and labor interests, and accept a broad concept of "rights" that includes material well-being and might be administered by the national government. They are, in general, pro–public interest, and often pro–government intervention.[2] "Right" policies, by contrast, rest on the assumption that market forces need to be unfettered to improve productivity, that taxation distorts incentives, and that "rights" pertain to negative liberty, that is, the right of the citizen to be left alone, free from governmental interference. They are in general pro–private business.

Even though "left" and "right" policies both address a jumble of sometimes conflicting concerns, two simple points can be made about Chinese policy with confidence. First, China has swung toward the left in almost every significant area of social and economic policy since the turn of the new century. Second, it is pointless and meaningless to judge the "left" as being "good," "bad," or "dangerous" even from a strictly economic standpoint. A "left turn" is definitely not equivalent to a rollback or halt in reform. There is plenty of middle ground. Moreover, many "left" policies may contribute to economic growth by reducing individual risk and broadening the social consensus in favor of a market economy. A broad ideological shift of the kind now taking place in China is leading to parallel shifts in many different policy arenas and creating many new policies, each of which will work out in a different way and at a different pace. The responsibility of outside observers is to recognize the broad shift and to consider the likely outcomes and different implications in specific policy arenas.

The Left Tilt in Economic Policy

A short chapter cannot adequately cover all of the many strands of economic policy, so I will briefly examine five of its most striking changes, all showing momentum toward a stronger, more intrusive, and more consistently "left" tilt in Chinese society.

The Pro-Rural Shift

The shift in policies toward rural areas—much less prosperous than the flourishing cities—is the most unambiguous manifestation of China's leftward tilt. Since 2002, the tax rate on rural households has been slashed, and central government funding for rural education and cooperative medical insurance has increased from almost nothing to significant levels. For the first time in its history, the Chinese state probably puts more into rural areas than it takes out, with resources on balance now flowing *into* the agricultural sector.

The pro-rural shift began to gain momentum in 2003, when the state prohibited all local government fees for a wide range of specified activities. After years of experimentation, the blanket prohibition of fees marked a new stage in reducing financial burdens on farmers. By explicitly forbidding even apparently legitimate justifications for local fees, the central government was, for the first time, empowering farmers to resist fee payments. Attention then turned to rural taxes, culminating in the abolition of the formal agricultural tax at the beginning of 2006. Within a few years, all the overt taxes on farmers had been abolished.

At the same time, new rural social programs have been steadily rolled out. Funding for universal primary education has increased, and free primary education is on track to be achieved almost nationwide during 2007. The new Cooperative Health Care scheme should reach 80 percent of all counties in 2007. Implementation of both these policies accelerated markedly in 2006 and 2007. Rural welfare programs also under way now include minimum income support as well as welfare and social security payments for farmers who surrender their land. None of these programs are lavishly funded, and all have significant problems in implementation. To actually reach the poorest 20 percent in the countryside with affordable education and health care remains a daunting challenge. To this end, the central government has given these programs annual increases in funding over the past five years. These steady increases, combined with the tax cuts, have caused a fundamental change in the relationship between farmers and the national budget.

A Redistributive Budget

Inevitably, the rural policy shift required the central government to step in to prevent rural local governments from plunging into a fiscal crisis. It therefore replaced local funds with central and provincial budgetary resources. This is possible because China's government budget has grown substantially in recent years, from 10.8 percent of gross domestic product (GDP) in 1995 to 18.9 percent in 2006 (see later discussion and figure 8-1). With the increase in overall budgetary resources, the budget has become more redistributive. Local governments in rural areas (counties and townships) collect a smaller share of total budgetary revenue and spend a larger proportion of outlays.[3] The difference is made up by increased transfers from the central and provincial governments. Indeed, an especially strong component of regional redistribution has been built into the policies designed to increase the flow of resources to the countryside.

Figure 8-1. *Budgetary Revenues and Industrial Profits of State-Owned Enterprises (SOEs), 1978–2006*

Percent of GDP

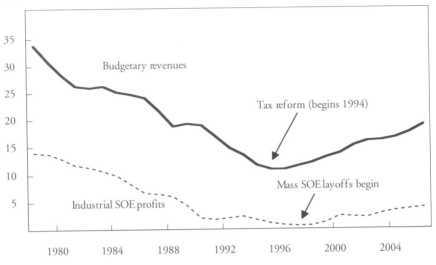

Source: *Statistical Communiqué*, National Bureau of Statistics, Beijing, February 28, 2007.

This is because of the way in which the government has funded the new rural policies, implementing them in an ad hoc "west to east" sequence, so the western provinces get money from the center sooner. Moreover, the center bears most or all of the costs for provinces in the west, center, and northeast. The prosperous eastern coastal provinces, however, are told to come up with resources from their own budgets to fund these programs: they do not receive new transfers from the central budget.

The result is a much more redistributive budget overall. After the fiscal reform of 1994, the central government had already begun collecting more revenue than it spent itself, transferring the rest to the provinces. In the mid-1990s, the center transferred about 3 percent of GDP net to the provinces, but nearly all of this was rebated taxes, so most of the "transfers" were actually repayments to the wealthy provinces where they had been collected. By 2006, net center-to-local transfers were almost 6 percent of GDP and were much more progressive, predominantly benefiting poorer inland provinces. Tax rebates were about the same, but other initially modest transfers had grown to significant size: earmarked transfers reached almost 2 percent of GDP in 2005; offsets for wage increases to government workers in poorer provinces, 0.5 percent; and general-purpose transfers, 0.6 percent. All these programs have a strongly redistributive character. Of the general-purpose transfers in 2005, for example, 48 percent went to western provinces, 47 percent to central provinces, and only 5 percent to coastal provinces.[4]

These changes are so recent that no good study of their net effect is yet available. It should not be overlooked that the government still pours money into infrastructure projects in developed areas and has injected billions into the financial system predominantly to the benefit of coastal financial centers. Even so, the redistributive parts of the budget are much larger than before. The government has even begun significant welfare expenditures: the number of people receiving government welfare payments in urban and rural areas has soared from 10 million in 2000 to 40 million in 2005.[5]

Environment

The central government has made a new—and long overdue—commitment to protect and ameliorate the environment, datable to the promulgation of the Eleventh Five Year Plan guidelines in November 2005.[6] Its dedication to environmental improvement during the 2006–10 plan period has reached a rhetorical level far beyond anything previously seen. In part, this is due to the dawning recognition that the steady improvement in energy efficiency registered since 1978 began to stall out a couple of years ago. Today, China's energy consumption is growing rapidly, while efforts to shift away from coal have failed completely. As a result, China's carbon emissions are increasing and local pollution worsening. In response, the government is acknowledging, for the first time, the damage done by an incentive system that motivates local government officials to push for economic growth at all costs. The Chinese government has begun to seriously contemplate paying a price in terms of economic growth in order to purchase the public benefit of a better environment.

Industrial Policy

During most of the period since 1978, China has attempted to shape the course of economic development through specific sectoral policies. However, this approach simply pulled policymakers in too many directions and never allowed them to formulate a coherent overall industrial policy. To improve upon previous efforts, the government has recently revamped its approach to industrial policy. Drawing on existing initiatives to restructure state-owned corporations and nurture high-technology industry, this new approach will have more impact than previous efforts. China began restructuring state-owned corporations in earnest in the mid-1990s. A first step was to downsize state-owned enterprises (SOEs)—half of all public enterprise workers were let go—and then stabilize government ownership. In 2003 central government corporations were transferred to a specialized "ownership agency," the State Asset Supervision and Administration Commission (SASAC). SASAC developed a complex mix of programs to prevent asset-stripping, maximize the value of state assets, and reshape the sectoral mix of central government firms. From the beginning, SASAC initiatives combined reform, modernization of management, and rehabilitation of government ownership.

In the past few years, though, SASAC has focused on conserving public ownership. The pace of privatization has slowed—and nearly stopped for the large central government firms. In September 2006, SASAC declared government majority ownership should remain predominant in seven industrial sectors: coal, oil, electricity, military industry, telecom, and air and ocean transport. This decision basically ratifies the status quo since central government firms are already overwhelmingly concentrated in those sectors, and the list does *not* exclude competing private firms in some of these sectors (such as coal and telecom value-added services). It does, however, represent a clear effort to stabilize public ownership and link it to specific sectors. Drawing a line around the public sector, it expresses the government's intent to maintain public ownership of key infrastructure and natural resources sectors.[7]

A complementary stream of industrial policy has come primarily from the National Development and Reform Commission (NDRC), successor to the old State Planning Commission. In recent years, the NDRC has become more active in promulgating sector-specific industrial policies and in charting long-range development programs. Its policy for the steel sector in July 2005, for example, set technical objectives but also abruptly prohibited foreign majority ownership in the sector. NDRC industrial policy draws its leverage from the Eleventh Five Year Plan. In itself, the Eleventh Plan was really an innovative vision statement. It called for a development model that would concentrate less on resource- and energy-consuming industry and more on a knowledge-intensive and environmentally friendly growth path. The improvements in rural education and social services described earlier were also an important focus of the plan.

However, the Eleventh Plan was short on implementation strategies, and the NDRC leaped to fill the gap, particularly to flesh out the "knowledge-intensive" part of the development vision with concrete measures for promoting high-technology industry. In tandem with the Ministry of Science and Technology, the NDRC has promulgated two plans: one, announced in early 2006, is a program for science and technology development over the long term (2006–20), and the other a five-year plan finalized in April 2007 for high-technology sectors. These plans do not call for a return to state enterprises in the high-technology sectors. Far from it. They accept the catalytic role of the dynamic private, foreign, and hybrid firms that have become the mainstay of China's high-technology development. But they do commit the government to significant expenditures directed at creating market-viable products and supporting high-technology enterprises.[8] Through procurement policy, directed credit, and government investment in applied research projects, the government will attempt to shape and accelerate China's development. These initiatives are complemented at the NDRC by a variety of regional development plans. The Western Development Plan began in 1999 and is now accompanied by a Northeast Revitalization Plan (since 2004) and a Central China Development Office (since 2007).[9]

Urban Land

To help rein in official corruption and abuse, the central government has decided to regulate urban land transactions strictly, under a new office, the National Inspector General of Land (*Guojia Tudi Zongducha*). In part this is simply an effort to inject some sunshine into secret sweetheart deals run by local governments. At the same time, the government has announced a raft of new price and expenditure controls, a mandate to build strictly defined affordable housing, and a new emphasis on having industrial land conversions follow national industrial policy. As of 2007, the inspector general of land will promulgate a list of forbidden and restricted industrial uses in line with the seventy-page industrial policy guidelines published by the National Development and Reform Commission in 2005. Land conversions that do not conform to this policy are forbidden.[10]

A Few Offsetting Trends

The left tilt in each of these five policy areas is clearly evident. At the same time, there are offsetting trends. Banking sector reforms clearly do not fit this framework yet have been remarkably successful. In addition, China's compliance with World Trade Organization commitments has been reasonable and has led to market-opening measures in several important areas. Clearly, there has not been any significant rollback of economic reform. But the thrust of government policymaking has shifted notably, making the government a stronger, more intrusive, and more consistently "left" advocate in Chinese society.

Tensions Implicit in the Current Policy Shift

Many of the policies described in the previous section stand in implicit tension with economic growth. They pose no immediate challenge to pro-growth policies, but such policies may erode growth over the long run if they are not well formulated. In their current form, these policies promise immediate benefits in exchange for long-run policies that are only vaguely formulated and will certainly need to be revised. Indeed, some will fail and will be scrapped altogether.

Environmental Policy

The Chinese government is still struggling to find an approach that can actually begin to ameliorate environmental problems. In an important breakthrough, however, it has recognized that government incentives overweight GDP growth and need to be replaced by indicators more broadly representative of social well-being. Still, it has not yet created new incentives that make waste expensive and environmental damage costly to local business and government decisionmakers. The idea, bruited in the Eleventh Plan, that local officials would be evaluated on "green GDP" rather than plain-old vanilla GDP is, quite simply, a nonstarter. Desirable as the idea might appear at first glance, it is in fact too complicated by conceptual issues, too hard to measure, and far too susceptible to manipulation to serve as the basis of bureaucratic incentives.

While the government has paid lots of attention to prices and subsidies in promoting high-technology industry, it has done much less along these lines with respect to the environment. In fact, taxes on resource consumption and quantitative caps on emissions—both of which can work and already have an embryonic existence in China—lie underutilized in their existing feeble incarnations. For the time being, the government has set itself a specific short-term target—by 2010 energy consumption per unit of GDP is to be 20 percent below the 2005 level. It has declared that this is a "hard target" that will not be abandoned. When it becomes clear that the target will not be met, China will finally have to decide whether it wants to cap, tax, and trade carbon emissions.

Urban Land Policy

In land policy, quantitative planning and direct national control are in danger of overuse. In the short run, in an overheated economy with the government focused on reducing the growth rate of investment, there is probably no big cost. But in the long run, the attempt to extend direct controls over local land-use decisions is likely to fail. The Chinese central government has, in the past, repeatedly attempted to raise revenues from urban land transactions and repeatedly failed. The current effort mixes macroeconomic motives, a desire to protect agricultural land, revenue considerations, and industrial policy objectives. However noble some of the objectives are, such a complex initiative is likely to slow down the decisionmaking process and impede development. Instead, the objective ought to be a hard-edged regulatory regime—tough, but transparent. The costs of the current initiative will become apparent over the next couple of years.

Industrial Policy

Some of the costs of China's industrial policy are already evident in the emergence of economic nationalism, which always finds many adherents since it promises support to local champions. Considering the current economic boom and consequent pride in China's new-found economic and technological successes, some degree of economic nationalism is no doubt inevitable. But like other forms of protectionism, it can produce easy short-run benefits at the expense of larger long-run costs. In any case, China has made its most dramatic technological advances through intensified cooperation with multinational corporations as a result of globalization.

Yet the long-run technology development plan emphasizes domestic sources: "Experience shows us that we cannot buy true core technologies in the key fields that affect the lifeblood of the national economy and national security." Perhaps this is true, but overemphasis on domestic development will lead to costly duplication of international knowledge and delays in the adoption and diffusion of technology. Suppose, for example, that the homegrown 3G telecom standard (TDS-CDMA) turns out to be a fiasco, causing economic losses to whichever phone company gets stuck with it, and that a significant number of customers fail to adopt it despite years of government investment. This would strike a significant blow not only to China's economy but also to its credibility.

Redistribution and the Pro-Rural Shift

The shift to a more redistributive budget—one that works more to the benefit of rural people—is clearly a positive step. As tax revenues mount, the government will be able to direct incremental funds to rural and western beneficiaries. The biggest problem is that the system for redistribution has evolved in an almost entirely improvised manner. Money is directed to the needy, and those who are well off are asked to wait. This is the fastest way to get results, but in the long run it creates perverse incentives. Since good performance is penalized, localities have an incentive to emphasize their problems. Laggard regions are encouraged to allocate effort to lobbying and manipulating the fiscal environment. The urgent need over the medium term is to move to a more regularized system that clearly defines the rules and formulas for revenue sharing.

The other great challenge in devising redistributive policies is to avoid creating expectations that may be disappointed. Thus far economic growth, with the help of antipoverty programs, has brought poverty rates down, and the new rural policies buffer rural residents from some of the worst outcomes. But over the long term, the new redistributive policies are unlikely to shrink the urban rural gap or the coastal-western gap very much. China is experiencing enormous growth momentum, powered by economic forces that also drive differentiation and thus enable the developed coastal centers to continue to pull away from the rest of the economy. If existing policies produce modest outcomes and mounting frustration, there may be pressure to adopt more extreme policies at a greater cost.

It should be stressed that these rather skeptical remarks should not be construed as criticisms of the policies themselves. As I stated at the outset, the new policies are "moderate and overdue." Furthermore, China has a track record of introducing policies that were at first feeble and ineffective, only to reformulate and relaunch them later with improved results. So it would be foolish to discount policies to which the Chinese government has committed a substantial share of its credibility. But the current policies are nevertheless quite different from initiatives generated during much of the reform period, and this difference is rooted in their common swing to the left.

Earlier, successful reform policies typically provided an opening for personal enrichment. Being empowered to pursue their own interests, specific individuals or groups were able to push for a broader scope and test the limits. The new policies do not have the same built-in dynamics. Although they respond to public opinion and public pressures, in general they do not motivate specific individuals to push changes or monitor outcomes. Who will correct the shortcomings of green GDP, urban land planning, or government sponsorship of state-run firms? No individual has the incentive and authority to push hard for the expansion of the public interest implied in such policies. In other words, these policies "lean against the wind" of private self-interest, whereas most reform-era policies exploited private self-interest to sail with the prevailing wind. Adopted as modest midcourse corrections, the most recent policies will probably need to be pushed harder in the future if they are to be effective. When that occurs, the policies will likely become increasingly controversial.

Implications for the Chinese Political System

These policies appear to be responding to public opinion and the general mood of (especially urban and informed) citizens of China. Since the onset of mass layoffs at SOEs in the mid-1990s, the public has clearly wanted more attention and resources to go to "disadvantaged social groups" (*ruoshi qunti*) and the repair of social safety nets. Prejudices against rural residents and rural-urban migrants have diminished, and the politics of compassion has gained a hearing. Thus a kind of populist logic seems to be at work in the general tilt to the left, while many of the individual policies have a strong political logic. Even if redistributive policies do not succeed economically—for example, in compressing income differentials—they may well succeed politically. The government and the Communist Party may be perceived to be "taking the side of" poor and rural Chinese even if the outcomes fall short of the declared goals.

This trend is somewhat paradoxical: democratization as such is virtually non-existent, yet China's political leaders are making every effort to identify and move with, even preempt, opinion among informed citizens. In that sense, Hu Jintao and Wen Jiabao have pulled off one of the great acts of political reinvention and repositioning in recent times. At a minimum, they have forestalled the dawning of public perception that the Communist Party was nothing more than a front group for the wealthy and powerful in the new market economy and created a plausible image of themselves as defenders of the poor and the broader social interest. While not yet successful perhaps as a positive piece of propaganda, it has certainly made them less vulnerable to political attack and "negative campaigning." Wen seems to be a very popular political figure. But as a result, there is more pressure on the leaders to deliver on their promises: their credibility is on the line. There is more incentive to protest mistreatment at the local level because the center has committed to rectifying mistreatment. The policies do not necessarily reduce the pressure on the system.

The policy process now acknowledges the existence of interest groups, and policies are adapted to the interests of groups that have a seat at the table. The interests of large-scale social groups are routinely brought into the decisionmaking process: farmers, nonfarming rural residents, migrants, regional interests, and, of course, workers. There is nothing "fair" or "representative" about this process—since China has no representative institutions—but the number of voices that can be heard has expanded greatly. In the Jiang Zemin era, there was plenty of space for business interests—especially state-owned, but also private and foreign interests—and it was not difficult for them to get a message to (or an audience with) the top leadership. The Communist Party would readily represent any one of the three elite forces of society. But under Hu and Wen, the party in principle represents the interests of all social groups yet is subject to the actual supervision of none.

With politicians now playing to broader sets of interest groups, the nature of political patronage has changed. Hu and Wen have many more resources at their disposal as a proportion of total GDP than did Jiang and Zhu. As figure 8-1 shows, budgetary revenues have recovered robustly, and other financial institutions are in a much less precarious position. Hu and Wen have not hesitated to use these resources to cultivate clients in regional governments in the northeast and in western China.[11] Moreover, they have rewarded (more sparsely) much larger groups of people, especially in rural China. Thus Hu and Wen have extended government patronage to much larger groups of people than in the recent past.

But this is not the whole story. Hu and Wen have also tentatively moved against the patronage system that defined the Jiang Zemin era. Jiang could seldom use budgetary resources to build political coalitions because recurring fiscal and financial crises ate into those resources and forced the government to impose policies with real costs on a number of social groups, especially state-enterprise workers. As a result, the only way Jiang and his political faction could muster patronage was to allow local government and party officials to hook up with local businesses in projects that enriched both sides. Local graft was permitted as long as it was pro-growth. Elites from business and government joined together in mutually beneficial ways and in return for these opportunities gratefully gave their loyalty to Jiang Zemin. This combination was most effective in the rapidly growing coastal provinces.

From the beginning, then, Hu and Wen's policies were in mild tension with the local interest groups based in coastal cities. As discussed earlier, when the central government started funding rural programs through budgetary transfers, wealthy eastern provinces had to fund the programs from their own resources. The tension intensified under the macroeconomic re-control policies adopted in 2004 and again in 2006. For the most part, however, the central government left the regional interest groups alone until 2006—when the arrest of Shanghai party secretary Chen Liangyu on corruption charges, combined with the crackdown on local government allocation of urban land, signaled a much more aggressive policy toward local government–business combinations. The move toward re-control and the local crackdown unambiguously constitute an attack on the most powerful local political leaders and on the most important basis of patronage that local factions control, namely, land. These actions have the potential to significantly shift the dynamics of local power, political patronage, and factional alignment. For that to happen, however, the center must follow through with a sustained political effort—and be successful.

So far, there has been no sign of a real political opening, despite dramatic shifts in policy. Important repositionings have taken place, but they all fall within the framework of what Minxin Pei calls "illiberal adaptation."[12] Policy has been adopted and implemented in a top-down fashion, often through the direct imposition of central government rules on diverse local situations. Of course, such an implementation style might be necessary to tackle entrenched local business–government combinations. But equally important is the fact that central politicians are deeply familiar and fully comfortable with such a style. Thus policy is adapted in a way that anticipates and seeks to preempt popular pressures but does not actually respond to them. The left tilt in Chinese economic policy is not incompatible with the talk about democratization that seems to be emerging from Beijing these days, and to optimists it may even look like groundwork for a future move in this direction. But the democratizing process itself is nowhere in evidence, nor is Beijing becoming more democratic. If anything, the current left tilt has a clearly undemocratic component, at least in one respect. The reassertion of government control over certain kinds of speech marks a de facto alliance between the Hu-Wen leadership and the ideological apparatchiks currently headed by Li Changchun. Indeed, this could be considered an alliance of the "left" as the term is traditionally used in China.

Given the top-down and nondemocratic fashion in which these more left policies were adopted, their implementation is highly dependent on the expertise of the economic bureaucracy—a small group of technocrats whose policymaking will determine whether this increased social emphasis is compatible with strong economic growth. As it happens, the current group is both extremely competent and extremely long-serving. For example, four of the outstanding individuals in the most important economic management positions are Zhou Xiaochuan, head of the People's Bank of China; Lou Jiwei, vice minister of finance (who was transferred to an important new post in April 2007 where he is in charge of diversifying China's foreign exchange investments); Zeng Peiyan, vice premier (and former planning head); and Li Rongrong, the head of SASAC. All four are highly intelligent and have dominated active policymaking in their respective arenas since the mid-1990s, if not earlier. Zeng Peiyan is the oldest (sixty-eight) and the highest-ranking person in the group (vice premier, Politburo member), but all four played important policymaking roles in the reform renewal of 1993–94 in a variety of less formal posts. Then in 1998 all four were moved into the top formal posts in their areas. Thus all four are "holdovers" from the Jiang-Zhu administration, with long experience and commitment that transcends a specific administration.[13] They are certainly not of a single mind in all matters and have been known to clash heatedly on some issues, most notably macroeconomic re-control in 2004. Nevertheless, they represent a relatively stable configuration that provides high-quality policy advice and a range of opinions.

The resulting technocratic continuity has important political implications because these elite technocrats are unusually well qualified to balance the populist needs of the left tilt with the productivity needs of the economy. They are good at adapting policy to minimize its economic costs, and at modifying policies when costs first become apparent. This economic team is comparable to the best such teams in developed economies and is probably capable of managing the trade-offs between social needs and market reforms in the short term. However, it has been in charge of the Chinese economy for over a decade, with few significant changes in personnel. This longevity is striking but cannot last forever. This team will break apart after the Seventeenth Party Congress in October

2007, and it will become more difficult thereafter to manage the necessary policy trade-offs.

Conclusion

At this point, it is impossible to construct an unambiguous vision of China's future political system. However, the political shifts described in this chapter will obviously play a critical role in shaping the framework of China's future political processes. China is becoming richer, more diverse, more sophisticated, and more complex, and these economic and social changes are indeed precipitating changes in the way the political game is played. So far, they have not translated into a democratization trend. Whether the important policy shifts described here portend a fundamental reorientation of policymaking, amount to strategic maneuvering, or are midcourse corrections is uncertain, but three scenarios come to mind.

In the first, most "cynical" scenario, Hu Jintao's policy positions would serve his general goal of consolidating power. Hu would take a "populist" position in order to overwhelm the remnants of the Jiang Zemin political coalition. Since Jiang's coalition was based in coastal cities—especially Shanghai—Hu would assemble a coalition of western and northeastern localities and national interests in Beijing. By tilting left, Hu would pick up popular support and also the backing of the ideological apparatchiks. In this scenario, the left tilt might have economic implications but limited political implications. If, however, Hu is able to overcome his opponents in the run-up to the Seventeenth Party Congress, as seems likely, he will then be free to absorb their clients and constituencies into his own coalition. Indeed, it has been common in past Chinese factional struggles for the winner to adopt his rival's ideology and policy positions after the rival has been disposed of. Some hint of this cautious outcome may be seen in the decision to replace fallen Shanghai leader Chen Liangyu with Xi Jinping. Xi is a politician who has served in Fujian (1985–2002) and Zhejiang (2002–07), so his entire political career has basically been in the coastal urban power centers. Moreover, Xi is generally considered a protégé of Jiang Zemin. Thus Hu Jintao may be trying to incorporate parts of Jiang Zemin's faction into the largest possible support coalition. Yet Xi Jinping is also an intelligent and capable leader, and a candidate for future top leadership positions; he has thus far avoided too much taint from the corruption around him—and he is a "princeling" whose father was an important patron of reformers in the past.

A second, middle-of-the-road scenario, would have a second-term Hu-Wen administration attempting to continue the combination of populist policies and political control that have marked the first term. Although the safest prediction, simple continuity will not be easy to achieve because of pressure to deliver on promises already made, the turnover among technocrats, and the inevitable shocks and growth fluctuations that will roil Chinese growth achievement. In a middle-of-the-road scenario, the top leadership can be expected to adopt a more decisive policy style to try to hold competing interest groups in line. Moreover, a reselected leadership group might feel that it has the political capital to insist on a more assertive policy mix, for better or for worse.

The third scenario is by far the most optimistic. It places the left tilt in a hopeful light as an essential precursor to the democratization of Chinese politics, broadening the spectrum of issues under discussion in Chinese politics while bringing a diversity of voices into the political process, including new interest groups. Even more important, in this scenario the left tilt would help restructure the political patronage relationship, a crucial step in breaking the association between patronage and corruption that tainted the Jiang Zemin era. New forms of patronage—still highly political, but more overt and more legitimate—would be used to build political coalitions that could survive in an electoral contest. Patronage would continue, but it would be carried out more and more through the budgetary process, as the budget is used to reward supporters with infrastructure projects and budgetary transfers.

Is this optimistic scenario realistic? The left tilt represents a pragmatic political response by China's authoritarian rulers to the growing diversity of Chinese society and the increase in governmental resources that comes from successful economic performance. In moving left, they have adapted to sweeping social changes that many expect to ultimately lead to democratization. Yet as of now there is nothing in the Communist Party's political practice that portends a smooth transition toward deeper democratization or even suggests movement in this direction. All that can be said for sure is that after the Seventeenth Party Congress, a reselected leadership group will face a set of economic challenges that might lead them to consider bottom-up change as one way to help realize their vision of a harmonious society.

Notes

1. Scott Kennedy, *The Business of Lobbying in China* (Harvard University Press, 2005).
2. This description of "left" combines elements of the term in common usage in China and the West. In China, the term is also associated with ideological rigidity and controls on speech, because it is inextricably tied to the fixed point of the Cultural Revolution that defines "extreme left." Since this chapter focuses on social and economic policy, I generally avoid discussing this aspect of the Chinese Left. It could be argued, however, that in some instances the Hu-Wen administration has also adopted a left policy toward speech, trying to keep a lid on China's increasingly vibrant public discussion.

3. County and township revenues declined from 20 percent to 17 percent of total revenues between 1998 and 2004 and undoubtedly were much less by 2006. Expenditures from those two layers increased from 28 percent to 31 percent of the total over the same period and again would have grown even larger in the two years since. See Christine Wong, "Challenges in Rural Local Government Fiscal Management in China," paper presented at the Conference on Pro-Poor Fiscal Reforms and Building New Socialist Countryside in China, Beijing, November 14–15, 2006.

4. Ministry of Finance. "Report on the Implementation of the Central and Local Budgets for 2006 and on the Draft Central and Local Budgets for 2007," National People's Congress, March 5, 2007; and Wong, "Challenges in Rural Local Government Fiscal Management in China."

5. National Bureau of Statistics, *China Statistical Yearbook 2006* (Beijing: Zhongguo tongji), p. 904.

6. Barry Naughton, "The New Common Economic Program: China's Eleventh Five Year Plan and What It Means," *China Leadership Monitor,* no. 16 (Fall 2005) (media.hoover.org/documents/clm16_bn.pdf).

7. See SASAC, "Guanyu tuijin Guoyou Ziban tiaozheng he guoyou qiye zhongzu de zhidao yijian" (Guiding opinions on advancing the readjustment of state capital and the reorganization of state-owned enterprises) (www.sasac.gov.cn/2006rdzt/2006rdzt_0021/gzw/03/200702050217.htm [February 5, 2007]); Xinhua News Agency, "Guoziwei: Guoyou jingji ying baochi qige hangye de juedui kongzhili" (SASAC: The state-owned economy ought to maintain absolute control over seven sectors) (www.gov.cn/jrzg/2006-12/18/content_472256.htm [December 18, 2006)].

8. State Council, People's Republic of China, "Guidelines for the Medium- and Long-Term National Science and Technology Development Programme (2006–2020)" (Beijing: PRC State Council, 2006); Xinhua Domestic Service, Federal Broadcast Iinformation Servise, February 9, 2006; National Development and Reform Commission, "The 11th Five Year Plan for High Technology Sector Development," *Fagai gaoji 911* (www.ndrc.gov.cn/zcfb/zcfbtz/2007tongzhi/W020070514615556997089.pdf [April 28, 2007]); Cong Cao, Richard P. Suttmeier, and Denis Fred Simon, "China's 15-Year Science and Technology Plan," *Physics Today,* December 2006, pp. 38–43.

9. "National Office for Promoting the Rising of Central Part of China Was Established," April 10, 2007 (en.ndrc.gov.cn/newsrelease/t20070410_128098.htm).

10. Barry Naughton, "The Assertive Center: Beijing Moves against Local Government Control of Land," *China Leadership Monitor,* no. 20 (Winter 2007) (media.hoover.org/documents/clm20bn.pdf).

11. An unchanged aspect of the system is that in all periods Chinese politicians have dispensed substantial patronage through their control of the nomenklatura, or professional personnel system.

12. Minxin Pei, *China's Trapped Transition: The Limits of Developmental Autocracy* (Harvard University Press, 2006).

13. "Holdovers" from the Jiang-Zhu administration is not just a polite way of saying that they are Zhu Rongji protégés. On the contrary, Zeng Peiyan was very closely linked to Jiang Zemin, while Lou Jiwei was a personal protégé of Zhu Rongji. The others are in between.

Part IV

Agents of Change:
Media, Law,
and Civil Society

9

Political Implications of China's Information Revolution: The Media, the Minders, and Their Message

RICHARD BAUM

> It is unrealistic to expect the Chinese media to open up immediately. But, ultimately, a controlled press is incompatible with the information age.
>
> WANG RUOSHUI, "China's Ban on Bad News," *Los Angeles Times*

Media liberalization is widely, though not universally, regarded as a precursor of political liberalization in authoritarian states.[1] In post-Mao China, expectations of a more pluralistic, open media environment were raised in the early 1980s, only to be dashed in the repressive aftermath of the 1989 Tiananmen crackdown. Since then, not even the rampant commercialism and creeping tabloidization of China's newspapers, magazines, television, and radio have effectively broken the Chinese Communist Party's (CCP's) grip on media content. Political censorship remains tight: reporters who probe sensitive issues are harassed and their editors reprimanded—or worse. In its year-end Press Freedom Index for 2006, Reporters without Borders ranked China 163rd in the world (out of 168 countries)—four slots lower than the previous year.[2]

The new electronic media—the Internet, mobile phones, and short message service (SMS), once heralded as avatars of an irreversible process of global liberalization—have not proved immune from the heavy hand of the state. Tens of thousands of Internet police have been employed to monitor Chinese websites, electronic bulletin boards, and chatrooms. Meanwhile, a sophisticated array of software filters—the so-called Great Firewall of China—exercises silent, robotic surveillance over China's 167 million Internet users, blocking access to controversial websites and screening out thousands of "offensive" key words and phrases.

To judge by these benchmarks, China's much-heralded Information Revolution has failed to live up to its promise of promoting political liberalization and openness. The communist party-state has seemingly tamed both the conventional media and the Internet. Consequently, the voices of dissent have been stifled and the People's Republic of China (PRC) remains a closed, authoritarian system. *Plus ça change. . . .*

As this chapter suggests, such conventional benchmarks conceal as much as they reveal. Beneath the surface continuity of tight media censorship, intimidation of journalists, stringent regulatory barriers, and the ubiquitous Great Firewall, a quiet revolution is under way. Social pressures at the state-society boundary are building, tectonic plates are starting to shift, and the media are beginning to find an independent, critical voice.

The Changing Political Economy of the Mass Media

Since 1978, all major media in China have experienced explosive growth. Four strong new institutional forces help to explain this growth: (a) *the loosening of ideological restrictions on content,* which has allowed the media to present more varied and interesting stories; (b) *fiscal and administrative decentralization*, which has introduced local managerial discretion, responsibility-based accounting, and performance-based incentives in media units; (c) *commercialization*, which has tied operational success and survival to bottom-line performance in the media marketplace; and (d) *new technologies of electronic communication,* which have exponentially increased both the amount and the flow rate of spontaneous, unscripted information in China. These forces began to converge in the early 1980s, with the onset of Deng Xiaoping's reforms; and all have contributed importantly to the rise of a more diverse, consumer-friendly, and profit-driven media environment.

The Print Media

In the post-Mao period, the number of newspapers and magazines published in China has increased tenfold, while readership has trebled. Today there are more than 1,900 newspapers and 9,700 magazines in print. Newspaper circulation in China is by far the highest in the world, with an average of 93.5 million copies sold daily.[3] Print-based media advertising has also risen dramatically since the early 1980s, with ad revenues showing spectacular growth far in excess of the country's overall growth of gross domestic product (GDP).[4]

Although state-owned publications (especially those directly run by party organs) remain the presumptive "mouthpiece" of the Leninist regime, the profusion of new, locally managed newspapers and magazines has made the task of enforcing uniform guidelines more complex. Under the principle of "one-level-down" administrative control, in effect since the 1980s, only national media such as *People's Daily,* Xinhua News Agency, and *Guangming Daily* come under direct supervision by central party and state organs, while provincial, county, and municipal-level publications enjoy somewhat greater de facto reportorial and editorial discretion. To compensate for the loss of direct control over press content, propaganda organs in many provinces have supplemented traditional censorial "sticks" with incentive-based financial "carrots," offering cash and promotional rewards to local reporters and editors whose "positive" news stories are picked up by the national media.

Along with the greater number and diversity of print outlets and expanded managerial discretion over local press operations, the decentralization and commercialization of the print media have served to expand the social roles of the press. In addition to their traditional mandate to inform and inspire, newspapers are now expected to entertain, excite, and *sell.* Even the crusty old *People's Daily*—flagship of the CCP media empire—has been constrained to improve its bottom line, expanding both sales and ad revenues by diversifying and enlivening its content and, starting in the 1990s, spinning off new, eye-catching commercial media ventures. The latter include a highly popular tabloid-style newspaper, *Huanqiao ribao* (Global Times), and a lively, interactive website, *Renmin wang* (People's Net), featuring diverse editorial commentaries, interviews, and an online public forum.

As newer, more dynamic newspapers have met with success in the marketplace, the old mainstream party press has lost readership. Between 1990 and 2005, *People's Daily* circulation dropped by 40 percent. Meanwhile, dynamic new regional and local papers such as *Southern Metropolitan Daily, Southern Weekend, Beijing Evening News,* and *Beijing Youth Daily* began to attract large numbers of new, generally younger readers—and substantially larger ad revenues—with their lively reportage and bold exposés.[5]

Special-interest publications, targeted at niche audiences, have also flourished in the newly marketized media environment. With over 300 titles currently available, business-oriented newspapers such as the Guangdong-based *21st Century Economic Herald* have been particularly successful. One hard-hitting glossy economic journal, *Caijing,* became a commercial success through the in-depth investigative reporting of its staff, led by crusading editor Hu Shuli.

Although China's print media continue to enjoy broad popularity in the post-reform marketplace, recent evidence suggests that newspapers and magazines alike have begun to experience a downturn in readership and advertising revenues since 2005 owing to the dramatic explosion of Internet use in China. If this proves to be a long-term trend, it would not be unique to China, as a steady decline in newspaper readership has been widely noted in the United States and elsewhere since the mid-1980s.[6]

One important and often overlooked by-product of the growing commercialization of the Chinese press has been the increased public availability of previously restricted (*neibu*) hard news and statistical information. China's National Bureau of Statistics, as well as a number of commercial and state-owned publishing houses, now routinely make available—usually at a hefty market price—vast amounts of once-classified statistical data. Even the traditionally restricted circulation of *Cankao xiaoxi* (Reference News), with its accurate, albeit carefully abridged, translations of major foreign press articles and editorials, has been eased, with the paper now openly available at newsstands and by subscription. Since going public, *Cankao xiaoxi*, operated by the Xinhua News Agency, has become the leading printed source of international news and opinion in China, with a daily circulation of more than 3.5 million newspapers.

Not all the consequences of increased media decentralization, diversity, and commercialization are salutary, however; at least three problematic effects have also been noted. First, since the early 1990s, the amount of soft news (or "infotainment") in the Chinese media has increased sharply, often featuring dumbed-down stories presented in a provocative, titillating format (think *National Enquirer* or *London Daily Mirror*). When infused with patriotic symbolism and pageantry, such reportage can take on the characteristics of what Xiao Qiang has called "bread and circuses" journalism.[7]

Second, there has been a serious blurring of the distinction between news and advertising. In recent years many journalists, encouraged by performance-based pay incentives and bottom-line-conscious editors, have engaged in the questionable practice of "paid news"—accepting (or even demanding) cash payments from business firms in exchange for favorable press coverage. Worse yet has been the growing wave of journalistic blackmail, wherein reporters extort hush money to suppress unfavorable investigative reports.[8]

Third, an increasing trend toward media conglomeration since the mid-1990s has served to concentrate ownership in some media even as the total number of media outlets has risen dramatically and administration has become more decentralized. By 2002 there were more than 100 publishing and broadcasting groups in China. One consequence of the trend toward media mergers and acquisitions has been to render the resulting corporate conglomerates—which must answer to the concerns of their financial stakeholders—potentially more, rather than less, sensitive to censorial pressure from above.

Clearly, the decentralization and commercialization of the print media cut both ways. Although a lively, diverse array of new information is now available to a far larger audience, there has been a clear cost in terms of rising ownership concentration and increasing vulgarity, corruption, and degradation of journalistic standards.

The Broadcast Media

With some variation, the same forces that have driven the diversification and popularization of the print media have also altered the shape and nature of China's broadcast media. Under the current four-level system of administration introduced in the early 1980s, governments at each level (center, province, municipality, and county) are authorized to establish their own stations, catering to "local public requirements" under the general guidance and oversight of the State Administration of Radio, Film, and Television (SARFT). Within this framework, control over the management, revenues, and programming of radio and TV stations is also deconcentrated, allowing for substantial local editorial initiative, hiring and firing of personnel, and more consumer-oriented programming.

The deconcentration of control over broadcasting has fostered a rapid increase in the number of new radio and television outlets at the provincial, county, and municipal levels. In the first decade of reform, the number of TV stations rose from 38 to 541. Following Deng's "southern tour" of 1992, an even more rapid blossoming of new stations occurred, with the total number reaching 3,200 in 2006. Of these, 209 were owned and operated by the central government, 31 were provincially owned, and nearly 3,000 were locally run.[9] Today there are more than 340 million TV households in China, including 110 million cable subscribers. Fifty-one satellite channels transmit programming from international media providers such as Star-TV, Phoenix, and MTV.[10]

With its near-total saturation of the national market, television has proved to be an ideal platform for generating revenue growth through commercial advertising. TV ad revenues have increased at a rate of 35 percent annually for more than a decade, greatly outpacing the revenue growth of print media.[11] Along with the rising importance of commercial TV advertising has come increased competition for market share, and with it a tendency for local broadcasters to appeal to the widest (if not the lowest) common denominators of mass taste. This is reflected in the proliferation of such low-brow, crowd-pleasing TV fare as soap operas, sit-coms, patriotic holiday galas, game shows, and talent contests—including the highest-rated Chinese TV show of all time, the *Supergirl's Voice* (*Chaoji nusheng*) competition of 2005. Patterned after the U.S. TV hit *American Idol*, the final round of the *Supergirl's Voice* competition was viewed by 400 million Chinese.

Bucking the trend toward low-brow commercial infotainment, CCTV's sixteen national channels offer a good deal of prime-time public service programming, including the country's most controversial daily newsmagazine, *Jiaodian fangtan* (Focus Report), which pioneered the field of televised investigative journalism in China. Breaking a long-established media taboo against negative reporting and the publicizing of bad news, *Jiaodian fangtan* has been compared to CBS's *60 Minutes* and has become the second most popular regularly scheduled program on Chinese television, with an estimated daily audience of 300 million.[12]

CCTV also connects to the global media through a range of transnational programming, including American, Japanese, and South Korean television dramas and Hong Kong action movies. International satellite broadcasting has brought additional in-depth coverage of global events and issues to Chinese television viewers. Hong Kong–based Phoenix TV, which reaches an estimated 140 million people in China, provided extensive real-time coverage of the September 11 terrorist attacks on the World Trade Center and Pentagon.

Radio stations have also shown substantial, though less spectacular growth. More than 1,500 radio stations are currently operating in China, with programming ranging from news, music, sports, and entertainment to listener call-in shows. Since first appearing in the early 1990s, two-way talk shows have proved particularly popular, enabling listeners to participate in candid discussions on a wide range of sometimes controversial (though normally apolitical) issues, while also affording them a modicum of anonymity. Time delays of several seconds are used to prevent off-color or politically incorrect comments by callers from being broadcast.

While market competition has contributed to livelier, more diverse, and cutting-edge radio programming, radio audiences have not grown at nearly the same rate as print and television audiences; and advertising revenues from radio broadcasting are far smaller than from the other media, accounting for only about 2 percent of the country's total ad revenues. Though reliable statistics are hard to come by, it has been credibly reported that the Chinese radio market has been shrinking in recent years because of the rising popularity of the Internet; and future radio programming (and advertising) is consequently expected to be targeted increasingly toward specific demographic niches—such as the millions of middle-class, urban Chinese automobile owners who spend up to ten hours a week commuting on China's overcrowded roads.[13]

The Internet

Since the mid-1990s, the Internet has been the fastest-growing, most dynamic of all mass media in China. When Deng Xiaoping undertook his "southern tour" early in 1992, China had a total of only six electronic mail systems, each with a maximum capacity of 3,000 e-mailboxes—and no online data services.

Within the next decade, a geometric explosion in Internet use took place. By 2007 there were 167 million Internet users in China, along with 75 million individual Internet service provider addresses, 2.5 million registered Internet domain names, and more than 700,000 China-hosted websites. Although blogging is a relatively recent phenomenon, there are said to be 17 million active bloggers in China (up from only 2 million as recently as 2005). On average, one new blog is posted in China *every second*.[14] (By the time this book appears in print, the statistics just cited will be badly out of date.)

Internet users tend to be younger, better educated, middle-class, and more urban than non-users. Seventy percent of China's netizens are under thirty years of age, 59 percent are male, and 54 percent have at least some college education. Saturation is heaviest in major eastern cities such as Beijing, Shanghai, and Tianjin, where between 25 and 30 percent of the population is "wired." Consumer surveys reveal that the most popular uses of the Chinese Internet are news (67.9 percent of all users), search engines (65.7 percent), e-mail (64.7 percent), instant messaging (41.9 percent), bulletin boards and community forums (41.6 percent), music downloading and listening (38.3 percent), electronic games (33.2 percent), and chatrooms (23.1 percent).[15] One also suspects that access to pornography—a category not included in most consumer surveys—is among the more popular uses of the Internet in China, as elsewhere.

Some popular websites, such as Sina.com, permit readers to post comments about news items. At times these comments can be more interesting and controversial than the stories themselves. And if a tabloid paper or website somewhere in China publishes a relatively sensitive item, for example, about an emerging local corruption scandal, the story will quickly be propagated on blogsites and chatrooms around the country—notwithstanding current laws prohibiting print and broadcast media from publicizing stories that cross provincial boundaries.

Cellphones and SMS

When one adds to the veritable blizzard of online communications the extraordinary propagative capabilities of the newest mass electronic medium to hit China, mobile phone–based SMS, the task of controlling the flow of information becomes even more daunting. According to industry sources, in the first quarter of 2007 alone, China's 449 million mobile phone subscribers sent 135.8 *billion* text messages—an average of 17,500 messages *a second*.[16]

In what has been called the largest experiment in electronic direct democracy ever conducted, some *8 million* Chinese mobile phone subscribers cast electronic votes via SMS in the final round of the 2005 *Supergirl's Voice* competition. So nervous were the government's media minders about the possible political implications of such a large-scale electronic plebiscite that they decided to cancel the competition the following year—on the grounds that it was "exploitative" and embodied "the perversions of an unprepared democracy"—until a wave of public indignation forced them to reverse their decision.[17]

The State's Regulatory Apparatus

Although the party-state's regulatory, propaganda, and security agencies have been hard pressed to keep up with the extraordinary growth and diversification of the media, they have hardly given up the ghost. Neither the traditional print and broadcast media nor the new electronic media are "free and open" in the sense of providing a solid platform to support vigorous public debate on issues of political concern or controversy. Indeed, in the regime's efforts to stay abreast of new developments in the Information Revolution, media minders have sharpened their tools of censorship, surveillance, and supervision. And while enforcement of content restrictions is by no means universally effective or consistent, a substantial number of media access points—and a wide range of possible sanctions—remain available to agents of the party-state to restrain and, if restraint fails, to punish those who stray too far, or too often, from official guidelines.[18]

The regulation of media content begins with a series of internal information controls applied directly by central party organs. These include classification of state secrets (barring open reporting on specific topics), controlled dissemination of internal reference news (with access tied to bureaucratic rank and status), and preparation of periodic situation reports guiding the work of lower-level units (including description of incidents in which the media violated guidelines, and the penalties imposed in each instance).[19]

Broadly speaking, there are three levels, or concentric circles, of media control. The innermost circle comprises the "mainstream" media—centrally owned party and government news organizations like Xinhua, *People's Daily*, and CCTV. Control over content is tightest at this level. An intermediate circle is made up of government-owned trade papers and regional media outlets not directly operated by the central party-state. These midlevel media are somewhat more likely to publish information and opinion lying outside (though rarely in defiance of) established guidelines. Third are the "fringe media"—local products of the newly commercialized marketplace, including most Internet portals and local content providers. Financially and administratively independent of state management (if not ownership), they are least subject to state-imposed political and financial constraints; and some have even developed into alternative media voices.[20]

Control of the Print Media

According to the 2001 Regulations on the Administration of Publishing, state control over the print media is exercised through a licensing system that gives the State Administration of Press and Publication (SAPP) indirect authority over all media outlets in the country. Under these regulations, it is illegal to publish a newspaper without explicit permission from, and sponsorship by, an agency of the state. The regulations also specify that the government directly controls the amount, structure, distribution, and coordination of all publishing in the country.

With respect to day-to-day monitoring of mainstream print media, content is routinely scrutinized at four levels: (1) the editor, (2) the branch director in charge of the editor's work, (3) the editor-in-chief of the agency, and (4) the umbrella company over the agency. According to one veteran Chinese journalist, "As an article makes its way up the ladder, the content becomes more politically conscious and less politically sensitive."[21]

The author of this passage, Jiao Guobiao, was relieved of his Beijing University teaching duties after publishing a blistering critique of the party's Central Propaganda Department on the Internet in 2004, in which he savaged CCP media minders for their "voodoo-style thinking" and their "totally groundless, absolutely arbitrary" censorship directives.[22] While Jiao's rhetoric was unusually provocative, his punishment was hardly an isolated case. Over the past few years, there has been a steady stream of alarming news about tightened regulatory controls, censorship, and coercion against print media in China:

—Between 2003 and 2005 the government canceled the registration of 202 news bureaus and shut down an additional 73 "illegal" bureaus.

—In 2004 the government prohibited newspapers from reporting stories about changes of leadership or political reform unless the source was the official news agency Xinhua.

—In 2005 the CCP Central Propaganda Department dismissed the respected editor of the investigative journal *Bingdian* (Freezing Point), Li Datong. When Li's dismissal provoked a strong outcry from other journalists, the government closed *Bingdian,* banning all media references to the incident.

—In June 2006 the National People's Congress tabled a draft law on "emergency management" imposing fines of up to ¥100,000 on media that published unauthorized reports on natural disasters or other emergency situations involving large-scale public disorders.

—In 2006 Xinhua announced stringent new regulations on the distribution of foreign news agency content within China, including the requirement that all foreign agencies must annually report to Xinhua on their news-gathering and publishing activities.

—In 2006 reporters for two foreign newspapers, the *Straits Times* of Singapore and the *New York Times*, were criminally convicted in Chinese courts on dubious charges of "espionage," "fraud," and "revealing state secrets."

—In February 2007 SARFT, SAPP, and the CCP Propaganda Department jointly announced a new list of twenty restrictions on topics that could be openly discussed in the media. Banned subjects included the 1957 anti-rightist campaign, the Cultural Revolution, the Nanjing Massacre of 1937, judicial corruption, and media freedom.

While by no means exhaustive, these examples confirm the general observation that the print media in China today are neither free nor open politically. When journalists and their editors decide to violate official policy guidelines by illuminating "gray areas" and crossing into "forbidden zones," they do so at their own considerable risk.

Control of the Broadcast Media

As in the case of print media, the state controls the licensing of all radio and television outlets. SARFT and the CCP Propaganda Department share responsibility for monitoring radio and TV stations and for providing "guidance" on programming and content.

Over the years, a number of TV programs have been banned (or canceled) for political or ideological reasons; the controversial 1988 documentary miniseries *Heshang* (River Elegy) being a prominent case in point. Its criticism of Mao's narrow-minded provincialism and its unabashed glorification of Western culture, commerce, and democracy were simply too much for the CCP's traditionalists to bear.

In an effort to limit foreign media influence, the Chinese government in 2004 prohibited television broadcasters from showing programs that promoted "Western ideology and politics." A year later, the authorities launched a crackdown on illegal satellite dishes (said to number as many as 40 million). To minimize the impact of multinational broadcast media, the Ministry of Culture in 2005 also banned Chinese television and radio stations from forming partnerships and leasing channels to foreign companies.

In 2006 SARFT unveiled new censorship rules for television dramas and news reports. The new rules stipulate that historical soap operas involving "major or sensitive" issues must receive pre-broadcast government approval. Along similar lines, in January 2007 SARFT announced that henceforth Chinese television stations would only be allowed to run "ethically inspiring TV series" during prime time. The move followed an earlier ban on foreign cartoons between 5:00 p.m. and 8:00 p.m. and an announced intent to crack down on vulgar reality shows.[23]

Control of the Internet

While the party-state has policed conventional media at the mainstream and intermediate levels with some success, Internet use has presented a more formidable challenge because of its very nature as a broadly decentralized, acephalous "network of networks." For this reason, the authorities in charge of Internet surveillance have tried to foster a climate that maximizes self-censorship and self-deterrence. The psychology behind this effort was explained by an official of the Public Security Bureau: "People are used to being wary, and the general sense that you are under surveillance acts as a disincentive. The key to controlling the Net in China is in managing people, and this is a process that begins the moment you purchase a modem."[24]

Under the watchful eye of the Internet Affairs Bureau of the State Council Information Office, tens of thousands of cyber police have been recruited and trained since 2000.[25] Collectively known as Big Mama (*dama*), the I-police have, among other things, cracked down heavily on unlicensed Internet cafes, shutting down more than 100,000 nationwide since 2002. On college campuses around the country, thousands of student monitors, called "little sisters," have been hired to scrutinize postings in chatrooms and on electronic bulletin boards and blogsites, to remind users to observe self-restraint while promoting the regime's goal of a "civilized web." When self-policing proves ineffective, little sisters are expected to report offenders to local I-cops.[26]

Finally, powerful filtering hardware and software (some of it supplied by Western vendors such as Cisco Systems) has been installed by Chinese webhosts and Internet portals to screen out undesirable political content, including such prohibited search terms as "Tiananmen incident," "June 4," "Dalai Lama," and "Taiwan independence." A recent report from the Open Net Initiative—a consortium of British, American, and Canadian universities—concluded that "China's Internet-filtering regime is the most sophisticated effort of its kind in the world."[27]

Major commercial web hosts and Internet portals find themselves under particularly strong pressure to police their own web content. When the head of Bokee.com, China's largest blog host, was asked to explain why his company voluntarily screened out "offensive" subject matter, he responded in terms of narrow corporate expediency: "We are a commercial company. . . . We have a responsibility to our shareholders. . . . If we allow anyone to publish sensitive content, the whole site will be blocked."[28] In similar fashion, major global Internet companies like Yahoo, Google, and Microsoft have agreed voluntarily to remove offensive content from their hosted services in order to ensure continued access to China's fast-growing electronic market. Foreign news media have also come under pressure to sanitize their online content. When they fail to do so, they may find their websites blocked in China—sometimes indefinitely, as has happened to the BBC and *New York Times,* among others.

To further defend against "unhealthy tendencies," the government periodically launches mass movements. In one recent campaign—a two-year drive to "Sweep Away Pornography and Strike Down Illegal Publications"—some 996,000 "illegal political publications" and 4,620,000 Falun Gong and other "evil cult organization propaganda materials" were reportedly purged from the Internet.[29]

Netizens who openly criticize the CCP or challenge its authority online can expect to receive harsh treatment. In 2002 the notorious free-speaking Chinese blogger Liu Di, better known by her sobriquet "Stainless Steel Mouse," was detained by police without charges for more than a year after she criticized party leaders and policies on her blog. Although Chinese government spokesmen routinely claim that no one is arrested solely for exercising their right of free speech on the Internet, at the end of 2006 Amnesty International reported that at least fifty-seven Chinese netizens were under arrest merely for discussing democracy online.[30] Veteran Chinese political bloggers like Li Xinde and Michael Anti (Zhao Jing) play a continuous cat-and-mouse game with the authorities to avoid detection, detention, or both.[31]

Even personal cellphone communications are increasingly subject to official intervention. Major mobile service providers like China Mobile and Unicom routinely post official state "advisory" notices to their subscribers. One such advisory was sent to more than 3 million Beijingers in May 2005, following the eruption of anti-Japanese demonstrations in the nation's capital. "Express patriotism rationally," exhorted the boldfaced text message. "Don't take part in illegal protests. Don't make trouble."[32]

The government's concern with heading off ultranationalist zeal among mobile phone and Internet users had valid roots. In May 1999 and again in April 2001, young male Chinese netizens flooded Internet bulletin boards and chatrooms with radical anti-American rhetoric in the aftermath of two controversial American military actions: the "accidental" bombing of the Chinese embassy in Belgrade and the forced landing of a U.S. EP-3 spy plane on Hainan Island. In the latter case, a spate of emotional anti-American polemics on *Strong Country,* the online chat forum of the *People's Daily,* quickly morphed into bitter criticism of the Chinese government for its "shameful incompetence" in releasing the captive American aircraft and flight crew without an apology. The more inflammatory postings were quickly removed from the site. Since then, fear that the Internet and SMS could become launch pads for massive, populistic explosions of nationalist fervor has led the government to closely monitor electronic expressions of patriotism.[33]

The Limits of Media Control

Notwithstanding the wide array of weapons available to limit the impact of the Information Revolution, there is reason for optimism. For one thing, as a result of the sheer fragmentation of administrative command and management of the media, the number of salient pressure points at which state monitoring and regulatory authority must be applied to reasonably staunch the flow of problematic communications is extraordinarily large.

Second, and greatly compounding the problem of fragmented management, are the perverse incentives built into the very structure of principal-agent relations at each level in the media hierarchy. Evaluation and promotion of cadres at each level are based principally (though not exclusively) on the fulfillment of financial targets. This tends to reinforce existing fiscal and property rights arrangements under which local governments are constrained to privilege market success (profitability) over cultural and political correctness. Although mainstream state media operate on a relatively tight political leash and enjoy little latitude, in the less closely controlled intermediate (local) and third-tier (fringe) media, when the bottom line conflicts with the party line, the former increasingly takes precedence.

Third, the ongoing revolution in information technology has made it easier for sophisticated saboteurs to discover and exploit weak links in the state's media systems. Thus, for example, on at least three occasions since 2001, tech-savvy hackers affiliated with the outlawed Falun Gong have used remote radio signals to successfully hijack satellite transponder signals beamed to millions of Chinese television viewers.

Fourth, and finally, the acephalous nature of the new electronic media, in particular the Internet, has rendered effective, comprehensive top-down command and control increasingly problematic. Given the staggering volume of electronic messages flying into, out of, and around China at any given moment, total content control of the Internet has become impractical, if not impossible. The Great Firewall has numerous leaks, and many netizens have become adept at navigating around it, using proxy server addresses to access blocked websites. As fast as the authorities can block or delete access to these proxy servers, new ones are added.

Text messaging has proved particularly vulnerable to massive violations of political correctness. Following the 2003 Severe Acute Respiratory Syndrome (SARS) epidemic, for example, a wave of sarcastic doggerel was propagated on mobile phones throughout the country, lampooning the party leadership's inept handling of the outbreak. One particularly caustic SMS transmission slammed the CCP's inability to control official corruption:

> The Party can't stop officials from feasting at public expense, but SARS did!
> The Party can't stop junketeering officials, but SARS did!
> The Party can't stop endless futile meetings, but SARS did!
> The Party can't stop the deception of superiors and the cheating of subordinates, but SARS did!
> The Party can't stop prostitution, but SARS did![34]

Taken together, these various limiting factors—administrative fragmentation, perverse principal-agent incentives, continuous technological innovation, and a decentralized, acephalous Internet/cellphone universe—make it highly unlikely that Chinese authorities will be able to halt either the relentless, market-driven expansion of the information cascade or the increasing envelope-pushing licentiousness of local and fringe media. In a rare acknowledgment of the impracticality of exercising effective content control, the deputy director of the Guangdong provincial propaganda bureau recently noted: "Every day we receive phone calls from various government offices demanding that this not be reported or that not be reported. We basically consider their requests, but speaking from a long-term perspective . . . it is not a workable control strategy."[35]

Civil Society and the "Rights Defense" Movement

Another reform-induced development complicating the media regulatory task is the emergence of a self-organizing civil society in China stemming from the substantial expansion of "public space" available for addressing issues of civic concern. According to Chinese sources, there were over 317,000 nongovernment-organized civil society associations in the country in 2006, though no one knows the true number.[36] For the most part, these associations are small and narrowly focused on issues of substantive local concern (pollution, poverty, rural education, HIV/AIDS awareness, and the like). They are also mostly apolitical. But their rising numbers and heightened civic awareness have visibly enlarged the arena of public discourse where policies and actions of the party-state and its agents can be discussed, debated, and, with increasing frequency, contested.

Energized by marketization and informatization, and enabled by the party-state's retreat from micromanaging individual behavior, Chinese citizens have begun to use legally prescribed channels to articulate their interests. Between 1993 and 2002, for example, the number of lawsuits filed annually by Chinese citizens against agents of the state, under the terms of the 1990 Administrative Litigation Law, rose from 27,000 to almost 100,000. In the single year 2005, the All-China Federation of Trade Unions reported 314,000 labor disputes, up 20 percent from the previous year. Also in 2005, according to the State Council, 30 million Chinese citizens submitted petitions, both individual and collective, to "letters and visits" offices around the country, requesting government intervention to resolve a range of individual and collective grievances—marking a threefold increase over 2004.[37]

When peaceful petitioning fails, direct action increasingly ensues. Between 1993 and 2005, the number of annual "mass disturbances" in China grew from 8,700 to over 83,000—an average increase of almost 20 percent a year. According to Xinhua, in 2005 alone there were more than 540,000 violent "public incidents" (*gonggong shijian*) of all kinds, resulting in 200,000 deaths and financial losses of ¥325 *billion*.[38] In the past few years, angry groups of homeowners and farmers—sometimes numbering in the tens of thousands—have confronted local officials and property developers in dozens of Chinese cities and hundreds of rural townships to protest illegal land seizures and corrupt real estate development deals. One recent estimate put the number of rural dwellers who have been victimized in fraudulent land deals at more than 50 million.[39]

Rising civic activism in China has been further spurred by the emergence of a *weiquan* (rights defense) movement. Lawyers affiliated with this movement have represented, among others, the victims of real estate scams, industrial waste-dumping, consumer fraud, and illegal commerce. Equally important, they have defended vulnerable whistleblowers against reprisals from well-connected scofflaws and their local state patrons. In the process, the lawyers have themselves become increasingly vulnerable to state intimidation and coercion. In the past few years, several lawyers associated with the *weiquan* movement have been beaten up, and at least two dozen have been jailed.[40]

Although the regime's continued willingness and ability to silence unwelcome voices could be taken as evidence that little has changed in China, and that the party-state remains omnipotent and invincible, the opposite conclusion can also—and perhaps even more credibly—be drawn. In China today, where an emerging, rights-conscious civil society has begun to push back against the traditional boundaries and symbols of state dominance, the *weiquan* movement's tactic of persistently appealing to the *letter* of the law to expose flaws in a system purportedly based on the *rule* of law serves as a growing reminder of the glaring gap between legal theory and political reality.[41]

As public awareness of rights and rules grows, civil society begins to bump up against the system-preserving political logic of the regime. The media are on hand to record and amplify the resulting frictional encounters. The state then responds with a combination of new rules, new monitoring devices, new sticks, and new carrots. Seeking to deter the propagation of bad news, the state security apparatus punishes a few chickens to scare off the gathering monkeys, while the state's media chiefs offer lucrative material inducements to those editors and journalists who publish uplifting stories and feel-good news reportage. But the media have become, in some measure, the natural ally of civil society—its voice—and so the bad news continues to bleed through. As one observer has remarked, "various repressed discourses" keep "bubbling to the surface."[42]

From Feedback to Pushback: The Role of Investigative Journalism

While no aggregate data are available to confirm the importance of the media's new role as civil-society watchdog, anecdotal evidence abounds. For example, the frequency and efficacy of investigative journalism has risen dramatically in such areas of growing public awareness as environmental protection. In 2003 pressure jointly generated by environmental nongovermental organizations (NGOs) and the local media in Sichuan Province mobilized public opinion against a planned dam near Dujiangyan, an ancient irrigation system designated as a World Heritage site. The plan was eventually dropped. Similarly, in 2004 plans to construct a massive hydropower station on Yunnan's Nujiang River were placed on hold pending detailed environmental impact studies—the result of negative publicity generated by NGOs, their lawyers, and the media.[43] An even more dramatic display of the newfound potency of media-activated public opinion was the May 2007 announcement that in response to 1 million SMS protest messages sent by citizens of Xiamen on their mobile phones, the construction of a new, environmentally hazardous $1.4 billion petrochemical plant in the city was being halted indefinitely.[44]

Increased media scrutiny of courts, prosecutors, and police has also begun to push China's judicial institutions to become more fair, impartial, and transparent. The case of Sun Zhigang provides a relevant illustration. Sun, a university graduate from Wuhan, was beaten to death in a Guangzhou migrant detention center in 2003 after having been taken into custody for failing to display his temporary residence card. Guangzhou's *Southern Metropolis Daily* broke the story, which was then widely circulated on the Internet. The resulting public outcry led the central government to abolish the temporary residence permit requirement and convert migrant detention centers into voluntary service centers.[45]

The role of the media in exposing cadres' misdeeds is also growing. In the fall of 2006, in Chongqing Municipality, an education bureau employee was transferred from his job and briefly jailed for circulating on the Internet a satirical poem criticizing local governmental incompetence. Despite an order by the Central Propaganda Department banning media coverage of the incident, *Liaowang*, an official outlet of the Xinhua News Agency, published the story. A wave of public indignation ensued, directed at the Chongqing municipal government. Subsequently, Chongqing's mayor was called on the carpet by the central government.[46]

In the area of public health advocacy, the record of media pushback is mixed. The 2003 SARS outbreak in China initially appeared to provide a breakthrough opportunity for the media to gain traction—propelled by public outrage—against the state's traditional ban on the spread of bad news. After an initial surge of investigative reporting by journals such as *Caijing* and the *Sanlian shenghuo zhoukan* (Sanlian Life Weekly) revealed the existence of a deliberate governmental cover-up of the SARS epidemic, Beijing's chastened leaders called for greater governmental openness and transparency. But when Hu Shuli, the envelope-pushing editor of *Caijing,* openly championed the original SARS whistle-blower, renowned surgeon Jiang Yanyong, and criticized the public health authorities for having maligned him, *Caijing* was promptly pulled from the newsstands, and the empire struck back with fresh media restrictions.[47]

Corruption within the mass media has also been targeted for exposure by investigative journalists. Since 2001, the magazine *News Reporter* has annually published a list of "ten top fabricated news stories."[48] In another widely publicized case, after the *China Youth Daily's* weekly supplement, *Bingdian,* was shut down by censors in late 2005, its feisty editor, Li Datong, posted on the Internet a lengthy exposé denouncing the introduction of a controversial "credit point system" by the chief editor of *China Youth Daily*, under which journalists were awarded cash bonuses according to the frequency with which their stories were favorably mentioned by high-level party and government officials.[49]

In January 2007 the well-known print journalist Wang Keqin of the *China Economic Times* wrote a 13,000-word exposé concerning the death of fellow journalist Lan Chengzhang, who had been brutally beaten by thugs after threatening to publicly expose an illegal coal mining operation in Shanxi Province. (The case was further muddied by allegations of attempted extortion against Lan.) When censors at the *China Economic Times* red-penciled the sensitive concluding remarks of Wang's article, he boldly posted the entire, uncensored piece on his blogsite, whereupon the story—now including the censorship issue—was recycled back into the print media via *Southern Weekend*, a Guangzhou based weekly known for its bold investigative reporting.[50]

Humor, too, has played a role in the media's pushback against state censorship. At CCTV's annual Spring Festival staff party in 2002, two news anchors performed a self-parodying rap on the lack of integrity and the prevalence of cheerful, sanitized news reportage in CCTV programming. Modeled after Cui Jian's hit song, *Bushi wo bu mingbai* (It's not that I don't understand), the musical parody contained the following lyrics:

No news presentations are not truthful
No information is not timely
No programs are not excellent
No audiences are not loyal
No official speeches are not important
No applause is not thunderous
No participation is not enthusiastic
All these years we could only do what we've been told
Tonight let's be the masters for once![51]

Even a few pro-establishment media voices have begun to speak out on the need for accelerated political reform. In a February 2007 interview appearing in Guangzhou's *Southern Metropolis,* retired editor of the *People's Daily* Zhou Ruijin candidly acknowledged that China was weighed down by a series of crushing social and economic problems and argued that the only reasonable cure lay in "pushing forward political system reform above all [other] reform." He specifically called for expanded direct elections and strengthened protection for China's emerging civil society.[52]

A final example of the newfound efficacy of the pushback by media-voiced civil society is provided by the recent saga of the Chongqing "nail house." In this extraordinary case, which burst into the public's awareness in March 2007, a Chongqing couple held out against intense pressure applied by property developers and local government agencies, refusing to evacuate their home without adequate financial compensation. Enlisting the support of local resident groups and a generally sympathetic mass media (who obligingly portrayed the couple's struggle as a confrontation between David and Goliath), the couple parlayed widespread public sympathy—and the acute embarrassment this caused the Chongqing government—into a nationwide media blitz. Hundreds of web forums, chatrooms, and mobile phone networks all over China provided daily updates of the nail-house saga, complete with stunning photos of the small house perched atop a tiny spit of land at the center of a gigantic excavation pit; after the *Southern Weekend* and a few other tabloids picked up the story in mid-March, the nail-house occupants received a generous financial settlement; and on March 29, the Beijing *Youth Weekend* hailed the "most awesome nail-house" event as heralding "the birth of citizen journalism."[53]

Writing about this remarkable triumph of citizens pushing back against the state, the *New York Times* commented:

On the face of it, theirs was a hopeless task, two simple citizens against a mighty and murky alliance of an authoritarian state and big development money.

In reality, though, the couple was anything but alone . . . because they figured out how to glue millions of discrete individuals together in sympathy for a cause not directed from above. . . .

None of this mobilization would have been possible without media to transmit the message, and Chinese journalists, both traditional and virtual, carried the ball, spreading the word far and wide, turning this into a truly national story.[54]

Obviously, no random sample of anecdotes can "prove" the efficacy of the mass media as guardians of civil society or advocates of political liberalization. In fact, the record to date is spotty at best. But it is still early in China's ongoing Information Wars; and what does seem clear is that *some* media voices, interacting with *some* sectors of civil society, have begun to amplify and articulate the policy concerns of *some* hitherto voiceless individuals and groups, and that the resulting commotion is causing *considerable* consternation within the Chinese party-state.

Conclusion: Toward Political Liberalization?

No one can be certain just how—or how quickly—this ongoing drama will play itself out, or just where it will end. Some observers have placed their hopes for a more liberal, pluralistic Chinese political future on the CCP's emerging Fifth Generation leaders, who will come into their own early in the next decade.[55] Others foresee, in lieu of liberal political reforms, the emergence of an increasingly responsive, paternalistic (but undemocratic) "nanny-state," employing administrative remedies cloaked in neo-Confucian homilies to bolster its "authoritarian resilience."[56] Still others see China caught in a "trapped transition," doomed to flounder, if not fail, owing to inherent structural flaws in its marketized Leninist institutions.[57] And a stubborn few continue to cling to their predictions of imminent chaos and collapse.[58]

For myself, I am strongly inclined to echo the words of Wang Ruoshui, the late editor of the *People's Daily* quoted at the head of this chapter, who argued that ultimately a controlled press is incompatible with the sociopolitical dynamics of the Information Age. To be sure, political liberalization, if and when it does occur, will require a degree of political will heretofore lacking in China's top leadership. Up to now, the only relevant precedent available to Chinese leaders to instruct them in the potential perils and pitfalls of post-Leninist liberalization has been a catastrophic one—the Gorbachev-led, *glasnost*-induced implosion of the Soviet Empire. Few in China, Leninists or liberals alike, would welcome such a devastating outcome.

Notwithstanding the inertial implications of the preceding point, the observed trend toward an expanding, increasingly "noisy," and contentious public sphere is likely to become even more pronounced with the passage of time. This is true not merely because a rising tide of information is relentlessly lapping at the dikes of party censorship, but also because of collateral developments in other parts of the Chinese polity, including ongoing legislative pressure to strengthen private property rights and growing public demand for greater transparency and openness in local government. These developments cannot but further erode the presumptive power monopoly enjoyed by the Leninist party-state.

The erosion process—measured for our present purposes by the frequency with which unauthorized, "off-message" media content is propagated—is already well under way. But it is not occurring evenly throughout the system. It is more evident at the periphery than at the core, in fringe media rather than in mainstream media. It is thus at the outer edges of China's state-society media frontier—where the political logic of top-down command and control is directly contradicted by the market logic of bottom-up consumer demand—that the most unsettling, discordant voices are most frequently, and most audibly, heard.

In accordance with the known laws of physics, as social pressure builds at the system's periphery, it will eventually move inward and upward toward the core; and at some point, the party-state at the system's command center will either have to ratchet up still farther its repressive controls or begin to accommodate rising societal demands for greater media (and ultimately political) openness and pluralism. Arguably, such a calculus was at play in Chiang Ching-kuo's momentous decision to liberalize Taiwan's political system in 1987, followed less than a year later by Chun Doo Hwan's equally bold decision to terminate South Korea's military dictatorship.

Although the likelihood of outright regime failure must be reckoned as rather low, the intensifying contradiction between rising levels of public information and awareness, on the one hand, and the CCP's determination to hold onto political power at all costs, on the other, constitutes a long-term invitation to a legitimacy crisis. The fact that even relatively small increments of civil society activism and media pushback have recently provoked intense, heavy-handed responses from the party-state's control apparatus suggests that the current state-society equilibrium is a fragile one, lacking in long-term metastability.

In a Darwinian universe, species confronted with rapidly changing environmental conditions are free to choose maladaptive behaviors. But the price they pay is a stiff one: an increased likelihood of extinction. So it is with Leninist regimes, whose in-built (and ultimately self-defeating) resistance to the free flow of ideas and information must be reckoned as a serious obstacle to their own long-term survival. With three-fourths of the world's existing communist regimes having been swept away in the Leninist "Mass Extinction" of 1989–91, this is no mere liberal delusion, as James Mann has suggested.[59] Since I assume China's present and future leaders are not particularly suicidal and will therefore first seek to exhaust relatively congenial alternatives—including their current flirtation with paternalistic neo-Confucianism—before undertaking liberalization as a last resort, I would suggest that it is not unreasonable to expect a more open and information-friendly China to emerge within a decade or so.

Since China is a vast, rapidly developing country facing a daunting set of developmental challenges (including severe income polarization, a devastated natural environment, and pandemic official corruption), and since, in government as in nature, form must ultimately follow function, China is unlikely to blindly imitate Western-style institutions—as Sun Yat-sen once did after the ill-fated Chinese Republican Revolution of 1911. China will have to find its own way out of its current political bind. But whatever institutions are ultimately adopted, they will have to bear the added weight of an increasingly vibrant, contentious, information-rich, and rights-conscious civil society. About the only thing that can be said with confidence at this point is that those institutions will not be Leninist in nature.

Notes

Works from 2005 and 2006 attributed to the China Media Project at Hong Kong University may not give a web address because they are no longer available online.

1. Patrick O'Neil, ed., *Communicating Democracy: The Media and Political Transition* (London: Lynne Rienner, 1998); and Richard Gunther and Anthony Mughan, *Democracy and the Media: A Comparative Perspective* (Cambridge University Press, 2000).

2. Reporters without Borders, "Worldwide Press Freedom Index 2006" (www.rsf.org/rubrique.php3?id_rubrique=639).

3. By comparison, average daily U.S. newspaper circulation in 2005 was 55.6 million. See World Association of Newspapers, "World Press Trends: Newspaper Circulation and Advertising Up Worldwide," May 30, 2005 (www.wan-press.org/article7321.html); and "China to Inspect Newspaper Circulation Data," Xinhua News Agency, September 5, 2006.

4. Research and Markets, "China Newspaper Industry" (www.researchandmarkets.com/reports/297002/china_newspaper_industry.htm). Also (Singapore) *Straits Times,* April 25, 2006; and *China Media Project* (online), October 20, 2005.

5. "Chinese Officials Gather to Discuss Circulation Future of Party Pubs," *People's Daily,* October 17, 2005, p. 4.

6. "Newspaper Readership Giving Way to Internet," *South China Morning Post,* April 15, 2006; also "Chinese Papers Hit by Falling Ad Profits" (Singapore) *Straits Times,* April 25, 2006; and "The State of the News Media, 2005: An Annual Report on American Journalism" (www.stateofthenewsmedia.org/2005/narrative_newspapers_audience.asp?cat=3&media=2).

7. Xiao Qiang, remarks at the Conference on Changing Media, Changing China, University of California, San Diego, May 5–6, 2006.

8. "Corruption in Regional News Bureaus: An Analysis," *China Digital Times,* August 15, 2006 (http://chinadigitaltimes.net/2006/08/corruption_in_regional_news_bureaus_an_analysis_zhan_ji.php).

9. Paul SN Lee, "Mass Communication and National Development in China: Media Roles Reconsidered," *Journal of Communication* 44 (Summer 1994): 27; and Central Intelligence Agency, *World Factbook 2006* (www.cia.gov/cia/publications/factbook/geos/ch.html).

10. Hamburg-Shanghai Network, "Looking at Chinese Media Industries," Newsletter 9, 2006 (www.hamburgshanghai.net/de/index.php?).

11. *Renmin wang,* April 30, 2004 (http://english.peopledaily.com.cn/200404/29/eng20040429_141890.html).

12. Alex Chan, "From Propaganda to Hegemony: *Jiaodian Fangtan* and China's Media Policy," *Journal of Contemporary China* 11, no. 30 (2002): 35–51.

13. *China Media Project,* August 8–14, 2005 (http://cmp.hku.hk/look/article.tpl?IdLanguage=1&IdPublication=1&NrIssue=1&NrSection=70&NrArticle=188).

14. See, for example, "Internet Use in China Jumps by almost 25pc in 2006," *China View,* January 24, 2007 (www.chinaview.cn); also Congressional Research Service, "Internet Development and Information Control in the People's Republic of China," February 2006 (www.fas.org/sgp/crs/row/RL33167.pdf).

15. China Internet Network Information Center, "Internet Statistics: 2005." See also Guo Liang, *Surveying Internet Usage and Impact in Twelve Chinese Cities* (Beijing: Research Center for Social Development, 2005).

16. *PanAsianBiz,* May 4, 2007 (www.panasianbiz.com/2007/05/).

17. Reporters without Borders, "WTO Members Urged to Oppose a New Wave of Chinese Media Restrictions" (www.ifex.org/en/content/view/full/73753/ [April 17, 2006]).

18. On state regulation of the media, see Daniel Lynch, *After the Propaganda State* (Stanford University Press, 2001).

19. He Qinglian, *Media Control in China* (New York: Human Rights in China, 2004), chap. 4.

20. Betty Winfield and Zengjun Peng, "Market or Party Controls: Chinese Media in Transition," *International Journal for Communication Studies* 67, no. 3 (2005): 262.

21. Jiao Guobiao, transcript of a talk at the University of California, Los Angeles, Center for Chinese Studies, November 29, 2004.

22. Paul Mooney, "China Wages a New War on Academic Dissent," *Chronicle of Higher Education,* June 17, 2005.

23. "SARFT Throws in with Market-Driven TV," *Danwei,* April 12, 2006 (www.danwei.org/media_and_advertising/sarft_throws_in_with_marketdri_1.php); and "Only 'Ethically Inspiring' TV Allowed," *News.com.au,* January 22, 2007 (www.news.com.au/story/0,10117,21099868-1702,00.html?from=public_rss).

24. Quoted by James Mulvenon, Testimony to the Congressional-Executive Commission on China, April 15, 2002 (www.cecc.gov/pages/roundtables/041502/mulvenon.php).

25. The figure 30,000 is the one most frequently reported, but no authoritative source has been located for it.

26. *Renmin wang,* April 23, 2006 (www.people.com.cn); and *Xinhuanet,* April 13, 2006 (www.xinhuanet.com/English).

27. Open Net Initiative, "Internet Filtering in China in 2004–2005: A Country Study" (www.opennetinitiative.net/studies/china/).

28. "Media Explosion Tests China's Control," *BBC News* (Shanghai), October 25, 2006.

29. U.S. Congressional-Executive Commission on China, "China Human Rights and Rule of Law Update," May 2006 (www.cecc.gov/pages/virtualAcad/newsletterListing.phpd? NLdate=20060503&show=ALL).

30. *BBC News,* December 18, 2006 (http://news.bbc.co.uk/2/hi/technology/6191171.stm).

31. See "Blogging in China: The Michael Anti Interview," *China Digital Times,* September 4, 2005 (http://chinadigitaltimes.net/2005/09/blogging_in_chi_1.php).

32. "Beijing Warns Off Protestors with SMS," *Taipei Times,* May 2, 2005.

33. Susan Shirk, *China: Fragile Superpower* (Oxford University Press, 2007).

34. I am grateful to David Cowhig for bringing this incident to my attention.

35. "Top Guangdong Propaganda Official Comments on News Control and the Role of the Press in China," *China Media Project,* February 7, 2007 (http://cmp.hku.hk/look/article.tpl?IdLanguage=1&IdPublication=1&NrIssue=1&NrSection=100&NrArticle=786).

36. Congressional-Executive Commission on China, *Annual Report 2006* (U.S. Government Printing Office, 2006), p. 120; also Ying Ma, "China's Stubborn Anti-Democracy," *Policy Review,* February–March 2007.

37. Yuen Yuen Tang, "When Peasants Sue En Masse," *China: An International Journal* 3, no. 1 (2005): 30; and "The Time Magazine Office of Letters and Visits," in *China Blog,* January 23, 2007 (http://time-blog.com/china_blog/2007/01/the_time_magazine_office_of_le_1.html).

38. "Highlights of Draft Law on Emergency Response" (in Chinese), *Xinhuanet,* June 24, 2006 (http://news.xinhuanet.com/politics/2006-06/24/content_4744089.htm).

39. He Qinglian, "Where's the Boom of the Chinese Property Industry Coming From?" (part 4), *Epoch Times,* May 8, 2004 (http://en.epochtimes.com/news/4-5-8/21287.html).

40. Congressional-Executive Commission, *Annual Report 2006.* See also Joseph Kahn, "Rivals on a Legal Tightrope Seek to Widen Freedoms in China," *New York Times,* February 25, 2007.

41. This point was brilliantly made by the Czech political dissident Vaclav Havel, in an extended 1979 essay, *Living in Truth* (London: Faber and Faber, 1990).

42. Yuezhi Zhao, "Media and Elusive Democracy in China," *The Public* 8, no. 4 (2001): 41.

43. Ashley Palmer, "The Role of the Media in China's Environmental Protection" (Michigan State University, July 8, 2004) (forestry.msu.edu/China/New percent20Folder/Ashleyppt.pdf); and Yiyi Lu, "Environmental Civil Society and Governance in China" (London: Chatham House Asia Programme, August 2005).

44. Associated Press (Beijing), May 31, 2007.

45. Benjamin Liebman, "Watchdog or Demagogue? The Media in the Chinese Legal System," *Columbia Law Review* 105 (January 2005); and Sophie Beach, "Rise of Rights?" *China Digital Times,* May 27, 2005 (http://chinadigitaltimes.net/2005/05/rise_of_rights.php).

46. "Xinhua News Agency Revisits the Qin Zhongfei SMS Story," *China Media Project,* November 15, 2006 (http://cmp.hku.hk/look/article.tpl?IdLanguage=1&IdPublication=1& NrIssue=1&NrSection=100&NrArticle=759).

47. Mure Dickey, "The Chinese Press Rebuts SARS Claims," *Financial Times,* June 10, 2003; and Arnold Zeitlin, "SARS and the Chinese Media: A Brief Opening," *China Brief* 3, no. 13 (July 1, 2003).

48. Transparency International, "National Integrity System Country Study Report: China 2006," p. 31 (www.transparency.org/content/download/12696/125523/file/China_nis_2006.pdf).

49. "Freedom Row at China Youth Daily," *South China Morning Post*," August 16, 2005; also "Let a Thousand Blogs Bloom," (London) *Times*, February 16, 2006.

50. "Debate Begins in the Lan Chengzhang Case," *China Media Project*, January 17, 2007 (http://cmp.hku.hk/look/article.tpl?IdLanguage=1&IdPublication=1&NrIssue=1&NrSection=100&NrArticle=765); and Jonathan Ansfield, "Dirty Newsrooms: Wang Keqin's Missing Ending," *China Digital Times*, January 27, 2007 (http://chinadigitaltimes.net/2007/01/dirty_newsrooms_wang_keqin_uncensored.php).

51. Lyrics translated by Xiao Qiang, *China Digital Times*, February 17, 2007 (http://chinadigitaltimes.net/2007/02/elfmockery_of_cctv_broadcasters_and_employees.php).

52. Chris Buckley, "China Editor Makes Bold Call for Democracy," Reuters (Beijing), February 5, 2007.

53. Chen Wanying, "The Most Awesome 'Nail-House' Gives Birth to Citizen Journalism," *China Youth Weekend,* March 29, 2007 (http://zonaeuropa.com/20070331_1.htm).

54. Howard French, "A Couple's Small Victory Is a Big Step for China," *International Herald Tribune*, April 6, 2007, p. 2.

55. Cheng Li, "The Emergence of the Fifth Generation in the Provincial Leadership," *China Leadership Monitor*, no. 6 (Spring 2003), pp. 75–90.

56. Andrew Nathan, "Authoritarian Resilience," *Journal of Democracy* 14, no. 1 (2003): 13–16; and Dali Yang, *Remaking the Chinese Leviathan* (Stanford University Press, 2004).

57. Minxin Pei, *China's Trapped Transition: The Limits of Developmental Autocracy* (Harvard University Press, 2006).

58. Gordon Chang, *The Coming Collapse of China* (New York: Random House, 2001).

59. James Mann, *The China Fantasy: How Our Leaders Explain Away Chinese Repression* (New York: Penguin Books, 2007).

10

Legalization without Democratization in China under Hu Jintao

JACQUES DELISLE

> A harmonious society should feature democracy, the rule of law, equity, justice, sincerity, amity and vitality.
>
> HU JINTAO, "Address to Party School Training Course" (2005)

Throughout the reform era, China's leaders have expected law and the legal system to play unprecedented and important roles. The resulting gains have been impressive: laws and legal institutions have contributed greatly to the diffusion of international norms, construction of a market-oriented economy, and amelioration of problematic features of authoritarian rule. In some areas, demand and supply are growing, or threatening to grow, beyond the leadership's expectations and preferences. These trends have broadened and deepened since the Deng era and are likely to continue despite some friction between the emphasis on law (particularly law with pro-market, international norm-conforming content) and the populism associated with the current leadership.

At the same time, this "legalization" has not much supported democratization, and is not likely to do so following the Seventeenth Party Congress. In the Chinese leadership's immanent strategy, laws and the legal system have sought to substitute for democracy and postpone effective demand for democratization. This approach may prove sustainable for a relatively long time, given that the relationship between rule by law (in the sense of effectively and consistently applying legal rules, whatever their content, as a principal means for regulating economic, social, and political behavior)—or even the rule of law (which goes beyond rule by law, in that laws and the legal system are a reliable constraint upon, and not merely a tool of, government, or meet some minimal substantive standard of protecting human rights or citizen's liberties)—and democracy, while broadly positive, is not simple or linear. Ideological readjustments under

185

Hu Jintao (including discussions of constitutionalism and a turn to populism) do not imply a basic shift on the question of democracy or a course reversal on legalization and the forces favoring its development, but they do create tensions with some aspects of legalization. China may democratize, and legal change and related developments may contribute to democratization, but that transformation is not yet on the horizon or likely to enter the leadership's strategy in the near future.

Through the Open Door: Law, International Norms, and Chinese Reforms

The most significant effect of the laws and legal institutions developed in the People's Republic of China (PRC) during the reform era has been to provide a framework for economic growth, specifically of a market-oriented and internationally open type. Major policies for pursuing this goal have relied extensively on laws and the legal system.

Economic Law

A vital foundation for Chinese enterprises' engagement in market-based transactions was the Economic Contract Law of 1981, the broader Contract Law that superseded it nearly two decades later, and other related laws. More nearly arm's-length and rule-governed ownership and fiscal relationships between firms and the state were gradually established through laws governing enterprise management, taxation, and related matters. Additional laws established the propriety and powers of new, more market-oriented entities, including township and village enterprises, partnership organizations, private firms, and share-issuing and exchange-listed companies, as well as foreign-invested enterprises. The Company Law and Securities Law of the 1990s, their 2005 successors, and kindred laws and regulations authorized, ratified, or encouraged diverse forms of ownership and new modes of transferring ownership and control. These laws and laws on bankruptcy, secured interests, banks, and the like adopted more market-conforming rules for credit and capital.

With these increasingly expansive reforms, Chinese law has begun to converge with its foreign counterparts. More than its predecessors, the 1999 Contract Law accepts freedom of contract, protection of party autonomy, limits on permissible grounds for state interference in or invalidation of contracts, and other features familiar to contract lawyers from market economies. The 2005 Company Law and Securities Law similarly move well beyond prior legislation and adopt provisions analogous to laws in developed capitalist economies concerning investor rights, director and officer duties, disclosure obligations, protections for minority shareholders, and access to judicial redress. Compared with its 1987 progenitor, the 2006 Bankruptcy Law envisions a significantly greater role for creditors and protection of their interests, and a lesser role for the state and protection of what was left of employees' iron rice bowls. The 2007 Property Law faced fierce opposition largely because critics thought it too thoroughly abandoned socialist principles to strengthen private parties' land use rights against government encroachment or expropriation.[1]

These developments—via mechanisms that are now well-entrenched and unlikely to face reversal—reflect, in part, the diffusion of legal norms from abroad. Chinese law reformers routinely study foreign laws and legal systems. Their access to such models has increased as more of them have acquired extensive foreign language skills, legal education and research experience abroad, and contact with foreign lawyers and legal scholars. Structured programs of foreign legal assistance have grown numerous and varied. Examples in the law-drafting area include those addressing torts, insolvency, intellectual property, and equities.[2]

Some receptions of external law have enjoyed strong and deep-rooted commitment. For a regime that has based its legitimacy on economic performance and its strategy for growth on deepening engagement with the outside world, the logic was simple and compelling: foreigners could provide the markets, capital, and know-how that China needed, but they required a legal framework with familiar content. Accordingly, economic laws that went furthest toward international standards early in the reform era addressed foreign economic contracts, foreign investment vehicles, and special foreign investment zones. Many of these laws became models for subsequent reforms to domestic economic laws. Almost all key foreign investment laws themselves have been revised to become more market- and investor-friendly and thus international in style. The earlier separation between economic laws for the domestic and foreign-linked sectors has faded, with convergence generally bringing the former into line with the latter. The 1999 Contract Law, the 2005 Company Law, and the unification of the Enterprise Income Taxation Law are examples of formal legal changes of this type.

China's entry into the World Trade Organization (WTO) at the end of 2001, legal reforms undertaken earlier to secure accession, and the phase-in of China's commitments since accession have created another channel for diffusion. Significant revisions to China's foreign trade, intellectual property, foreign investment, administrative, and other laws were among the thousands of legal changes in anticipation or implementation of WTO obligations. In key areas, including intellectual property, this specifically meant adopting legislation that tracked international standards.[3]

Foreign investors and, increasingly, PRC enterprises seeking capital or markets abroad favor harmonization between Chinese and foreign economic laws. They can, and do, use their now-considerable clout to support reforms that bring Chinese laws more fully into line with international standards and market principles. Major PRC firms and the state have become more interested in adopting such reforms for several reasons: to improve their access to foreign capital markets, to "go out" into the world as foreign investors, and to protect themselves (with more active state assistance) against unfair practices of other states and companies or foreign allegations of Chinese unfair trade practices.[4]

The elite politics behind adopting economic laws that conform to global standards has been about more than these economic issues. It also has been about establishing China as a "normal" state. Initially, this meant overcoming the autarchic isolationism and economic radicalism of the Mao years. A decade later, the task was to recover from the damage to China's image following the violent suppression of the Tiananmen Movement. During the late Jiang Zemin and Hu Jintao years, the agenda has been to be accepted as an emerging great power. A legal system that "lives up" to Western standards is a significant factor in China's current quest for international stature and respect, as it has been since the unhappy nineteenth-century origins of China's modern encounter with the West.

Those goals remain elusive today, however, because external assessments continue to be critical of Chinese behavior and suspicious of PRC motives. Even the tempered statement of then Deputy Secretary of State and now World Bank president Robert Zoellick, calling upon China to become a "responsible stakeholder" in the international system, spotlights the international concern about Beijing's perceived irresponsibility in international economic and security regimes.[5] Those worries extend to legal aspects of such international regimes, including China's compliance with WTO obligations and weapons proliferation laws.[6] Washington has also questioned China's motives in the attempted acquisition of Unocal by a subsidiary of the China National Offshore Oil Company and the role of Chinese oil companies in developing African resources, especially in Sudan. Such ostensibly and arguably business-driven and market-consistent moves have occasioned sharp charges of political motivation and threats of retaliation, as well as skepticism about China's commitments to applying its market-consistent laws to a key group of state-owned enterprises and to taking international human rights law seriously.[7]

Implementation and Institutions

China's reforms to economic law have gone so far that foreign complaints now focus less on the content of the laws and more on their implementation. The much-criticized "implementation gap" is in significant part the result of modeling laws on U.S. or other capitalist or common law systems so closely that they do not fit China's developmental and institutional circumstances. Two examples are the Contract Law, which gives a major role to "reasonableness" and "good faith" and permits "anticipatory breach," and the revised Company Law, which adopts provisions concerning fiduciary duties and shareholders' derivative suits that resemble Anglo-American models. The meaning of these terms in Chinese law is uncertain and potentially problematic given the absence of rich judicial precedent, experienced courts, expert and professional enforcement agencies, specialized bars, sophisticated investors and directors, and so on that shape laws' meanings and effects in states from which China borrows.[8]

Despite these and other serious implementation problems that stem from ambivalent commitment, limited resources, bureaucratic indiscipline or corruption, and the like, China's economic law-in-practice has been converging toward international standards, particularly in the more advanced regions—and in contrast to the benchmark of the early reform era, and, still more so, the Mao years. Progress in building a legal system adequate to foreign investors' demands has been sufficient to keep perceived shortcomings from deterring tens of billions of dollars in foreign investment annually. The bulk of this investment has come in the last decade-and-a-half as legal reforms have advanced. The lion's share flows to already-developed areas that have been losing their production cost advantages while gaining legal-institutional capacity. A growing portion has come as portfolio or small-stake strategic investments that generally provide weaker extralegal means for foreigners to protect their stakes.[9]

Shanghai, Beijing, and other first-tier cities have many large law firms with highly compensated and foreign-educated lawyers whom Chinese and foreign enterprises pay handsomely to assess and ensure the legality of their businesses and business dealings, and to represent them in litigation and arbitration. Though evidence and assessments are mixed, many lawyers and businesspeople perceive that having the law on their side—which increasingly has meant international-style economic law (and not merely connections [*guanxi*] or corruption)—is important for the transactions and the enterprises they create.[10]

Millions of Chinese citizens and enterprises each year seek redress in courts that have become more like courts in developed legal systems. Unlike judicial opinions of the early reform era—which often consisted of only a few lines, cited little law and much party policy, and seemed focused on educating an audience beyond the participants in the case about regime agendas—court decisions now tend to be more elaborate, cite formal sources of law and analyze them carefully, and address only the parties and issues formally before the court. The judges who staff these courts, as well as the lawyers who practice before them, are trained in universities that have become more like those—or are those—of the West, Japan, Hong Kong, and the like. Judges in top-tier cities now almost uniformly have undergraduate degrees. In higher courts, many have postgraduate law degrees.[11]

Trends in other means of handling economic disputes, including arbitration and mediation, have been broadly similar. Although official mandates and practice have been mixed, reform era China has developed arbitration and mediation laws and institutions that are more formal and closer to international models. Laws and policy directives and, on some accounts at least, behavior have moved toward handling disputes according to law and legal rights (ones that increasingly resemble their foreign counterparts) rather than "fairness" or "feeling."[12]

"Political" Law

Although China's openness to external influence has been less extensive in noneconomic areas of law, it is emerging there, too, with potential for further growth. The reform era turn to law has been partly an act of borrowing political law. The Deng legalization project, the Jiang call to "rule the country by law" and "build a socialist rule-of-law country," and the continuation of such ideology under Hu reflect a vision of the role of law in a developing, stable state that owes much to the observed successes of neighboring East Asian "tigers" (in versions that predate democratization in Taiwan and Korea). The reform era rehabilitation of traditional Chinese culture, the Jiang flirtation with "Asian values" in international human rights law, and the Hu pursuit of a "harmonious society" and support for "Confucius Institutes" abroad suggest further affinities for an East Asian model in politics and law.

External influence has also flowed from more liberal sources. A striking example is the norms and, increasingly, the institutions of international human rights law. China acceded to the UN Convention against Torture in 1988; accepted the idea of universal human rights in the early 1990s; signed and ratified the International Covenant on Economic, Social and Cultural Rights; signed and pledged to ratify the International Covenant on Civil and Political Rights; made or promised to make conforming changes to criminal and other laws; and became an inaugural member of the UN Human Rights Council (an entity that has been, however, only a mixed blessing for human rights).[13]

On these fronts and in other public law areas, the impetus to international legal conformity has been, in part, a reflection of China's broader desire to win acceptance as a normal state and great power. In the human rights and public law context, this has meant trying to overcome the legacies of "rejectionism" from the Mao years, Tiananmen, and the fallout of the regime's more recent handling of Falun Gong, house churches, and worker and peasant protesters and their advocates. It also surely reflects recognition that China's abnormal

(and international norm-nonconforming) alegality of the late Mao era was part
of China's disastrous internal politics that needed to be laid to rest.

More concretely, officially welcomed or tolerated foreign aid projects, offering advice rooted in foreign models, have reached areas of "political" law. Examples include a long-running project on administrative procedure law that continued into the 2000s, technical assistance for legislation-drafting during the
1990s, and support for and monitoring of the implementation of village election laws since the late 1980s.[14]

Influential reformist Chinese intellectuals offer prescriptions for further public or political law reform that clearly, and sometimes explicitly, bear the imprint
of foreign, including U.S., models. Examples include proposals for a freedom of
information act, a revamping of the courts to adopt broadly Western-style
notions of judicial independence and judicial review or aspects of the American
federal court of appeals structure (with its centrally funded budget and multi-
state jurisdictions), and constitutional principles such as more robust notions of
individual rights and federalism.[15]

Guardians and the Vanguard:
Law, the Party-State, and Autonomous Legality

A major objective of China's legal development project during the reform era has
been to use law to control and constrain agents of the party and state. This
agenda does not show a deep commitment to the rule of law. It may reflect nothing more than a sense of law's usefulness in pursuing the regime's self-interest in a
more effective, disciplined, and legitimate party and state apparatus. That does
not mean that this portion of the law reform project is insignificant. Indeed, law
often fares best when proponents see it as a means, not as an end in itself.

Law as a Check on Party-State Behavior

China's leaders during the reform era have come to appreciate that law can help
address corruption, *guanxi*, parochialism (including local protectionism),
incompetence, excessive rent seeking, the failure to restrain extreme abuses by
those wielding governmental power, and the failure to avoid, discern, and correct badly crafted or badly executed policies—all of which can imperil economic
development, fuel social unrest, and undermine political order. Laws and legal
institutions have emerged as means to provide greater discipline, transparency,
and accountability in governance, so as to sustain rapid growth and avoid disorder among the discontented. (Such disorder is a growing regime concern, given
official reports that put the annual number of "incidents" at more than
80,000).[16]

Administrative law has been the most prominent development here. Under the Administrative Litigation Law, courts handle tens of thousands of suits each year challenging state decisions that affect individual citizens and enterprises concerning matters such as land use, business licenses, fines, environmental harms, abuse by law enforcement authorities, and so on.[17] The Administrative Reconsideration Law provides a formal structure to press a government office (and its superiors) to reverse its decision. The State Compensation Law provides a legal framework for citizens to seek damages when harmed by some unlawful government actions.

Criminal law and administrative punishments—imposed on government or party functionaries and sometimes quite severe (including the death penalty)—are another part of this public law repertoire. Authorities have deployed these legal weapons repeatedly during the reform era, most aggressively in anticorruption drives that began under Deng, accelerated under Jiang, and continued under Hu. A prominent recent example is the ouster of Shanghai Party boss Chen Liangyu on corruption charges before the Seventeenth Party Congress.

Much of what law can do to check problematic official behavior in China lies beyond the conventional enforcement of public law. For example, substantive legal norms can be invoked somewhat informally outside of judicial or prosecutorial contexts. Key mechanisms include "letters and visits" and less established forms of entreaties to party and state authorities. Through such means, citizens often invoke laws and legal norms in beseeching higher-level authorities to use their discretion to intervene or impose discipline on lower-level functionaries who flout laws.

The "public law" function here includes much that lawyers in developed market economies ordinarily regard as private or economic law. In reform era China, economic litigation and dispute resolution in the shadow of the law have been tolerated or encouraged as means to address market-subverting and citizen-angering acts by party and state functionaries or others acting with their backing. In the early reform years, contract suits in the countryside often revolved around local cadres' attempts to expropriate contract-based rights from peasants who had prospered from collective assets they had leased, or cadre self-dealing in which the politically well-connected contracted valuable assets at low prices.[18]

During the Hu years, economic law and administrative law remedies have addressed a different form of party-state-linked expropriation of contractual land-use rights. Contract law, constitutional amendments enhancing private property rights and concerning takings for public use, directives on compensation for expropriation and court jurisdiction to hear land disputes, and the 2007 Property Law all address problems of collaboration between local governments and developers to strip peasants of land rights without fair compensation.

Broadly parallel problems and responses have arisen in the cities, where rapid redevelopment—and related real estate speculation—have brought similar displacements. A handful of successful cases have received extensive attention, including a joint action lawsuit victory by dispossessed Zhejiang peasants and Chongqing authorities' negotiations to provide increased compensation to the holdout owners of the mediagenic *dingzi hu*—the nail house—that perched on a small, soaring plateau in the middle of a massive construction site.[19]

In the urban industrial sector, litigation and disputes over contracts, particularly during the early reform era, often involved breaches attributable to official misbehavior, as in the paradigmatic cases of a state-owned or collective enterprise's governmental "owner" extorting revenues or issuing orders that prevented an enterprise from fulfilling its obligations, or an enterprise's refusal to perform because it expected political intervention to prevent the court from issuing or enforcing an adverse judgment.[20] Later years added other official malfeasance-linked cases to the mix. For example, township or county governments were sometimes found liable for the obligations of sham enterprises—or "briefcase" companies—that they had put into business but never properly funded.

More recently, China's increasingly "corporatized" enterprises have generated new legal issues and new types of cases in which state-linked misbehavior lies behind economic disputes. For example, the problems of minority shareholder rights addressed by reforms to the Company Law and the Securities Law—through shareholder suits and other means—often stem from abuse by dominant state or state-linked shareholders who combine the opportunism ordinarily expected of unrestrained controlling shareholders and the more peculiarly Chinese (or transitional economy) pursuit of agendas that do not respond to material incentives, much less seek to maximize share values.[21]

Assessing "Supply"

Law clearly has not fulfilled its promise to check abuses of power, unlawful actions, and reform-undermining behavior in the party-state. But just how far practice has fallen short of promise is difficult to assess. A few examples suggest a pattern. In administrative litigation lawsuits, plaintiffs prevail 20 to 40 percent of the time—a respectable to high rate by international standards. But the rate's significance is uncertain given the difficulties of controlling for cross-national differences in base rates of inappropriate state action and the proportion of claims that are meritorious. Some surveys and studies, especially those focusing on Shanghai, indicate a relatively high level of trust in the administrative litigation system's fairness and a belief that having legal right and skill on one's side is important. Other accounts, especially those focusing on poorer or rural areas, often paint a darker picture, in which local authorities wield influence over unskilled or pliable courts, use coercion to deter potential litigants, and retaliate against victorious ones. Moreover, Chinese administrative law does not permit challenges to party actions, or laws, regulations, or many other matters that are not "concrete administrative acts."[22]

Criminal and formal administrative penalties are infrequently used against officials. They reach only a few percent of identified instances of corruption and often are employed selectively and politically. Still, they likely yield some deterrent effect, given the potential severity of sanctions, the uncertainty about when anticorruption campaigns or shifting factional politics may make a particular official a target, and the attraction of using such sanctions to slake public anger over official abuses.

The story for civil and economic law is similar. As noted earlier, legal and other mechanisms for protecting economic rights have worked well enough to permit or sustain rapid growth and large-scale foreign investment. As discussed in the next section, they also have underpinned comparatively strong "rule-of-law" rankings for reform era China. The courts are satisfactory enough that parties turn to them in more than 4 million civil cases annually. International and domestic arbitration commissions have sizable case loads as well. Rates for enforcement of judgments are difficult to acquire or assess (not least because of their feedback effect on plaintiffs' willingness to sue), but some analyses suggest they may be similar to American levels.[23]

Still, China's courts and less formal dispute resolution mechanisms have received severe, pervasive, and partly justified criticism for their delivery of justice in economic cases. The complaints are strikingly "statist," focusing on structural bias toward, or targeted influence on court decisions by, party or state actors; party or state control of, or intervention in, fully or partly state-owned enterprises that are parties to disputes; and local protectionism, produced by entanglement among state-linked firms that are important to the local economy, local officials whose prospects depend on their area's economic health, and courts that depend on local governments for funding and whose judges are beholden to the local party for appointment.[24]

The indictment is thick with accounts of such phenomena, as well as the more conventional evils of bribery or incompetence of judges (which also are problems in the state and its agents), or judicial or governmental deference to, or bias toward, independently powerful economic actors. While these factors also figure prominently, in the Chinese context they, too, involve a strong party-state element, given the close personal and structural links and murky entwining between the party and state, on one hand, and managers of large firms and the now formidable cohort of entrepreneurs, on the other.[25] Another major critique focuses on "state" factors as well. Critics generally do not see China as an incapable state on a par with many developing or post-socialist countries. They argue, rather, that China could more effectively handle the problems in its legal system—and the political, economic, and social problems the legal system fails to address—if it tried harder.

Increasing "Demand" (and "Supply")?

Several broadly related phenomena—some of them products of the first waves of reform—suggest potent pressures or fertile soil among key constituencies for increasing demand for, and supply of, legality. China's small but rapidly expanding and increasingly influential contingents of judges and lawyers have institutional and professional interests and intellectual and normative preferences that support stronger and more autonomous courts and a more central role for law and lawyers in China's economy and polity. Agendas favoring these ends surface regularly in informal comments from attorneys, jurists, and others, as well as in more formal media such as the Supreme People's Court's annual work reports to the National People's Congress (NPC), the court's "five-year plans," and the writings of influential legal scholars.

These often propose specific reforms, for example, that career advancement for judges should depend more on performance evaluations by their superiors and less on the support of local party and state functionaries; that the control of court budgets should be moved from provincial or local authorities to the central government; multiprovince appellate courts should be established to undercut provincial party and state influence; burdensome regulation and intrusive state oversight of law firms should be reduced; and legal aid, pro bono work, and other "access to justice" initiatives should be expanded to make the legal system more effective for ordinary citizens.[26] Notably, the legally trained have begun to enter the upper reaches of the party-state elite, and reformist legal intellectuals have gained access both as well-connected informal counselors to some top leaders and as participants in relatively regular channels for providing advice to the leadership.[27] These trends suggest rising influence for China's legal elites.

More heterodox segments of China's legal cohort have emerged as striking and sometimes strident sources of pressure for greater legality. Perhaps most remarkable are the bold and innovative lawyers associated with the *weiquan* (rights protection) movement who seek enforcement of civil and other rights that are on the books and who link that effort to further advancement of government under law.

Broader social constituencies are also showing significant (and likely increasing) support and demand for law and the legal system. Although difficult to measure, popular "rights consciousness" is widely believed to have been rising. Official encouragement or acquiescence may have helped. With the regime touting legality and embracing law for many years, social expectations of greater legality have increased—as indicated by the millions of litigants and claimants who pursue suits, arbitration, and mediation each year; the millions more who invoke legal norms through letters and visits and other informal approaches to party and state organs; and the modestly encouraging rates of success and accounts of parties' beliefs that processes are reasonably efficacious and amenable to legal argument. Also contributing to growing popular rights consciousness may be the efforts of *weiquan* and other public interest lawyers, as well as the central roles that ideas of legal rights and legal accountability have played in gripping public controversies in recent years, including the Sun Zhigang case, the Chongqing nail-house incident, and controversies over rural land seizures.

Among somewhat more elite social strata, voices from the past have joined the chorus calling for greater legality. Strikingly, 2,000 of those—mostly intellectuals—who had been branded as "Rightists" in 1957 wrote an open letter calling on the Seventeenth Party Congress to declare the Anti-Rightist Campaign unconstitutional and to recognize the still unmet need it revealed for more institutionalized rule-of-law procedures.[28] Long-term trends from *guanxi* toward law in business decisionmaking are another important, if limited and disputed, example of growth in legal orientation and consciousness.[29] If venerable social science theories and impressionistic evidence from contemporary urban China hold up, rising social and economic status accompanying entry into China's burgeoning middle class portends a growing demand for the legal protection of rights.

China's top political elite may find it too costly not to acquiesce in greater roles for law and the rule of law, even where this exceeds their agenda or comfort level. "Legality" is a lumpy good with somewhat opaque characteristics. Establishing the level and forms of legality that the leadership's somewhat unstable and fragmented strategy envisions may mean also having to satisfy unwelcome demands for more (or having to acquiesce in "oversupply").

Mast binding may have worked. After so many years of endorsing law (including at the Seventeenth Party Congress[30]), attempts to resist or roll back legal developments or commitments may now pose too much risk of undermining confidence in the regime's broader and perhaps indispensable commitment to legality and, in turn, law's contribution to development and stability.

The functional logic of the reform era agenda may make "adequate" legality a rising target. Sustaining economic growth may require "more developed" laws and legal institutions as the relatively easy gains of moving from plan toward market are exhausted, the economy becomes more complex, economic integration with the outside world deepens, and China's cost advantage dissipates. This imperative may draw further strength from a perceived need to redress the threat that "bureaucratic capitalism" and the fusion of political and economic power may pose to continued growth.[31] Maintaining social order and stability has been a growing concern that may require stronger legal controls on state behavior and, increasingly, on private actions (including market-responsive or market-driven behavior), especially where they yield concentrations of wealth and power.

Recently, the leadership has turned to law (or discussions of using law) to address additional challenges, alongside the familiar ones of supporting a market economy and political stability. Examples of new or newly emphasized issues include SARS and other public health threats, mistreatment of internal migrants, disregard for workers' rights in private and foreign-invested firms, and the need to protect Chinese industry from foreign competition and peasants from unlawful land seizures.

Finally, a more supportive orientation toward law may be growing among China's top elites during the Hu years because of changes in the composition of those elites and their advisers. The legal thinkers who have gained unprecedented access to current senior leaders and the unprecedentedly large group of lawyers who have joined the rising cohort of leaders can be expected to hold relatively sympathetic and sophisticated views of law.

Legalization without—or against—Democratization

The "legalization" project in China is not meant to advance, and has not been advancing, democracy, at least in the relatively narrow but mainstream sense of institutionalized processes that allow citizens meaningfully to choose among diverse candidates for positions that wield ultimate governmental power and, in so doing, alter the way in which or ends to which that power is wielded.[32] Rather, a key assumption during the reform era has been that law and (this type of) democracy can be disjoined. Law and legal processes have been relied upon to provide substitutes for democracy and to dampen or delay demand for democratization. From this perspective, the contemporary Chinese version of expanded but still-limited legality and constrained public participation may be functional.

Legality and Democracy

The operative democratic content of Chinese law remains thin. Democratic elements in the Chinese constitution can perhaps be reconciled with even a relatively narrow or demanding notion of democracy, but they are among the constitutional provisions that are taken least seriously. The Law on Legislation, rules governing administrative rulemaking, and their implementation have brought greater opportunities for public input into legislative and regulatory processes, but these remain modest in reality and even in theory are a far cry from democratic control. Notably, orthodox commentary and official agendas for the Seventeenth Party Congress assigned law little role in implementing the goals of opening party and government affairs to the public and strengthening public supervision over administration.[33]

The major law with the most substantive democratic content—the law governing village elections—has been unevenly implemented, often fails to live up to hopes for open and contested elections, and reaches only the most local of posts.[34] The electoral law for local people's congresses is still weaker as an instrument of democracy, as are procedures for the indirect selection of higher-level people's congresses. The imperfectly implemented village elections law and the elections held thereunder allow very bounded participation, monitor potentially explosive peasant discontent, and strengthen the capacity of the regime. The elections serve these functions by sometimes weeding out the most ineffective and despised agents of the regime and by recruiting new cadres who can command popular support as well as their superiors' confidence.[35] These gains, however, are pursued while moving very slowly, if at all, toward genuinely contested elections for higher-level government offices.[36] Recent favorable discussions of democracy, including electoral democracy, from Wen Jiabao, Hu Jintao, other leaders, and prominent policy intellectuals remain vague, long-term, or ambivalent projects and sometimes suggest little change from existing approaches. More concrete or near-term discussions more often focus on intraparty democratization and related reforms, including modest extensions of pluralism at elite levels and initial steps to expand contests at the party's grass roots.[37] Law plays only a peripheral role in such plans, not going much beyond exhortations to party members and state officers to follow the law and boilerplate assertions that the rule of law ranks alongside leadership by the party and socialist democracy as guiding principles.[38]

Similarly, hearings and other permitted public input on proposed regulations and legislation provide party and state actors with information about the preferences and complaints of affected constituencies. This may enhance the receiving institution's leverage in intraregime wrangling over power or policy, especially given the emphasis now placed on empirical policymaking or "scientific" concepts of development and the rhetorical embrace of democracy or the emphasis on a "harmonious society." The constrained format may limit these upsides, but that is the obverse of avoiding such mechanisms' potential for encouraging sustained, organized, autonomous, and institutionalized political participation.

Administrative litigation has kindred authoritarian virtues. It promises to provide useful redress and monitoring in a way that "atomizes" or "individuates" citizen complaints and thus does not produce much collective action or create harbingers of participatory democracy. The regime's continuing aversion to full-fledged class actions and impact litigation reflects and underscores this point. Much the same can be said about the continued official preference for informal "letters and visits" (which avoid judicial articulation of legal rights and which, archetypically, assert highly particularistic grievances) and recently imposed restrictions that reflect the leadership's chronic concern about large groups using the petitioning process and litigation in politically charged contexts.[39] Law's authoritarianism-supporting roles are also evident in the ongoing use of media regulations and criminal laws to silence critical voices that might galvanize and mobilize public opinion, and in the top elite's conception of government entities' organic laws and rules of procedure as means primarily of strengthening—not constraining—the state.[40]

It is hardly eccentric to characterize China as having made significant progress in developing laws and legal institutions over the past three decades without much movement toward democracy.[41] This comports with China's place in prominent cross-national measures. China ranks at the 40.6th percentile in the World Bank ratings of the rule of law but only at the 17th percentile in the Economist Intelligence Unit's democracy index, 6.3rd percentile in the World Bank's "voice and accountability" metric, and a lowly −7 in Polity's −10 to +10 scale for democracy. In another survey, China's democracy ranking of 126th lagged far behind its ranking of 57th for corruption (which may only partly reflect rule of law issues, as the gap between China's 30.5th percentile ranking in the World Bank "control of corruption" measure and its higher rule-of-law ranking suggests).[42]

This pattern does not make China such an aberration that it casts doubt on the relatively near-term viability of the regime's approach. The connection between legality and democracy was also weak among the ostensibly similar East Asian countries during their long transitional phases, and even beyond: Japan from the Meiji Restoration to the Occupation Constitution, Taiwan under Kuomintang dictatorship, Korea during the same period, Singapore under People's Action Party hegemony, and Hong Kong under British rule were all undemocratic, though not easily characterized as similar in terms of ordinary notions of the rule of law. Today, those five entities exhibit very different levels of democracy despite their similarly high rule-of-law rankings.[43]

Legality, Constitutionalism, and Democracy under Hu Jintao

The Hu era has brought new emphasis on the constitution, but this does not imply a rising legality that has qualitatively greater democratic implications. In one of his first major speeches as China's top leader, delivered at a celebration of the current constitution's twentieth anniversary, Hu declared the constitution the country's "fundamental" law, to be safeguarded and implemented by all state and private entities. The constitution's "inviolability" was the object of an early Hu era Politburo study session.[44] The period following the Sixteenth Party Congress has seen the most significant amendments since the 1982 constitution was adopted. References to the importance of upholding and implementing the constitution occur throughout Hu's Seventeenth Party Congress report.

Still, this new emphasis on the constitution has not greatly advanced legal development, much less its possibly democracy-promoting effects. Rhetorical embraces do not necessarily precipitate—and recently have not precipitated—major change in its operational content. Under Hu, as throughout the reform era, legal change has occurred mostly below or outside the constitution. The 1982 constitution did depart sharply from its 1975 Gang of Four or Cultural Revolution predecessor, as well as from the short-lived transitional constitution adopted in 1978. But, especially in comparison with striking subconstitutional legal developments, the current charter was largely a product of restoration, returning to pre–Cultural Revolution roots. Amendments since 1982 have addressed issues of political and policy import, such as foreign and private property rights, market economics, the political acceptability of entrepreneurs, and human rights. But these are mostly nonstructural and nonfundamental alterations or broad policy exhortations, and they do not address the charter's fallow democratic provisions.

More to the point, the constitution has had little legal and political traction. The long-standing PRC orthodoxy that constitutional provisions generally are not directly operative retains considerable force. The debate that raged into 2007 over the Property Law in part reflected this perspective, largely accepting that the property rights provision previously added to the constitution meant little until the NPC adopted a statute. Constitutional review and even review of regulations or local legislation for conformity with the constitution or national laws remains in the hands of the legislature, not the courts, and lies largely dormant. Reformist legal scholars had hoped that the Sun Zhigang case would provide an occasion for the NPC's Standing Committee to use this power to address abuses in the system of "custody and repatriation" of internal migrants that resulted in Sun's death in 2003, but those aspirations were disappointed when more ordinary and discretionary bureaucratic means were used to revise the rules.[45] Henan judge Li Huijian unsuccessfully tested the limits of judicial review in 2003 when she tried to reject a local law because it did not conform to national law—a move that would have vindicated the constitutional principle of the supremacy of national laws. Since the early 2000s, courts have occasionally invoked constitutional provisions, typically concerning individual rights, to accord relief to individual claimants or to fill interstices of statutes or regulations. Such sprouts of constitutionalism have remained fragile and sparse, however.[46]

Senior judicial and well-connected intellectual proponents of constitutionalism continue to lament its limitations. According to Supreme Court president Xiao Yang, the current situation is one in which a "reform constitution" has not yet reached the level of "constitutionalism." Prominent theorist Yu Keping, widely regarded as an important adviser to Hu, has expressed concern that constitutionalism is being subordinated to other political values. More heterodox intellectuals such as Cao Siyuan are a good deal harsher in their assessment of the weakness of constitutionalism under Hu and his predecessors.[47]

Moreover, much of what most nearly approximates constitutionalism under Hu (as in preceding periods) has occurred apart from the written constitution and formal legal structures. While its extent and durability are debatable, this informal constitutionalism has emerged largely in the form of implicit or immanent rules of the political game among top elites and in their dealings with constituencies among, or mediated by, party and state organs.[48] Such informal constitutionalism has uncertain or contradictory implications for making the formal constitution more functional (and for moving toward democracy).

Populism and Legalization under Hu Jintao

More than constitutionalism, "populism" has been the ideological hallmark of the Hu years. This populism has a complex or ambivalent relationship to democracy. It also has created friction with the reform era project of legalization, including incipient constitutionalism. The populist turn thus does not promise enhancement of whatever positive implications legalization has for democratization.

Under Hu, populism has meant a greater focus on the needs of ordinary Chinese, including those who have not fared so well in the reform era's long boom (such as rural-to-urban migrants, dispossessed peasants, tax-and-fee-burdened farmers, displaced factory workers, coal miners, and so on) and other vulnerable groups (AIDS victims and others).[49] Placing greater emphasis on these people and seeking a "harmonious" society are not, however, democratic moves in the relatively narrow or demanding sense used here. Nor do they promote constitutionalism. They reflect discretionary authoritarian decisions to represent popular interests, not institutionalized and obligatory responses to popular preferences. He Weifang, a leading intellectual advocate of constitutionalism and the rule of law, tellingly decries the Hu-Wen leadership's populism and endorsement of letters and visits as a traditional Chinese-style reliance on a wise and benevolent emperor to dispense justice as a matter of grace and something therefore at odds with the development of rule by law and constitutionalized rights.[50]

Hu's populism encourages "pushback" against perceived excesses of "market fundamentalism" and the costs of WTO compliance and other aspects of opening to the outside world (which critics see as having "sold China"—cheaply—to foreigners).[51] This has produced tensions with the project of legalization, given the particular content of China's laws in the mid-2000s. Simply, by the time the populist agenda ascended, the law on the books (including that in the constitution and WTO-related and other external legal obligations, as well as many other reform laws) deeply reflected the Jiang ethos of relatively unbridled capitalism and deep international integration.

In principle, a populist ideological readjustment need not be at odds with a continuing or deepening emphasis on law, including the constitution. In theory, it is feasible in China's system of legislative supremacy, party-dominated legislature, and largely coequal status of domestic statutes and properly received international law simply to change the laws' content. The substantive conflict also is less sharp than it might seem, given the residua of statism and discretion in PRC economic legislation and tolerance for illiberalism in international economic legal rules and states' legal and diplomatic practices. Adopting more populist content is not easy in practice, however. The processes of constitutional reform, legislation, and implementation of international obligations are ponderous and inertial. Many lawmaking processes and agendas continue pre-Hu trends, and many entrenched constituencies at home and abroad are influential and prone to resist populist reorientations.

Legalization and Democracy in the Later Hu Era and Beyond

Hu's populism and related developments are unlikely to stall, much less reverse, China's long march toward greater conformity to international legal norms and stronger laws and legal institutions, nor are they likely to blunt growing pressures for greater legalization. They are no more likely to prompt basic rethinking by the leadership of the strategy of nondemocratization.

After the Seventeenth Party Congress, choices about legal development may become more difficult and contested. Whereas debates under Deng and Jiang were often about how fast to move toward international norms and a more robust legal order, the issues under Hu increasingly may be about whether to move farther in those directions now that China has already traveled so far down that path.

This is not to say that China will not become democratic, or that the reform era's accomplishments and trends in legal development, or even the turns to constitutionalism and populism, will not expand and contribute to democratization in the longer run. Significant forces and plausible assessments point in that direction, but not powerfully in the near term.

International norms, external pressure, and foreign expectations that have helped advance legalization also contain pro-democracy elements. These include citizen participation in governance and perhaps a "democratic entitlement" as international human rights, democracy-promotion agendas in foreign policies of other states (particularly the United States), and the prospects raised by the post–cold war resurgence and the broader "third wave" of democratization.[52] Still, democracy remains much weaker than civil liberties as a global human rights imperative. And civil liberties enjoy notably weak legal protection in China. The United States and others generally have been less zealous, or at least less effective, in promoting democracy than in pressing legality, not least because democratization often encounters sharper host regime resistance (as it has in China), particularly because it is less easily packaged as merely a technical, politically neutral, and development-sustaining objective.[53] High-level Chinese sources pointedly reject the idea that China will democratize to "cater to the tastes" of other countries.[54] Any seeming ineluctability of near-term global democratization has been undercut by the post–third wave "democratic recession."[55]

China's "legalization" in the reform era and the robust economic development and nascent political accountability that it has promoted may produce powerful unintended consequences in fostering democracy or demands for it. In the long run and at the extremes, democracy remains strongly positively correlated with high levels of legality and economic development. The pattern broadly holds for the five exemplars of the East Asian model—the apparent inspiration for much of China's reform strategy. Three of these have become democratic. The city-states of Hong Kong and Singapore may be special cases because of their small size, and they arguably are incipiently democratic. Factors often thought to account for the correlation—growing social and elite demands, expectations, and constituencies for legal rights and legal rules—have been on apparently strongly upward trajectories in China and were notably on display at the time of the Seventeenth Party Congress.[56] Nonetheless, these are long-term trends from very low baselines. Moreover, relatively full-fledged electoral democracy for the foreseeable future raises prospects—such as illiberal democracy, or social disorder, or radically redistributionist or xenophobic policies—that would not be welcomed by emergent urban middle classes, liberal-reformist intellectuals, or political elites.[57]

The Chinese leadership's immanent strategy might become more tolerant or supportive of democracy, perhaps in response to such influences from abroad and pressures from within. And law may play a substantial role in any such development. Some elite advisers, such as Yu Keping, see building the rule of law as a prerequisite to the development of democracy. Premier Wen Jiabao recently declared that democracy ultimately will be appropriate for China. The constitutionalist and populist strands in Hu era orthodoxy are in some respects pro-democratic, at least in their openness to a government that operates under legal constraints and is more responsive to the people. Still, Wen's notion remains unclearly articulated, redolent of nonelectoral and uninstitutionalized concepts of democracy, and compatible with China's remaining distinctively "socialist" for a very long time, probably for decades.[58] Even Yu envisions a relatively long transitional period of "incremental" democracy. Others—including Hu, official sources, and prominent political thinkers—stress that China's model of democracy will be distinctive and differ from the West's.[59] Relatively pro-democracy and robust rule of law advocates also must contend with other influential law and policy intellectuals such as Pan Wei, who rejects democracy while endorsing a "consultative" rule of law.[60]

Any strategic embrace of democracy is likely to remain more tepid than the leadership's still-ambivalent support for the still-far-from-completely-realized agenda for legal development. Absent an exogenous shock, the remainder of the Hu Jintao years offer little prospect for a fundamental shift from the long-running reform era strategy of significant legalization without significant democratization.

Notes

1. See, for example, Jiang Ping, "Drafting the Uniform Contract Law in China," *Columbia Journal of Asian Law* 10 (Spring 1996): 245–58; Wang Liming and Xu Chuanxi, "Fundamental Principles of China's Contract Law," *Columbia Journal of Asian Law* 13 (Spring 1999): 1–34; Mo Zhang, "Freedom of Contract with Chinese Legal Characteristics," *Temple International and Comparative Law Journal* 14 (Fall 2000): 237–62; Robert C. Art and Minkang Gu, "China Incorporated: The First Corporation Law of the People's Republic of China," *Yale Law Journal of International Law* 20 (Summer 1995): 273–308; Craig Anderson and Bingna Guo, "Corporate Governance under the New Company Law," *China Law and Practice* 20 (April 2006): 17–24; Charles Booth, "Drafting Bankruptcy Laws in Socialist Market Economies: Recent Developments in China and Vietnam," *Columbia Journal of Asian Law* 18 (Fall 2004): 93–147; E. J. Chua, "China's New Bankruptcy Law: A Legislative Innovation," *China Law and Practice* 20 (October 2006): 17–20; Huen Wong and Adam Arkel, "China's New Property Law: Practical Issues," *China Law and Practice* 21 (June 2007); Patrick A. Randolph Jr., "The New Chinese Property Law," *Probate and Property* Magazine, September/October 2007, pp. 14–20.

2. See Jacques deLisle, "Lex Americana?" *University of Pennsylvania Journal of International Economic Law* 20 (Summer 1999): 179–308; Katharina Pistor, Daniel Berkowitz, and Jean-François Richard, "The Transplant Effect," *American Journal of Comparative Law* 51 (Winter

2003): 163–203. See also the sources cited in note 1, which include discussions of the influence of foreign models on specific legislation.

3. See in general Nicholas R. Lardy, *Integrating China into the World Economy* (Brookings, 2002), chaps. 1–3; Kong Qingjiang, *China and the World Trade Organization: A Legal Perspective* (Singapore: World Scientific, 2002); Supachai Panitchpakdi and Mark L. Clifford, *China and the WTO: Changing China, Changing World Trade* (Hoboken, N.J.: John Wiley, 2002), chaps. 3, 5.

4. Margaret M. Pearson, *China's New Business Elite: The Political Consequences of Economic Reform* (University of California Press, 1997); Scott Kennedy, *The Business of Lobbying in China* (Harvard University Press, 2005); Wang Heng, "Chinese Views on Modern Marco Polos: New Foreign Trade Amendments after WTO Accession," *Cornell International Law Journal* 39 (2006): 329–69.

5. Robert Zoellick, "Whither China: From Membership to Responsibility?" (usinfo.state.gov/eap/Archive/2005/Sep/22-290478.html [September 21, 2005]); Thomas L. Friedman, "The Axis of Order?" *International Herald Tribune*, January 14, 2006, p. 7; Caroline Daniel, "Bush Trip Designed to Demonstrate Asia High on Washington's Agenda," *Financial Times*, November 14, 2005, p. 7; Catherine Armitage, "Chinese Urged to Allay U.S. Anxiety," *Australian*, September 23, 2005, p. 11.

6. "USCBC Analysis of China's WTO Compliance" (Washington: U.S. China Business Council, 2007) (www.uschina.org/public/wto/); *Report to Congress on China's WTO Compliance* (Washington: U.S Trade Representative, 2004); Robert Shuey and Shirley Kan, "China Missile and Nuclear Proliferation: Issues for Congress" (Washington: Congressional Research Service, 1995) (www.fas.org/spp/starwars/crs/92-056-1.htm); "China Weapons Proliferation Threat a Major U.S. Concern" (Washington: Department of State, 2005) (http://usinfo.state.gov/eap/Archive/2005/May/02-538299.html).

7. Joseph Kahn, "A Deft Balance in Orchestrating China's Oil Offer," *New York Times*, July 6, 2005, p. A1; Keith Bradsher, "China Retreats Now, but It Will Be Back," *New York Times*, August 3, 2005, p. C1; Jacques deLisle, "Into Africa: China's Quest for Resources and Influence" (www.fpri.org/enotes/200702.delisle.intoafricachinasquest.html [February 2007]).

8. Jacques deLisle, "Traps, Gaps and Law: Prospects and Challenges for China's Reforms," in *Is China Trapped in Transition? Implications for Future Reforms* (Oxford, U.K.: Oxford Foundation for Law, Justice and Society, 2007); Anderson and Guo, "Corporate Governance"; John H. Matheson, "Convergence, Culture and Contract Law in China," *Minnesota Journal of International Law* 15 (Summer 2006): 329–82.

9. See, for example, U.S. Department of State, "2007 Investment Climate Statement—China" (www.state.gov/e/eeb/ifd/2007/82189.htm); International Financial Services, London, "External Finance for Emerging Markets" (www.ifsl.org.uk/pdf_handler.cfm?file=External_finance_EM_2007&CFID=798994&CFToken=65046836).

10. On the uneven distribution of legal resources and its economic consequences, see "China's Lawyers Failing to Provide Nationwide Service," Xinhua News Agency, July 10, 2006; Cui Yuqing, "China Has a Strong Demand for Lawyers," *China Economic Net*, October 11, 2005; World Bank, *China—Governance, Investment Climate and Harmonious Society: Competitiveness Enhancements in 120 Cities in China* (Washington, October 2006); on the roles of law and *guanxi*, see Doug Guthrie, *Dragon in a Three-Piece Suit: The Emergence of Capitalism in China* (Princeton University Press, 1999); but compare David L. Wank, *Commodifying Communism: Business, Trust, and Politics in a Chinese City* (Cambridge University Press, 1999).

11. See "Zhongguo faguan jianchaguan zhengtisuzhi tigao faguan benke bili guoban" (The overall quality of China's judges and prosecutors has been raised, with more than half holding bachelor's degrees), *Zhongguo xinwen wang* (China News Network), July 17, 2005; Veron Mei-Ying Hung, *Judicial Reform in China: Lessons from Shanghai* (Washington: Carnegie Endowment for International Peace, 2005); Randall Peerenboom, *China's Long March toward the Rule of Law* (Cambridge University Press, 2002), pp. 290ff.; Minxin Pei, *China's Trapped Transition: The Limits of Developmental Autocracy* (Harvard University Press, 2006), pp. 67–69; see also Stanley Lubman, *Bird in a Cage: China's Post-Mao Legal Reforms* (Stanford University Press, 2000), chap. 9.

12. Lucie Cheng and Arthur Rosett, "Contract with a Chinese Face: Socially Embedded Factors in the Transition from Hierarchy to Market, 1978–1989," *Journal of Chinese Law* 5 (Fall 1991): 143–244; Lester Ross, "The Changing Profile of Dispute Resolution in Rural China," *Stanford Journal of International Law* 26 (Fall 1989): 15–66; Wang Sheng Chang, "Resolving Disputes through Conciliation and Arbitration in Mainland China" (Washington: Association of Trial Lawyers of America, 2000); Jun Ge, "Mediation, Arbitration and Litigation: Dispute Resolution in the People's Republic of China," *UCLA Pacific Basin Law Journal* 15 (Fall 1996): 122–37; see also Lubman, *Bird in a Cage*, chap. 8; Benedict Sheehy, "Fundamentally Conflicting Views of the Rule of Law in China and the West and Implications for Commercial Disputes," *Northwestern Journal of International Law and Business* 26 (Winter 2006): 225–66.

13. On China's engagement with the international human rights regime, see Jacques deLisle, "Pressing Engagement: Uneven Human Rights Progress in China, Modest Successes of American Policy and the Absence of Better Options" (www.carnegieendowment.org/files/delisle.pdf); Ann Kent, *Between Freedom and Subsistence: China and Human Rights* (Oxford University Press, 1995); Information Office of the State Council of the People's Republic of China, *China's Progress in Human Rights in 2004* (www.china.org.cn/e-white/20050418/index.htm); Michael C. Davis, ed., *Human Rights and Chinese Values: Legal, Philosophical, and Political Perspectives* (Oxford University Press, 1995); U.S. Department of State, Country Reports of Human Rights Practices: China 2006 (www.state.gov/g/drl/rls/hrrpt/2006/78771.htm [March 6, 2007]).

14. See deLisle, "Lex Americana"; Ann Seidman, Robert B. Seidman, and Janice Payne, *Legislative Drafting for Market Reform: Some Lessons from China* (New York: St. Martin's Press, 1997); International Republican Institute, *Election Observation Report, Fujian, People's Republic of China, May 1997* (www.iri.org/asia/china/pdfs/97Fujian.pdf).

15. "Judge Sows Seeds of Law-Making Dispute," *People's Daily*, November 24, 2003 (english.people.com.cn/200311/24/eng20031124_128871.shtml); Cao Siyuan, *Xiugai xianfa* (Revising the Constitution) (Hong Kong: Tidetime Media, 2003); Tahirih V. Lee, "Exporting Judicial Review from the United States to China," *Columbia Journal of Asian Law* 19 (Spring–Fall 2005): 164–65; Pitman Potter, "Governance of China's Periphery: Balancing Local Autonomy and National Unity," *Columbia Journal of Asian Law* 19 (Spring–Fall 2005): 295–96; Wu Changhua, "Improving the Legal and Policy Foundation for Public Access to Environmental Information in China," *Temple Journal of Science, Technology and Environmental Law* 24 (Spring 2005): 300–03; Cao Jianming, "WTO and the Rule of Law in China," *Temple International and Comparative Law Journal* 16 (Fall 2002): 379–90; He Weifang, *China Rights Forum, Straight Talk from China's Best and Brightest* (hrichina.org/public/PDFs/CRF.2.2006/CRF-2006-2_StraightTalk.pdf); He Weifang, "Quannengxing yamen: Chuantong yu yingxiang" (Omnipotent government: Tradition and influence), *Nanfang zhoumo*

(Southern Weekend), January 16, 1998; see also Supreme People's Court, *Second Five Year Reform Program for the People's Courts* (Beijing: Supreme People's Court, 2005).

16. See, for example, Irene Wang, "Incidents of Social Unrest Hit 87,000," *South China Morning Post*, January 20, 2006 (quoting Public Security Ministry Official Wu Heping).

17. Minxin Pei, "Citizens *v.* Mandarins: Administrative Litigation in China," *China Quarterly* 152 (December 1997): 832–62; Veron Mei-Ying Hung, "Judicial Reform in China: Lessons from Shanghai" (Washington: Carnegie Endowment for International Peace, 2005) (www.carnegieendowment.org/files/CP58.Hung.FINAL.pdf); Randall Peerenboom, "Globalization, Path Dependency and the Limits of Law: Administrative Law Reform and the Rule of Law in the People's Republic of China," *Berkeley Journal of International Law* 19, no. 2 (2001): 161–264.

18. See David Zweig and others, "Law, Contracts and Economic Modernization: Lessons from Recent Rural Reforms," *Stanford Journal of International Law* 23 (Summer 1987): 319–64.

19. Accounts of these developments include Wu Zhong, "A Step toward the Rule of Law," *Asia Times,* April 18, 2007 (www.atimes.com/atimes/China/ID18Ad01.html); "The Nail House Is Gone but the Questions It Raised Linger On," *China Daily*, April 6, 2007; Howard W. French, "A Couple's Small Victory Is a Big Step for China," *New York Times*, April 6, 2007, p. 2.

20. See, for example, Donald C. Clarke, "Regulation and Its Discontents: Understanding Economic Law in China," *Stanford Journal of International Law* 28 (Spring 1992): 283–322; Sun Xinqiang, "Reform of China's State-Owned Enterprises: A Legal Perspective," *St. Mary's Law Journal* 31, no. 1 (1999): 19–47.

21. See, for example, Yuwa Wei, "An Overview of Corporate Governance in China," *Syracuse Journal of International Law and Commerce* 30 (Winter 2003): 23–48; Donald C. Clarke, "The Independent Director in Chinese Corporate Governance," *Delaware Journal of Corporate Law* 31, no. 1 (2006): 125–228.

22. See note 18; Kevin O'Brien and Li Lianjiang, "Suing the Local State: Administrative Litigation in Rural China," *China Journal,* no. 51 (January 2004): 76–96; Isabelle Thireau and Hua Linshan, "The Moral Universe of Aggrieved Chinese Workers: Workers' Appeals to Arbitration Committees and Letters and Visits Offices," *China Journal* 50 (July 2003): 83–103.

23. See, for example, Donald C. Clarke, "The Enforcement of Civil Judgments in China," *China Quarterly*, no. 141 (1995): 65–81; Randall Peerenboom, "Seek Truth from Facts: An Empirical Study of the Enforcement of Arbitral Awards in China," *American Journal of Comparative Law* 49 (Spring 2001): 249–327.

24. See in general Lubman, *Bird in a Cage*, pp. 265–76; Pei, *China's Trapped Transition*, pp. 72, 126–30; Peerenboom, *China's Long March toward the Rule of Law*, pp. 302–15; He Weifang, "Tongguo sifa shixian shehui zhengyi" (Realization of social justice through judicial means), in *Zou xiang quanli de shidai: Zhongguo gongmin quanli fazhan yanjiu* (Toward an age of rights: Research on the development of Chinese civil rights), edited by Xiao Yang (Beijing: China University of Politics and Law Press, 1995), pp. 245–83.

25. Xueliang Ding, "The Illicit Asset-Stripping of Chinese State Firms," *China Journal*, no. 43 (2000): 1–28; Bruce J. Dickson, *Red Capitalists in China: The Party, Private Entrepreneurs, and the Prospects for Political Change* (Cambridge University Press, 2003).

26. See note 16.

27. Li Cheng and Lynn White, "The Sixteenth Central Committee of the Chinese Communist Party," *Asian Survey* 43, no. 4 (2003): 553–97; and Jacques deLisle and Cheng Li, "Constitutional Change and Foreign Policy in China," *Orbis* (forthcoming 2008). Under Hu, law has been among the principal topics of frequent presentations by scholars to the Politburo. This practice builds upon precedents established under Jiang Zemin and Li Peng. See *Xin yijie zhongyang zhengzhiju jiti xuexi neirong yilan* (A view of the contents of the Politburo collective study for the new session) (http://news.enorth.com.cn/system/2004/04/01/000760835.shtml); *Li Peng: jiujie quanguo renda changweihui fazhi jiangzuo zuo de xuyan* (Li Peng's preface to lecture series on the legal system for the Ninth NPC Standing Committee Meeting) (2003) (http://www.hwcc.com.cn/newsdisplay/newsdisplay.asp?Id=61432). Legal thinkers' ascension as influential informal advisers to the top leadership appears to be qualitatively greater under Hu.

28. "Some 2000 Rightists Call for Political Reforms, Rehabilitation, Reparations and Freedom of Speech," *Ming Pao*, October 18, 2007.

29. See note 11.

30. Hu Jintao, *Political Report to the 17th Party Congress* (October 15, 2007), sections III, IV, VI (describing past accomplishments and contributions and future roles of law in pursuing goals of economic development, democracy, and better governance).

31. See, for example, Wu Jinglian, *Huhuan fazhi de shichang jingi* (A market economy crying out for the rule of law) (Shanghai: Sanlian, 2007); Xiaobo Hu, "The Future of SOEs: From Shortage Economics to 'Enron-omics'?" in *China under Hu Jintao: Opportunities, Dangers and Dilemmas,* edited by Tun-Jen Cheng, Jacques deLisle, and Deborah Brown (Singapore: World Scientific, 2006).

32. See, for example, Robert A. Dahl, Ian Shapiro, and Jose Cheibub, *The Democracy Sourcebook* (Cambridge, Mass.: MIT Press, 2003), pp. 31–45 (discussing minimalist, Schumpeterian definitions of electoral democracy, definitions of liberal democracy, and other definitions of democracy). Typically, this will mean regular, near-universal suffrage and free and fair elections for national (and some subnational) offices in which candidates representing a range of policy views—including those reflecting much of the range of policy preferences and interests in society—can compete effectively. This is not to say that these are the only, or highest, democratic values. Rule of law, civil society, accountability of government and individual officers, effective mechanisms for receiving popular input, and heterodox views in law- and policymaking are important as well, and democracy's value may be largely its ability to secure those ends. The analysis here, however, focuses specifically on how PRC leadership in the reform era has sought to pursue, or has tolerated, some development of those features while rejecting or limiting movement toward "democracy" in the narrower sense used here.

33. See, for example, Yang Ching-lin, "China's Democratization Pushed Forward in Four Major Areas," *Ta Kung Pao*, October 18, 2007 (quoting Wang Changjiang of the Central Party School); see also Hu, *Political Report*, section VI(1)-VI.(3).

34. Laura Paler, "China's Legislation Law and the Making of a More Orderly and Representative Legislative System," *China Quarterly*, no. 182 (2005): 301–18; Wang Xixin, "Administrative Procedure Reforms in China's Rule of Law Context," *Columbia Journal of Asian Law*, no. 2 (Fall 1998): 251–77; State Council, *Xingzheng fagui zhiding chengxu tiaoli* (Procedural rules for enacting administrative regulations); Kevin J. O'Brien and Lianjiang Li, "Accommodating 'Democracy' in a One-Party State: Introducing Village Elections in China," *China Quarterly,* no.162 (June 2000): 465–89.

35. O'Brien and Li, "Accommodating 'Democracy'"; Amy Gadsden, "The Evolution of Elections in China," and Yawei Liu, "What Does Buyun Township Mean in the Context of China's Political Reform," in *China under Hu Jintao: Opportunities, Dangers and Dilemmas,* edited by Cheng and others.

36. "Interview: Chinese Premier on Reforms, Foreign Policy," Deutsche Presse-Agentur, September 9, 2006.

37. Gang Lin, "Ideology and Political Institutions for a New Era," in *China after Jiang,* edited by Xiaobo Hu and Gang Lin (Stanford University Press, 2003); Richard McGregor, "China Opens Up to Redefine Democracy," *Financial Times,* June 13, 2007, p. 3; "Socialist Democracy Means Enabling People to Oversee, Criticize Government," Xinhua News Agency, March 16, 2007 (quoting Wen Jiabao); Yu Keping, *Zou xiang shanzheng he shanzhi zhi lou* (The path toward good politics and good governance) (www.hi.chinanews.com.cn/hnnew/2005-10-20/29705.html); Yang, "China's Democratization Pushed Forward"; "At Least 8 Percent of Nominees Eliminated in Polls at Chinese Party Congress," Xinhua News Agency, October 20, 2007; see also note 61.

38. Hu, *Political Report,* section VI; Yu Zheng, "Communist Reform Broadens Democracy," Xinhua News Agency, October 17, 2007.

39. Eva Pils, "Land Disputes, Rights Assertions and Social Unrest in China," *Columbia Journal of Asian Law* 19 (Spring/Fall 2005): 235–92; Joseph Kahn, "Legal Gadfly Bites Hard and Beijing Slaps Him," *New York Times,* December 13, 2005, p. A1; Joseph Kahn, "Rivals on Legal Tightrope Seek to Expand Freedoms in China," *New York Times,* February 25, 2007, p. 1; "Implementation Program for Comprehensively Promoting the Exercise of Administrative Functions in Accordance with the Law," Xinhua News Agency, April 20, 2004; "Guiding Opinions of the All-China Lawyers Association on Lawyers Handling Mass Cases" (Beijing: All-China Lawyers Association, March 20, 2006, adopted on a "trial basis"); State Council, *Xinfang tiaoli* (Letters and Visits Rules) (Beijing: State Council, 2005).

40. Hu, *Political Report,* section VI; "Hu Jintao Mentions 'Democracy' More than 60 Times in Landmark Report," Xinhua News Agency, October 15, 2007; Human Rights Watch, "China's Olympian Human Rights Challenges: Media Freedom" (October 2007) (http://china.hrw.org/issues/media_freedom).

41. Jacques deLisle, "Chasing the God of Wealth while Evading the Goddess of Democracy," in *Development and Democracy: New Perspectives on an Old Debate,* edited by Sunder Ramaswamy and Jeffrey W. Cason (University Press of New England, 2003); Randall Peerenboom, *China Modernizes: Threat to the West or Model for the Rest?* (Oxford University Press, 2007); see also Pei, *China's Trapped Transition.*

42. World Bank, *World Governance Indicators 1996–2005* (info.worldbank.org/governance/kkz2005/sc_chart.asp); Economist Intelligence Unit, *Democracy Index2006* (www.economist.com/media/pdf/DEMOCRACY_INDEX_2007_v3.pdf); *Polity IV Country Reports 2003: China* (www.cidcm.umd.edu/polity/country_reports/ Chn1.htm); *World Democracy Audit* (www.worldaudit.org/democracy.htm).

43. DeLisle, "Chasing the God of Wealth"; compare Peerenboom, *China Modernizes,* chaps. 2, 9.

44. "Hu Jintao Values Role of Constitution in Progress," Xinhua News Agency, December 5, 2002. See www.china.org.cn/english/2002/Dec/50396.htm; James Kynge, "China Sets Up Secret Review of Constitution," *Financial Times,* June 11, 2003, p. 12.

45. Keith J. Hand, "Using Law for a Righteous Purpose: The Sun Zhigang Incident and Evolving Forms of Citizen Action in the People's Republic of China," *Columbia Journal of Transnational Law* 45 (2007): 114.

46. "Judge Sows Seeds of Law-Making Dispute," *People's Daily Online*, November 24, 2003; Jim Yardley, "A Judge Tests China's Courts, Making History," *New York Times*, November 28, 2005, p. A1: "Supreme People's Court Reply on Whether the Accused Shall Bear Civil Liability for the Infringement of the Citizen's Fundamental Right of Receiving Education under the Protection of the Constitution" and "Case of Infringement of Citizen's Fundamental Rights of Receiving Education under the Protection of the Constitution (Qi Yuling *v.* Chen Xiaoqi et al.)" in *Supreme People's Court Gazette*, no. 5 (2001): 152, 158–62; "First Case Ruling Based on Chinese Constitution" (www.junhe.com/junhewebsiteold/junhe/law_archive_2001_L.htm).

47. Xia Yong, "Zhongguo xianfa gaige de jige jiben lilun wenti—cong gaige xianfa dao xianzheng xianfa" (Some basic theoretical issues in China's constitutional development: From reform constitution to constitutionalist constitution), *Zhongguo shehui kexue* (China Social Sciences), no. 2 (2003); China Sociology and Anthropology Net, "Zhongyang fanyi ju fujuzhang Yu Keping: Zhongguo tese gongmin shehui xingqi" (Central Committee Translation Bureau Deputy Chief Yu Keping: The rise of civil society with Chinese characteristics) (www.sachina.edu.cn/Htmldata/news/2005/12/656.html).

48. Cheng Li, "The New Bipartisanship within the Chinese Communist Party," *Orbis* 49 (Summer 2005): 384–400; Joseph Fewsmith, "Political Succession: Changing Guards and Changing Rules," in *China under Hu Jintao*, edited by Cheng and others.

49. See Li, "The New Bipartisanship"; deLisle and Li, "Constitutional Change"; Jacques deLisle, "SARS and the Pathologies of Globalization and Transition in Greater China," *Orbis* 47, no. 4 (2003): 587–604.

50. "Judicial Independence Should Come First" (www.bjreview.com.cn/En-2005/05-45-e/china-2.htm; and http://law-thinker.com/show.asp?id=2280).

51. Jacques deLisle, "China and the WTO," in *China under Hu Jintao*, edited by Cheng and others; Li, "The New Bipartisanship"; Yasheng Huang, *Selling China: Foreign Direct Investment during the Reform Era* (Cambridge University Press, 2003).

52. Thomas M. Franck, "The Emerging Right to Democratic Governance," *American Journal of International Law* 86 (January 1992): 46–91; Thomas Carothers, *Aiding Democracy Abroad: The Learning Curve* (Washington: Carnegie Endowment for International Peace, 1999); Samuel P. Huntington, *The Third Wave: Democratization in the Late Twentieth Century* (University of Oklahoma Press, 1991).

53. See in general deLisle, "Lex Americana."

54. "Socialism Does Not Contradict Democracy in the Least: Hu Deping," Xinhua News Agency, October 19, 2007 (quoting United Front Work Department chief and Hu Yaobang's son, Hu Deping).

55. Larry Diamond, "Is the Third Wave Over?" *Journal of Democracy* 7, no. 3 (1996): 20–37.

56. Richard McGregor, "More Powerful than Ever: How the Communist Party is Firming Its Grip on China," *Financial Times*, October 12, 2007, p. 9 (quoting argument from Xie Tao, former Beijing University vice dean, as example of the "old cadres" arguing that "political reform"—including democracy—needed to keep up with economic development in order to sustain economic development); Minnie Chan, "12,000 Petitioners Send Letter Urging Democratic Reform," *South China Morning Post*, October 10, 2007, p. 10.

57. Arthur Waldron, "How Would Democracy Change China?" *Orbis* 48 (2004): 247–61; Edward Friedman, "Jiang Zemin's Successors and China's Growing Rich-Poor Gap," in *China under Hu Jintao,* edited by Cheng and others, pp. 97–134. Hong Kong Special Administrative Chief Executive Donald Tsang made and had to retreat quickly from—a statement that an "excess of democracy," rather than insufficient democracy (which the party secretary of Jiangsu contemporaneously cited as the cause), produced the Cultural Revolution in China, and that too much democracy too soon now might risk similar results. Robin Kwong, "Tsang in 'Cultural Revolution' Gaffe," *Financial Times,* October 15, 2007; Mary-Anne Toy, "Leader Strikes Blow for China Democracy," *The Age,* October 19, 2007, p. 12.

58. "Interview: Chinese Premier on Reforms, Foreign Policy."

59. See Yu, "Communist Reform Broadens Democracy" (Hu Jintao speech at Yale); Bill Smith, "Free Elections 100 Years Away for China's Communists," Deutsche Presse-Agentur, October 15, 2007 (quoting Party Congress spokesman Li Dongsheng); *Shiqida qian gefang tanxun Zhongguoshi minzhu* (On eve of Seventeenth Party Congress, all sides discuss Chinese-style democracy), May 30, 2007 (discussing views of political scientist Liu Xirui, Wen Jiabao, and others) (http://gb.chinareviewnews.com/doc/1003/7/8/3/100378354.html?coluid= 7&kindid=0&docid=100378354).

60. See note 38; Yu Keping, "Minzhu shi ge hao dongxi" (Democracy Is a Good Thing), *Xuexi shibao* (Study Times), January 5, 2007; Yu Keping, "Toward an Incremental Democracy and Governance: Chinese Theories and Assessment Criteria," *New Political Science* 24, no. 2 (2002): 181–99; "Wen Jiabao Says We Should Push Forward the Construction of Socialist Democracy and the Legal System," Xinhua News Agency, March 5, 2007; "Chinese Premier Wen: '100 Years' More of Socialism," Deutsche Presse-Agentur, February 27, 2007; Pan Wei, "Toward a Consultative Rule of Law Regime in China," *Journal of Contemporary China* 12, nos. 3–4 (2003): 3–43; Pan Wei, "Falu yu weilai Zhongguo zhengti" (The rule of law and China's future polity), *Zhanlue yu guanli* (Strategy and management), no. 5 (1999), pp. 30–36.

11

Staying in Power: What Does the Chinese Communist Party Have to Do?

JOSEPH FEWSMITH

> Democracy is a good thing.
> YU KEPING

After some years of relative quiescence, the question of China's possible democratization has once again been raised, both by those in China who hope that progress toward democracy can be speeded up and by observers abroad who believe that democratization is likely to occur quickly and by critics who are frustrated that it has not.[1] Observers note that China's economy is developing rapidly, the middle class is growing ever larger, society is pluralizing, and globalization is bringing external forces to bear on China in unprecedented ways. To this list, one should add generational turnover, which certainly brings new attitudes to prominence among the population and leadership alike. Generational change also raises questions about legitimacy and leadership selection.

Mao Zedong and Deng Xiaoping could base their legitimacy on their participation in the revolution, but that link becomes ever more tenuous as new generations of leaders take the stage. As a result, economic performance, the maintenance of social stability, and procedural legitimacy have become increasingly important, and these new sources of legitimacy in turn exert increasing pressure for political institutionalization even as many of the old rules about the need to accumulate personal power continue to co-exist.[2] In short, economic, societal, and political pressures appear to make the continuation of Leninist rule impossible, yet the Chinese Communist Party (CCP) continues to hold power. What explains this apparent contradiction?

One answer, explored in chapter 15 of this volume, is that the CCP has very carefully studied political successes and political failures around the world and derived from them a series of policies that aim to maximize the CCP's ability to retain power well into the future. One outcome of this study was the decision to promulgate Jiang Zemin's theory of the "Three Represents," which admitted private entrepreneurs and other "new elements" into the party. As Li Junru, vice president of the Central Party School explained, "One lesson of political parties that have lost their ruling positions in the late 20th and early 21st centuries is that they have lost the support of youthful entrepreneurs and young intellectuals."[3] Excluding the most dynamic elements of society, in other words, is a sure way to commit political suicide. Although co-optation undermines Leninist organization, co-opted entrepreneurs, whether they have joined the party or not, have so far sought to work with, not against, the party.[4]

The CCP's ability to maintain power is also related to the changing relationship between the central and local levels. Since the implementation of tax reform in 1994, central revenues have increased dramatically, from some ¥95.7 billion in 1993 to over ¥1.6 trillion in 2005. As a percentage of total revenues, central revenues have increased from 22 percent in 1993 to 52.3 percent in 2005 (somewhat down from their highest point, 55 percent, in 2002).[5] In short, the central government simply has a lot more resources with which to address serious social and distributional needs (see chapter 8), increase the salaries of government and party workers, and dispense patronage of one sort or another. The capacity of the central government has increased significantly.

As the economy has expanded, personal incomes have also increased greatly: between 1989 and 2005 urban incomes rose from ¥1,374 to ¥10,493, while rural incomes, though well behind, grew from ¥602 to ¥3,255.[6] The gap between urban and rural residents, and particularly between the very wealthy and the poor, whether urban or rural, has become a major point of social commentary in recent years, and as Dorothy Solinger points out in chapter 13, the attitudes of the poor differ significantly from those of their better-off counterparts. Although this gap in income has contributed to social discontent in recent years, the more immediate cause appears to be the abuse of power by local authorities. For urban residents, rising incomes have enabled them to purchase residences, in many cases at relatively low prices. The urban middle class has also benefited from the escalating real estate prices of recent years and from the runup in stock prices. There is little question that many urban residents have become stakeholders in the current system, while the poor remain unable to buy housing.

Despite the inequities that have developed, the CCP has adapted to a changing society and been the beneficiary of rapid economic growth. Although complaints about contemporary Chinese society are numerous and at times find expression in protest and violence, overall Chinese society appears fairly stable. One indication of the vast change in attitude from the late 1980s is that today there are serious people who argue that China can develop rule of law without democratizing.[7] Certainly there is still pressure for democratization, particularly for the incremental expansion of democratic procedures, but it seems to be less than just a few years ago, as indicated by data on public attitudes.

Public Attitudes

The relative satisfaction of most citizens is worth emphasizing because it conflicts with U.S. perceptions of China. In one recent survey, a majority of the population (more than 63 percent) indicated that their income has increased "somewhat" or "greatly" over the past five years, and most (54 percent) believe their incomes will continue to grow "somewhat" or "greatly" over the next five years. Such figures suggest a fair amount of confidence in the future, although a significant degree of uncertainty is evident as well; after all, almost 20 percent responded "hard to say" when asked about future income increases. Put in negative terms, 15 percent said that their incomes had decreased "somewhat" or "greatly" over the past five years, while about 9 percent believed that their incomes would decrease "somewhat" or "greatly" over the next five years.[8] Such figures suggest that there is reason for social contention, but that a strong majority of people are still optimistic about their own personal circumstances.

Other data reinforce such conclusions. For instance, when asked about their individual employment circumstances, urban residents have expressed generally rising satisfaction over the past six years.[9] When asked about overall satisfaction with life, urban residents report an increasing sense of satisfaction, while rural residents' sense of satisfaction has declined somewhat after by and large increasing between 2000 and 2004. On a five-point scale, urban residents' satisfaction rose from 3.27 in 2000 to 3.52 in 2006. Rural residents, who generally register greater satisfaction than their urban counterparts, registered 3.22 on the same five-point scale in 2000, increasing to 3.59 in 2004, before declining somewhat to 3.47 in 2006—still higher than six years ago.[10]

What Western observers will find most surprising is that the data currently available suggest a high degree of trust in the ability of the central government to manage the problems the country faces. For instance, when asked if the party and state are capable of managing the country well, more than 91 percent of respondents gave a positive or strongly positive answer (see table 11-1). Similarly, when asked about the level of trust in various institutions, they rated the central government highest (3.56 on a 5.0 scale), so it beat out such competitors as consumer associations (2.92), environmental and social organizations (2.9), and Internet news (2.27).[11]

Table 11-1. *Distribution of Views on the Circumstances of China's Economic and Social Development*[a]

Percent

Question	Very much agree	Relatively agree	Don't really agree	Very much do not agree	Uncertain
The social developmental problems China is facing are temporary.	27.7	55.7	8.8	0.8	6.9
The party and state are capable of managing our country well.	43.8	47.8	4.3	0.5	5.4
China's current status in the world is something to be proud of.	44.1	44.8	5.2	0.6	5.4
The overall circumstances of China's socioeconomic development are good.	36.3	54.2	4.7	0.6	4.2

Source: Li and others, "2006 nian Zhongguo shehui hexie wending zhuangkuang diaocha baogao," p. 21.

a. This survey was conducted in May–June 2006 throughout 28 provinces and covered 7,140 respondents.

Perhaps such attitudes explain why China's political elite feel little compulsion to initiate democratic reform. Surveys of bureau-level (*ting*) cadres studying at the Central Party School have repeatedly revealed that cadres see economic growth, not political reform, as the single most important factor in maintaining social stability. For instance, when asked the most important factors for smoothly promoting reform, 68 percent of these cadres chose "maintaining social stability." When asked the most important factor for maintaining social stability, 51 percent identified rapid economic development (a significant number, 23 percent, chose accelerating the reforms in the social security system).[12]

Such surveys highlight the fact that most cadres view political reform as administrative reform, not as opening the system to competition. As table 11-2 reveals, most cadres think transforming the functions of government is much more important than strengthening the supervision of public opinion, expanding the role of the "democratic" parties, or increasing the functions of the local people's congresses. Perhaps surprisingly, "inner-party democracy" also gets low marks despite official encouragement.

Overall, these data suggest that a substantial majority of the Chinese population, most especially the urban population, is fairly satisfied with the status quo and that China's political elite is focused on maintaining that prosperity. Public

Table 11-2. *Decisive Factors for the Success of Political Reform, 2004 and 2006*[a]
Percent

Decisive factor	First place		Second place		Total	
	2006	2004	2006	2004	2006	2004
Transform government functions	38.4	24.3	10.7	12.7	49.1	36.4
Step up struggle against corruption	17.0	4.7	18.8	6.5	35.8	11.2
Manage well party-state relations	12.5	29.0	9.8	15.9	22.3	44.9
Strictly implement cadre term limits	4.5	3.7	17.0	6.5	21.5	10.2
Raise function of people's congresses	5.4	9.3	9.8	14.0	15.2	23.3
Expand inner-party democracy	5.4	20.6	8.9	17.8	14.3	38.4
Strengthen supervision of public opinion	2.7	2.8	8.9	8.4	11.6	11.2
Reduce party organs	3.6	4.7	3.6	7.5	7.2	12.2
Improve decisionmaking mechanism	6.3	0.0	8.9	10.3	4.5	10.3
Expand functions of democratic parties	2.7	0.9	0.9	0.9	3.6	1.8

Source: Qing, "Dangzheng lingdao ganbu dui 2006–2007 nian Zhongguo shehui xingshi de jiben kanfa," p. 39.

a. The 2004 survey had 107 respondents, and the 2006 survey had 112 respondents.

satisfaction is, of course, contingent on continuing prosperity, so a sharp economic downturn, perhaps precipitated by a crash in the stock market or plummeting real estate values, could change the public's mood quickly, but for the present there appears to be a willingness to accept economic growth even if it comes with nondemocratic rule. Not everyone is happy, of course—especially with local government.

Local Government

Confidence in the central government may still be high, but it seems that lower levels of government are not fulfilling important social tasks, as indicated by citizen concern about their ability to improve the social mood and increase the integrity of cadres.[13] Moreover, when one looks at citizens' trust in the government's ability to manage social affairs, it is apparent that there is substantially less trust at the local level and that what trust does exist has been declining in recent years.[14]

Note, however, that most people do not interact with the government very much; when they do, their experiences are not always happy. In a 2005 survey, for instance, only 5.8 percent of respondents had interacted with the government directly in the previous year. Of these people, 52.7 percent reported being dissatisfied with the government's response, whereas only 46.7 percent reported being satisfied. Reasons cited for feeling dissatisfied included red tape (that is,

Table 11-3. *Views of Different Strata on Interest Conflict between Cadres and Masses*[a]

Percent

Stratum	No conflict	Very little conflict	Some small conflict	Much conflict	Serious conflict
Highest	9.1	22.7	31.8	22.7	13.6
High	5.6	18.9	42.7	22.4	10.5
Upper middle	6.2	19.5	48.6	19.7	5.9
Middle	5.8	17.9	46.6	21.6	8.1
Lower middle	5.6	14.9	46.3	23.7	9.5
Lower	3.6	13.3	41.4	30.4	11.4
Lowest	5.4	6.2	36.4	28.0	24.0

Source: Li and others, *Shehui chongtu yu jieji yishi*, p. 219.

a. This survey was conducted in November–December 2002 and had 11,094 respondents in 31 cities.

one department saying the matter was the responsibility of another department), the bad attitudes of government officials, the slow management of affairs, and complicated procedures.[15]

Relations between cadres and the "masses," as citizens in China continue to be called, have been sensitive for many years; most "mass incidents" appear to be a direct result of clashes of interest between citizens and cadres. It is relevant in this regard that the masses see cadres as the chief beneficiaries of reform, according to 71.4 percent of those asked.[16] Moreover, 28.3 percent believed that tension between the cadres and people was high, easily mounting into conflict. Such conflicts were most likely to occur at the local level, where contact between people and cadres was the most frequent, rather than between people and cadres at a higher level.[17] This, too, shows that citizens place more trust in the central government than that in local government.

Not surprisingly, a person's status in society affects how he or she is likely to view relations between cadres and the masses (see chapter 13), with those at the lowest levels of the system likely to see substantially more conflict than those at higher levels. In a 2002 survey of citizens in thirty-one cities, 83.2 percent of those who perceive themselves to be in the "lower" stratum of society and 88.4 percent of those who see themselves as in the "lowest" stratum of society perceive "some," "much," or "serious" conflicts of interest between cadres and masses (table 11-3). Interestingly, those in the highest social strata also perceive a high degree of conflict, whereas those in the middle perceive much less.

These findings along with those cited earlier confirm what is often observed about China, namely, that localized conflict is widespread but no threat, at least for the moment, to overall stability. Even so, this scenario generates a significant amount of pressure for governmental reform, particularly at the local level. To complicate matters, the central government, despite its enhanced capacity, is having an increasingly difficult time controlling its agents, especially at the lower reaches of the political system. This desire to reduce conflict at the local level, to prevent social conflicts from growing larger and perhaps raising more difficult challenges to CCP rule, and the desire of the central government to better monitor local agents continue to generate modest but important political change, just as they did in the late 1980s when village elections were first allowed.

Government Innovation

Although China's elite seem reluctant to view political reform in more systemic terms, local tensions are forcing at least some local governments to experiment with new ideas. Such reforms fall into two broad and sometimes overlapping categories: those that would readjust the party-state's relationship with society and those that would promote "inner-party democracy." An example of the former is the development of nongovernmental organizations (NGOs). Although the CCP has been extremely vigilant about discouraging the growth of NGOs, especially since the "color revolutions" of 2004–05 overturned autocratic governments in Georgia, Ukraine, and Kyrgyzstan, the party has nevertheless recognized that NGOs can play a beneficial role in society. The growth of chambers of commerce in Wenzhou Municipality in Zhejiang Province suggests that such groups can play an important role in regulating the economy and aiding government without posing a threat to the authority of the CCP. Two examples of the latter are the development of "democratic consultation meetings" in Wenling, Zhejiang Province, and the implementation of the "public recommendation and public selection" system in parts of Sichuan and Jiangsu Provinces.

Chambers of Commerce

The development of chambers of commerce and of industry associations in Wenzhou are interesting not because they are typical in China—they are not— but because they suggest the outer limits of what is possible for NGOs in contemporary China. Wenzhou, in southern Zhejiang Province, became famous in the 1980s for its development of the private economy. For years, the "Wenzhou model" of private, family-owned enterprise vied with the "Sunan model" of collective ownership (in the southern part of Jiangsu Province) to become the leading pattern for China's economic development. Wenzhou built its reputation on the ability of its industrious population to make goods more cheaply and in larger quantities than anywhere else. Unfortunately, it also developed a reputation for shoddy and fake goods. This practice threatened Wenzhou's economic future as consumers grew unhappy with Wenzhou products, so much so that residents of Hangzhou, the capital of Zhejiang, publicly burned 5,000 shoes made in Wenzhou.[18] Wenzhou manufacturers now faced a serious public relations problem that was threatening the local economy, particularly in Lucheng District, where most of the shoe industry was concentrated.

In response, the Lucheng District government took immediate action, forming the Lucheng District Shoe Industry Association (Lucheng qu xieye xiehui) and requiring all shoe manufacturers in the district to join the association. Working with the industry, the government arrived at a set of industry standards—Management Regulations on the Rectification of Quality of the Lucheng District Shoe Industry and Provisional Regulations on After Sales Service of the Shoe Industry—and enterprises that did not comply were shut down. Later, when all manufacturers were no longer required to join the association, the association still retained authority to enforce standards throughout the industry. Thus the Lucheng District Shoe Industry Association was initially formed as a government-organized nongovernmental association (GONGO) even as it reflected and utilized the social capital developing in Chinese society.

Another organization that grew up with the aid of government was the Wenzhou Federation of Industry and Commerce, a united-front "mass organization." It played an important role in nurturing chambers of commerce primarily because it understood something of the history of chambers of commerce in Wenzhou (the first had been founded in 1906), as well as the government's structure. As a result, the federation was in a position to promote chambers of commerce among entrepreneurs who were initially skeptical of joining a government-sponsored organization. Uncertainty about policy following the Tiananmen crackdown in 1989 slowed the development of associations, but Deng Xiaoping's journey to the south helped spur the organization of additional chambers of commerce and other industry associations. By 2002 there were more than 100 chambers of commerce and industry associations in Wenzhou.[19]

Originally, many chambers invited government officials to serve as directors or "advisers," but over time they became less and less involved in the internal affairs of trade associations. Although the government still appoints a few trade association heads, 77 percent report that they freely elect their chairmen in accordance with their own rules of operation.[20] Moreover, the internal organization of trade associations—the number of directors and committees, and training and consulting activities to raise funds for the association—seems to be free of government interference. Indeed, the fact that Wenzhou's trade associations receive no government funding makes them quite entrepreneurial. In addition to imposing membership dues, trade associations organize training classes to impart technical expertise and provide consulting services to raise funds.

Wenzhou merchants have not confined their organizational activities to this region but have a well-deserved reputation for traveling throughout China and, indeed, the world, and organizing in those distant places much as traditional Chinese merchants once formed native place guilds (*hui guan*). These outside activities began in 1995, and by 2005, some 134 associations of Wenzhou merchants had been established elsewhere. The Wenzhou government has even set up an Office of Economic Cooperation (Jingji xiezuo bangongshi) to help its merchants make connections with each other abroad so as to establish such associations. This geographic spread outward is particularly interesting because it seems to violate the corporatist framework of China's associational regulations. Not only is such organizational activity horizontal in nature but it also represents *all* Wenzhou merchants in a particular area to the local government, thus contravening the "one industry, one association, one area" rule.[21]

In allowing NGOs (or at least some NGOs) to play a larger role than in the past, this development marks an important change in state-society relations. But it does not imply that "civil society" is about to break out in China. Although Wenzhou chambers of commerce are relatively independent of the government (and in that respect far ahead of most chambers of commerce elsewhere in China), their legitimacy still depends on the government.[22] There is no chamber of commerce law, and when there is one, which seems likely in the relatively near future, the deference generally given to administrative units in China is likely to prevail. In short, the third-party enforcement normally associated with independent associations and civil society is unlikely to exist for some time.

To the extent that China's chambers of commerce fill a gap left by the uncertain legal environment, they may actually *delay* the building of a sounder legal framework. After all, chambers of commerce represent the interests of business, particularly large business, whose interests are quite similar to those of government officials. Chambers press their concerns more through informal channels than formal channels, and, to the extent that the interests of chambers and government officials converge, there may be an implicit agreement to limit the number of interests that can be represented and the effectiveness of formal legal institutions. Such an understanding, however implicit, would work against the sort of legal institutions that are a necessary part of civil society.

Chambers of commerce are but one of many organizations (such as labor unions and environmental groups) interested in promoting good government. However, the playing field is far from level. Some groups get represented and others do not, and it has been government policy to differentiate carefully among different types of NGOs. Although relations between state and society are changing to allow more room for the expression of certain societal interests, pluralism seems a long way off, especially since these sorts of associations often give organizational expression to corrupt links between politics and economics (see chapter 12).

Democratic Consultation Meetings

In 1996 the county-level city of Wenling, in southern Zhejiang Province, began convening "democratic consultation meetings" (*minzhu kentanhui*) when yet another political campaign came through the area, much to the apathetic populace's resentment. Instead of forcing people to listen to numerous mobilization meetings, local cadres decided to invite the discontented to vent their feelings. At subsequent meetings, the discussion reportedly became very lively, making some cadres feel as if they were facing a Cultural Revolution–style mass criticism meeting. But with the support of the local Propaganda Department and several outside intellectuals, townships and villages in the area began to institutionalize the process. In the beginning, these meetings dealt with whatever issues were on people's minds. Later, as they evolved and became more institutionalized, they generally focused on specific financial issues, such as capital construction. Townships generally hold such meetings once a quarter; villages have been known to hold them even more frequently. As is well known, the level of elections has never been raised (except in rare, experimental cases) from the village to the township level, leaving citizens voiceless at that higher level. In allowing citizens to express their concerns, democratic consultation meetings fill this gap to a certain extent.[23]

Although useful as a mechanism for opening the policymaking process at least somewhat, democratic consultation meetings have no legal or constitutional foundation and thus have a precarious existence, even in the areas where they have sprung up. For this reason, local authorities have been looking for ways to merge these meetings with local people's congress sessions. At the township level, people's congresses generally meet only one day a year for the purpose of ratifying government decisions on the budget and personnel changes. Starting in 2005, one township, Xinhe, decided to extend the length of the congress session to three days, to hold a democratic consultation meeting in conjunction with the people's congress session, and to make details of the budget open (or relatively open) to public inspection. This is an effort to combine democratic consultation with participatory budgetmaking.

However, circumstances make it difficult to sustain such efforts. Although the party secretary in Xinhe township was supportive of the idea, he has since been transferred away (in a normal rotation) and the new secretary is not as interested. Higher-level authorities have been tolerant but not willing to promote the experiment, so local authorities are looking for other townships that might be open to such experimentation. Even when democratic consultation meetings seem fairly well institutionalized, as they are in this area, it will clearly be difficult to extend them in directions that could force greater openness and accountability. The state-society relationship may be shifting somewhat, perhaps relieving some social tensions, but the party remains very much in control.[24]

Public Recommendation and Public Election

Some of the potentially most far-reaching reforms—if they are continued—are occurring inside the party itself. An important reason for the party's willingness to reform is the need to break up local networks, particularly the power associated with "number one" officials (*yibashou*). These networks are the sources of local corruption and of conflict with the local population, and they are generally impenetrable by the central authorities. This problem is a classic principal-agent problem, with the state (the principal) not being able to monitor and control its agents at the local level. The state and the local population have a common interest in curbing the arbitrary use and abuse of authority at the local level, but their interests may not converge on how to solve this dilemma.

In any event, this combination of tensions at the local level and the state's inability to control its own agents has been the stimulus for much of the innovation that has gone on in recent years. In 1991, for instance, peasants in the village of Daiyudian in Shanxi Province demanded the right to elect their own party secretary. Panicked county leaders thought long and hard about how to reconcile the public's demand for electoral control with the party's regulation requiring party secretaries to be elected by the party. Eventually, they came up with the "two-ballot" system, in which a preliminary vote—a public opinion poll—is taken and then the party committee takes a separate vote that ratifies the choice of the villagers.[25] Similarly, clashes between the party committee and the village committee in a village in Handan, Hebei Province, sparked a search for a means to harmonize the conflicting interests of these two bodies. The result, known as "one mechanism, three transformations" upheld the authority of the party secretary but included the village chief and others in a committee that considered all financial matters.[26]

Perhaps the most interesting of these innovations is the "public recommendation and public election" (*gongtui gongxuan*) system that has been tried out in Sichuan and other places since 1995. This system is used for the election of township heads, and because township staff and people's congresses include nonparty members, the system allows nonparty people to participate (although it is dominated by party members). The basic idea behind the public recommendation and public election system is that, since direct election of township heads is not allowed, elections at the township level should nevertheless be opened up to a certain extent. In the past, county party organizations simply appointed the heads of the townships under their jurisdiction. By contrast, the new system is intended to make township heads more responsive to the township itself (or at least the leadership of the township) by enlarging the number participating in the selection of township heads and deputy, which now includes:

—All staff of the township (about 80–120 people)

—The top three cadres from each village under the township (so if there are ten villages, that would be 30 people)

—The heads of the small groups (*xiaozu*) in villages (usually 5 per village, so about 50 people)

—Delegates to the township people's congress (perhaps 30–50 people).

In addition, the county sends 5–20 delegates. In the past, these were superdelegates who collectively were given 40 to 60 percent of the vote. But in some places now, they are beginning to implement a "one-person, one-vote" rule.

In total, some 200–300 people participate in the selection process. This is still a very limited electorate, but nevertheless a considerable expansion from the half-dozen county officials who used to make these decisions. These 200–300 people are allowed to nominate as many people as they want (reminiscent of the "sea elections" prevalent at the village level) and then vote to determine the winner. In the 2001–02 term elections, this system was adopted in about 2,000 instances, constituting about 40 percent of Sichuan's counties. It should also be noted that the system was more readily adopted in economically backward places where social tensions were high.[27]

Conclusion

Perhaps the most interesting aspect of the CCP's evolution at this stage is the tension between the political, economic, and sociological underpinnings of its governance system and the organizational need to confront—at least to a limited extent—those very underpinnings. The Leninist system has concentrated enormous power in the hands of leaders, and it may well be that such leaders are least constrained by other political and institutional forces at the local level. The temptation to engage in corruption has grown as the economy has developed and as the interests of the economic and political elite have converged. "Socialist rents" (the ability to earn above-market returns based on power inequities inherent in the socialist system) are now part of the glue holding the polity together. It is at this level that China's political economy most resembles the "trapped transition" described by Minxin Pei.[28] This ingrown, often collusive local leadership is what alienates citizens and defies central authority.

It is thus in the interests of both the central leadership and the citizenry to curb the power of this local elite, at least to some extent. In response, the party is looking at ways to expand participation of both party and nonparty people in local governance, allowing at least a limited role for NGOs and subjecting "number-one" officials to greater scrutiny and procedural requirements. None of this suggests the party may be interested in democratizing China. It does suggest, however, that in order to remain in charge, the party must change.

The changes described in this chapter are still quite small and have taken place mostly along the east coast, where many resources are available to deal with social discontent, and in Sichuan, where capable leadership has turned to political reform to defuse social tensions. In the interior, unfortunately, harsher methods usually prevail.[29] Hence government innovation is quite uneven and is likely to remain so for a long time to come.

As suggested at the beginning of the chapter, high levels of public trust mean that the central government is not under extreme pressure to carry out extensive reform or democratization. It does, however, face problems of discontent at the local level and an organizational inability to control these local agents of the state. There is thus pressure to adjust the relationship between state and society, make more room for societal interests (especially privileged interests), and to undertake limited inner-party reforms in order to make local leaders more responsive to citizens' needs. Compared with a decade ago, it is apparent that there are increasing pressures on the party to undertake institutional reforms, especially to make Leninist organization more compatible with a marketizing and pluralizing society. In another decade from now, the sorts of innovations described here may well spread to more areas and become more institutionalized. Whether they will be sufficient to ward off the twin dangers of organizational sclerosis, on the one hand, and demands for real democracy, on the other, remains to be seen. They do, however, suggest that the CCP, as an organization, understand the pressures that it is facing and that it is capable of devising measures to respond to those pressures.

It is not clear at this point whether the sort of changes described in this chapter are improving local governance; the changes are too new and the study of them too limited to know for sure. But if it turns out that the CCP can be responsive to societal demands and that the center can better monitor its agents, it is likely that the CCP will be around for a long time. This is both good and bad. China's economy has grown very rapidly during the past twenty-five years, and that has improved the lives and individual freedoms of the Chinese people. But abuses of authority will continue and China will continue to be a country in which human rights do not have the priority that they should enjoy. For outsiders, particularly in Washington, the frustration over "Why hasn't China democratized yet?" will continue to mount and such frustration, combined with economic and security issues, will add to the challenges of dealing with a rising China.

Notes

1. Bruce Gilley, *China's Democratic Future: How It Will Happen and Where It Will Lead* (Columbia University Press, 2004); and Jim Mann, *The China Fantasy: How Our Leaders Explain Away Chinese Repression* (New York: Penguin, 2007).

2. Joseph Fewsmith, "Political Succession: Changing Guards and Changing Rules," in *China under Hu Jintao,* edited by Tun-jen Cheng, Jacques deLisle, and Deborah Brown (Singapore: World Scientific, 2006), pp. 27–46.

3. Li Junru, "Zhengque lijie he jianchi dangde jiejixing" (Correctly understand and uphold the party's class nature), *Lilun dongtai* (Theoretical trends), July 20, 2001, p. 3.

4. Bruce Dickson, *Red Capitalists in China: The Party, Private Entrepreneurs, and Prospects for Political Change* (Cambridge University Press, 2003).

5. *Zhongguo tongji nianjian 2006* (Chinese statistical yearbook 2006) (Beijing: China Statistics Press, 2006), p. 286.

6. Ibid., p. 347.

7. Suisheng Zhao, *Debating Political Reform in China: Rule of Law versus Democratization* (Armonk, N.Y.: M. E. Sharpe, 2006).

8. Li Peilin, Chen Guangjin, and Li Wei, "2006 nian Zhongguo shehui hexie wending zhuangkuang diaocha baogao" (A report on the situation of social harmony and stability in China in 2006), in *2007 nian: Zhongguo shehui xingshi fenxi yu yuce* (China's social situation: Analysis and predictions, 2007), edited by Ru Xin, Lu Xueyi, and Li Peilin (Beijing: Shehui kexue wenxian chubanshe), p. 22.

9. Yuan Yue and Zhang Hui, "2006 nian Zhongguo jumin shenghuo zhiliang diaocha baogao" (An investigative report into the quality of life of urban residents in China in 2006) in *2007 nian,* edited by Ru and others, p. 59.

10. Ibid., p. 49.

11. Wang Junxiu, Yang Yiyin, and Chen Wuqing, "Dangqian Zhongguo shehui xintai fenxi baogao" (Survey report on the social mood in contemporary China), in *2004 nian: Zhongguo shehui xingshi fenxi yu yuce* (China's social situation: Analysis and predictions, 2004], edited by Ru Xin, Lu Xueyi, and Li Peilin (Beijing: Shehui kexue wnxian chubanshe) p. 65.

12. Qing Lianbin, "Dangzheng lingdao ganbu dui 2006–2007 nian Zhongguo shehui xingshi de jiben kanfa" (The basic views of leading party and state cadres on China's social situation in 2006–2007), in *2007 nian,* edited by Ru and others, pp. 38 and 41.

13. Yuan and Zhang, "2005 nian Zhongguo jumin shenghuo zhiliang diaocha baogao," p. 61.

14. Ibid.

15. Ibid., pp. 61–62.

16. Wang and others, "Dangqian Zhongguo shehui xintai fenxi baogao," p. 67.

17. Ibid., p. 68.

18. Chen Shengyong, Wang Jinjun, and Ma Bin, eds., *Zuzhihua, zizhu zhili yu minzhu* (Organization, self-governance, and democracy) (Beijing: Zhongguo shehui kexue chubanshe, 2004), p. 38.

19. Ibid., p. 228.

20. Yu Jianxing, Huang Honghua, and Fang Liming, eds., *Zai zhengfu yu qiye zhijian, yi Wenzhou shanghui wei yanjiu duixiang* (Between government and enterprise: Chambers of commerce in Wenzhou as a case study) (Hangzhou: Zhejiang renmin chubanshe, 2004), p. 286.

21. Joseph Fewsmith, "Chambers of Commerce in Wenzhou Show Potential and Limits of Civil Society," *China Leadership Monitor*, no. 16 (Fall 2005) (http://media.hoover.org/documents/clm16_jf.pdf).

22. He Zengke, *Zhongguo zhengzhi tizhi gaige yanjiu* (A study of China's political system reform) (Beijing: Zhongyang bianyiju chubanshe, 2004), p. 254.

23. Joseph Fewsmith, "Taizhou Area Explores Ways to Improve Local Government," *China Leadership Monitor*, no. 15 (Summer 2005) (http://media.hoover.org/documents/clm15_jf.pdf).

24. Joseph Fewsmith, "Exercising the Power of the Purse?" *China Leadership Monitor*, no. 19 (Fall 2005) (http://media.hoover.org/documents/clm19_jf.pdf).

25. Li Lianjiang, "The Two-Ballot System in Shanxi Province: Subjecting Village Party Secretaries to a Popular Vote," *China Quarterly*, no. 42 (July 1999): 103–18.

26. Jing Yuejin, *Dangdai Zhongguo nongcun "lianghui guanxi" de weiguan jiexi yu hongguan youshi* (Micro-analysis and macro-views of "relations between the two committees" in contemporary China's villages) (Beijing: Zhongyang wenxian chubanshe, 2004), pp. 137–66.

27. Lai Hairong, "Jingzhengxing xuanju zai Sichuansheng xiangzhen yiji de fazhan" (The development of competitive elections at the township-level in Sichuan Province), in *Jiceng minzhu he difang zhili chuangxin* (Grassroots democracy and innovations in local governance), edited by He Zengke and others (Beijing: Zhongyang bianyi chubanshe, 2004), pp. 51–108.

28. Minxin Pei, *China's Trapped Transition: The Limits of Developmental Autocracy* (Harvard University Press, 2006).

29. Kevin O'Brien and Lianjiang Li, *Rightful Resistance in Rural China* (Cambridge University Press, 2006).

Part V

*Forces for and against
Democracy in China*

12

Fighting Corruption:
A Difficult Challenge for Chinese Leaders

MINXIN PEI

> The task of fighting and preventing corruption determines the party's legitimacy
> and survival.
>
> HU JINTAO, "Political Report to the 17th Party Congress" (2007)

Of all the potential risks for instability that dot China's changing political landscape, none may be more lethal than corruption by government officials. The abuse of power for personal gain, the classic definition of corruption, today permeates nearly all layers and departments of the government.[1] Anticorruption investigations have ensnared officials of all ranks, from members of the powerful Politburo of the ruling Chinese Communist Party (CCP) to senior generals and commanders of the armed forces, provincial party secretaries and governors, top executives in financial institutions and state-owned enterprises, county magistrates, and village chiefs. In September 2006, the CCP dismissed Chen Liangyu, Shanghai's party chief and a member of the Politburo, for alleged involvement in a corruption scandal. Each year since the 1980s, the CCP's top antigraft agency, the Central Discipline Inspection Commission (CDIC), metes out various forms of disciplinary action and punishment to roughly 100,000–170,000 CCP members and officials for various forms of wrongdoing (see table 12-1). And each year Chinese courts prosecute more than 30,000 cases of corruption involving "large sums of money." Yet repeated campaigns against corruption and harsh penalties for lawbreakers, including the death sentence and life in jail for the worst offenders, have failed to restrain rapacious officials and curb abuses of power.

Despite some optimistic, though questionable, observations that corruption in China has not hurt its economic growth, endemic corruption threatens China's future prospects in many ways.[2] Politically, corruption by the members of the ruling elite undermines the legitimacy of the CCP, erodes the authority of the state, impedes the effective implementation of government policies, and fuels public resentment against the government. Economically, corruption creates distortions, increases the costs of commerce, causes waste and inefficiency, and stunts growth and employment. Socially, corruption exacerbates inequality, harms public safety, victimizes the poor and the powerless, and increases social injustice.[3] Ultimately, if the party fails to curb corruption, China will most likely witness the rise of a form of authoritarian crony-capitalism that marries unaccountable political power with ill-gotten private wealth. Such a development would pose an enormous hurdle to the democratization of China in the future because the socioeconomic inequality embedded in a society dominated by crony-capitalists hinders democratic transition and subverts democratic processes (this often continues to be true even after a democratic transition occurs).[4] Given the corrosive effects of corruption, it would be hard to imagine how China could confront its manifold economic, social, and political challenges in the decade ahead without waging a more committed and effective campaign against official corruption.

Corruption in China: Enforcement, Magnitude, and Scope

A frustrating difficulty in understanding corruption in China is the dearth of quality time-series data that accurately capture both the magnitude and the trends of corruption. For obvious reasons, the Chinese government does not publish such data. even though it is reasonable to assume that the CDIC collects such information. Another difficulty lies in interpreting the data on the investigation and punishment of corrupt officials.

The Enforcement Record

While such data can be used to gauge the magnitude and trends of corruption, they actually reflect only the intensity of anticorruption efforts. In other words, although more intense anticorruption efforts yield more investigations and prosecutions, and therefore increase the number of corruption cases exposed and prosecuted, this does not necessarily indicate a worsening of corruption per se. However, any such worsening could be masked by lax enforcement, and to judge by the three key measurements of enforcement effectiveness—the rate of investigation, the rate of prosecution, and the rate of imprisonment—China does not have a tough enforcement record against corrupt officials.

If the number of CCP members punished for corruption and misdeeds is taken as an indicator of the scope of corruption, it seems that corruption grew significantly in the 1990s: the average number of CCP members disciplined

Table 12-1. *CCP Members Punished by the Party's Disciplinary and Inspection Committees, 1982–2006*

Years	Average number punished and disciplined a year[a]	Percent expelled	Percent criminally prosecuted[b]
1982–86	130,000	23.4	n.a.
1987–92	146,000	21.0	5.8
1993–June 1997	190,000	18.2	5.6
October 1997–September 2002	169,230	16.2	4.5 (37,790)
December 2002–November 2003	174,580	n.a.	5.0 (8,691)
2004	170,850	n.a.	2.9 (4,915)
2004–05	115,143	21.0	13.1 (15,177)
2006	97,260	21.7	3.6 (3,530)

Sources: Yan, Corruption and Market in Contemporary China, p. 47; Xinhua News Agency, November 19, 2002; www.chinanews.com.cn, February 22, 2004, January 21, 2005, and February 14, 2007; and People's Daily Online, February13, 2006.

n.a. Not available.

a. I use the twelve-month average for this column because the CDIS provides only five-year aggregate numbers for the period 1982–2002.

b. Number of members prosecuted in parentheses.

each year was about 50 percent higher in the mid-1990s than in the early 1980s (table 12-1). Then in the early years of the twenty-first century, especially after 2004, these figures dipped: the number of CCP members punished from December 2004 to November 2005 was about 55,000 fewer, or about a third less, than in 2004. In 2006 only 97,260 CCP members received disciplinary actions, about 18,000 fewer, or 16 percent less, than in 2005. Furthermore, the punishment meted out to CCP members found to have committed wrongful deeds is generally mild (tables 12-1 and 12-2). A huge majority—two-thirds— got away with only a mild to serious warning that appeared to have no real punitive consequences. Less than 3 percent were stripped of their CCP positions, only 9 percent received expulsion on probation, and roughly 20 percent were immediately expelled from the party. Only 6 percent were criminally prosecuted in the 1980s and 1990s. In more recent years, with the exception of the spike in the prosecution rate in 2004, only about 3 percent of the CCP members disciplined were prosecuted as criminals.

Is such relatively light punishment for wayward CCP members justified? Further details on the exact nature of the various violations and misdeeds perpetrated by such CCP members (table 12-3) indicate that 48 percent of the CCP members disciplined and punished in 2006 committed very serious, and most likely, criminal offenses (such as obstructing and harming social order, violating the rules of integrity and self-discipline, or engaging in corrupt financial prac-

Table 12-2. *Types of Disciplinary Actions against CCP Members, 2004–06*

Action[a]	December 2004– November 2005	2006
Warning	44,836 (38.9)	37,343 (38.4)
Serious warning	32,289 (28.0)	27,185 (28.0)
Dismissal from CCP positions	3,173 (2.8)	2,744 (2.8)
Expulsion, on probation	10,657 (9.3)	8,777 (9.0)
Expulsion	24,188 (21.0)	21,120 (21.7)
Criminal prosecution[b]	15,177 (13.1)	3,530 (3.6)
Total number disciplined	115,143 (100)	97,260 (100)

Sources: People's Daily Online, February 13, 2006; www.chinanews.com.cn, February 14, 2007.

a. Figures in parentheses are percentages.

b. The numbers in these two columns are most probably already included in the "expulsion" category since only expelled CCP members are criminally prosecuted.

tices). The unspecified types of wrongdoing committed by 49 percent of the disgraced CCP members in 2006 also most likely included serious criminal acts. On this evidence, the severity of administrative and criminal sanctions against corrupt CCP members is fairly low.

The near quadrupling of the prosecution rate in 2004–05 appears to be an aberration. Intriguingly, it occurred during the transition from the Jiang Zemin era to the Hu Jintao era, which suggests a connection with inner-party political rivalry. Conceivably, the new leadership might have been motivated to use corruption charges to remove officials perceived as loyalists of the retired leadership, thus prosecuting many more miscreants within the CCP and causing the prosecution rate to spike in 2005. Alternatively, the high prosecution rate in 2005 might indicate that the new leadership is far more committed to fighting

Table 12-3. *Types of Infractions Punished by the CCP Disciplinary and Inspection Committees, 2006*

Infraction	Number punished	Percent
Negligence	3,196	3.3
Obstructing and harming social ordera	31,218	32.1
Violating rules of integrity, self-discipline, and financial mattersb	15,350	15.8
Other	47,496	48.8
All	97,260	100.0

Source: www.chinanews.com.cn, February 14, 2007.

a. The Chinese term is *fanghai shehui guanli zhixu*.

b. The Chinese term is *weifan lianjie zilu he caijing jilu*.

corruption and has taken a tougher approach. Unfortunately, the facts do not support this hypothesis because, after the unusual rise in 2005, the rate of prosecution fell to 3.6 percent in 2006—the second lowest level recorded since 1982. At least one thing seems clear about the new leadership's record on fighting corruption: the number of CCP members punished by the CDIC since 2004 has inexplicably collapsed, despite the prosecution of several high-level CCP and government officials in the same period (see table 12-1).

What does this recent decline in the number of CCP members punished signify? As depicted in table 12-1, it gives the government's anticorruption campaign an inverted U-shape: the number punished was low in the 1980s, began to rise steadily and apparently peaked during the period of 1992–97 (on an average annual basis), held steady until 2004, then fell dramatically after 2004. Unfortunately, the evidence points only weakly to declining corruption and more reasonably to lax enforcement as the cause, as corroborated by the falling rate of prosecution since the late 1990s. This rate declined by almost half between the mid-1990s and 2006 (see table 12-1).

Indeed, paralleling the fall in the number of CCP members punished for corruption, the number of cases received by prosecutors began a precipitous decline after the mid-1990s (table 12-4).[5] From 1996 to 2005, this number fell by nearly two-thirds. Moreover, only about half of the cases received by the prosecutors led to investigation and prosecution, demonstrating further a relatively low rate of prosecution of corrupt officials.

At the same time, the government appears to have been focusing greater attention on the more egregious cases (see table 12-5). An estimate of the magnitude of corruption, as measured by the percentage of so-called "major cases" (defined in terms of the sums of money involved) and the number of cases involving officials at and above *xian* (county) and *chu* (division) levels, is telling. Roughly half of all prosecuted corruption cases involve large sums of money, called *da'an* (literally "big cases"). Apparently this category was reclassified in 1998 (when the sum was adjusted upward to reflect inflation); this led to a dramatic fall in the share of such cases among all cases filed. Subsequently, however, the share of *da'an* began to rise rapidly, reaching 52 percent in 2005. Note, too, that the absolute number of *da'an* fell considerably after the reclassification in 1998 but has stayed at around 18,000 a year in the past five years, which suggests that such cases are of some concern.

Similarly, the number of officials with the rank of *xian* or *chu* and above prosecuted for corruption in the so-called *yao'an* (key) cases has held remarkably steady, at about 2,700–2,900 in the past decade, despite the significant decline in 1998 and 1999. Because of the huge decline in the number of cases filed by the prosecutors in this period, however, the relative share of major

Table 12-4. *Cases of Corruption and Abuse of Power Prosecuted by Courts,*
1996–2005

Year	Number received by prosecutors	Number filed	Number concluded	Cases filed as a share of cases received	Major cases (da an)[a]	Key cases (yao an)[b]
1996	180,186	82,356	88,574	45.7	39,727	2,700
1997	153,946	70,477	62,336	45.7	42,194	2,577
1998	108,828	35,084	34,081	32.2	9,715	1,820
1999	103,356	38,382	34,806	37.1	13,059	2,200
2000	104,427	45,113	40,770	43.2	16,121	2,872
2002	86,187	43,258	40,776	50.2	18,496	2,925
2003	71,032	39,562	37,042	50.1	18,695	2,728
2004	68,813	37,786	35,138	54.9	18,611	2,960
2005	63,053	35,028	32,616	55.5	18,416	2,799

Source: *Zhongguo falu nianjian* (Law yearbooks of China) (Beijing: *Zhongguo falu chubanshe*, various years).

a. Major cases, based on the amount of money involved (filed cases only). Such cases meet one of the following criteria applied since 1998: embezzlement or bribes involving more than ¥50,000; misuse of public funds in excess of ¥100,000; collective misappropriation of public funds, unexplained wealth, and undeclared foreign bank accounts in excess of ¥500,000.

b. Key cases based on involvement of xian-chu officials (filed cases only).

cases has more than doubled (from 3.3 percent to 8 percent). Again, this signals that the government has maintained its focus on addressing corruption by key officials even though the overall anticorruption efforts appear to have grown much less intense. Also significant is the increase in the number of bribery and embezzlement cases involving more than ¥1 million: from January to November 2005 this number rose by 8 percent over the comparable period in 2004; the number of corruption cases involving officials at, or above, the *ting*-level also rose 8 percent.[6]

If anything, the stabilization of the number of prosecuted key cases (at about 18,000) and the number of *xian-chu* officials prosecuted (now averaging 2,800 a year) may indicate the existence of a fragile anticorruption equilibrium. The Chinese government may have, in other words, routinized its anticorruption work, prosecuting a fixed number of key cases and officials each year. This equilibrium may have several implications. First, given the CCP's limited commitment to combating corruption (and its fear of undermining its own political authority and support base), the CDIC is not likely to refer as many corrupt CCP members as possible to government prosecutors. Second, the CCP nevertheless has an interest in maintaining a minimum level of internal discipline and

Table 12-5. *Share of Major (da an) and Key (yao an) Cases in Total Filed by Prosecutors, 1996–2002*

Year	Total number filed	Major cases		Key cases	
		Number[a]	Percent	Number[b]	Percent
1996	82,356	39,727	48.2	2,700	3.3
1997	70,477	42,194	59.9	2,577	3.7
1998	35,084	9,715	27.7	1,820	5.2
1999	38,382	13,059	34.0	2,200	5.7
2000	45,113	16,121	35.7	2,872	6.4
2002	43,258	18,496	42.8	2,925	6.8
2003	39,562	18,695	47.3	2,728	6.9
2004	37,786	18,611	49.3	2,960	7.8
2005	35,028	18,416	52.6	2,799	8.0

Source: *Zhongguo falu nianjian* (Law yearbooks of China) (Beijing: *Zhongguo falu chubanshe*, various years).

a. Major cases based on amount of money involved.

b. Key cases based on involvement of xin-chu officials.

wants to keep corruption by its own agents within certain limits. As a result, it uses criminal prosecution to punish officials whose actions blatantly exceed the CCP's implicit levels of tolerance, thus deterring those who might be tempted to follow suit. Third, without external political pressure, such as a mass political movement or extreme agitation in public opinion, it will probably be hard to break this equilibrium.

Although the data in tables 1–5 do not reveal definitively whether corruption is increasing or decreasing in China, they do confirm that corruption is a very serious problem and involves large numbers of CCP and government officials. From October 1997 to September 2002, 28,996 *xian* or *chu*-level and 2,422 *ting* (department) or *ju*-level (bureau) officials were prosecuted. According to official statistics, China has 170,000 *difang ganbu* (local officials). This means that almost one in five local officials were prosecuted for corruption in a five-year period (assuming the number of officials did not expand significantly during the same period).[7] Despite the epidemic proportions of official corruption, anticorruption efforts are less intense today than before, and the number of cases filed for prosecution has been declining, as has the rate of prosecution of CCP members found to have committed wrongful acts. Indeed, for all the CCP members punished for misdeeds today, only 3 percent are eventually prosecuted. Astonishingly, the actual punishment meted out to these individuals after they are prosecuted and convicted appears to be very mild. According to an official report, of all the 33,519 individuals convicted of using their official positions to commit crimes (*zhiwu fanzui*, a term referring mostly to official corruption) during 2003–05, 52 percent received suspended sentences and did not serve jail time. In comparison, only 20 percent of convicted common criminals receive suspended sentences.[8]

Magnitude and Scope

By its very nature as an illicit activity, corruption is inherently difficult to measure in magnitude and scope. In this section, I employ a variety of measures to this end, ranging from public opinion surveys to officially reported figures and scholarly estimates.

Polling data suggest that the elite and the public consider corruption a serious social problem. In surveys conducted by researchers at the CCP's Central Party School, which trains midlevel and senior officials, the officials who participated in these surveys have consistently rated corruption as one of the most serious social problems in China since 1999. From 1999 to 2004, corruption was ranked either the most or second most serious problem facing the country. Only in 2005 and 2006 did other social problems—such as income inequality, crime, and lack of access to health care—top their concerns.[9]

Recent public opinion surveys show similar concerns with corruption. In a survey of 5,000 readers conducted by the influential official publication *Banyuetan* (Semi-Monthly) in July 2006, the issue of "intensifying anticorruption measures" was the fifth top concern of the respondents (behind rising income inequality; high costs of health care, education, and housing; unemployment; and an inadequate social safety net).[10] In an August 2006 survey of 4,586 business executives (87 percent of them in nonstate firms) by the State Council's Development Research Center, only 20 percent rated their local officials as "very good" or "quite good" in terms of integrity, 45 percent rated them "so-so," 23 percent said "bad," and 12 percent said "very bad." In addition, 30 percent reported that they had to pay "extra fees" on top of standard interest rates in order to secure bank loans.[11]

Second, the magnitude of corruption may also be measured by the amount of misspent or misappropriated public funds found each year by the National Audit Agency's investigations. When the agency audited 22,000 government officials from January to November 2005, for example, it found that ¥290 billion had been spent in violation of laws and regulations (*weifa weigui*). In a two-year period (2004 and 2005), government auditors uncovered ¥14.5 billion in misspent funds by the various departments and ministries of the central government.[12] From 1996 to 2005, the National Audit Agency uncovered, altogether, ¥1.29 trillion in government spending categorized as *weigu* (in violation of the rules), averaging ¥129 billion a year, or about 8 percent of the on-budget spending in 2000.[13]

Third, the economic costs of corruption may be derived from a set of certain assumptions. One notorious example of corruption is officials' misuse of government-provided automobiles. In 2006 the government spent about ¥70 billion on purchasing such automobiles (and an undisclosed but presumably very large amount for the maintenance of said vehicles). If even as little as 10 percent of the spending on such automobiles is unjustified, then the cost of automobile-related corruption alone would amount to ¥7 billion in 2006. The total government procurement budget in 2005 (which includes the purchase of official automobiles) was ¥300 billion. If at least 10 percent of the procurement budget goes to corruption, then the amount that can be misappropriated from the procurement budget is, at a minimum, ¥30 billion (or 0.25 percent of gross domestic product [GDP] that year). If the price tag of corruption includes the costs of unjustified overseas visits by government officials, it rises considerably. In 2004 alone, officials' overseas visits cost Chinese taxpayers ¥480 billion. Assuming that a quarter of these trips are junkets, the costs of corruption in this area of spending would be ¥120 billion.[14] The so-called administrative spending in the budget, about 20 percent of the total budget (¥470 billion in 2003), is easily subject to misappropriation and theft. If illegal activities constitute 10 percent of the administrative spending budget, this would cost ¥47 billion in 2003, or 0.4 percent of GDP that year.[15]

The cost of corruption in land transactions, known to be one of the most tainted economic activities, is presumably very high. In 2005 the government claimed that it generated ¥580 billion in revenues from land leases.[16] It is common knowledge that local governments underprice land leases for well-connected developers, often by a very significant margin. If these land transactions were underpriced by 20 percent, then the loss of revenue to the government in 2005 from land leases would be ¥115 billion. The biggest black hole of corruption appears to be fixed-asset investment, mainly infrastructure projects. In 2003, for example, state-owned firms and institutions spent ¥2.1 trillion (19 percent of GDP that year) on fixed-asset investments. If 10 percent of this massive amount of government spending were siphoned off in corruption, China would lose roughly 1.9 percent of GDP.[17] Thus a conservative estimate of the direct costs of corruption in the areas of government procurement, administration, and state spending on fixed-asset investments in 2003 would be 2.5 percent of GDP, assuming that 10 percent of such spending is diverted to private benefits illegally every year. If the loss of revenue from land transactions is added, then the cost of corruption would be 3 percent of GDP. Previous estimates by various scholars put the costs of corruption at 3–17 percent of GDP.

At the high end of the estimate, Hu Angang argued that corruption cost the Chinese economy about 13.3–16.9 percent of GDP in 1998. He included both the direct and indirect costs of corruption resulting from tax evasion (7.6–9.1 percent), siphoning off government investments and public expenditures (3.4–4.5 percent), income from the underground economy (0.4–0.5 percent), and "rents" from monopoly industries (1.7–2.7 percent).[18] At the lower end, I estimated that corruption in 1998 cost the Chinese economy about 3–4 percent of GDP. The share of tax evasion was much lower in my estimate. I also excluded the costs of rents from government-run monopolies.[19]

High-Risk Sectors

By and large, corruption in China springs from the same causes as in other societies: a combination of political and economic monopolies (that is, a lack of political and economic competition). According to official reports, it tends to be concentrated in the sectors where China's government exercises a monopoly or has extensive involvement. Termed "commercial corruption" (*shangye huiru*), such illegal practices typically consist of bribes, kickbacks, and misappropriations.[20] Anticorruption agencies have repeatedly identified the high-risk areas, as reflected in their priorities. In 2006 the Supreme People's Procuratorate listed the following six priorities in prosecuting corruption: (1) attacking bribery and embezzlement involving CCP and government officials; (2) battling corruption committed by government officials using their power of personnel appointment and project approval; (3) fighting corruption committed by officials in the process of the restructuring, bankruptcy, and management of state-owned enterprises; (4) combating corruption in the judiciary and law enforcement agencies; (5) rooting out corruption in major infrastructural projects, the financial sector, and land management; and (6) uncovering and punishing bribes paid to officials in order to advance illegal private interests.[21] In April 2007, the Supreme People's Procuratorate announced that four economic sectors, all highly lucrative, would receive special attention: urban infrastructural projects, land sales and leases, construction, and real estate.[22]

Infrastructural Projects

Given the huge amounts of public investment in infrastructural projects, it is no surprise that kickbacks are common in this sector. Kickbacks range from about 10 percent to 20 percent of the total costs of infrastructural projects.[23] Proportionally, infrastructural projects account for a large share of all corruption scandals. Of all the commercial corruption cases investigated by government prosecutors from January to July 2006, one-quarter were related to infrastructure projects.[24] Anecdotally, the pervasiveness of corruption in the infrastructure sector can be seen in the downfall of many local officials in charge of transportation (mainly highway construction) and urban planning (project approval) policies. In Henan, three successive directors of the provincial transportation department were jailed for corruption. The same pattern was observed in many other provinces. Altogether, provincial transportation chiefs in almost half of the provinces have been arrested and sentenced for corruption.[25] During 2002–07, three successive directors of the bureau of urban planning of Kunming, which approves real estate projects, were arrested for corruption. One was sentenced to life in prison and another to thirteen years.[26] Government officials have generally engaged in the following corrupt practices in the infrastructure sector: demanding bribes in exchange for project approval, colluding with architects and designers, reporting inflated expenses for relocation, rigging the bidding process, subcontracting to favored firms in exchange for bribes, accepting illegal commissions from suppliers of building materials, lowering quality control standards, inflating the costs of finished projects, and conducting superficial inspections and certifications following the completion of the projects.[27]

Land Acquisition and Leases

Since only a small proportion of all land transactions are market based, corruption here consists largely of bribes paid by developers to the local officials in charge of land leases. Moreover, these officials often use illegal means to acquire the land that they later lease to developers at low prices. Following a satellite survey of sixteen cities in 2005, the Ministry of Land Resources concluded that half of the land used for development was acquired illegally.[28] Zhang Xinbao, director of the Regulatory Enforcement Bureau at the Ministry of Land Resources, disclosed that between 1999 and 2005 the government uncovered more than 1 million cases of illegal land acquisition, affecting more than 5 million *mu* (about 825,000 acres) of land. Provinces that are more developed appear to have fewer violations than less developed ones. In some cities on the coast, about 10 percent of all land acquisitions violated government rules. In some cities in the central region, about 60–70 percent of land acquisitions violated government rules.[29]

Violations of government regulations and illegal acquisitions allow local officials to pocket the lion's share of the proceeds from land deals or divert the benefits to their family members and friends. According to one study, 60 percent of village and township cadres who had been accused of using their powers to commit a crime were under suspicion of embezzling revenues from land deals.[30] Corruption in the real estate sector often implicates senior leaders. A vice governor of Anhui, the chief prosecutor of Tianjin, a vice mayor of Beijing, a large number of local leaders in Fujian, and many other local party bosses, have been arrested and sentenced for getting involved in corrupt real estate transactions.[31]

The Financial Sector

Poor regulation, weak governance, and inadequate internal control have made the financial sector (banks, brokerage houses, trust companies, insurance firms, and credit cooperatives) a rich target for corrupt officials and thieving insiders. In 2004 alone, bank regulators uncovered ¥584 billion in misused funds, 244 senior executives in the industry were arrested or dismissed, and a total of 1,219 individuals were deemed to be involved in corrupt practices in one way or another. In 2005 the situation seemed worse: regulators uncovered ¥767 billion in misused funds, and 1,466 individuals were allegedly involved in their misuse.[32] That same year, the Bank of China disciplined eight provincial branch chiefs and dismissed another eleven provincial branch chiefs (totaling two-thirds of its top provincial executives) for various causes, most likely corruption and negligence.[33] Several senior executives in the four mega state-owned banks have been jailed for corruption, including Wang Xuebing (chairman of the Bank of China), Liu Jingbao (chairman of the Bank of China Hong Kong), Zhang Engzhao (chairman of the China Construction Bank), and dozens of provincial branch chiefs.

As just mentioned, bank insiders are often involved as well. In 2006 the influential investigative business publication, *Caijing*, exposed evidence of collusion between senior state-owned bank officials and real estate developers who used fraudulent means to get loans from the state-owned banks, causing billions of yuan worth of losses to the banks in the form of nonperforming loans.[34] In one particularly egregious case, according to the chief auditor of the State Audit Agency, Li Jinghua, one company took out ¥1.1 billion in fraudulent bank loans and used ¥300 million of it to bribe various officials, presumably including bank insiders.[35] Indeed, corruption and fraud are rife in the financial services sector. In a survey of 3,561 employees in banks, state-owned enterprises (SOEs), private firms, brokerage houses, and farming households in 2003, 82 percent of the respondents said that corruption was "pervasive" or "quite pervasive" in financial institutions. Because of corruption, firms and borrowers were forced to pay bribes averaging roughly 9 percent of the loan amount.[36] China's nascent insurance industry is similarly plagued by the pervasive use of kickbacks, which sometimes amount to as much as 50 percent of the premiums paid out.[37] Media reports, too, charge that corruption in the financial sector often entails collusion between outsiders and bank insiders.[38] *Caijing* published a long investigative story in 2006 that exposed a real estate developer who colluded with two branch chiefs of the Beijing City Cooperative Bank in an elaborate scheme to defraud various state- and city-owned banks of as much as ¥2 billion.[39]

State-Owned Enterprises

Transactions in the restructuring, privatization, and transfer of state-owned assets, especially in SOEs, breed corruption because such activities are monopolized by insiders—usually local officials or SOE executives, or both. Because market forces play a negligible role in these transactions, insiders can more easily underprice state assets and thereby reap huge profits. In 2004 SOEs owned by the central government declared asset losses close to 10 percent of the value of their net assets. It is suspected that a large portion of these losses were siphoned off by SOE executives.[40]

The Pharmaceutical Industry

Official reports indicate corrupt practices are common in the approval, sale, purchase, and prescription of pharmaceuticals. Kickbacks are prevalent and often involve doctors, who can get illegal commissions from pharmaceutical companies for prescribing their products. Even top industry regulators are routinely bribed to get them to approve drugs of dubious effectiveness. Zheng Xiaoyu, the director of the State Drug Administration, which regulates the pharmaceutical industry, was arrested in March 2007 after investigators found that he had taken ¥5 million to ¥6 million in bribes from drug companies in exchange for approving their products.[41]

Corruption across Sectors

The extent of corruption across various sectors can be assessed from the findings of a major study conducted by the prosecutor's office of Jiyuan City in Henan Province, as reported in the weekly newspaper *Lianzheng zhoukan* (Government Integrity Weekly) in 2006. In 3,067 "representative" cases of *zhiwu fanzui* (using one's official position to commit crime), about half related to infrastructural projects and land transactions, 20 percent to government procurement scandals, and 13 percent to corrupt or fraudulent loan approvals. When the ranks of the corrupt officials were examined in more detail, those at or above the *chu*-level, 1,348 altogether, accounted for almost 44 percent of all the cases in the study. Of this group, 608 (45 percent) were implicated in infrastructure and land transaction scandals, 216 (16 percent) in *maiguan-maiguan* (the buying and selling of government appointments), 120 (9 percent) in illegal loan approvals, 95 (7 percent) in questionable sales practices such as kickbacks, and 67 (5 percent) in asset-stripping during SOE restructuring.[42]

Corruption in Key Institutions

China's most vital political institutions—the CCP, the judiciary, law enforcement, and local bureaucracies—have all been severely damaged by corruption. Perhaps most serious of all is its easy penetration of the legal system, which remains heavily politicized and lacking in transparency despite small efforts at modernization. In the absence of systematic data, the extent of judicial corruption is unclear, but several anecdotes provide strong hints of its depth. In 2003, for example, thirteen judges of Wuhan's Intermediate Court, including two vice presidents, were arrested and sent to jail for corruption; forty-four lawyers were also implicated in the same scandal. Surprisingly, even all of these arrests combined failed to curb corruption in this particular court: in 2006 the president of the court, Wu Zhenghan, was arrested for taking ¥3 million in bribes.[43]

In Fuyang City, one of the most corrupt regions in Anhui, a large number of senior judges of the Fuyang Intermediate Court were implicated in corruption scandals, including three successive presidents of the Fuyang Intermediate Court who were arrested and tried for corruption. Other disgraced judges included a vice president of the court, the chief and deputy chief of the criminal tribunal, the chief and deputy chief of the enforcement division, and the chief judge of the economic chamber.[44] In Shenzhen, one vice president and four senior judges (heads of the civil tribunals) of the Intermediate Court were arrested for corruption in 2006. They all took huge bribes.[45] In addition, the chief prosecutor of Jiangsu Province, Han Jianlin, and the chief prosecutor of Tianjin were both brought down in corruption scandals in 2006.

Like the judiciary, China's other key institutions are now rife with the most insidious forms of corruption: the buying and selling of government appointments (*maiguan-maiguan*) and collusion among local ruling elites. These activities usually signify late-stage political decay.

Buying and Selling Government Appointments (maiguan-maiguan)

The practice of *maiguan-maiguan* was practically unheard of in the 1980s but has become prevalent since the 1990s, as is evident from shocking news accounts of local officials taking large bribes in exchange for appointments to desirable government positions. This is a particularly pernicious activity because it completely undermines the integrity of the state and turns government positions into nothing more than investments for rapacious individuals. In one of the most notorious cases, Ma De, the party boss of Suihua in Heilongjiang Province, sold hundreds of government appointments in return for millions of yuan in bribes. Han Guizhi, a long-serving powerful Heilongjiang CCP organizational chief, also sold government positions for bribes. A similar scandal brought down Xu Guojian, the CCP organizational chief of Jiangsu Province in 2004. Xu sold positions to the province's deputy chief prosecutor, the provincial chief of the anticorruption bureau, and the head of the provincial transportation department, the chairman of the provincial toll road operations board, the director of the provincial state-asset investment and trust company, and the head of the provincial state-asset management group. Altogether, these individuals oversaw state-owned assets in excess of ¥60 billion.[46]

Just a few examples can serve to illustrate how lucrative this practice can be. In a fourteen-month period during 2003–04, Wu Bao'an, a county party boss in Shanxi Province, took in ¥5 million in bribes from individuals who paid him to secure government appointments.[47] Xu Guojian, Jiangsu's organization chief, netted ¥6.4 million (¥2 million from one deal alone).[48] Han Guizhi, the provincial CCP organization chief in Heilongjiang, pocketed ¥7 million in bribes from officials seeking promotions between 1993 and 2003. And Tian Fengshan, former governor of Heilongjiang, received ¥4.4 million in bribes from 1996 to 2003 for handing out juicy government positions to those willing to pay.[49] The national record for *maiguan-maiguan* belongs to the aforementioned Ma De, the former CCP boss in Suihua prefecture in Heilongjiang. From 1997 to 2002 he collected bribes worth ¥24 million, for an average of more than ¥10,000 (approximately US$1,250) a day.[50] The most extreme case of *maiguan-maiguan*, which occurred in Heilongjiang, involved 265 officials, including five officials at the deputy governor level.[51]

Collusion

Widespread collusion among members of the ruling elite completely subverts the political hierarchy and state authority and thus is widely regarded as a symptom of almost incurable institutional decay. Previously unknown or rare in China, collusive corruption—termed *wo'an* (literally, nest cases)—has become common since the 1990s. In retrospect, its emergence was predictable. Since the Cultural Revolution, members of the ruling elite have become quite negative about mass political movements, and since Tiananmen, they have been shielded from the scrutiny of the mass media and civil society by the conservative political environment. As a result, those engaged in corrupt activities are under no serious threat other than denunciation by their colleagues. Collusion and the sharing of the spoils of corruption have therefore become the preferred strategies of cooperation among the ruling elite.

Anecdotal evidence from various localities indicates that 30–65 percent of all corruption cases can be classified as *wo'an*.[52] In the previously cited study of more than 3,067 corruption scandals, 552 (or 18 percent), were *wo'an*. Collusive corruption has brought down numerous senior officials, sometimes numbering in the hundreds. In one study it was blamed for 29 of 36 corruption cases involving officials at the vice ministerial level and above.[53] In Suihua, where Ma De ran a racket of selling government appointments for years, 260 officials, including the chiefs of fifty government agencies and party organizations, were involved in the scandal.[54] Collusive corruption can turn an entire city or town into a local mafia state, as in the case of Fuyang City, a major region in Anhui with a population of 9 million. The impoverished city has the distinction of producing a string of corrupt party chiefs and mayors. Hundreds of local officials above the rank of *ke* (section) were investigated and punished for corruption. Most of the chiefs of the city's main bureaucracies, including the police and the finance bureau, have been involved in corruption.[55]

In a very large number of jurisdictions, local officials even collude with and protect mafia elements. The government reported that, as of January 2004, nearly 1,000 officials had been exposed for providing protection for organized crime. From March 2006 to March 2007, the government prosecuted fifty-four cases involving sixty-two officials who protected organized criminal groups.[56] He Qinglian, a leading social critic, has gone so far as to argue that the behavior of the state has increasingly assumed the style of organized crime (*hei shehui hua*).[57]

In one of the most notorious such cases, Hou Wujie, a vice governor and third highest official in Shanxi Province, was arrested in 2004 for protecting a local mafia boss. In another highly publicized case, the deputy chief of police of Jiangxi Province, Xu Xiaogang, asked a local crime boss to pay ¥450,000 to his mistress in 2003 to set up a business. Xu had provided protection for the crime boss for years.[58]

Collusion and protection have made it much harder for the authorities to crack down on corruption, with the result that many corrupt officials have been able to engage in extended predatory activities and even get promoted through the CCP and government hierarchies. For a full fifteen years, from 1990 to 2005, Wang Zhaoyao accepted bribes totaling ¥7 million on 294 occasions while he was a vice governor of Anhui Province. He could not explain where another ¥8.1 million came from. Another official, the toll-road administration chief of Hunan Province, took in nearly ¥3 million in bribes from 1994 to 2004 (in addition to ¥2.6 million in unexplained wealth); despite his actions, he kept getting promoted during this period.[59] Collusion also appears to account for as much as 61 percent of all financial corruption and crime cases.[60]

Conclusion: Corruption and Prospects for Democracy

To be sure, the Chinese government has promulgated numerous laws and rules to combat corruption. By one account, China has more than 1,200 laws, rules, and regulations designed to curb official corruption. Clearly, the problem is not a lack of legal injunctions against corruption but their weak implementation and effectiveness.[61] In recent years, Beijing has taken additional measures and begun various experiments to combat corruption.

Recent Anticorruption Measures

In fighting corruption within the elite, the CCP is forced to strike a delicate balance. On the one hand, it needs to restrain greedy officials from undermining economic development and stoking public resentment. On the other hand, it is afraid of unleashing popular opinion and unwanted civic participation that could threaten its legitimacy and rule. As a result, most recent measures tend to be top-down organizational initiatives or administrative adjustments that attempt to curb corruption within the current institutional framework of the one-party state.

In one of its most notable moves, the CCP Central Committee has begun rotating provincial anticorruption chiefs (known as secretaries of the provincial CCP discipline and inspection committees) and dispatching the CDIC's own senior personnel to assume such provincial positions. By the end of 2006, ten of the newly appointed fifteen provincial discipline chiefs (*jiwei shuji*) were either from another province or from the CDIC.[62] Even though these new discipline chiefs now occupy a lower rank because the number of deputy provincial party secretaries has been reduced (the discipline chief is now a member of the standing committee of the provincial party committee), they are supposedly more accountable to the central government since the CCP Central Committee controls the nomination and appointment of such officials.[63] Through similar recentralization initiatives in 2004 and 2005, the CDIC eliminated the previous system of "dual control," under which the CDIC's inspectors stationed in fifty-six critical government ministries, agencies, and SOEs used to report both to the CDIC and the bureaucracy's party organization. As a result, the inspectors now report only to the CDIC, without the threat of interference from these bureaucracies. In another move to overcome local obstruction, Beijing established nine land supervisory bureaus to enforce land laws. In addition, five environmental inspection centers, directly reporting to Beijing, were set up in 2006 to monitor local compliance with environmental regulations.

In August 2003, the CCP had already formed roving local inspection teams to increase the monitoring of powerful provincial party chiefs. A staff of forty-five serves five "central teams," which report to the CDIC and the Central Organization Department. Each team is headed by a ministerial official who has recently stepped down but is not yet formally retired. In a period of three years, the inspection teams visited 150 cities. However, such teams are unlikely to be effective because the heads of inspection teams lack political power, their staffs are too small, and they have restricted local access.[64] According to a former head of the Central Organization Department, when the CCP evaluates a senior provincial official, it usually solicits opinions of *ju* (bureau) and *ting* (department) officials. But local social and political networks are so complex that the CCP's evaluation team rarely obtains an accurate picture of the official being evaluated.[65]

With the aid of modern technology, the Supreme Procuratorate plans to publish the names of those who pay bribes and wants to set up a national electronic database on the individuals who have committed bribery in construction, finance, education, pharmaceuticals, and government procurement (though it has yet to implement these plans).[66] In 2004, during the height of the campaign against *maiguan-maiguan*, the Central Organization Department set up a special hotline, 12380, to allow whistle-blowers to report cases of corruption involving organizational matters, especially *maiguan-maiguan*.[67]

While these are welcome measures that should have some effect in Beijing's campaign against corruption, more drastic political reforms are needed to root it out among officials. International experience suggests that the most effective weapons against official graft are greater governmental transparency (often enforced by democratic political institutions), judicial independence (which ensures punishment of the guilty and maintains deterrence), a free media, and monitoring by nongovernmental organizations (NGOs). Indeed, some inside the CCP have recognized the need for outside pressure. In the opinion of Lu Dingyi, a veteran revolutionary who was the party's propaganda chief before the Cultural Revolution, "self-discipline" alone cannot solve the corruption problem within the CCP, which cannot be its own "referee" in this fight. The power to adjudicate and monitor corruption within the CCP, said Lu, must reside outside the party, in the hands of the people and the mass media. This, added Lu, was the only effective solution.[68]

Prospects for Democratic Change

Ironically, worsening corruption may precipitate democratic change even as it threatens to undermine China's democratic prospects by giving birth to crony-capitalism and derailing economic development. The CCP's incremental steps to fight corruption could gradually help expand the role of the media and civil society, thus introducing political liberalization through the back door. Indeed, China's mass media today already function as key players in exposing official wrongdoing and galvanizing public opinion against corruption. If it is serious about combating corruption, China must also strengthen the autonomy of the judiciary. Such a move, if adopted by the CCP, would contribute to the rule of law.

Alternatively, runaway corruption could accelerate regime decay, induce collapse, and in that way trigger a democratic transition. Uncontrolled corruption could, at some point in the future, conceivably destroy the legitimacy of the CCP, corrode the authority of the state, cause serious economic hardship or even a financial crisis, fuel social unrest, and contribute to environmental degradation. However, a crisis of those proportions may not necessarily spawn a stable liberal democracy. The transition costs would likely be extremely high, and the resulting new democracy could easily fall under the control of China's own oligarchs, whose illicitly acquired wealth could accord them great resources to manipulate an infant democratic system.

Notes

1. For recent literature on corruption in China, see Yan Sun, *Corruption and Market in Contemporary China* (Cornell University Press, 2004); Shawn Shieh, "The Rise of Collective Corruption in China: The Xiamen Smuggling Case," *Journal of Contemporary China* 14, no. 42 (2005): pp. 67–91; Andrew Wedeman, "The Intensification of Corruption in China," *China Quarterly*, no. 180 (December 2004): 895–921; Xiaobo Lu, "Booty Socialism, Bureau-Preneurs, and the State in Transition: Organizational Corruption in China," *Comparative Politics* 32 (April 2000): 273–94.

2. Li Shaoming and Judy Jun Wu claim that corruption has not hurt China's economic growth because of high social trust. But the only empirical evidence they offer is a survey by the World Values project showing that 54 percent of the people in China reported they trust other people. Li Shaoming and Judy Jun Wu, "Why China Thrives Despite Corruption," *Far Eastern Economic Review*, April 7, 2007, pp. 24–28.

3. Chinese press reports show that corruption is frequently behind major environmental accidents, mining disasters, and the sale of counterfeit products, including dangerous, fake pharmaceuticals.

4. In the Chinese context, *crony-capitalism* refers to government officials' practice of giving sweetheart real estate deals, government contracts, and state-bank loans to companies owned by their children, friends, and bribe-givers. Two high-profile scandals in Shanghai are representative. Zhang Rongkun, a well-connected thirty-five-year old private entrepreneur from Zhejiang, managed to borrow more than ¥10 billion to invest in toll roads. Most of his loans came from the Shanghai Social Security Fund. Zhou Zhengyi, a Shanghai private real estate developer, made a huge fortune mainly by gaining access to cheap land and easy credit from state-owned banks. *Gaige neican* (Internal reference materials on reform), no. 26 (2006), pp. 14–16.

5. Chinese prosecutors usually get most of their cases from the CCP's in-house discipline and inspection committees, which decide whether to transfer to the courts for criminal prosecution the cases they investigate and conclude.

6. See www.chinanews.com.cn, January 19, 2006.

7. *Gaige neican*, no. 6 (2006), pp. 910; in 2006 the number of *difang* officials was 170,000. *China Newsweek*, August, 21, 2006, p. 32.

8. The trend seems to be worsening. In 2001, 51 percent of individuals convicted of *zhiwu fanzui* received suspended sentences; in 2005, 67 percent did. *Gaige neican,* no. 23 (2006), p. 17; www.chinanews.com.cn, July 26, 2006.

9. Corruption was rated the most serious social problem in 2000 and 2002, and the second most serious in 1999, 2003, and 2004. In 2006 the top three issues were crime, income inequality, and lack of access to health care. In 2005 the top three were income inequality, regional income disparities, and declining public morality. In 2004 income inequality was tops; in 2003, unemployment. The number of midlevel officials who participated in each survey ranges from 100 to 150. *Blue Book on Chinese Society* (Beijing: Shehui kexue chubanshe, various years); *Gaige neican,* no. 35 (2006), p. 19.

10. *Banyuetan* (Fortnightly Discussion Forum), August 15, 2006, p. 4.

11. *DRC Research Report* 285, December 13, 2006.

12. Such violations include overstating the number of staff, setting up slush funds, misappropriating special funds, and collecting illegal fees. See www.chinanews.com.cn, October 16, 2006, and December 26, 2005.

13. Xu Sitao, "Shengzhi Jiasu nan," *Caijing* (Finance), July 24, 2006, p. 68; I decided to use the on-budget expenditures in 2000 as a reference point because this happened to be the midpoint for this period. See *Zhongguo tongji nianjian 2004* (Chinese Statistical Yearbook 2004) (Beijing: Zhongguo tongji nianjian chubanshe, 2005), p. 291.

14. Huang Genglan, "Gaige neican pinglun ban," *Gaige neican,* no. 15 (2006), p. 46.

15. *Zhongguo tongji nianjian 2004*, pp. 53, 293.

16. Xiao Hua, "6000 Yi xingzheng shoufei jingle sheide yaobao?" *Beijing wanbao* (Beijing Evening News), May 9, 2007, p. 16.

17. *Zhongguo tongji nianjian 2004*, p. 187.

18. Hu Angang, *Zhongguo: Tiaozhan fubai* (China: Challenging corruption) (Hangzhou: Zhejiang renmin chubanshe, 1999), p. 61.

19. Minxin Pei, "Will China Become Another Indonesia?" *Foreign Policy,* Fall 1999, pp. 94–109.

20. Xie Shan, "Shangye huilu shida paixingbang," *Fanfubai daokan* (Anti-Corruption Herald), no. 4 (April 2006), pp. 7–16.

21. "Zhanwang 2006: liuda yaoan cheng fangfu zhongdian," *Jiancha fengyun* (Prosecutorial Storm), no. 2 (2006), p. 8.

22. See www.chinanews.com.cn, April 29, 2007.

23. Xie Shan, "Shangye huilu shida paixingbang," *Fanfubai daokan*, no. 4 (April 2006), pp. 7–16.

24. See www.chinanews.com.cn, October 17, 2006.

25. These officials include Zhao Zhanqi, director of the provincial transportation department of Zhejiang. Reported by *Jiancha ribao* (Prosecutors' Daily) (www.chinanews.com.cn, April 12, 2007).

26. Ibid.

27. Ibid., April 29, 2007.

28. Ibid., February 7, 2007.

29. Ibid., June 20, 2006.

30. Ibid., March 27, 2007.

31. Ibid., August 4, 2006.

32. Xie Shan, "Shangye huilu shida paixingbang," *Fanfubai daokan*, no. 4 (April 2006), pp. 7–16.

33. Wang Yuanfu, "Fanfu zaixian," *Fanfubai daokan,* no. 5 (May 2006), p. 5.

34. Lu Lei, "Guatou zhimeng—fangdichan paomo yu jinrong anliu," *Caijing,* September 4, 2006, pp. 39–70.

35. See www.chinanews.com.cn, September 25, 2006.

36. Xieping and Lu Lei, "Jinrong fubai qiujie," *Caijing,* January 10, 2005, p. 48.

37. Xie Shan, "Shangye huilu shida paixingbang," *Fanfubai daokan*, no. 4 (April 2006), pp. 7–16.

38. See www.chinanews.com.cn, April 12, 2007.

39. Li Qing and Hu Jiao, "Fantan guanyuan shetan," *Caijing,* no. 4 (2006): pp. 39–58.

40. Xie Shan, "Shangye huilu shida paixingbang," *Fanfubai daokan*, no. 4 (April 2006), pp. 7–16.

41. Nicholas Zamiska, "China's Probe Vindicates Drug Critic," See www.chinanews.com.cn, April 7, 2007; *Wall Street Journal,* April 5, 2007, p. B2.

42. See www.cinanews.com.cn, March 27, 2007.

43. Wang Heyan, "Wuhan zhongyuan zaimeng yinying,"*Caijing,* September 4, 2006, p. 126; www.chinanews.com.cn, May 3, 2007.

44. Ren Jianming, "2005 Fangfubai Zhanwang," *People's Daily Online,* May 11, 2005; Xiao Zhong, "Zhuoyang zhongyuan sanren yuanzhang qi shoushen," *Jiancha fengyun* (Prosecutors' Storm), no. 22 (2006), pp. 22–25.

45. See www.chinanews.com.cn, November 10, 2006.

46. Bao Yonghui, "Guo Bensheng, Toushi guanchang 'quanzhi bing,'" *Liaowang xinwen zhoukan* (Outlook News Weekly), no. 2 (2005), p. 8.

47. "Zhonggong zhongyang guowuyuan guanyu shishi keji guihua ganyao, zhengqiang zizhu cuangxin nengli de jueding," *Xinhua yuebao* (Xinhua Monthly), March 2006, p. 43.

48. Huang Shan and Xia Lin, "Shengwei zuzhi buzhang de 'qinpeng maiguan tuan,'" *Xiangzhen luntan* (Township and Village Forum), no. 4 (2006), p. 30.

49. *Gaige neican,* no. 6 (2006), p. 9.

50. See www.chinanews.com.cn, May 3, 2007.

51. Ibid.

52. Minxin Pei, *China's Trapped Transition: The Limits of Developmental Autocracy* (Harvard University Press, 2006), p. 160.

53. *Gaige neican,* no. 6 (2006), pp. 9–10.

54. See www.chinanews.com.cn, March 27, 2007.

55. *People's Daily Online,* May 11, 2005; Xiao Zhong, "Zhuoyang zhongyuan sanren yuanzhang qi shoushen," *Jiancha fengyun,* no. 22 (2006), pp. 22–25. The following Fuyang officials have been arrested or sentenced for serious corruption: the director of the Bureau of State Security, who collected ¥10 million in bribes; the deputy police chief, sentenced to life in prison for taking ¥5.5 million in bribes; a former party secretary responsible for law enforcement, arrested for accepting "huge" bribes; the head of the traffic division of the local police, found guilty of pocketing ¥14 million in bribes; Wang Huaizhong, a former party secretary and vice governor, executed for taking tens of millions of yuan in bribes; Wang Zhaoyao, another former party secretary and vice governor, arrested; and Xiao Zuoxin, a former mayor, executed for corruption. Other corrupt officials included a party chief and the city's police chief. Altogether, eight members of the city CCP standing committee and 11 *ting*-level officials were brought down by corruption over the years.

56. See www.chinanews.com.cn, November 21, 2005, and April 29, 2007.

57. See He Qinglian, "Zhongguo zhengfu xingwei de heishehui hua" (The criminalization of the behavior of the Chinese government), Report for Human Rights in China (New York: 2007).

58. See www.people.com.cn, January 12, 2007.

59. Ibid., March 27, 2007.

60. Ibid.

61. Ibid., September 1, 2006.

62. The new provincial discipline chiefs in Henan, Shanxi, Chongqing, Shanghai, and Beijing were from the CDIC; the newly appointed discipline chiefs in Guangdong, Zhejiang, Anhui, Fujian, and Tianjin were from other provinces; www.chinanews.com.cn, April 18, 2007.

63. See ibid.

64. Ibid.

65. *Gaigen neican*, no. 35 (2006), p. 47.

66. Zong Jian, "Fanfu liqi: gongbu xinghui 'heimingdan,'" *Jiancha fengyun*, no. 1 (2006), p. 4.

67. See www.thebeijingnews.com, October 25, 2005.

68. Xu Shuiya, "Lu Dingyi: Chengzhi fubai lingyou waili," Quoted in *Beijing ribao* (Beijing Daily); www.chinanews.com.cn, May 5, 2007.

13

The Political Implications of China's Social Future: Complacency, Scorn, and the Forlorn

DOROTHY J. SOLINGER

> Big Bluffer Ye [the Party boss of a Nanjing district] was chauffeured everywhere—to business meetings, Party confabs, his equestrian club, the Party's exclusive tennis courts in his black Audi 6. . . . I was at the gate waiting when the Audi swerved up the street, blaring its horn in the rush-hour traffic. . . . As the car sped up to me, cutting into the bicycle lane, Ye reached over to open the door. The door smacked an old man on a bicycle, sending him face-forward onto the asphalt. "Don't worry about him," Ye shouted from inside the car as it screeched to halt. "Get in." . . . "Hey . . ." the old man shouted, as he struggled to his feet. The click of the door silenced him in mid-sentence. The motor purred; the air conditioner blasted. Bicyclists glared into the car.
>
> JOHN POMFRET, *Chinese Lessons: Five Classmates and the Story of the New China* (2006)

A pair of poignant themes emerges from John Pomfret's anecdote: the hauteur of China's "haves" toward the poor and the old, and the anger and powerlessness of its "have-nots" in their hardscrabble existence. Not surprisingly, today's China is a society in which a concern for social justice leaps from the lips of more than 90 percent of the people, including some of the country's top politicians, according to one account. To address these concerns, the regime is striving to produce some elements of the rule of law.[1]

While protests and labor disputes abound, the Chinese Communist Party (CCP) seems to be listening and attempting to alleviate the inequities and inequalities at their roots. To cite a few examples, the central government has planned fee exemptions and subsidies for students in 592 poor counties; allocated increasing amounts of investment to the western, less developed part of

251

the country and eliminated the rural tax; recently announced subsistence allowances for rural residents in abject poverty and increased the funds for the rural sector by 15.6 percent a year from 2003; and raised the *dibao* (minimum living guarantee) such that the outlay in 2002 was twentyfold that of 1992.[2] Although the job market is severely compromised and the majority of workers go without welfare guarantees, the government claims it is giving these problems high priority.[3] The results of its efforts remain somewhat clouded, however, by the mixed reviews it has been receiving: some say the numbers of "incidents" and "disturbances" are steadily escalating, others that the reverse is true.[4] When people have been surveyed directly, a majority claim to be contented, with their incomes climbing year by year.[5]

China's ultimate goal, its leaders state, is to build a "harmonious society," defined by the *China Daily* in autumn 2006 as "one that respects the rights of people, sticks to the principles of human civilization and abides by the laws of nature." This would seem a challenging task, given that the poorest 10 percent of the citizenry control a mere 1.4 percent of total income, whereas the top 10 percent own a full 45 percent of China's total assets.[6] That such information can now be accessed through the official media underscores the leadership's awareness of the urgency of the problem, as too does the government's decision to mete out billions of yuan in order to pull up the income of the indigent and expand the size of the middle class, even as it simultaneously seeks to wipe out corruption and clamp down on what it terms "excessively high salaries."[7] Clearly, the political elite are determined to stay atop and ahead of the tides of discontent.

To assess the leadership's chances of making things better, one might look for clues in several social trends and the segments of the population involved: aging and the aged; growing imbalances in sex ratios and their effects on bachelors; urbanization and migrant workers; increasing poverty and unemployment in the cities, with the concomitant birth of an urban underclass; and rising upper- and middle-class incomes, especially those of private entrepreneurs. These trends should also indicate whether China's social structure is undergoing major realignments; at least in the short term, however, there are few signs that they herald the rise of democracy. Instead, the next decade or so is likely to see a progressive advance of the better-off, both in their advisory capacity and in their clout, along with a few gestures (some substantive, others symbolic) to the disadvantaged, whose members will become entrenched as the socially and politically excluded. China's social future thus appears headed for a politics of complacency and sometimes scorn among the better-off, with a persistence of the present status of the forlorn.

Five Trends and Their Associated Groups

The issues surrounding the five social groups I have just identified will undoubtedly leave a large mark on China's coming politics.

Aging and the Aged

One striking social trend, confirmed by recent research, is a change in the age structure of the Chinese population. Demographic calculations indicate that from 2007 to about 2015, those aged sixty-five or older will increase from about 7–8 percent of the populace to 15 percent. As soon as 2025, their numbers could amount to a full one-fifth of the population and continue to climb steadily thereafter. As a result, the proportion of working-age people (aged fifteen to sixty-four) is expected to decline steadily from its level of more than 70 percent of the population in 2000, such that the growth rate of the working-age population in the cities is expected to drop from 1.5 percent in 2005 to zero in subsequent years.[8] Indeed, two leading demographers have predicted that "China will soon enter a long period of decline in labor supply, and will face a rapid increase in the elderly population that cannot be reversed easily and quickly."[9]

Numerically, the population over the age of 65 is expected to rise from 100 million in 2005 to as many as 329 million in 2050, with their proportion of the total population swelling from 7.6 percent to 23.6 percent over that period. Another estimate, by Zhang Yi, a researcher at the Chinese Academy of Social Sciences, puts the proportion at 14 percent by 2028.[10] In part, this aging trend is a function of the one-child policy and resulting slowdown in the birth rate over time; it is also an effect of the increase over time in life expectancy, which rose from 35 years in 1950 to over 71.4 years by the time of the 2000 census.[11] With the increase in the marriage age and greater numbers of young people extending their years in school, the birth rate is expected to decline even more, further increasing the proportion of elderly citizens in the total population.[12]

What will become of this ever-larger section of the populace? Social scientists do not present an optimistic outlook. While just 8 percent of those aged sixty to sixty-nine are likely to be unable to provide for themselves, 49 percent of those aged eighty-five to eighty-nine will require assistance in caring for themselves. Their offspring, who will be down to just one per generation within coming years, will be under severe strain, even as the "baby boom" generation starts to retire around 2015.[13] Moreover, certain aspects of China's economic reforms are likely to exacerbate this problem. The demise in the cities of widespread *danwei* (work unit) welfare and the failure, to date, to replace it with an adequate social security or pension system, combined with the decay of collective health care

systems in the countryside, are likely to make health care for the elderly a popular concern in China in coming years. There was already a serious issue of inadequate welfare provision in the late 1990s, at which time nearly 90 percent of the
rural population and 40–50 percent of urbanites were without health care insurance. As a result, the government began to work on constructing new social
safety nets in the urban and rural areas, though even now these are not yet fully
functional.[14]

Two additional aspects of older people's lives give cause for worry. First, the
2000 census revealed a decline in household size in urban China, down to just
about three people per household, a development that is related to a growing
tendency of the elderly to live by themselves. At that time, 8.4 percent of males
and 13.7 percent of females over sixty-five lived alone, while 16.9 percent of
men in that age group were residing just with their spouse.[15] Second, as pointed
out by recent research, people of lower socioeconomic status age faster than
those with higher incomes. These trends suggest that many of those advancing
in age are likely to be short on funds.[16]

All in all, many elderly may soon be indigent, unhealthy, and living without
sufficient support. Their level of satisfaction is already lower than that of other
age groups.[17] Research suggests that many in this group, such as the large numbers who protested over unpaid pensions in the late 1990s, may still be tied to
the Maoist past, remembering nostalgically all the socioeconomic benefits they
received back then.[18] If this is widely the case, they are not apt to become politically active, much less to press for democratization.

Research conducted in the second half of the 1990s shows people over the
age of fifty-six having the highest level of support for the political regime of any
age group, with those over sixty-five exhibiting the strongest support of any
group. Of course, some of these surveys were done in 1995 and 1997, before the
most extreme of the market reforms took hold, and thus reflect an attachment
to the Maoist system, which granted them pensions, nearly free housing, and
health care. But their continuing support for the regime in 1999 could reflect
that—again, except for those who protested over nonreceipt of pensions—many
were ill-disposed to fight for change of any kind. As the author of the study
pointed out, "The relationship between aging and resistance to change is a phenomenon widely observed."[19]

Growing Imbalance in Sex Ratios and Bachelors

Another expanding demographic group that may be even less likely to agitate
for democracy consists of multiplying numbers of bachelors, young men unable
to find wives, mainly because the one-child policy and China's age-old preference for male offspring has induced many women to abort or abandon female

babies. Reportedly, "since 1995, an average of more than one million females have been 'missing' each year from the birth population alone." Here, "missing" simply means that there is no record of their births, not that they have all died.[20] If this trend prevails, by 2020 China should have between 29 million and 33 million "surplus" males in the age group fifteen to thirty-four.[21] Most of these men will be rural-born, poor, and of low status, making it even more difficult for them to attract female partners. Migrating to the cities will not enhance their chances, since the women there will constitute a sellers' market, most of them having their choice among young, better-off, urban-registered males.

Some speculate that men living in these conditions could end up like their historical predecessors: often transient and without steady work, undereducated, and easily stirred to conflict, violence, crime, and even rebellion.[22] If that turns out to be correct, this subgroup could become active—capable, possibly, of causing mayhem well beyond its numbers—but probably not in politically positive ways. Indeed, to date, there are no data describing them as democracy advocates. It is, of course, possible that the regime, aware of this issue, could attempt to install reforms to address the grievances of these frustrated males. So far, it is not clear what these might turn out to be.

Urbanization and Migrants

According to demographer Judith Banister, China's urban population increased from 18 percent of the total population in 1978 to 42 percent in 2004.[23] Although the redefinition of some townships and the expansion into the countryside of some urban jurisdictions can account for some of this metamorphosis, a more important force for urbanization has been the massive rural-to-urban migration, which is said to account for "60 percent of all urban population growth during the 1990s." While the 2000 census tabulated only 80 million as migrants on the move, if people who had lived at their then-current place of residence for less than six months had been included, the total number of temporary dwellers would have been as high as 120 million. In major east coast cities, where the largest concentrations of sojourners are located, one-third or more of the populace is composed of these "outsiders."[24]

Migrants often take part in labor protests, especially in the Pearl River Delta, although these actions are, for the most part, little more than cries for unpaid wages.[25] At this point, these people are not politically relevant in any "democratic" sense, not only because of the nature of their demands but also because of the barriers imposed by the registration system, which prevents them from remaining in urban areas and does not permit them to take part in elections. As a result, they cannot receive urban benefits such as unemployment insurance, pensions, or medical insurance, though reforms that would offer them some of these goods are currently under experimentation. Migrant parents also have to contend with the higher education costs for migrant children should they try to enroll in urban schools.[26] Alternatively, they have attempted to create their own schools but have constantly faced obstacles here. In 2006, for instance, sixteen of the schools that migrant parents had set up for their children in Shanghai were shut down, and there have been "scores of closings in China's big Eastern cities recently . . . [where] most of the nation's 20 million or more migrant children live. . . . In some instances as few as 10 percent of the students were absorbed into the public school system."[27]

Despite recent reforms, the household registration (*hukou*) system continues to exclude most rural migrants from permanent settlement in the cities.[28] As a result, "a new urban underclass that includes a significant proportion of temporary migrants has been gradually developing in many Chinese cities."[29] This rigid barrier to urban residency affects not only the migrants themselves but also the children and wives left behind in the countryside. A recent survey in Anhui Province found 74 percent of rural school children living with only one parent, and 31 percent having neither parent at home—a situation that is damaging their schoolwork and entices many into hooliganism.[30] According to the official organ *China Daily*, more than 20 million children throughout China have been left in the countryside with either one or no parents.[31]

Although more women have begun moving into towns, reportedly up to 47 million have been at least temporarily abandoned in the countryside, left to care for the land, the young, and the old, and at increased risk of becoming targets of violent crime.[32] In late 2006, an officer in the public security bureau of Jiangsu Province noted that authorities were investigating ninety recent sexual attacks in the rural areas, as well as numerous instances of property damage and robbery.[33]

The rise in migrant population is likely to accelerate as rural land is appropriated for development use, environmental pollution in the countryside continues unabated, rural wages remain at approximately half of those along the coast, and labor-age urbanites begin to decline. In the next twenty years, demographers predict, as many as 300 million people will leave the countryside and move to urban places.[34] Some research suggests that these migrant workers—despite being better educated and better dressed than their parents, more comfortable with modern technology, and more experienced in factory protests—will be "no nearer to gaining a foothold in the city than [their] predecessors were."[35]

In the two and a half decades since migrant workers began leaving the farms, concludes demographer Fei Guo, "changes in migrant occupational structure have been insignificant"; too, "migration has not brought significant social transformation to millions of rural migrants . . . who have hardly become an integrated part of [the city]."[36] Since central policy seems unable to spark fundamental changes in these phenomena, the majority of migrants are likely to remain on the fringes of urban society, scratching out a livelihood and not expressing political inclinations. Neither the emptying out of the countryside into the cities—mostly of young males, who are compelled to subsist there as an unwelcome, unentitled, undervalued, and socially excluded presence—nor the rise of crime back in the rural home, where the victims have no real recourse to justice, suggests that political activism will take hold. Indeed, there has been no sign of any demands for democracy among these groups so far. A rising trend of children dropping out of school in rural areas and a concomitant decline in the percentage of educated rural youth also seem to augur poorly for democracy.[37]

Urban Poverty, Unemployment, and the New Underclass

Just how much poverty is there in China's cities today? This is a subject for various sorts of calculation and speculation, complicated by changing prices over time, differing definitions and standards (whether according to consumption or income), and regional variation. According to the China Human Development Report of 2005, prepared under UN auspices, 300 million to 400 million Chinese were living on the margins in rural areas that year. Another estimate around the same time, arrived at in a World Bank study using the norm of US$1 a day to divide the poor from the rest, put the number of poor in all of China at just 130 million.[38] However, the World Bank's Development Report, as cited in the Chinese Academy of Social Sciences' 2006 Blue Book of Social Development, put the total at 200 million, while the Asian Development Bank, using expenditure data, found a mere 37 million poor living in the cities.

Using the Chinese government's preferred standard—namely, an annual per capita income of less than ¥683 (about US$85)—the State Council found only 23.65 million rural residents living in abject poverty at the end of 2005.[39] When measured by farmers' net incomes and urbanites' disposable incomes reported in the China Statistical Yearbook for 2004, the rural figure rises to 64.3 million, with another 27.15 million in the cities, for a total of 91.45 million poor in China.[40] For the urban areas alone, estimates for the early 2000s range from a low of 14 million to a high of 37 million.[41]

Whatever the actual figures, they are being fanned by China's worsening unemployment. The government had aimed to keep the official urban unemployment rate under 4.6 percent for 2006, but that goal was apparently not reached, as the target figure was subsequently revised to "below 5 percent" for the years 2007 through 2010.[42] A researcher at Beijing University's China Center for Economic Research recently estimated the true rate of unemployment to be 10–15 percent and rising, while another scholar found it to be even higher, citing a rate of 16.36 percent.[43] Meanwhile, roughly 10 million new workers are entering the labor market each year, even as the manufacturing sector's ability to absorb labor is on the decline.[44]

A particularly worrisome development is the mounting number of unemployed college graduates. In 2006 a reported 1 million applicants competed for a mere 10,000 posts in the national examination for civil servants, and three of every five new university graduates were likely to be jobless. In 2007 the number of young people in search of jobs was expected to rise by 22 percent over the previous year, while the positions available were down by more than 20 percent.[45] Clearly concerned, the government is making an effort to alleviate the situation, but it will be difficult, if even possible, to find a solution. Yet these sorts of exigencies do not seem to have affected the political process or produced any political demands for greater inclusion or representation. Protests by baccalaureates have been narrowly focused on the demand for jobs rather than pleas for systemic political change, while neither the poor nor the unemployed have gone to the streets demanding democratic transformation.[46]

The CCP's efforts to bring the excluded into the political process have not been encouraging. What has been occurring is that worker and farmer representation in the party has dropped markedly, from nearly two-thirds of the CCP membership in 1994 to less than half by the end of 2003.[47] Figures for workers and farmers in the National People's Congress (NPC) suggest that by the late 1990s their representation had fallen to just 11 percent and 8 percent, respectively, after a high of 27 percent and 21 percent in the early 1980s. Further symbolizing the marginality of the lower classes in the NPC, migrant laborers were not represented at all.[48]

Rising Incomes, the Middle Class, and Private Entrepreneurs

In the words of the *China Daily Business Weekly,* "A substantial middle class has taken shape in China and is likely to keep growing given the country's galloping economic growth and the government's efforts to expand their ranks in a bid to maintain social harmony." The *Weekly* goes on to define the middle class as "a couple with one child, an urban apartment, no pets, and one car mainly used for weekend getaways." Other defining characteristics of this group would be its educational levels, good careers, and high social standing. According to the National Bureau of Statistics (NBS), the annual income of such a family in 2004 would have been between ¥60,000 and ¥600,000 (or US$7,500 to $75,000). Members of this stratum are civil servants, company managers, technicians, or private business owners—in other words, professional white-collar workers as well as private entrepreneurs.[49]

Because the boundaries of this division of the population are so indeterminate, estimates of its numbers vary considerably. Some put its total at about 65 million in 2005 (which would be 5.04 percent of the population) and expect the figure to reach perhaps 750 million (45 percent) by 2020.[50] Others calculate that the "middle stratum" had already reached about 260 million in 2003 (20 percent of the population) and will be close to 633 million (38 percent of the total population) by 2020.[51]

Despite the wide range of these predictions, the upward trend is unmistakable, but the figures must be considered alongside China's 100 million aged population, its 150 million migrants, and the 90 million to 440 million people living in poverty.[52] Each of these population segments is likely to continue growing steadily as well (along with the unemployed and the bachelors making up the broader category of "the poor").

One of the newer categories, private entrepreneurs, is also on the rise. The owners of businesses who belong to this group have an average of ¥1.31 million of registered capital, and numbered 3.65 million in 2004, after increasing at the rate of 810,000 a year since 1995.[53] The category could also be viewed as people participating in China's 2.44 million privately operated firms, and if so its numbers rise to 34 million for 2002 (or 4.62 percent of the employed population); of this total, 6.23 million were investors. Another 6.43 percent small proprietors, small traders, and individual entrepreneurs (*getihu*).[54] Again, it is difficult to draw hard conclusions from this set of disparate data, except to note that this stratum is quickly expanding and attracting much attention.

The activities of the richer segment of the populace clearly demonstrate its elitism. Upper-income women are enrolling in classes on image-designing, adult ballet, social etiquette, and communication skills ("only women with decent incomes have such demands and can afford such costs," remarked the president of a Women's Training Club). At the same time, private education in Beijing can cost as much as ¥14,500 (US$1,788) a year for primary school students, while wealthy parents might well lay out another ¥800 a month for dance, music, and English classes. In Shenzhen, the Zuanyuan (Diamond Affinity) Information Company offers courses to prepare young women to attract rich bachelors at a cost of ¥20,000 to ¥50,000 per course, while their prospective mates are willing to put out ¥60,000 to ¥1 million for such matchmaking services.[55] The costs for the activities of those on the rise in China's urban consumer society—bowling, disco dancing, purchasing luxury housing apartments, and buying bridal gowns—surpass the purchasing power of those who are not already members of the "middle class."[56] One particularly striking indication of the growth in personal income is the competition for parking on many college campuses because growing numbers of students drive their personal cars to school. In the past few years, Xiamen University, seeking to cater to the changing tastes of the *nouveau riche*, was planning to offer classes in golf, mandatory for some majors, and a

Beijing businessman was putting ¥12 million into the construction of polo grounds specifically targeted at a new generation of Chinese elites.[57] The wealthiest of its individuals cluster mainly in the large, modern cities along the eastern coast and are apt to have foreign contacts. These brushes with Western bourgeoisie, one might surmise, could dispose them to dream of democracy, but the evidence shows no clear trajectory leading to this outcome.

Politically, most indications are that the middle class and even more so the wealthy are wedded to, and benefit from, the current status quo. True, these people are sometimes willing to engage in resistance, but so far only in defense of their homes. In any case, the record of success in "pushing back" is not promising,[58] and these people are not inclined to pursue any fundamental political change.[59] Perhaps as a consequence—and also out of the leaders' own hopes— the regime takes these people as its supporters, to judge from official intentions as expressed in the media. Recently, for instance, the party has been making much of the "new social classes," meaning private businesspeople and self-employed intellectuals, who numbered some 20 million as of 2006. Such elites are publicly praised for their tremendous contribution to both the economic and social progress of the country. In the words of a *China Daily* article, "The Party says it will give reverence, assistance and guidance" to these people, as they "set the trends for the young generation."[60]

The party-state is obviously keen to co-opt persons of this type, no doubt in the interest of stabilizing society, calling them the future "backbone of Chinese society."[61] Quite unlike those in the lower sections of society, who are becoming increasingly marginalized, many from these new social classes have been incorporated into urban-level branches of the Federation of Industry and Commerce, local people's congresses, and people's consultative conferences. As of late 2006, 38 of the top 100 business tycoons in the latest edition of China's version of the *Forbes* list were members of the top organs of the state: 19 were deputies to the National People's Congress (a doubling of such individuals in that body in just one year), with the rest belonging to the National Committee of the Chinese People's Political Consultative Conference. On top of that, more than 200 members of the legislature—or nearly 7 percent—were private entrepreneurs.[62] The Sixth Plenum of the Sixteenth Party Congress even *required* that the provinces pick a certain number of party members from this segment of society to serve as deputies to the Seventeenth Party Congress.[63]

In a related development, in the party's late 2005 statement celebrating its building of democracy, the section on "the system of multi-party cooperation and political consultation under the leadership of the CPC" preceded the one on grassroots democracy, making much of the nine "democratic" political parties that purport to represent wealthy businesspeople, and with which the Communist Party allegedly "collaborates." If that document is any indication, inner-party cooperation and consultation are becoming institutionalized and standardized, and thus more important. Equally telling are the important roles that entrepreneurs are playing in people's congresses. They also hold leading positions in government and judicial organs and exercise democratic supervision over the party and the state.[64] It is these personages, in particular, whom the party approaches for advice on constructing its "harmonious society."[65]

Conclusion

Clues to China's near-term political future can be found not only in the overt political behavior of its population but also in the composition and activities of select social groups whose numbers are increasing. These factors suggest that change, when it comes, is more apt to be initiated by the top political decision-makers than by the popular strata within society. Furthermore, the discontented segments of the populace, those with the potential to become activists—ranging from members of nongovernmental organizations, netizens, intellectuals, and artists to peasants rioting over pollution or against the dispossession of their land, people newly conscious of their rights, and those enraged by official corruption—are too geographically dispersed to create broadly based influential movements. Thus there seems to be little potential for organizational success, since many social barriers separate the members of these groups. Besides, perilous risks await anyone who would aspire to lead these groups in demanding sociopolitical change.

Therefore instead of predicting change to issue from any of these groups, I looked at the place of each of them within society and their near-term prospects, along with the regime's stancees toward each of them. The government appears set to concentrate on building its "harmonious society," in part through the new alliance with the upper strata of the population. At the same time, it will likely use a growing portion of the state's coffers to quiet those at the base—to keep them minimally satisfied but still politically excluded. As a result, the Chinese polity appears to be moving not toward democratization, in which numbers count, but toward elitism. This, then, is a politics of complacency and scorn among those in the social strata who matter, and a politics of the forlorn for those who do not.

Notes

1. Mary E. Gallagher, "Mobilizing the Law in China: 'Informed Disenchantment' and the Development of Legal Consciousness," *Law and Society Review* 40, no. 4 (2006): 783–816. The regime's public stance is referenced in note 4.

2. *China Daily*, March 21, 2005, p. 6.; Gu Wen and Yang Yiyong, "2005–2006 Nan: Zhongguo shourur fenpei wenti yu zhanwang" (2005–2006: The issue of Chinese income distribution and the outlook), in *Shehui lanpishu: 2006 nian* (Social blue book: 2006), edited by Ru Xin, Lu Xueyi, and Li Peilin (Beijing: Shehui kexue wenxian chubanshe (Social science documents company, 2006), p. 277; Zhao Huanxin, "Subsidy Net to Cover All Rural Poor in China," *China Daily*, December 25, 2007; and Tang Jun, "Zhongguo chengshi jumin zuidi shenghuo baozhang zhidu de 'tiaoyueshi' fazhan" (The leap forward style of development of Chinese urban residents' minimum livelihood guarantee), in *Shehui lanpishu: 2003 nian: Zhongguo shehui xingshi fenxi yu yuce* (Social blue book: 2003: Analysis and predictions of China's social situation), edited by Ru Xin, Lu Xueyi, and Li Peilin (Beijing: Shehui kexue wenxian chubanshe, 2003), pp. 243–45.

3. "Social Formula of Hope," *China Daily*, October 12, 2006, states that the Sixth Plenum of the Communist Party in October 2006 promised "guarantees of civil rights under a framework of law," a "reasonable and orderly income distribution system," "decent job supply and a social security network" for city and rural residents, plus improved public administration and services.

4. Guan Xiaofeng, "Labor Disputes Threaten Stability," *China Daily*, January 30, 2007, states that worker altercations are increasing (the 314,000 cases of 2005 were a 20 percent rise over the number in 2004). But see Zhao Huanxin, "Farmers' Protests Decline Sharply," *China Daily*, January 31, 2007. Zhao claims that since the State Council called on local governments to raise compensation payments to farmers whose land was taken over for development projects and to provide job training and reemployment assistance plus social security for them, protests in the countryside declined by the same 20 percent.

5. Satisfaction rose between 2000 and 2005, with a peak in 2004: also, 70 percent of the respondents expressed satisfaction toward their overall situation in 2002, while 73.7 percent felt optimistic about their own future livelihood in 2005. See Yuan Yue and Zeng Huizhao, "2002 nian Zhongguo jumin shenghuo zhiliang diaocha" (An investigation of Chinese urban residents' quality of life in 2002), in *Shehui lanpishu: 2003 nian,* edited by Ru and others, pp. 140–50; and Zhang Hui and Yuan Yue, "2005 nian Zhongguo jumin shenghuo zhiliang diaocha baogao" (Report of an investigation of Chinese urban residents' quality of life in 2005), in *Shehui lanpishu: 2006 nian,* edited by Ru and others, pp. 52–66). On incomes, see Zhu Qingfang, "Jumin shenghuo he xiaofei jiegou de xin bianhua" (New changes in residents' livelihood and consumption structure), in *Shehui lanpishu: 2006 nian,* edited by Ru and others, pp. 85–86.

6. Qin Xiaoying, "Harmonious Society to Be a Model for the World," *China Daily*, October 13, 2006 (www.chinadaily.com.cn/bizchina/2006-10/13/content_707731.htm). Statistics are from the *Hindu,* December 27, 2006, citing an investigation published by the NBS in June 2006.

7. From July 1, 2006, the central government would spend ¥34.7 billion for these purposes. See "China Strives to Narrow Yawning Income Gap for Social Equality," Xinhua News Agency, October 1, 2006 (www.chinadaily.com.cn/china/2006-10/01/content_700784.htm).

8. Barry Naughton, *The Chinese Economy: Transitions and Growth* (Cambridge, Mass.: MIT Press, 2007), pp. 17–76.

9. Wang Feng and Andrew Mason, "The Demographic Factor in China's Transition," in *China's Economic Transitions: Origins, Mechanisms, and Consequences*, edited by Loren Brant and Thomas Rawski (Cambridge University Press, 2008), p. 32.

10. Zhongwei Zhao and Fei Guo, "Introduction," in *Transition and Challenge: China's Population at the Beginning of the 21st Century,* edited by Zhongwei Zhao and Fei Guo (Oxford University Press, 2007), p. 8; Zhang Yi, "13 yi zhihou Zhongguo renkou de xin tezheng" (New characteristics of China's population after 1.3 billion), in *Shehui lanpishu: 2006 nian,* edited by Ru and others, p. 104. Judith Banister, "Poverty, Progress, and Rising Life Expectancy," in *Transition and Challenge,* edited by Zhao and Guo, pp. 140–59, also addresses this.

11. Zhang, "13 yi," pp. 97–98, 101, states that between 1978 and 2004 the birth rate fell from 18.25 per thousand to 12.29 per thousand.

12. Ibid., pp. 102, 106–07.

13. Naughton, *The Chinese Economy,* p. 175.

14. Zhao and Guo, "Introduction," p. 8; Banister, "Poverty, Progress," p. 143.

15. Wang and Mason, "The Demographic Factor," p. 13.

16. "Poor Are Worse Off in Aging Process," *China Daily,* July 21, 2006 (www.chinadaily.com/cn/cndy/2006-7/21/content_645867.htm).

17. Raymond Chou, "Folks, Are You Happy with Your Lot?" *China Daily,* December 16, 2004.

18. William Hurst and Kevin J. O'Brien, "China's Contentious Pensioners," *China Quarterly,* no. 170 (June 2002): 345–60. Other accounts of the nostalgia for Maoism among members of the older population are in Ching Kwan Lee, "The 'Revenge of History': Collective Memories and Labor Protests in Northeastern China," *Ethnography* 1, no. 2 (2000): 217–37; and Eva P. W. Hung and Stephen W. K. Chiu, "The Lost Generation," *Modern China* 29 (April 2003): 204–36.

19. Jie Chen, *Popular Political Support in Urban China* (Stanford University Press, 2004), pp. 78–79.

20. Valerie M. Hudson and Andrea M. den Boer, *Bare Branches: The Security Implications of Asia's Surplus Male Population* (Cambridge, Mass.: MIT Press, 2004), p. 157. Wang and Mason, "The Demographic Factor," pp. 26–27, explain how these numbers could be exaggerated, partly through the underreporting of female births. See also Yong Cai and William Lavely, "China's Sex Ratios and Their Regional Variation," in *Transition and Challenge,* edited by Zhao and Guo, pp. 108–23.

21. See Hudson and den Boer, *Bare Branches,* pp. 179–81; and Wang Shanshan, "30 Million Men Face Bleak Future as Singles," *China Daily,* January 12, 2007. Both report on a study by the State Population and Family Planning Commission indicating that about one in every ten men aged twenty to and forty-five will be unable to marry. See also Jane Macartney, "China Faces Population Imbalance Crisis," in *Times Online,* January 12, 2007 (www.timesonline.co.uk/tol/news/world/asia/article1292295.ece).

22. Hudson and den Boer, *Bare Branches,* chap. 5.

23. Banister, "Poverty, Progess," p. 157. Lu Xueyi, "Tiaozheng shehui jiegou, goujian shehuizhuyi hexie shehui" (Adjust the social structure, construct a harmonious socialist society), in *Shehui lanpishu: 2006 nian,* edited by Ru and others, p. 197, concurs (he cites 41.8 percent).

24. Wang and Mason, "The Demographic Factor," p. 12.

25. Ching Kwan Lee, *Against the Law: Labor Protests in China's Rustbelt and Sunbelt* (University of California Press, 2007).

26. Dorothy J. Solinger, *Contesting Citizenship in Urban China: Peasant Migrants, the State, and the Logic of the Market* (University of California Press, 1999). More recently, Lin Qi, "Club Warms the Hearts of City's Migrant Women," *China Daily,* March 15, 2005;

Wang Zhuqiong, "Female Migrants Suffering at Work," *China Daily,* November 30, 2006; "Migrant Workers Earn Monthly Income of 120 Dollars," *China Daily*, October 23, 2006 (www.chinadaily.com.cn/language_tips/2006-10/23/content_714825.htm); Fei Guo, "The Impact of Temporary Migration on Migrant Communities," in *Transition and Challenge*, edited by Zhao and Guo, pp. 216–50; and Wang Chunguang, "Nongmingong qunti de she-hui liudong" (The social mobility of the peasant worker mass), in *Dangdai Zhongguo shehui liudong* (Social mobility in contemporary China), edited by Lu Xueyi (Beijing: Shehui kexue wenxian chubanshe, 2004), chap. 10.

27. Howard W. French, "China Strains to Fit Migrants into Mainstream Classes," *New York Times*, January 25, 2007. In an NBS survey of 5,065 migrants who brought children with them to cities, 49.2 percent had to pay an average registration fee of ¥1,226 in addition to their regular tuition fees; see "Migrant Workers Earn Monthly Income of 120 Dollars."

28. Kenneth Roberts, "The Changing Profile of Labor Migration," in *Transition and Challenge*, edited by Zhao and Guo, p. 242.

29. Guo, "The Impact," p. 217.

30. Roberts, "The Changing Profile," p. 243.

31. Zhao Xiaolu, "Rural Women Left to Hold the Fort at Home," *China Daily*, December 23, 2006.

32. Roberts, "The Changing Profile," pp. 246–47; Zhao, "Rural Women." The statistic comes from research by Bai Nansheng, professor at the School of Agricultural Economics and Rural Development at Renmin University.

33. Zhao, "Rural Women Left."

34. Macartney, "China Faces Population Imbalance Crisis," citing the report from the State Population and Family Commission mentioned earlier.

35. See Cheng Li, "Hu's Policy Shift and the Tuanpai's Coming-of-Age," *China Leadership Monitor*, no. 15, p. 6, from *Zhongguo xinwen zhoukan* (China News Weekly), December 28, 2004, p. 1. Wang Chunguang notes that perhaps 80 percent of the 150 million migrants at work in cities belong to this category ("Peripheral citizens—The 2nd generation of migrant workers" [www.chinadaily.com.cn/english/doc/2005-12/27/content_507066.htm]).

36. Guo, "The Impact," pp. 231, 232.

37. A recent survey conducted by the Central Committee of China Association for Promoting Democracy found that nearly 40 percent of junior high students in the countryside have dropped out of school, about half of whom stayed at home to farm; "China Experiences Rising School Dropout Rate," Xinhua News Agency, March 4, 2005 (www.chinadaily.com.cn/english/doc/2005-03/04/content_421618.htm). See also Shi Xiuying and Li Wei, "Zhongguo zhiye jiegou de qu gaojihua ji yuanyin fensi" (Analysis of the tendency toward a rise in quality of China's professional structure and the reasons), in *Dangdai Zhongguo*, edited by Lu, pp. 90–92, 197–200. Shi and Li discuss the unfairness in educational opportunity and the lower chances for rural children to go on to higher levels of education. Lu, "Tiaozheng shehui," p. 202, states that less than 70 percent graduate from primary schools in large parts of seven poor provinces. The government announced that in 2007, tuition fees would be waived for all 150 million rural children eligible for the nine-year compulsory schooling requirement, and that the fees for 50 million of these were exempted in 2006 (news.xinhuanet.com/politics/2006/19/content_5507946.htm).

38. Xin Dingding, "Rich-Poor Divide Serious, Study Finds," *China Daily*, December 26, 2006.

39. State Council Leading Group of Office of Poverty Alleviation and Development" (bbs.chinadaily.com.cn/viewthread.php?tid=547282&extra=page). Zhu, "Jumin shenghuo," p. 92, notes that the NBS counted a total low-income population in the countryside of 75.87 million in 2004.

40. For farmers, the standard was ¥1,000 per capita net annual income; for urbanites, a daily average income of ¥6.4. Zhu, "Jumin shenghuo," p. 93.

41. He Xuesong, *Shehuixue shiyexia de Zhongguo shehui* (Chinese society in sociological perspective) (Shanghai: Huadong ligong daxue chubanshe [East China Science and Engineering College Publishing Co.], 2002), pp. 168–69, cites 15 million to 31 million. Mo Rong, "Jiuye: Zai tiaozhanzong guanzhu kunnan qunti" (Employment: In challenge, pay close attention to the masses in difficulty), in *Shehui lanpishu: 2003 nian*, edited by Ru and others, p. 40, cites Asian Development Bank data of 37 million. See also Li Peilin, "Dangqian Zhongguo shehui fazhan de rogan wenti he xin qushi" (Some issues and new trends in contemporary China's social development), in *Shehui lanpishu: 2003 nian*, edited by Ru and others, p. 23.

42. "China Aims to Keep Unemployment Rate Below 4.6 percent," Xinhua News Agency, December 20, 2005 (www.china.org.cn/english/null/152504.htm); and "China Aims to Keep Urban Jobless Rate below 5 Percent," Xinhua News Agency, November 9, 2006 (www.chinadaily.com.cn/bizchina/2006-11/09/content_728940.htm).

43. He Huifeng, "Robust Economy Masks Legions of Unemployed," *South China Morning Post*, September 17, 2006.

44. Lu, "Tiaozheng shehui," p. 200.

45. "University Graduates Line Up for Government Posts," *China Daily*, October 29, 2006 (www.chinadaily.com.cn/bizchina/2006-10/29/content_719221.htm). According to another *China Daily* story, Shanghai government department statistics show that young jobless people are increasing, and that people between the ages of sixteen and twenty-five accounted for over 40 percent of the total of Shanghai's unemployed, one-third of whom are college students. See "Foolhardy Graduates Sure of Future with No Action," *China Daily*, June 27, 2005 (www.chinadaily.com.cn/english/doc/2005-06/27/content_454969.htm).

46. Kay Lehman Schlozman and Sidney Verba, *Injury to Insult: Unemployment, Class, and Political Response* (Harvard University Press, 1979).

47. Membership dropped from 63 percent to 44 percent. See Bruce J. Dickson, "Beijing's Ambivalent Reformers," *Current History*, September 2004, pp. 250, 252.

48. Li, "Hu's Policy Shift," p. 5.

49. Liu Jie, "Middle Kingdom," *China Daily Business Weekly*, November 13, 2006; Luigi Tomba, "Creating an Urban Middle Class: Social Engineering in Beijing," *China Journal* 51 (January 2004): 1–26.

50. Liu, "Middle Kingdom."

51. Lu, "Tiaozheng shehui," p. 204.

52. Zhang Houyi, "Siying qiyezhu jieceng chengzhang de xin jieduan" (The new stage of the growth of private entrepreneurs), in *Shehui lanpishu: 2003 nian*, edited by Ru and others, p. 341. Zhang puts the number of registered private entrepreneurs at 55.65 million in mid-2005, an increase of nearly 20 percent over the year before.

53. Lu, "Tiaozheng shehui," p. 198, states that another 50 million people were employed in these firms, and that there were another 23.5 million smaller-scale individual firms, with 25.21 million people working in them.

54. Zhang Wanli, "Shehui zhongjian jieceng de jueqi" (The sudden appearance of the social middle stratum), in *Dangdai Zhongguo*, edited by Lu, pp. 275–78.

55. Xiao Changyan, "High-Income Women Seek New Image," *China Daily*, March 10, 2006; Zhang Yu, "Private Education Struggles for Survival," *China Daily*, March 6, 2006; Liu Jie, "Purchasing Patterns," *China Daily*, March 6, 2006; "Matches for Aspiring Cinderellas?" Xinhua News Agency, November 13, 2006 (www.chinadaily.com.cn/china/2006-11/13/content_731058.htm).

56. Deborah S. Davis, *The Consumer Revolution in Urban China* (University of California Press, 2000).

57. "Parking a Headache for School Campuses," *Eastday*, May 23, 2005 (www.chinadaily.com.cn/english/doc/2005-05/23/content_444971.htm); "Confidence Building," *Shanghai Star*, January 11, 2005 (www.chinadaily.com.cn/english/doc/2005-01/11/content_407898.htm); "Elitism in Education," *China Daily*, October 29, 2006; "Sport of Kings for New Elite," *China Daily*, September 28, 2006.

58. Yongshun Cai, "China's Moderate Middle Class: The Case of Homeowners' Resistance," *Asian Survey* 45 (September/October 2005): 777–99; Howard W. French, "Chinese Boomtown, Middle Class Pushes Back," *New York Times*, December 18, 2006.

59. Bruce J. Dickson, *Red Capitalists in China: The Party, Private Entrepreneurs, and Prospects for Change* (Cambridge University Press, 2003); and Kellee Tsai, "Capitalists without a Class," *Comparative Political Studies* 38 (November 2005): 1130–58.

60. "United Front Expands," *China Daily*, September 4, 2006.

61. This was the label used by Xiao Mingchao, chief researcher of the national research project, China's New Middle Class Life Survey, as reported in Liu Jie, "True Picture," *China Daily Business Weekly*, November 13, 2006.

62. "Private Business People Gain More Political Influence in China," Xinhua News Agency, October 30, 2006 (www.chinadaily.com.cn/china/2006-10/30/content_720213.htm).

63. Zhongzhou He, "The Emergence; 'New Social Stratum' Playing Important Role in China," Xinhua News Agency, February 14, 2007 (www.chinadaily.com.cn/china/2007-02/14/content_809712.htm); and Zhang, "Siying qiyezhu," p. 346.

64. "Bid to Build Democracy Comes to Fruition," *China Daily*, October 20, 2005.

65. "CPC Seeks Advice on Building Harmonious Society," Xinhua News Agency, October 13, 2006 (www.chinadaily.com.cn/china/2006-10/13/content_707558.htm).

14

Straining against the Yoke? Civil-Military Relations in China after the Seventeenth Party Congress

JAMES MULVENON

> *General Jack D. Ripper:* Mandrake, do you recall what Clemenceau once said about war?
> *Group Capt. Lionel Mandrake:* No, I don't think I do, sir, no.
> *General Jack D. Ripper:* He said war was too important to be left to the generals. When he said that, 50 years ago, he might have been right. But today, war is too important to be left to politicians. They have neither the time, the training, nor the inclination for strategic thought.
>
> *Dr. Strangelove or: How I Learned to Stop Worrying and Love the Bomb* (1964)

As China enters the homestretch for the Seventeenth Party Congress, the Chinese People's Liberation Army (PLA) is firmly under the civilian control of the Chinese Communist Party (CCP) leadership. Yet there is a growing body of evidence suggesting that the military is straining against the yoke of this arrangement. The cause of this tension is not the stereotypical complaints of the South American or Southeast Asian junta (inept civilian policymaking, perceived loss of national prestige or purity, or inadequate resources devoted to defense), but the growing quality and range of Chinese military forces. With their expanded patrolling activities and greater strategic war-fighting capabilities (in the way of road-mobile intercontinental ballistic missiles [ICBMs] and anti-satellite weapons [ASATs]), China's armed forces are challenging the CCP's traditional, post-Mao military command and control mechanisms and coming into increasing conflict with the civilian foreign policy apparatus, thereby posing large questions for the party-military dynamic of the Seventeenth Party Congress, not to mention party-military relations overall.

Post-Mao Civil-Military Relations: Conditional Compliance

The best term to describe the post-Mao civil-military arrangement in China (more accurately, its party-military relations) is Ellis Joffe's notion of "conditional compliance."[1] The Chinese military is compliant with civilian wishes in two critical respects. First, it supports the legitimacy of the CCP paramount leader and the CCP's single-party rule with the full political and coercive weight of the military institution itself. Second, the PLA has accepted a somewhat circumscribed role within the Chinese political system, by and large staying out of the management of nonmilitary policymaking arenas such as the economy and focusing on professional development instead of factional conflict. In areas of corporate identity such as military modernization and defense planning, however, the military seems to retain virtual autonomy, unfettered by civilian control. In areas of corporate interest (such as relations with the United States, Japan, or Taiwan; South China Sea issues; energy security; and arms control), the military seeks to influence the policymaking process, whereas in matters of nondefense and nonsecurity, the PLA appears to have ceded or lost the ability to influence policy.

The reasons for this conditional compliance are complicated. Viewed over the past seventy-plus years, the major continuity in Chinese civil-military relations is the party's domination of the military, manifest in the lack of a historical legacy of praetorianism or coups d'état by the PLA. In the past, this relative quiescence could be explained largely in terms of personal and institutional variables: the Chinese military was for decades subordinated in a system dominated by powerful, paramount leaders with personal connections to the senior military leadership; to reinforce that subordination, the military was penetrated from top to bottom by a political work system intent on maintaining the military's loyalty to the party. In recent years, however, both of these patterns have changed significantly. As Joffe has pointed out, neither Hu Jintao nor Jiang Zemin before him has enjoyed the same type of relationship with the PLA that Mao Zedong or Deng Xiaoping had, a fact that gives the military a degree of leverage over Hu and Jiang that it did not have with previous leaders.[2] As a result, military legitimation of Hu's leadership requires a complicated mix of formal institutional authority, patronage, and bureaucratic bargaining over resources and influence. As Michael Swaine writes: "Senior Party leaders undoubtedly play a complex and nuanced game in their policy interactions with the military leadership, seeking to retain the initiative and maintain overall flexibility by alternately placating, resisting, or diluting military views and pressures through a complex mixture of personal persuasion, balancing of bureaucratic interests, and direct control over formal organs and policy channels."[3]

For his part, Hu Jintao has spent a substantial amount of time cultivating a relationship with the PLA and catering to its interests. He regularly pays his respects to military elders, visits units, extols military heroes, supports budget and procurement increases, honors PLA traditions, and listens to their concerns about issues related to internal and external affairs. Nonetheless, Hu, like Jiang before him, remains critically dependent on the political support of the military.

In the first twenty years of the post-Mao era, two important trends—the professionalization of the officer corps and an unprecedented generational shift that has led to an effective separation of military and civilian elites—constrained the extent to which the PLA could exploit this leverage.[4] The generational shift separating military and civilian elites has been particularly important in this regard. China has undergone a tectonic generational transformation of the civilian and military leaderships from a symbiotic revolutionary guerrilla generation to a technocratic pairing of bifurcated military and civilian elites. The deaths of the revolutionary generation and changes in the political setting, especially the passing of Deng Xiaoping and the ascension of a collective leadership under Jiang Zemin and now Hu Jintao, mean that the current military leaders do not possess the same level of political capital as their predecessors and therefore are less able to act as power brokers within the system. As a result, the institutional and individual opportunities and capacities for the military to intervene in the policy process have been reduced, thereby strengthening civilian control of critical realms. Moreover, the military's intervention in politics in general and the policy process in particular has both narrowed and deepened, depending on the particular issue or individuals involved. The relative weakness of the collective civilian leadership means that bureaucratic wrangling is still required on key policy and resource distribution issues, but the parties to this bargaining cannot be considered "equals." Thus it could be argued that the PLA's conditional compliance is as much a function of the transitional trends in the Chinese system writ large as it is a result of the changing dynamic between the paramount leader and the military. Together, the interaction of these two structural changes is producing the dynamic seen in party-military relations in China today.

Since the mid-1990s China's military has become truly modern, with its expanded "normal" patrolling activities and greater war-fighting capabilities. Thus, as already mentioned, it is posing more and more command and control dilemmas for the CCP, which finds particularly troublesome the units operating at the outer edge of the PLA's impressive command, control, communications, computers, intelligence, surveillance, and reconnaissance (C4ISR) infrastructure, where Beijing's traditional penchant for close control comes into conflict with operational requirements. The imminent fielding of a new generation of road-mobile, solid-fueled ICBMs (DF-31), for example, will provide China's leadership with a credible nuclear second strike capability for the first time in its history, but operational deployment of road-mobile ICBMs presents a profound challenge to Beijing's traditional close control of nuclear weapons, since the full deterrence capability of mobile ICBMs requires provision of at least limited targeting data and rules of engagement to independent missile units to protect against an enemy decapitation strike. Similarly, the PLA's deployment and now-regular patrolling of significant numbers of quiet diesel-electric submarines creates a new and dangerous threat to U.S. carrier strike groups; but, like those manning the road-mobile ICBMs, the crews of these boats also require at least limited rules of engagement should they encounter a carrier strike group (CSG), since surfacing to send a "Mother, may I?" request to Beijing could fatally expose them to the strike group's antisubmarine-warfare operations.

A second tension in the civil-military dynamic arises from the discrepancy between China's military modernization and Beijing's attempts to present this trend as a "peaceful rise" or "peaceful development" to the international community. At least four times in the past six years, Chinese military forces have come into contact with foreign forces, each time causing a crisis in one of Beijing's most important bilateral relationships. Moreover, in all four cases the military and foreign policy bureaucracies were, it seems, not fully coordinated in their responses, causing Foreign Ministry personnel to complain privately that the military was acting as an independent entity beyond civilian oversight. After the April 2001 collision between an American EP-3 reconnaissance aircraft and a Chinese F-8II fighter, the PLA apparently presented the civilian leadership with an inaccurate version of the incident, possibly prolonging the crisis.[5] In 2004 a Han-class nuclear attack submarine violated Japanese territorial waters, much to the annoyance of Foreign Ministry officials because the PLA, they said, had not received prior approval for the operation. In 2005 a Song-class, diesel-electric attack submarine broached within 5 nautical miles of the USS *Kitty Hawk* carrier strike group, again allegedly without prior Foreign Ministry notification. And in January 2007 the Chinese military's successful ASAT test was followed by twelve days of awkward official silence, in large part because the relevant foreign policy bureaucracies had been unaware of the planned test and were unprepared to deal with the intense international reaction. This last case merits closer scrutiny.

Case Study: China's 2007 ASAT Test

On January 11, 2007, a Chinese medium-range ballistic missile (MRBM) armed with a direct-ascent kinetic kill vehicle (KKV) destroyed a defunct PRC weather satellite, the Fengyun-1C. According to open sources, the Bush administration confronted Beijing about the test soon afterward but received no substantive reply.[6] As a result, the White House went public with details of the ASAT hit on January 18. At the same time, the U.S. government publicly complained about a 2006 incident in which a Chinese ground-based laser "painted" an American satellite.[7] At first, the Chinese Foreign Ministry continued to bob and weave, reasserting China's long-standing opposition to the weaponization of space but refusing to confirm or deny the test.[8] The Defense Ministry also claimed to be unaware of a test, calling foreign newspaper accounts "hearsay."[9] While the Beijing authorities dithered, a senior military academic, speaking on January 19 to a newspaper sponsored by the party's flagship propaganda organ, tried to downplay the furor but instead conveyed (inadvertently or not) a sense of military cockiness to the outside world by describing antisatellite weapons as "ordinary."[10]

Despite an international outcry and nonstop pointed questions from both the media and foreign governments, the Foreign Ministry waited another five days to confirm the test, tepidly telling the world on January 23: "This test was not directed at any country and does not constitute a threat to any country. . . . What needs to be stressed is that China has always advocated the peaceful use of space, and opposes the weaponization of space and arms races in space."[11] When asked about the delay in confirming the test, the Foreign Ministry spokesman responded: "China has nothing to hide. After various parties expressed concern, we explained this test in outer space to them."[12] On February 8, 2007, the Foreign Ministry added one more element to its stock answer, asserting that the test did not "violate any international treaty."[13]

The twelve days of silence from the Chinese bureaucracy sparked intense speculation among outside observers that part, or all, of the civilian leadership and bureaucracy may not have known about the test ahead of time. Indeed, the very leak of the information by the White House was explicitly aimed at eliciting further information about the civil-military dynamic surrounding the ASAT test. Sensing that key parts of the Chinese bureaucracy may not have known about the test, which was almost certainly conducted by the space-related components of the PLA's General Armaments Department, administration officials informed the *New York Times* that the United States "kept mum about the antisatellite test in hopes that China would come forth with an explanation."[14] The article quoted National Security Adviser Steven Hadley, musing about whether the civilian leadership was aware of the military test: "The question on something like this is, at what level in the Chinese government are people witting, and have they approved?" Hadley further suggested that the diplomatic protests were intended, in part, to force Hu Jintao to give some clue about China's intentions: "It will ensure that the issue will now get ventilated at the highest levels in China . . . and it will be interesting to see how it comes out."

While no public information is yet available about the inner bureaucratic coordination (or lack thereof) preceding or following the test, one can advance at least three analytical hypotheses for testing future data if, and when, they become available. These hypotheses are not exhaustive, but they provide a good framework for investigating intentions and process, as well as the possible implications for civil-military relations.

SPECULATION 1: *The civilian leadership, including Hu Jintao, was completely unaware of the testing program or the specific test.* As chairman of the Central Military Commission, Hu Jintao is the only civilian official with ex officio access to information about military testing programs, but his position alone does not guarantee knowledge about the test. In addition, it is not impossible that even a civilian-dominated military could hide information from its party overlords, either for pure, impure, or mixed motives. The pure military (but subversive) motive for testing an ASAT in this scenario would be to establish the credibility of the capability for both deterrence and offensive operations, with the goal of convincing both domestic and international skeptics of this. A mixed or impure motive would be a desire to force the hand of the civilian leadership to approve more aggressive operations like ASAT warfare against high-tech adversaries like the United States in a crisis, such as a Taiwan contingency. Having tested this capability, military proponents might even believe a successful ASAT capability would likely force satellite-dependent powers such as the United States to respond with the development of offensive or defensive ASAT capabilities and thereupon secure internal support for continued testing and deployment of new Chinese ASAT systems.[15]

The civil-military implications of this scenario are potentially serious, with the strong possibility of senior military officers at multiple levels of the system being cashiered. The personnel moves could be interpreted as a signal to other serving officers in the military, reminding them of civilian control of the military and deterring them from participating in rogue activities. It could also be interpreted as a message to foreign governments, especially if the punishments are publicized, assuring them that civilian control over the military has been restored. If, however, the civilian leadership found out about the program after the test and yet no punishments were forthcoming, one would have to come to the difficult conclusion that the civilian leadership cannot or does not want to punish military personnel involved with the test because of concerns for the potential loss of institutional prestige, the possible nationalist blowback from the military and civilian population, or a decision to accept the new strategic reality and move forward.

SPECULATION 2: *As chairman of the Central Military Commission, Hu Jintao was to some extent aware of the testing program but did not know the specific date of the test.* It is not necessary or realistic for the civilian oversight authority of a large, complex military to be aware of every detail of every program. The United States has one of the longest traditions of civilian control of the military, and its senior civilian leaders often have only top-level or, at best, incomplete cognizance of major research and development (R&D) efforts. If the R&D program was approved by the civilian leadership, then the motive for this specific test was likely pure in terms of military and strategic benefit, but the civilians should be faulted for not maintaining closer oversight of the program and not calculating the possible negative international diplomatic repercussions of a successful test.

The civil-military implications of this scenario are less serious than the first, but the resulting bureaucratic decisions will also be an effective indicator of civilian leadership attitudes. If military officials are quietly punished, it may be only an internal signal meant to reassert civilian control of the military while retaining the appearance of nationalist unity abroad. If military officials are publicly punished, it might indicate a desire to communicate reassertion of civilian control to foreign audiences and repair some of the damage to the country's international relations. If, however, no military officials are punished, then the civilian leadership has more likely accepted the existence of the new capability, though it will no doubt seek more intrusive oversight of similarly significant programs in the future so as to avoid a repeat of crises of this sort.

SPECULATION 3: *Hu Jintao or the rest of the senior civilian leadership, or both, were aware of the test but did not anticipate a strong international reaction, either because they had not fully prepared for the possibility that the test would succeed or because they did not foresee that American intelligence on it would be shared with allies or leaked.* American silence about the reported three previous failed tests might have led Beijing to believe that the White House would also remain quiet about a successful test, since publicity would only draw attention to U.S. vulnerabilities.[16] Yet such a decision would be a staggering case of mirror-imaging, with Beijing projecting its own fear of transparency onto another country. Instead, the Chinese authorities should have known that the United States could not have kept the test a secret, even if it wanted to, given the intense attention of the international space and astronomy communities. Moreover, Washington had multiple incentives for going public, not the least of which was a chance to hoist Beijing by the petard of its own stated "principles."

Yet why would a witting civilian leadership approve the test, given the possible negative implications of success? One theory offered by both Chinese and Western observers is that China tested an ASAT in order to force the United States to change its previous opposition to negotiating a treaty banning weapons in space.[17] If true, this is a startling misperception on Beijing's part, since it assumes that Washington would reverse its published National Space Policy and decades of public opposition to arms control in space.[18] Instead, a better-informed and more culturally nuanced analysis of possible American responses would come to the opposite conclusion, arguing that a successful ASAT test would likely strengthen the hands of those within the U.S. system lobbying for more aggressive offensive and defensive ASAT programs. Indeed, the Chinese test has been an early Christmas for advocates of this position, as it has removed the significant barrier of the informal international moratorium in place since the last known test in 1986.

Yet the twelve days of silence after the test argues against a premeditated desire on Beijing's part to force through negotiations of an international treaty banning space weapons. If arms control had been the goal, then the test should have been accompanied by a clear government statement to that effect, not denials and thin rhetoric. By contrast, the Beijing authorities had a presumably coordinated public statement ready on the day of China's first nuclear test in 1964: "The Chinese Government hereby solemnly proposes to the governments of the world that a summit conference of all the countries of the world be convened to discuss the questions of the complete prohibition and thorough destruction of nuclear weapons, and that as the first step, the summit conference conclude an agreement to the effect that the nuclear powers and those countries which may soon become nuclear powers undertake not to use nuclear weapons either against non-nuclear countries and nuclear-free zones or against each other."[19] A calculated, coordinated effort to coerce the United States to sit at the negotiating table would likely have included a similar statement of principles about opposition to the weaponization of space.

Of the three scenarios just listed, the second one seems the most plausible and corresponds most closely with the limited external evidence available thus far, but the true facts of the case may never be known for sure. The Foreign Ministry's continued hewing to its weak line suggests that the system still lacked a coordinated response strategy more than one month after the test, which is yet another example of the weaknesses of the country's crisis-management mechanisms.[20] The lack of comment from the military media is especially noteworthy. Two weeks after the Foreign Ministry's admission that China did conduct an ASAT test, the military media finally published what looked like an authoritative commentary on February 2, but then it made no mention of the January 11

KKV hit.[21] In an article entitled "PLA 'Not Involved in Arms Race,'" Lieutenant General Zhang Qinsheng, deputy chief of the General Staff (Intelligence), repeated the standard platitudes and tried to push back against international criticism, though in an indirect way:

—"The PLA's modernization is open and based on cooperation."

—"We do not conceal our intention to build a strong and modern national defense. But we also tell the world candidly that the Chinese defense policy is always defensive in nature."

—"The modernization of the Chinese armed forces aims to achieve the ability to defend national sovereignty, security and reunification of the country."

—"China has never joined any military alliance, never sought military expansion, nor built overseas military bases." And so on.

General Zhang blamed "a lack of understanding and communication" for "misunderstanding," "suspicions," "concerns," and "even strong criticism of China's military development." To correct these mistaken views, he "welcomed more foreign friends to visit the Chinese armed forces themselves," and cited the five defense white papers as "pro-active and pragmatic" measures to improve transparency of national defense. Yet the 2006 defense white paper did not proactively or pragmatically announce China's intention to test space weapons for the purposes of greater transparency. While sins of omission (deletion of mention of opposition to the weaponization of space) are slightly closer to the spirit of transparency than sins of commission (continuing to defend the principle while testing a weapon that renders the principle meaningless), the case of the ASAT test highlights Beijing's significant challenges in managing international perceptions of "China's rise," especially if that rise is coupled with a perception (correct or not) that the military dimension of that rise may not be completely under civilian control.

Discussion

To reiterate, the Chinese Communist Party retains effective control of the nation's military forces. Yet the preceding analysis suggests that the PLA's growing military capabilities are causing new strains in party-military relations, testing traditional command and control mechanisms, and exacerbating natural institutional rivalries between the military and the civilian foreign policy bureaucracy. In the short to medium term, however, it is unlikely that these dynamics will alter the CCP's unquestioned control over the military. Despite periodic editorials in military newspapers criticizing the idea of a "national" as opposed to a "party" army, which immediately leads people to speculate that the authorities are trying to tamp down an internal debate on the subject, the PLA does not appear to question its subordination or the terms of the "conditional compliance" bargain it has with the CCP. There is no open evidence that the military seeks to restore its participation in decisionmaking related to non-defense or non–foreign policy topics, and the lack of military representation on the Politburo Standing Committee has evolved into a systemic norm. Without formal representation on the Standing Committee and other less significant bureaucratic channels, it is increasingly difficult for the military to articulate its policy preferences outside of its narrow purview, much less "dictate" or "veto" decisions or personnel choices made by the leadership collective. For its part, the CCP shows no sign of seeking to interfere in the purely corporate interests of the PLA, such as doctrinal development or equipment procurement, and the party and government continue to support robust annual funding for the military's priorities.

Why is the bargain holding? On the whole, the military is fundamentally aligned with the party leadership. The reasons for this common alignment include a range of normative and instrumental factors. Normatively, the CCP has effectively portrayed the PLA as the embodiment of the country's muscular new nationalism, giving the military significant "face" after the prestige-crushing humiliation of the 1989 Tiananmen crackdown. The PLA has returned this favor by holding up the party as the progenitor of China's political and economic great-power status. Instrumentally, the fates of the PLA and CCP are inextricably intertwined. The CCP knows it cannot survive domestic turmoil without the full support of the army, and the military would not enjoy the same level of institutional and bureaucratic autonomy in any other conceivable political system, save that of a military junta, which is antithetical to the corporate ethos of the PLA. For this reason, it remains likely that the PLA, under orders from the civilian CCP leadership, would act quickly and decisively to quell a major political crisis similar to the 1989 Tiananmen incident.

At the same time, the experiences of the past five years strongly suggest that party-military tensions will continue and perhaps worsen as Chinese military capabilities develop further. Chinese military forces, particularly the "normal" operational patrols carried out by air force and naval assets, will very likely push farther away from China's shores over time, bringing them more regularly into possible conflict with regional forces operated by Japan and the United States. As a result of the internal coordination problems highlighted by the ASAT test, one could speculate the Hu Jintao might seek, in the run-up to the Seventeenth Party Congress, to identify and promote senior military officers who not only possess the requisite professional qualifications but are also inclined to coordinate more closely with the civilian leadership and its foreign policy apparatus so as to mitigate or even avoid creating the external impression that Chinese military forces are operating independently of civilian oversight. Nonetheless, trends within the current generation of military and civilian leadership cohorts might actually work against these objectives and further exacerbate relations between the two groups. In the future, Chinese civilian leaders, especially those in the so-called Fifth Generation, will no longer be dominated by technocrats, whereas in the military, young and well-trained technocrats will begin to advance their careers and will likely exert more influence and power over China's security and military development.[22] There is a danger that these new military leaders will conclude, much as General Ripper concluded in *Dr. Strangelove*, that their civilian overlords are not professionally qualified to make decisions on military and security affairs and will push for greater, and potentially more dangerous, autonomy. The consequences of such a trend would be deleterious to party-military relations as well as China's relations with the outside world. To quote the mapmakers of the Old World when they sought to denote the dangerous areas at the edges of the map that had yet to be explored: *beyond there be dragons.*

Notes

1. Comments made by Ellis Joffe at the CAPS/Rand PLA conference, Washington, July 8–11, 1999.

2. Ellis Joffe, "The Military and China's New Politics: Trends and Counter-Trends," in *The People's Liberation Army in the Information Age,* edited by James Mulvenon and others (Santa Monica, Calif.: Rand, 1999).

3. Michael D. Swaine, *The Role of the Chinese Military in National Security Policymaking* (Santa Monica, Calif.: Rand, 1996), p. x.

4. James Mulvenon, *Professionalization of the Senior Chinese Officer Corps: Trends and Implications,* MR-901-OSD (Santa Monica, Calif.: Rand, July, 1997); and Michael D. Swaine, *The Military and Political Succession in China: Leadership, Institutions, Beliefs* (Santa Monica, Calif.: Rand, 1992).

5. See James Mulvenon, "Civil-Military Relations and the EP-3 Crisis: A Content Analysis," *China Leadership Monitor,* Winter 2002 (www.hoover.org/publications/clm/issues/2906891.html).

6. On January 18, National Security Council spokesman Gordon Johndroe confirmed to reporters that the U.S. government had confronted Beijing about the test: "The U.S. believes China's development and testing of such weapons is inconsistent with the spirit of cooperation that both countries aspire to in the civil space area. We and other countries have expressed our concern regarding this action to the Chinese." That same day, the Australian government also reported little progress in getting answers. Foreign Minister Alexander Downer, traveling in New York, told reporters: "So far, the answer from the foreign affairs people in China, including the ambassador in Canberra, is that they are not aware of the incident and they are getting back to us." See Jim Wolf, "U.S. Tells China Concerned by Satellite-Killer Test," Reuters, January 18, 2007.

7. Donald M. Kerr, director of the National Reconnaissance Office, told reporters that a U.S. satellite had been "painted" (illuminated) by a ground-based laser in China in late 2006.

8. In an interview with Reuters, Chinese Foreign Ministry spokesman Liu Jianchao declined to confirm or deny the incident but said Beijing wanted no arms race in space: "I can't say anything about the reports. I really don't know; I've only seen the foreign reports. What I can say is that, as a matter of principle, China advocates the peaceful use of space and opposes the weaponization of space, and also opposes any form of arms race." See Chris Buckley, "Concern Grows over China's Satellite-Killing Missile Test," Reuters, January 19, 2007.

9. The representative of the Defense Ministry's foreign affairs office reportedly told Agence France-Presse: "We are not aware of that test. Usually the media writes stories on hearsay evidence; we don't have time to verify such stories." See "PRC Defense Official Spokesman Says PRC Not Aware of Satellite Killer Test," Agence France-Presse, January 19, 2007.

10. Li Wenming and others, "Rash U.S. Conjectures on China's Anti-satellite Weapon," *Huanqiu shibao*, January 19, 2007. Here, in its entirety, is the relevant quotation from Major General Peng Guangqian of the Strategic Studies Department of the Chinese Military Science Academy: "The United States has slight neurosis. China already has the capability to send astronauts into space and bring them back; with capability in such precision control of space-craft, technically speaking, destroying a satellite in space is just ordinary technology. What must be emphasized, however, is that all of China's space exploration is peaceful and com-pletely responsible, and it is also activity that creates happiness for mankind. China has always advocated the non-militarization of space. So far, China has not carried out any mili-tary activities in space."

11. On January 19, the White House told reporters that it had still not received a reply from Beijing. Deputy White House press secretary Dana Perino said Chinese officials had not yet responded to the concerns expressed by the United States. See Chisaki Watanabe, "Three Nations Join China Test Protest," Associated Press, January 19, 2007. On January 22, the Associated Press reported that the Chinese Foreign Ministry had confirmed the test in their January 20–21 meetings with U.S. Assistant Secretary of State Chris Hill. See George Gedda, "U.S. Wants Info on China Missile Test," Associated Press, January 22, 2007.

12. Chris Buckley, "China Confirms Satellite Test, Says No Threat," Reuters, January 23, 2007.

13. "PRC FM Spokesman: 'Satellite-Related Test' Violates No International Treaty," Xin-hua News Agency, February 8, 2007.

14. See David E. Sanger and Joseph Kahn, "U.S. Tries to Interpret Silence over China Test," *New York Times*, January 21, 2007.

15. This scenario is reminiscent of the plot of the film *Dr. Strangelove or: How I Learned to Stop Worrying and Love the Bomb*.

16. The first public mention of three previous tests came from CNN Pentagon correspon-dent Jamie McIntyre. See http://transcripts.cnn.com/TRANSCRIPTS/0701/18/ldt.01.html.

17. As an example of Chinese views, a "quasi-official" interview on January 25, 2007, with Teng Jianqun, director of the research department under the China Arms Control and Disarmament Association, appeared in the "quasi-official" *Ta Kung Pao*, a PRC-owned news-paper in Hong Kong. In the interview, Teng calls for the United States to abandon its space policy and negotiate a treaty banning weapons in space. See "Chinese Expert Urges the Enactment of 'Rules for Outer Space,'" *Ta Kung Pao*, January 25, 2007. As an example of Western views, Michael Krepon and Michael Katz-Hyman, while criticizing the Chinese test as "irresponsible," also encouraged the U.S. government to drop its resistance to negotiating

space-related arms control. See "Irresponsible in Space," *Defense News*, February 5, 2007. Theresa Hitchens of the Center for Defense Information outlines in even stronger terms the parallel criticism of the Bush administration's "head-in-the-sand position" on space arms control (www.cdi.org/friendlyversion/printversion.cfm?documentID=3800).

18. The White House National Space Policy, promulgated in August 2006, is summarized at www.globalsecurity.org/space/library/policy/national/us-space-policy_060831.htm.

19. "Statement of the Government of the People's Republic of China," October 16, 1964, quoted in John Wilson Lewis and Xue Litai, *China Builds the Bomb: Studies in International Security and Arms Control* (Stanford University Press, 1988), pp. 241–43.

20. See Michael D. Swaine, Zhang Tuosheng, and Danielle Cohen, eds., *Managing Sino-American Crises: Case Studies and Analysis* (Washington: Carnegie Endowment for International Peace, 2007) (www.carnegieendowment.org/publications/index.cfm?fa=view&id=18899&prog=zch).

21. "PLA 'Not Involved in Arms Race,'" *People's Daily*, February 2, 2007 (http://english.people.com.cn/ 200702/02/eng20070202_346971.html).

22. I thank Cheng Li for this insightful comment in his review of my chapter.

Part VI

---

*External Models
and China's Future*

15

Learning from Abroad to Reinvent Itself:
External Influences on Internal CCP Reforms

DAVID SHAMBAUGH

> Fresh experiences during the Party building process should be carefully summarized,
> and helpful practices of foreign political parties should be studied and borrowed
> from to enrich and develop the CCP's governance theories.
>
> HU JINTAO (2005)

A s in all spheres of its development, China has looked abroad for ideas
about political reform. The Chinese Communist Party (CCP) has assidu-
ously studied the causes of collapse of other communist and authoritarian party-
states in Eastern Europe, Central Asia, East Asia, Latin America, and the former
Soviet Union—but has also carefully observed social democratic states in
Europe, as well as those communist party-states that have survived (Cuba,
North Korea, and Vietnam). These internal analyses of foreign regimes shed
considerable light on the thinking behind CCP reforms of recent years.[1]

As Andrew Nathan correctly observes in chapter 2, "ideas matter" in the
shaping of those reforms. That is why foreign analysts must "get inside" the
intraparty discourse in order to understand how the CCP hopes to reinvent, res-
cue, and relegitimate the party-state. The CCP's key concepts appear to stem
from its assessment of (a) the events of 1989–91 in Eastern Europe and the
Soviet Union, (b) the "color revolutions" in former Soviet republics and Central
Asia, and (c) the political systems of a variety of noncommunist states in Asia,
the Middle East, Europe, and Latin America.

Assessing the Soviet and East European Cases

Throughout the autumn of 1989, the CCP leadership watched in shock and
trepidation as the communist party-states in Eastern Europe experienced popu-

lar uprisings and, one after another, fell from power. Ironically, the first communist regime to lose power did so on June 4, 1989—the very day of the martial law crackdown in Beijing. As the Chinese military shot its way through the streets of Beijing, voters in Poland peacefully went to the polls and gave the ruling Communist Party a resounding and humiliating defeat in National Assembly elections. The subsequent dénouements of other ruling communist parties across Eastern Europe were not as peaceful or smooth as in Poland.

While, over time, Chinese analysts produced a variegated picture of the multiple reasons for the collapse of these regimes, the immediate assessment pinned the blame on a single factor: Soviet leader Mikhail Gorbachev. A series of Politburo meetings held shortly after the Romanian uprising apparently castigated Gorbachev.[2] Deng Xiaoping, Chen Yun, Jiang Zemin, Wang Zhen, and other octogenarian leaders all argued that Gorbachev had *intentionally* undermined the East European communist party-states, seeking just such a collapse. Jiang Zemin labeled Gorbachev a "traitor like Trotsky."[3]

By mid-1990, though, Chinese analysts began to publish different interpretations of the causes. Not surprisingly, these appeared in the pages of the journal of the Institute of Soviet and East European Studies of the Chinese Academy of Social Sciences (CASS), *Sulian yu Dong'ou Wenti* (Soviet and East European Studies).[4] This institute came to play a central role in assessing and determining the causes of the Soviet collapse and had a long and important history in Sino-Soviet relations, Sino-Soviet polemics, and subsequent assessments of the Soviet Union.[5] In mid-1990, the institute's journal carried a variety of articles on the causes of the "drastic changes" (*jubian*) in Eastern Europe, the first of which stressed four themes:[6]

—Economic deterioration, high levels of debt, and a poor standard of living.

—"Dictatorships" (*zhuanzheng*), ruling parties divorced from the populace, and a lack of local-level party building (*jiceng dangjian*).

—Unions that were not a "bridge" (*qiao*) between the party and the working class.

—"Peaceful evolution" efforts by Western countries.

Subsequent analyses built on these initial themes. One criticized East European communist parties for being too factionalized in their leaderships and too lax in their memberships (suggesting the need to tighten membership criteria, have trial periods for membership, and weed out corrupt cadres).[7] This article also criticized the overcentralization of the party structure and failure to institute "democracy" in local party branches. Needless to say, many articles took aim at the Solidarity independent trade union movement in Poland, arguing that it had abandoned the "real working class" and become a tool in the hands of Western powers intent on destabilizing the country.[8] Another concurred that unions were the principal target and agent of Western "peaceful evolutionists." The governments of Great Britain and Sweden, as well as the U.S. National Democratic Institute (NDI), the National Endowment for Democracy (NED), and the George Soros Foundation, were all accused of funneling money and offering training to unions in Poland, Bulgaria, Czechoslovakia, Hungary, and Romania.[9] One classified (secret) inner-party document entitled "The Reasons for the Changes in Eastern Europe and Their Lessons" circulated in the summer of 1991 bemoaned the arrests, interrogations, and imprisonments of former East European communist officials.[10]

Curiously, the Chinese postmortems on Eastern Europe tended not to consider a variety of processes, forces, and causes of collapse generally emphasized by Western scholars.[11] There is no (public and published) evidence that the analysts considered the part played by civil society, the Velvet Revolution, or intellectuals—or the impact of economic reform in countries like Hungary, pressures to enfranchise opposition parties, the nature of civil-military relations and control of the security services, the Helsinki Process, Willy Brandt's *Ostpolitik* strategy, or the green light that Gorbachev gave that the Soviet Union would not intervene in the East European demonstrations. Nor was there any real disaggregation of the nature and composition of the East European regimes, their historical circumstances, and variance in the paths to power of the opposition. Chinese analysts tended to treat them generically and as a group and thus oversimplified the forces at play—perhaps because Chinese intelligence and understanding of the conditions in Eastern Europe were really rather poor at the time. Moreover, in the wake of China's own June 4 incident, the intellectual and political climate was hardly conducive to a discussion of the various reasons for, and means of, the East European uprisings (there was, in fact, a media ban on such topics).

Eventually, however, the postmortems became more variegated and sophisticated, especially with greater exposure to these countries after 1989. Also, political conditions inside of China improved. In the more relaxed environment of 1999, a team of Academy of Social Science researchers undertook a comprehensive, country-by-country assessment of the causes of the East European collapse.[12]

The principal causes in Poland, they concluded, were primarily economic in nature: high foreign debt, rising inflation, imbalances in industrial development, a price structure that did not respond to supply and demand, and a low standard of living. All of these economic conditions, plus the Helsinki pressures on human rights, were said to have stimulated demands for independent trade unions and the founding of Solidarity in Gdansk.

The change in Hungary, however, was attributed to political factors. The Hungarian Socialist Workers Party not only had a factionalized leadership but also admitted the entrepreneurial class (which had emerged as a result of economic reforms) into the party. Furthermore, Hungary's party elites had come under the influence of Gorbachev's "New Thinking" of "humanism and democratic socialism." All of these processes diluted and ultimately split the party, according to the CASS analysts. Finally, the Hungarian parliament passed a constitutional amendment on October 18, 1989, to establish a parliamentary democracy, allow the separation of powers, create a real republic, and privatize state-owned enterprises.

The German Democratic Republic's failures were traced to a combination of economic (too wed to command and planned economy) and political (ossified leadership and party organization) problems. Czechoslovakia's reforms, concluded the analysts, had come "from below," stimulated by intellectuals, while Romania's party leadership (Ceaușescu) was to blame for losing control of the military and security services. As for Bulgaria, it had simply experienced a "domino effect."

To the CASS analysts, these cases appeared to have three distinct features in common: [13]

—The ruling parties developed internal splits and became democratized.

—Ordinary people were discontent, and opposition forces took advantage of the malaise.

—The Western campaign of "peaceful evolution" undermined belief in the one-party system.

Hence the CASS team summed up the collapse of the East European regimes as the product of "three forces, namely, political discontent, the West, and revisionism within the ruling Communist Party."[14]

Two years after the fall of those regimes, the Communist Party of the Soviet Union (CPSU), and the Soviet Union itself, came crashing down. These events, on top of the crisis of 1989, left the Chinese leadership and the CCP profoundly shaken and worried about their own future, prompting considerable introspection among the party's rank and file. Their analysis of the Soviet collapse began well before the final implosion, insofar as the Chinese were carefully monitoring and critiquing the Brezhnev-Andropov-Chernenko transitional period, and then the reforms unleashed by Mikhail Gorbachev.[15]

In contrast to their succinct explanation of the East European collapses, Chinese analysts now pointed to a wide range of factors in the Soviet case. Unlike many Western discussions—which tended to emphasize Gorbachev's individual actions and failings—the Chinese discourse took a much broader view and offered a more systemic analysis of the multiple reasons for the Soviet collapse.

This discourse passed through six distinct phases (each of which reflects different schools of thought):

Skepticism → Support → Suspicion → Shock → Systemic Study → Conclusion
(1986–87)   (1987–89) (1989–91) (1991–92) (1993–2004)   (2004–05)

To be sure, the analysis and discussion continued long after the collapse—lasting more than *thirteen years* in fact, from 1991 until 2004. The Lessons drawn were set forth in a document titled *Decision of the CPC Central Committee on Enhancing the Party's Ruling Capacity*, adopted at the Fourth Plenary Session of the Sixteenth Congress of the CCP in September 2004.

Broadly speaking, the factors blamed for the Soviet collapse fall into four categories: economic, political/coercive, social/cultural, and international (see box 15-1). Interestingly, the Chinese critiques took a systemic turn after the initial assessments of the August 1991 failed coup (which blamed Gorbachev and Yeltsin for precipitating the dénouement). As Chinese analysts began to probe the causes more deeply, they found that, instead of emanating from a "perfect storm" of events that coalesced August 1991, the collapse was rooted in a *long-term* decline marked by mismanagement, wrong judgments and policy mistakes, systemic distortions, an inability to react to failures and innovate, excessive dogmatism, bureaucratic inefficiency, an inappropriate foreign policy, and a variety of other maladies.

The Chinese emphasis on *systemic causes* contrasted sharply with the prevailing Western views that tended to emphasize *immediate causes*, most notably the role of Gorbachev and the precipitating events of 1990–91. Most post-collapse analyses published in China were also historically retrospective. For example, one critique focused on Nikita Khrushchev's attempted reforms in the mid- to late 1950s. Today, some Chinese analysts see Khrushchev as the Soviet Union's first great reformer, arguing that had he not been overthrown and his policies undermined, the Soviet Union would not have sunk into the thirty-year stagnation of the Brezhnev-Chernenko eras.

The Survivors: North Korea, Vietnam, and Cuba

Needless to say, CCP analysts also paid close attention to the few communist states that survived: Cuba, Vietnam, and North Korea (and occasionally Laos). Generally speaking, these critiques were descriptive, not judgmental. Here the Chinese were interested in why these regimes escaped collapse when so many others did not and seem fairly optimistic about their chances for continued survival. As one analysis described it, "Obviously, the drastic changes in Eastern Europe and the Soviet Union in the late 1980s and early 1990s have seriously hampered the international socialist movement. However, after several years, the

---

Box 15-1. *Factors Contributing to the Collapse of the Soviet Union*

Economic

Economic stagnation

Overcentralized economy and retarded market mechanisms

Collectivized and large-scale state agriculture

Nonintegration into international economic systems and international financial institutions

Party dominance of government economic apparatus

Low tax base

Severe price distortions, owing to heavy subsidies

Overdevelopment of heavy industry, to the detriment of tertiary industries

Overemphasis on defense industries and military sector of the economy

State monopoly of property rights

Little revenue sharing between center and localities

Inefficiencies of scale of production

Dogmatic ideological bias against capitalism

Perestroika too little, too late, and too fast

Political/coercive

All features of "totalitarianism" (*jiquanzhuyi*)

Overconcentration of political power in top leader; personal dictatorship

Failure to replace political leaders systematically

No inner-party democracy

Ideological rigidity and distorted Marxism

Party dominance of the state

Prolonged "leftist" tendencies from Stalin to Gorbachev ("rightist")

Party given special privileges and allowed to become "ruling class"

Bureaucratic inefficiency

Overconcentration of power in *nomenklatura*; too large a bureaucracy

Poorly developed mechanisms to police party members for breach of discipline

"Crisis of trust" in party leaders, with resulting "crisis of faith" in socialist system

---

'period of shock' [*zhendang qi*] has passed and many signs of revival have emerged. The shocks that resulted from the collapse have already passed; we [the international socialist movement] have gone through a period of emergency and into a period of moving forward amidst difficulties" (the article then describes reforms in Cuba, Laos, and Vietnam).[16]

North Korea

While China's North Korea watchers undoubtedly know more about the Democratic People's Republic of Korea (DPRK) than any other country, they tend not to commit their views to print. A scouring of the literature reveals very little beyond superficial descriptions of North Korea and China-DPRK relations. Even studies by the CCP International Department, which has

Political reforms (*glasnost*) begun before economic foundation was ready

Emasculation in role of Supreme Soviets and local Soviets, causing state's checks and balances on party to become meaningless

Falsehood of federalism—Moscow's dominance of other Soviet republics and East European communist parties

Gorbachev efforts to democratize the CPSU (too much, too late) and remake it as a social-democratic party

Social/cultural

Intimidated population, because of totalitarian terror

Low standard of living

Society cut off from outside world in all respects

Alienation from workplace and party-state

Low levels of worker efficiency, poor incentives, shoddy production

Production slowdown and workplace unrest

Pervasive alcoholism

Repression of, and chauvinism toward, non-Russian ethnic groups—through

ethnic cleansing, forced labor, forced relocation of ethnic minorities, and other means

Rising autonomous nationalist identities separate from USSR

Moral vacuum, public cynicism, and public "crisis of faith" in the system

Persecution of intellectuals

Dogmatism among intellectuals

"Pluralization" of media under Gorbachev

Breakdown in the party's (CPSU's) relations with various social sectors

Disillusion of youth

International

"Peaceful evolution" campaign of the West

Economic stresses caused by cold war containment policies

Military stresses caused by cold war

Expansionist and hegemonic policies, especially under Brezhnev

Soviet chauvinism within the international communist movement

Domination of Eastern Europe and other client states (Cuba, Vietnam)

more extensive interactions with Pyongyang than any other organization in China, contain no analysis of the DPRK, although they do describe a half-century of interesting party-to-party exchanges between the two sides.[17] North Korea is clearly a proscribed topic even in internal (*neibu*) publications. The only insights to be gleaned are a few analyses of North Korean economic reforms, which are said to have begun in 2001—with the establishment of some special economic zones and acceptance of some foreign investment, abolition of the ration system for certain controlled commodities, some price reform, and the rise of some small-scale free markets. These developments are said to be in line with the government's decision to move from a planned to a collective and mixed economy.[18] They are specifically credited to Kim Jong Il.[19]

Unlike in publications, Chinese analysts of North Korea are much more candid—and critical—in discussions. They often speak with disdain, despair, and frustration about DPRK-China relations. Many of China's Korea watchers deplore the sycophantic cult of personality surrounding the Kim dynasty (not to mention the family political dynasty), the Stalinist security state, the command economy, the impoverishment of the population, the use of scarce resources for military purposes, the regime's mass mobilization techniques, the autarkic paranoia about the world beyond its borders, and so forth. Many draw explicit parallels with Maoist China (particularly during the Great Leap Forward and Cultural Revolution), and they argue that North Korea's only viable option if it is to avoid national suicide is to emulate China's reformist example.[20]

Vietnam

China is more interested in the Vietnamese Communist Party (VCP) and the situation in Vietnam, which laudably weathered the storm of the Soviet collapse and embarked on a reformist path. Its sustenance is attributed to a policy of reform (*Doi Moi*) adopted at the Sixth VCP Congress in December 1986, which called for economic development, trade liberalization, reform of the planned economy, and a diversified economic structure.[21]

Agricultural reform began in 1988 with the implementation of the Chinese-style "household responsibility system," and in 1989 the grain market was totally privatized while private ownership was permitted in farming, fishing, and forestry. As a result, grain production jumped, and Vietnam became the world's second largest rice exporter after Thailand. Industrial reform followed. The Vietnamese government closed down a number of inefficient state-owned enterprises (SOEs) and abolished their monopoly in the national economy. The ownership structure was then reformed, with an emphasis on "national capitalism," foreign investment, and export processing. All of these policy reforms are discussed approvingly by Chinese analysts.

In terms of political development, the VCP is credited with having launched a series of party-building and rectification (*dangjian zhengfeng*) initiatives from 1999 to 2001, which addressed the "moral degeneration" and countered "peaceful evolution" inside the party.[22] The VCP's primary goals are allegedly to strengthen ideological education, improve the moral quality and lifestyle of party cadres, combat corruption and bureaucratism, promote self-criticism and democratic centralism within the party, and streamline and consolidate basic party organs.[23] Chinese analysts are quite admiring in their praise of Vietnam's economic reforms and efforts to revitalize the party.[24]

Cuba

Chinese analysts have published entire books on the successes of Cuban communism.[25] These offer comprehensive assessments of the Cuban system of health care, education, politics, military affairs, foreign relations, economy, society, and culture. There seems to be a particular fascination in China with the "Cuban Way." Fidel Castro is admired for his tenacity and longevity in the face of intense pressure from the United States and other obstacles.[26] Other articles detail Cuba's economic system and reforms, and praise these efforts for their distinctiveness.[27]

The Cuban Communist Party's methods of rule and reasons for longevity are analyzed closely. One study by the CCP Organization Department attributes the party's longevity to three principal actions: it fused party building with anti-American nationalism, kept close ties to the people, and promoted social equality.[28] Another study by an official in the CCP International Department credits other factors: the promotion of younger officials and cadres, new party recruitment campaigns, downsizing of government agencies to improve efficiency, frequent inspection trips by party leaders to the countryside, national discussion of policy alternatives prior to adoption, growth of inner-party democracy, strong monitoring of party members and enforcement of anticorruption measures, and the establishment of party branches in all schools.[29] An analysis by China's leading "Cuba watcher," Mao Xianglin of the Academy of Social Sciences, agrees with many of these observations but stresses the priority placed on "inner-party democracy," party and government dialogue with different sectors of society, control over the military and security services, and strong nationalism.[30] Yet another assessment, by the International Department of the CCP, is effusive in its praise for the Cuban Communist Party's accomplishments, noting that it has successfully combined indigenous ideology (Marti Thought) with Marxism-Leninism, refused to adopt a Western multiparty system, rejected the Soviet model as incompatible, stressed social stability above all, organized special study sessions for party members, used the mass media to mobilize patriotism, created party organizational linkages to urban neighborhoods and rural villages, established a system whereby party officials must meet with and "report back" (*hui bao*) to citizens and conduct opinion polls among the population, allowed two or more candidates to stand for local party elections, prohibited officials and senior party members from gaining special privileges, maintained a "zero tolerance" policy toward corrupt officials, promoted party members on the basis of merit and careful vetting, and streamlined central and provincial government to promote efficiency.[31]

Clearly, the "Cuban model" is of great interest to the CCP. Exchanges between the two sides have increased considerably since the early 1990s. Hardly a month passes without an official party or state visit in one direction or the other.[32] CCP leader Hu Jintao is said to have heaped praise on the Cuban Communist Party at the Fourth Plenum of the Sixteenth Party Congress in 2004, which discussed the lessons of other ruling parties for the CCP.[33]

The Central Asian "Color Revolutions"

While the CCP may have taken some solace from the fact that the Cuban, Vietnamese, and North Korean Communist Parties have endured, Chinese analysts and leaders have been deeply alarmed by the so-called color revolutions that swept through post-Soviet Central Asian republics in 2003–04 and the implications for China's external security and internal political stability. To judge by the substantial analysis devoted to this subject, a considerable amount of inner-party hand wringing—at times verging on paranoia—has taken place behind the scenes, especially over the role of the United States in fomenting these revolutions and the role played by nongovernmental organizations (NGOs).[34]

In mounting alarm, the Chinese government began to scrutinize foreign NGOs operating in China—not only because of their activities in Central Asia but also apparently because of their subversive impact, which Vladimir Putin reportedly warned Hu Jintao about at a Shanghai Cooperation Organization (SCO) meeting in 2005, saying "If you don't get a grip on them [NGOs], you too will have a color revolution!"[35]

One of several other concerns, notes Liu Jianfei of the Central Party School, is that the "Community of Democracies," made up of 124 countries, will gain an increasing voice in the United Nations, "and those countries [that] are not members will be in a clear minority and a weak position. If this goes on, China's role in the U.N. will be severely constrained."[36] Liu also thinks that U.S. foreign policy, with its emphasis on promoting democracy, "stimulate[s] the anti-China tendencies of the American neocons [neoconservatives]," and that this "policy of 'ending tyranny' will cause some problems for Chinese diplomacy."[37] Furthermore, Liu believes the Taiwan issue will become "more complicated" because of the "tendency of the neocons and the military-industrial complex to support Taiwan independence," which will serve to stimulate and encourage "pro-independence forces by urging them to play the 'democratic reunification card.'"[38] All in all, Central Asia's "color revolutions" of 2003–04 seemed to renew earlier fears and to reinforce the notion that the U.S. strategy of "peaceful evolution" was alive and well.

Noncommunist Party-States

Being relatively open-minded, the CCP has endeavored to learn lessons from various systems, not just the communist and former communist party-states. Indeed, the CCP has scoured the globe to this end, one focal point being political parties in Asia.[39]

This exploration began with the pre-Tiananmen interest in "neo-authoritarianism" (*xin quanweizhuyi*) and post-Tiananmen interest in "neoconservatism" (*xin baoshouzhuyi*).[40] While the former embraced far greater pluralism than the latter, both schools of thought envisioned a single-party state, which would guide all facets of development: economic, political, intellectual, and cultural. Both schools rejected laissez-faire liberalism, in the long-established Chinese belief that a strong state was crucial—in order to attain wealth and power (*fuqiang*) and to maintain social stability.[41] To be sure, each school had its permutations, and some Chinese intellectuals even embraced a more liberal "Enlightenment tradition," as Joseph Fewsmith describes it, but the mainstream all worshiped a strong state that could guide and facilitate the development of China into a major world power.[42]

This drew CCP attention to Singapore, whose People's Action Party (PAP) and methods of rule have been under intense Chinese scrutiny since the early 1980s. Chinese observers are particularly intrigued by the PAP's low-key presence, but total control.[43] They admire Singapore's clean and efficient government, social order, rule of law, moral education, higher education, and high level of technological development.[44] They see Singapore as a "guided democracy."[45] They attribute the PAP's longevity of rule to (a) successful policies and (b) co-optation of the opposition.[46] Two other strengths of the PAP system, in their view, are party recruitment and continuous midcareer training of officials.[47] CASS scholar Li Wen also attributes PAP success to the creation of the "administrative state" (*xingzheng guojia*), which merges party and government (*dangzheng heyi*), and to its willingness to allow some Western culture as a "necessary evil" but refusal to tolerate pornography, criticism of the government, defamation of leaders, or political subversion.[48]

Looking at Malaysia's longevity, some Chinese analysts believe Mahathir Mohamad's time in office was an odd mix of strongman politics under the dominant United Malays National Organization (UMNO) and decentralized constituencies in which competing factions nominate candidates for office. However, Mahathir selected the final slate, thus ensuring the UMNO would continue to dominate the political process and government.[49] Other sources of UMNO's longevity are said to be its emphasis on patriotic and moral education, its dominance of government fiscal policy, and its anti-American rhetoric.

In the case of Japan's Liberal Democratic Party (LDP), researchers at the Central Party School are impressed by its long rule (except for a brief period in the minority during the 1990s), the close links between it and the business sector, the party's strong rural base, and its close ties with government bureaucracy.[50] They also believe the triangular relationship between party, bureaucracy, and business is a strength of the Japanese system. The authors are critical, however, of money politics in the LDP and Japanese system, factionalism within the party (*dangpai*), and the fact that the LDP is an "elite not a people's party."[51]

China has obviously put enormous effort into analyzing Taiwan politics and the political parties on the island. Its analysts repeatedly assess the potential for independence versus "reunification." They try to determine which individual politicians and factions in Taiwan's political parties might be susceptible to China's "united front" tactics. Third, China is interested in why the Kuomintang (KMT) failed as a ruling party and fell from power in 2000. A closely related concern is what the post-Kuomintang political transition may mean for China's political future (this is why China is interested in shifts from authoritarianism to democracy in other states as well). In essence, Chinese analysts blamed the KMT's loss of power on money politics ("black gold") and corruption, factional splits within the party, ineffectual leadership, the rise of a nativist (*bentu*) Taiwanese identity and the KMT's traditional ties to mainlanders, and the machinations of Lee Teng-hui.[52]

In examining the longevity of India's Congress Party and its fall from power, Chinese analysts believe it was weakened by the personalization of party power in the Gandhi family, the party's domination of the government bureaucracy (party = state = Congress), the loss of support among traditional poor constituencies on the lower rungs of the caste system, factional struggles as well as corruption within the party, and the difficulties in unifying such a large and diverse country.[53] In the case of Indonesia's Golkar Party, the principal blame was assigned to corruption within the Suharto family and ruling clique, and to an intolerant party ideology (which stimulated opposition across diverse sectors of society), rural poverty, geographical dispersion of the nation and the difficulties of enforcing rule, factional infighting within the party, and disloyalty of the military.[54]

In South Korea, the Philippines, and Thailand, the close links between the military and ruling parties were thought to be an aid to single-party dominance (if not outright military rule). At the same time, the decline of military praetorianism in these countries was viewed as a crucial cause of democratization in each case.[55] In East Asia, as well as in Latin America, military rule is considered inherently fragile, as such regimes never build social bases of support and usually do not form political parties.[56]

States that have captured Chinese attention in other parts of the world range from Syria to Mexico, both of which had a dominant party for some years. In the Syrian case, the ruling party's longevity is attributed to the tactics of its strongman president (Hafez Assad and his son) combined with a large political role for the military, although under the control of the party; party penetration of all sectors of society; the formation of mass organizations; and the party's dominance of all local officials.[57] In the case of Mexico, the Partido Revolucionario Institucional (PRI) had ruled for seventy-one years, then abruptly lost its power. Its dominance is generally attributed to a strong presidential style that played to the machismo political culture in Mexico, as well as to the PRI's ability to tap into a strong sense of nationalism, close identification with its rural base, and the implementation of economic policies that combined nationalization with marketization.[58] Although these tactics were good enough to keep the PRI in power for seven decades, nothing could forestall its undoing, which the Chinese blamed on mistakes in economic policy, the pursuit of social democracy, a party organization so rigid that it was unable to undergo self-reform, corruption, the impact of globalization and external pressures from the World Trade Organization (WTO) and North American Free Trade Agreement (NAFTA), U.S. support of opposition parties, and U.S. diplomatic pressure.[59]

Latin American corporatist systems—particularly in Argentina, Brazil, and Chile—have also gained China's attention, as demonstrated by the steadily rising number of delegations the CCP's International Department has sent to these countries and received from them.[60] Interestingly, China's Latin Americanists have been slow to comment on the shift to the political left and election of anti-American socialists in Venezuela, Bolivia, Peru, and Chile in 2003–05—although China has shown some irritation with the anti-American and anti-capitalism rhetoric of Venezuelan President Hugo Chávez.[61] While buying Venezuelan oil, the Chinese government has been careful to keep its distance from Chávez.

By the time the Chinese began to interact extensively with West European social-democratic parties during the 1980s, they found many of them in a state of political crisis and in the midst of self-reflection and in the early stages of reform. Britain's Labor Party and Germany's Social Democratic Party, for example, had both experienced consecutive defeats at the polls in the face of staunchly conservative opposition parties. Much soul searching was going on, and the Chinese observed it all with great interest. They witnessed the move away from the traditional base of support among trade unions and industrial workers, away from long-cherished beliefs about the nationalization of public services, away from beliefs about big government and the "welfare state," away from hostility toward market forces and the view that fiscal interventionism should stimulate production and not consumption, and so on.[62]

Chinese analysts were particularly interested in "New Labor" and the "Third Way" under Tony Blair in Britain.[63] They watched closely as these parties progressively shed the vestiges of state socialism in favor of a host of reforms: economic policies that shifted emphasis from social justice to economic efficiency, the revamping of welfare systems, the privatization of public utilities and transportation, the devolution of government decisionmaking to more local levels, the embrace of the high-tech revolution, the adoption of business-friendly policies and more flexible labor laws, less state intervention in the economy and education, and the recruitment into party membershp of younger people, entrepreneurs, and business.[64]

All of these reforms were successful in overhauling European social-democratic parties and returning many to office.[65] As a study by the CCP International Department concluded, "Overall, the reform of West European social democratic parties has been very effective—marking the shift from traditional and ideological socialism to more modern, popular, and improved socialism. As a result, by 2000, thirteen European countries were again under the rule of social democratic parties."[66] In this process of social-democratic reform, Chinese analysts also noted the increased marginalization of West European communist parties.[67]

Conclusion: Eclectic Borrowing

The CCP and various research institutes, universities, and individual researchers have made a truly impressive effort to track the successes and failures of a wide range of communist, noncommunist, and formerly communist political parties. This has not been an idle academic inquiry, but a quest with a specific and practical purpose: to anticipate the challenges the CCP may face in the future and to draw practical policy lessons about how to deal with them in order to keep the CCP in power.

This exercise has been remarkably eclectic in the systems examined and lessons derived from them. In the political sphere, as in virtually every other area of reform, the CCP has certainly been willing to search for useful ideas abroad, with a view to selectively borrowing, adapting, and grafting them to indigenous Chinese institutions and practices. Hence the CCP itself is evolving into an eclectic hybrid, composed of bits and pieces of a wide variety of systems.

Equally important, the CCP has taken to heart the lessons that brought down the communist party-states in Eastern Europe and the Soviet Union. Thus it has put considerable emphasis on expanding the economy and improving the standard of living, embracing globalization and integrating with the international economic community, maintaining tight control over the security services, keeping a watchful eye on NGOs, maintaining control over the media, being flexible in its ideology, retiring and rotating political elites, being somewhat careful to avoid repressing the intelligentsia, expanding party membership to include newly emergent social classes, and reinvigorating local party cells and committees.

From European social-democratic states, the CCP has learned the importance of a populist ideology and political program that the working classes support. It has also learned the value of privatizing national transportation and utilities, politically embracing the business sector and fashioning business-friendly growth policies, emphasizing social justice and the rule of law, devolving government decisionmaking to lower levels. reducing state intervention in the economy, and overhauling state provision of social welfare to allow for mixed public-private responsibility.

From East Asian and Latin American corporatist states, the CCP has learned the importance of marketizing the economy and reducing state intervention, giving priority to the provision of public goods, and maintaining civilian control of the military and security services. It has also recognized the importance of controlling corruption, preventing family oligarchies and political dynasties from forming, not empowering political factions, emphasizing moral education and controlling social vices, improving local-level governance and instituting a system of midcareer training for officials, and co-opting any potential political opposition.

Once finds evidence of all these lessons in the CCP's recent policies and reforms, many of which are detailed in other chapters of this volume.[68] Perhaps their most striking feature is the unprecedented manner in which the CCP arrived at them: by grafting a variety of foreign parts onto a core Leninist system.[69] Only time will tell whether China's new eclecticism and reforms will be sufficient to keep the CCP in power—or whether they will serve to erode the regime's capacity to rule and possibly foster a "democratic transition," as has occurred in a number of former communist and one-party authoritarian states around the globe.

Notes

1. David Shambaugh, *China's Communist Party: Atrophy and Adaptation* (University of California Press and Woodrow Wilson Center Press, 2008). Much of this chapter is drawn from chapters 4–5 of this book.

2. According to party documents and reports leaked to the Hong Kong pro-communist media. See Richard Baum, *Burying Mao: Chinese Politics in the Age of Deng Xiaoping* (Princeton University Press, 1994), p. 304, nn. 67–68.

3. Ibid.

4. This journal changed its name to *Dong-Ou Zhong-Ya Yanjiu* (Research on Eastern Europe and Central Asia) following the collapse of the Soviet Union in 1991.

5. See Gilbert Rozman, *The Chinese Debate about Soviet Socialism, 1978–1985* (Princeton University Press, 1987).

6. Bo Tingxiang and Cui Zhiying, "Dong-Ou jubian de lishi jiaoxun: Tan zhizhengdang yu gongren jieji de guanxi" (Drastic changes in Eastern Europe and their historical lessons: Discussing the relationship between ruling parties and the working class), *Sulian Dong-Ou Wenti*, no. 6 (1990), pp. 7–9.

7. Li Jingyu and Ma Shufang, "Liening guanyu zhizhengdang jianshe lilun he Su-Dong ge dang zhizheng shoucuo jiaocun" (Lenin's theories regarding party building and the lessons from the mistakes of East European ruling parties), *Sulian Dong-Ou Wenti*, no. 2 (1993), pp. 5–11, 26.

8. See, for example, Jiang Lieqin, "Guanyu minzhushehuiizhuyi sichao yu yuan Sulian he Dong-Ou gonghui de yuanbian" (On the ideological trend of democratic socialism and the evolution of trade unions in the former Soviet Union and East European countries), *Sulian Dong-Ou Wenti*, no. 4 (1993), pp. 12–15.

9. "Xifang zai yuan Sulian he Dong-Ou gongyun lingyu ruhe weixing heping yanbian zhanlue" (Types of peaceful evolution strategies by Western countries in the union movement in the former Soviet Union and Eastern Europe), *Sulian Dong-Ou Wenti*, no. 4 (1992), pp. 33–35.

10. Cited in James Miles, *The Legacy of Tiananmen: China in Disarray* (University of Michigan Press, 1996), p. 67.

11. See, in particular, Daniel Chirot, ed., *The Crisis of Leninism and the Decline of the Left: The Revolutions of 1989* (University of Washington Press); Gale Stokes, *The Walls Come Tumbling Down: The Collapse of Communism in Eastern Europe* (Oxford University Press, 1993); Michael Dobbs, *Down with Big Brother: The Fall of the Soviet Empire* (New York: Vintage Books, 1996); David Childs, *The Fall of the GDR* (Harlow, Sussex: Longman, 2001); Mike Dennis, *The Rise and Fall of the German Democratic Republic, 1945–90* (Harlow, Sussex: Longman, 2000); Renee de Nevers, *Comrades No More: The Seeds of Change in Eastern Europe* (Cambridge, Mass.: MIT Press, 2003); Bartlomiej Kaminski, *The Collapse of State Socialism: The Case of Poland* (Princeton University Press, 1991); Robert Strayer, *Why Did the Soviet Union Collapse? Understanding Historical Change* (Armonk, N.Y.: M. E. Sharpe, 1998); Leslie Holmes, *Post-Communism* (Cambridge, England: Polity Press, 1997); Timothy Garton Ash, *The Magic Lantern: The Revolution of '89 Witnessed in Warsaw, Budapest, Berlin, and Prague* (New York: Random House, 1993); John Gaddis, *We Now Know: Rethinking the Cold War* (Oxford University Press, 1998); Peter Rutland, "Sovietology: Notes for a Post-Mortem," *National Interest* 31 (Spring 1993): 109–23.

12. Zhou Xiancheng, Guan Xueliang, and others, eds., *Sulian Dong-Ou Guojia de Yanbian Jichi Lishi Jiaoxun* (The historical lessons of the collapse of the Soviet Union and East European countries) (Hefei: Anhui renmin chubanshe, 2000).

13. Ibid., pp. 119–20.

14. Ibid., p. 172.

15. See Rozman, *The Chinese Debate about Soviet Socialism*.

16. Shan Bianji, "21 shiji shijie shehuizhuyi qianjing zhanwang" (The outlook for socialism in the twenty-first century), *Dangjian Yanjiu Neican* (*neibu*), nos. 1–2 (2000), p. 33.

17. See Li Jian, *Tianqian tongtu: Zhongguo gongchandang duiwai jiaozhu jishi* (A natural moat and thoroughfare: Recollections of the Chinese Communist Party's foreign exchanges) (Beijing: Dangdai shijie chubanshe, 2001), pp. 867–77.

18. See, for example, Party Building Research Institute of the CCP Central Organization Department, *Zhongguo gongchandang zhizheng guilu yanjiu* (Research on the CCP's ruling laws and regulations) (Beijing: Dangjian duwu chubanshe, 2004), pp. 396–98.

19. Ibid.; and Editing Group, *Xingshuai zhilu* (The road of rise and decline) (Beijing: Dangdai shijie chubanshe he Zhonggong Zhongyang Dangxiao chubanshe, 2002), pp. 20–21.

20. These impressions have been gained from personal interviews in the Shanghai Academy of Social Sciences, China Institute of International Studies, and China Institute of Contemporary International Relations during 2000–03. For further analysis of China's views of North Korea see David Shambaugh, "China and the Korean Peninsula: Playing for the Long Term," *Washington Quarterly* 26 (Spring 2003): 43–56.

21. The following analysis is drawn from Party Building Research Institute of the CCP Organization Department, *Research on the CCP's Ruling Laws and Regulations*, pp. 372–74.

22. Party Building Institute of the CCP Central Organization Department, *Dangjian yanjiu zong-heng tan (1999)* (Discussion of party building research in a comprehensive way) (Beijing: Dangjian duwu chubanshe, 2000), pp. 344–48.

23. Ibid.

24. See Chen Yanhua, "Yuenan de gaige kaifang de chenggong he wenti" (Successes and problems in Vietnam's reform and opening), *Guoji Gongyun Shi Yanjiu*, no. 1 (1993), pp. 11–13.

25. Yue Gang and Wang Zongxian, *Guba shehuizhuyi* (Cuban socialism) (Beijing: Renmin chubanshe, 2004); Mao Xianglin, *Guba shehuizhuyi yanjiu* (Research on Cuban socialism) (Beijing: Shehui kexue wenzhai chubanshe, 2005).

26. See Yue and Wang, *Guba shehuizhuyi*, in particular.

27. See Mao Xianglin, "Guba gaige kaifang de neirong jichi tedian" (The content and characteristics of Cuba's reform and open door policy), *Dangjian Yanjiu Neican*, no. 5 (2002), pp. 11–13.

28. Party Building Institute of the CCP Organization Department, *Research on the CCP's Ruling Laws and Regulations*, pp. 380–87.

29. Li Jianhua, "Guba gongchandang shi ruhe shixian dang de jianshe" (How does the Cuban Communist Party carry out party building?), *Dangjian Yanjiu Neican*, no. 6 (2000), pp. 15–17.

30. Mao, *Guba shehuizhuyi yanjiu*, chaps. 3–4.

31. Editing Group, *Xingshuai zhilu*, pp. 60–70.

32. See, for example, "Castro, Other Cuban Officials Hold Official Talks with China's Luo Gan" (English translation), *Granma*, December 21, 2005, in Foreign Broadcast Information Service—China Report (FBIS-CHI); "CPC, PRC Government Attach Great Importance to Sino-Cuban Ties," Xinhua News Agency, December 22, 2005, in FBIS-CHI.

33. Willy Wo-Lap Lam, "Hu Jintao and Wen Jiabao Draw Inspiration from Castro," *Pingguo Shibao* (Hong Kong), October 24, 2005, in FBIS-CHI.

34. Personal discussions with analysts at China Institute of Contemporary International Relations and the Central Party School, November 2005.

35. Ibid.

36. Liu Jianfei, "The U.S. Strategy of Promoting Democracy as Viewed from 'Color Revolutions,'" *Zhongguo Dangzheng Ganbu Luntan*, August 1, 2005, in FBIS-CHI, August 1, 2005.

37. Ibid.

38. Ibid.

39. See Li Luyou, *Dangdai Ya-Tai Zhengdang Zhengzhi de Fazhan* (Development of contemporary political parties in East Asia) (Shanghai: Xueshu chubanshe, 2005); Sun Shulin, *Dangdai Ya-Tai Zhengzhi* (Contemporary Asia-Pacific politics) (Beijing: Shijie zhishi chubanshe, 2002).

40. For an evaluation of these schools of thought and debates between them, see Joseph Fewsmith, *China since Tiananmen* (Cambridge University Press, 2001), esp. pp. 86–93; Baum, *Burying Mao*, chaps. 9–10; Yan Sun, *The Chinese Reassessment of Socialism, 1976–1992* (Princeton University Press, 1995); Kalpana Misra, *From Post-Maoism to Post-Marxism: The Erosion of Official Ideology in Deng's China* (London: Routledge, 1998).

41. See David Shambaugh, *The Modern Chinese State* (Cambridge University Press, 2000).

42. Fewsmith, *China since Tiananmen,* esp. chap. 4.

43. Editing Group, *Xingshuai zhilu*, pp. 224–29.

44. Ibid.

45. Party Building Research Institute of the CCP Organization Department, *Research on the CCP's Ruling Laws and Regulations*, pp. 431–32.

46. Chen Feng, "Xinjiapo renmin xindongdang minzhu shehuizhuyi de ruogan lilun" (Some theoretical viewpoints on the PAP's social democracy), *Guoji Gongyun Shi Yanjiu,* no. 1 (1993), pp. 5–10.

47. Editing Group, *Xingshuai zhilu*, p. 227.

48. Li Wen, "Xinjiapo renmin xingdongdang de zhizheng mowu jichi jiejian yiyi" (Singapore's People's Action Party's ruling methods and enlightenment) *Dangdai Yatai*, no. 5 (2005), pp. 3–8.

49. Editing Group, *Xingshuai zhilu*, pp. 230–37.

50. Wang Changjiang and Jiang Yao, *Xiandai zhengdang zhizheng fangzhen bijiao yanjiu* (Comparative research on the ruling methods of modern political parties) (Shanghai: Shanghai renmin chubanshe, 2002), pp. 105–50.

51. Ibid.

52. Ibid., chap. 16.

53. Ibid., chap. 14.

54. Ibid., chap. 15.

55. Ibid., chap. 16; also Li, *Dangdai Ya-Tai Zhengdang Zhengzhi de Fazhan,* chap. 3.

56. See *Qiushi* Editing Group, *Jiaqiang dang de zhizheng nengli jianshe da cankao* (Main reference materials on intensifying the building of the party's ruling capacity) (Beijing: Hongqi chubanshe, 2004), pp. 199–201.

57. Editing Group, *Xingshuai zhilu*, pp. 253–62.

58. Party Building Research Institute of the CCP Organization Department, *Research on the CCP's Ruling Laws and Regulations*, pp. 418–19.

59. Wang and Jiang, *Xiandai zhengdang*, chap. 13; Liu Zicheng, "Moxige geming zhidudang xiatai de yuanyin" (Causes of the fall from power of Mexico's Institutional Revolutionary Party), *Dangjian Yanjiu Neican*, no. 6 (2002), pp. 11–14.

60. See the annual volume cataloguing such exchanges, *Zhongguo gongchandang duiwai gongzuo gaikuang* (Survey of the Chinese Communist Party's external work) (Beijing: Dang-dai shijie chubanshe, 1992–).

61. See "Chinese Envoy to Venezuela: Business Interests Prevail over Political Concerns," *Caracas El Universal,* August 29, 2005, in FBIS.

62. Editing Group, *Xingshuai zhilu,* pp. 311–21.

63. Ibid., pp. 357–63.

64. Cao Changsheng, "Ouzhou shehuizhuyidang lilun he shixian de xin tiaozheng" (On the adjustment of theory and practice by social democratic parties in Europe), *Guoji Zhengzhi Yanjiu,* no. 1 (2002), pp. 119–23; Shen Yihuai, "Ouzhou zhengdang zhengzhi xin bianhua jichi xiangxiang" (The political evolution and direction of European parties) *Xiandai Guoji Guanxi,* no. 4 (2002), pp. 24–28.

65. See, for example, Gu Junli, *Ouzhou zhengdang zhizheng jingyan yanjiu* (Research on European political parties' ruling experiences) (Beijing: Jingji guanli chubanshe, 2005).

66. Editing Group, *Xingshuai zhilu,* p. 321.

67. See, for example, Party Building Institute of the CCP Organization Department, *Dangjian yanjiu zong-heng tan (1999),* pp. 350–51, and *Dangjian yanjiu zong-heng tan (2002),* pp. 328–330; Jiang Jun, "Fenxi Ouzhou fada guojia gongchandang gaikuang zhuyao de sange wenti" (Analyzing three main problems with communist parties in West European countries), *Dangjian Yanjiu Neican,* no. 2 (2003), pp. 15–17.

68. For a fuller elaboration see Shambaugh, *China's Communist Party.*

69. I have developed this concept in "The Evolving and Eclectic Modern Chinese State," in Shambaugh, ed., *The Modern Chinese State.*

16

Taiwan and China's Democratic Future: Can the Tail Wag the Dog?

CHU YUN-HAN

> A long dike will collapse because of a termite-hole in it; a tall building will be burned down by a spark from a chimney's chink.
>
> HAN FEI, ca. 280–233 B.C.

In many ways, Taiwan's democratic experience has important implications for China's political future. Taiwan is the only democracy ever installed and practiced in a Chinese society, and its unique mode of transition illustrates a viable strategy for a peaceful and gradual departure from one-party authoritarianism on the basis of successful economic modernization. Taiwan has demonstration value not only for the leaders of the Chinese Communist Party (CCP) but also for the mainland population, many of whom see a strong similarity between the political fortunes of the Kuomintang (the Chinese Nationalist Party, or KMT) and the CCP. Ordinary citizens, Chinese intellectuals, and the CCP elite alike keep a close eye on the way democracy works in Taiwan, where political and social actors—academics, writers, members of the mass media, figures from popular culture, and nongovernmental organizations (NGOs)—have all served as agents of liberalization through the transmission and dissemination of information, ideas, and practical knowledge about democracy. On the other hand, Chinese leaders also feel threatened by the rising tide of Taiwanese nationalism that was unleashed during the democratization process. With all these forces at play, Taiwan's competing political elites may well have the potential to upset the strategic applecart of East Asia and to reconfigure China's domestic priorities and external environment.

A vital question to explore, then, is whether the popular orientation toward politics and authority in the People's Republic of China (PRC) today is susceptible to a set of transformative forces similar to those that prompted a shift in Taiwan's mass political culture some twenty years ago. Will the lingering influence of traditional social values, sometimes dubbed "Confucian values," stand in the way of a steady strengthening of a popular demand for democratic legitimacy? One way to approach these questions is to compare the CCP's current political predicament with that confronting the KMT elite in the late 1970s and early 1980s. That was when the KMT was wrestling with the daunting task of retaining the party's hegemonic presence in the face of a dwindling capacity for ideological persuasion and social control. In response, it co-opted the newly emerging social forces that came with a rapidly expanding private economy, accommodating the growing popular demand for political representation and participation, and coping with the political consequences of economic opening-up. Although the strategic options available to the CCP might be somewhat different, because of China's particular political legacies and structural conditions, the KMT's challenges are of direct relevance to the changing relationship between state and society on the mainland today.

Taiwan is also an important source of ideas, information, and practical know-how about the nuts and bolts of developing a *Rechtstaat* (modern law-bound state). At the same time, its political elites could trigger a cataclysmic outburst of nationalistic lava from below and cause a major rupture in China's external environment (especially in its relationship with the United States) if the Democratic Progressive Party (DPP) leaders push for Taiwan independence beyond the tipping point. Conversely, Taiwan could maximize its magnetic power over China if, first, it improved the overall quality of its young democracy, and second, if the island's political elite were willing to engage China over the long-term prospect of reunification under one democratic China. The tail can wag the dog if the tail is still attached to the dog.

Comparing Political Value Change in Taiwan and China

According to modernization theory, economic and social development causes traditional social values to decline and more modern values to increase, as embodied in civic culture and democratic political principles. These values are a by-product of greater social mobility, participation in modern economic sectors, and the cognitive mobilization that comes with the expansion of mass communications. Modernization and its effect on values can transcend differing cultural systems and transition experiences of differing political systems. Of late, proponents of so-called postmodernization theory have accumulated substantial empirical evidence to suggest that economic development brings rising levels of tolerance, trust, political activism, and greater emphasis on freedom of speech, and that it thereby foments a populace's demand for liberalization in authoritarian societies and the desire for direct participation in societies that are already democratic.[1] An offshoot of this theory, proposed by "Asian values" theorists and some cultural relativists such as Lucian Pye and Samuel Huntington, holds, however, that East Asia's traditional culture, in particular the Confucian culture, might pose an obstacle to the acquisition of democratic values.[2] According to Huntington, Confucianism—which privileges group interests over individual interests, political authority over individual freedom, and social responsibility over individual rights—is so sharply different from the precepts of Western civilization as to be intrinsically incompatible with the organizing principles of liberal democracy.[3]

To test this theory, my colleagues and I tracked the evolution of political culture in Taiwan for more than two decades, covering the entire span of the island's transition from an authoritarian system to a democratic one. We found among Taiwan's populace a generally steady increase in the proportions of the public expressing pro-democratic values and rejecting the paternalistic, collectivist, and illiberal norms identified as obstacles by the "Asian values" perspective. At the same time, the acquisition of democratic values has been uneven, which suggests some lingering influence of traditional values. Support for political equality was high from the very beginning, and endorsement of popular accountability rose dramatically during the 1980s and early 1990s, but a substantial segment of Taiwan's public still expressed a great fear of disorder and a strong preference for communal harmony over pluralism.[4]

To determine whether the trajectory of Taiwan's cultural shift may shed light on the political consequences of socioeconomic change in China and whether the pattern of transformation is similar in both, I examine data from comparable surveys conducted in mainland China and Taiwan at different points in time. In the interest of brevity, I focus on three surveys implemented in Taiwan in 1983, 1993, and 2002 and two conducted in China in 1993 and 2002.[5] These surveys employed a consistent battery of questions for measuring citizens' commitment to liberal democratic values by tapping into the dimensions of popular accountability ("Government leaders are like the head of a family; we should all follow their decisions"), separation of power ("When judges decide important cases, they should accept the view of the executive branch"), political liberalism ("The government should decide whether certain ideas are allowed to be discussed in the society"), and political pluralism ("Stability and harmony of the community will be disrupted if people organize lots of groups").

All four items were scaled in the authoritarian direction. Hence "agreement" indicates an authoritarian value orientation while "disagreement" reveals a democratic value orientation. Each question was designed around a four-point scale, consisting of "highly disagree," "disagree," "agree," and "strongly agree." The

Figure 16-1. *Government Leaders Are Like the Head of a Family;*
We Should All Follow Their Decisions

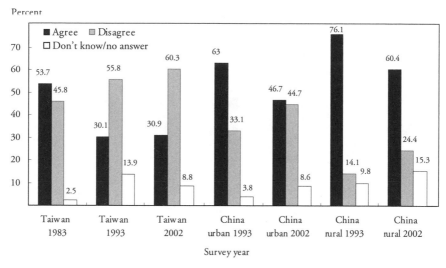

Source: The 1983 Taiwan survey is from the Political System and Change Project at National Taiwan University; the 1993 Taiwan and China surveys are from the Comparative Study of Political Culture and Participation in Taiwan, Hong Kong, and Mainland China Project at National Taiwan University; and the 2002 Taiwan and China surveys are from East Asia Barometer Survey at National Taiwan University.

distribution of popular political attitudes based on these four items over time is displayed item-by-item in figures 16-1 to 16-4. The mainland China sample is disaggregated into two subsamples, one representing the urban population and the other the rural population. The answers "highly disagree" and "disagree" are collapsed together, as are "agree" and "strongly agree."

The most significant finding across the two populations is the striking similarity in patterns of value change, suggesting that socioeconomic modernization has had a powerful impact on the growth of democratic values (indicated by the percentage of respondents who answered "disagree"). For instance, on the question "Government leaders are like the head of a family; we should all follow their decisions," only 45.8 percent of respondents in Taiwan answered "disagree" or "strongly disagree" in 1983, but the ratio rose to 55.8 percent in 1993 and to 60.3 percent in 2002 (figure 16-1). At the same time, the proportion of Taiwan's populace holding authoritarian orientations on this particular measure shrank from 53.7 percent in 1983 to 30.9 percent in 2002. In a similar vein, the proportion of China's urban residents embracing the notion of popular accounta-

Figure 16-2. *When Judges Decide Important Cases, They Should Accept the View of the Executive Branch*

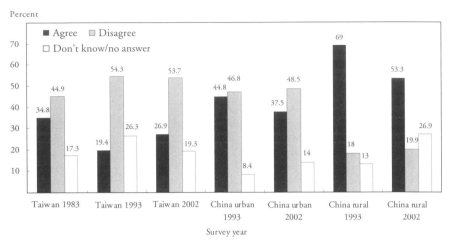

Source: See figure 16-1.

Figure 16-3. *Government Should Decide Whether Certain Ideas Are Allowed to Be Discussed in Society*

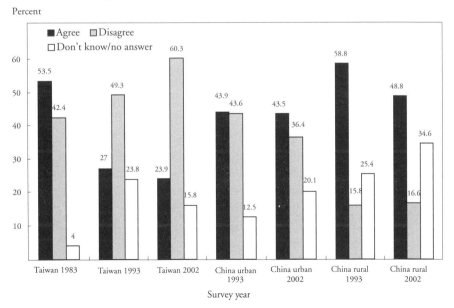

Source: See figure 16-1.

Figure 16-4. *Stability and Harmony of the Community Will Be Disrupted if People Organize Lots of Groups*

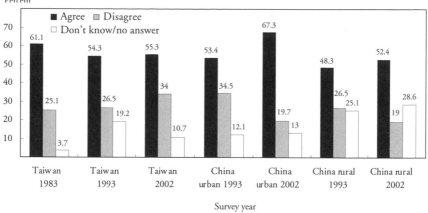

Source: See figure 16-1.

bility has risen from 33.1 percent in 1993 to 44.7 percent in 2002, approaching the level that Taiwan's electorate attained in 1983. China's rural population also showed a significant rise in democratic orientation over the decade, although the great majority of people there still embraced the notion of paternalistic government leaders (in excess of 60 percent by 2002).

This linear attitudinal shift holds up for the items measuring the concept of separation of power (see figure 16-2) and political liberalism (see figure 16-3), except that the pace of change is less dramatic. On the question "When judges decide important cases, they should accept the view of the executive branch," the proportion of Taiwan's respondents objecting rose from 44.9 percent in 1983 to 53.7 percent in 2002. In China, the percentage of rural residents expressing authoritarian orientation on this measure has dropped from 69 percent in 1993 to 53 percent in 2002, with a corresponding rise in the number of respondents answering "don't know" and "no answer," which could be interpreted as a subtle way of expressing "disagree" in many cases. On this particular measure, the attitudinal structure of China's urban population in 2002 again looks quite similar to that of Taiwan's electorate around 1983.

However, some constraining effect of traditional values can be detected across both of these Chinese societies, most notably in the fact that neither seems strongly attracted to the concept of political pluralism (see figure 16-4). In both Taiwan and mainland China, the number of respondents disagreeing with the statement "Stability and harmony of the community will be disrupted if people organize lots of groups" has never exceeded 35 percent. A persistently large number in both societies also seem worried about the effect competition and contestation among diverse interest groups may have on social stability and harmony. In 2002 this prospect bothered 55.3 percent of Taiwan respondents and 67.3 percent of China's urban residents. Furthermore, between 1993 and 2002 the percentage actually went up rather than down. This means that in both Taiwan and urban China, popular commitment to political pluralism actually lost ground during the 1990s, a period when many urban Chinese citizens had their first taste of an explosion of associational life.

Since patterns observed at the macro level provide only indirect supporting evidence for the transformative power of socioeconomic modernization, one needs to treat the survey data in a more rigorous way in order to ascertain the implied causal relationships. As table 16-1 shows, for example, the impact of age cohorts on democratic value orientation can be examined at the individual level by disaggregating the 2002 China sample into three age cohorts: (1) people who were born in or before 1948 (those fifty-five or older by the time of the 2002 survey), (2) those born between 1949 and 1968 (those aged thirty-five to fifty-four in 2002), and (3) those born after 1968 (those thirty-four or younger in 2002).[6] The value changes that emerge from this cross-generational analysis are highly consistent with the patterns identified earlier. The three age cohorts vary significantly in the measures of popular accountability and political liberalism, and to some extent in the separation of power as well. More important, there is an easily identifiable linear pattern across these three measures: the younger the generation, the lower the support for authoritarian values. As in the earlier analysis, this pattern does not hold up for the question about political pluralism. People from all three age cohorts harbored reservations about political pluralism, albeit to varying degrees. Most significant, it was the youngest generation (aged twenty to thirty-four) that showed a shift into positive territory in their average scores on all measures (except for political pluralism). That is to say, more people of this generation appeared to be embracing democratic values than people subscribing to authoritarian values. This pattern is in marked contrast to that of the two older generations.

With the progress of modernization and political liberalization, the influence of traditional values has steadily declined. Although the Confucian legacy might not have been conducive to the acquisition of liberal democratic values, it did not stop them from emerging either. If anything, China's rapid socioeconomic transition has precipitated a culture shift and has done so within two generations. A democratic culture is emerging among China's youngest generation, the generation that has received the best education ever and grown up virtually

Table 16-1. *Generation and Democratic Value Orientation, Mainland China Survey, 2002*

| Question[a] | ? | Orientation of respondents | | |
		Born before 1948	Born 1949–68	Born after 1968
Popular accountability				
1. Government leaders are like the head of a family; we should all follow their decisions.	Mean	−0.366	−0.231	0.017
	Standard	0.990	1.030	1.081
Separation of power (horizontal accountability)				
2. When judges decide important cases, they should accept the view of the executive branch.	Mean	−0.151	−0.150	0.011
	Standard	1.068	1.073	1.067
Political liberalism				
3. The government should decide whether certain ideas are allowed to be discussed in society.	Mean	−0.489	−0.308	0.044
	Standard	0.894	0.989	1.042
Political pluralism				
4. Stability and harmony of the community will be disrupted if people organize lots of groups.	Mean	−0.605	−0.494	−0.637
	Standard	0.917	0.949	0.873

a. Each question was designed around a four-point scale consisting of "highly disagree," "disagree," "agree," and "strongly agree." For the sake of statistical analysis, the four response categories are given numerical values: "highly disagree," 2 points; "disagree," 1 point; "don't know," 0 points; "agree," −1 point; and "highly agree," −2 points. Since "disagreement" reveals a democratic value orientation, all four items are scaled in the democratic direction.

exclusively in the reform era. Hence there is a ray of hope for China's further political liberalization and possibly eventual democratization. However, cultural shifts provide only a necessary condition for regime transition. Before political liberalization can be actualized and authoritarianism replaced, political structures and institutions must also change.

Comparing the Trajectory of Regime Evolution in Taiwan and China

The genesis and early organizational developments of the KMT and CCP were not only strikingly similar but also closely intertwined.[7] They both sprang up in the early twentieth century in an attempt to rebuild the state and society out of the ashes of imperial China and to save the nation from the predations of imperialist powers. At birth, both parties quickly adopted Leninist configurations—

with their clandestine activities, cellular structure, and organizational coherence based on the principle of democratic centralism—and they took on the role of political vanguards, presumably with mass support.[8] Having self-imposed (and competing) historical missions, a nationalist one for the KMT and a communist one for the CCP, both parties superimposed themselves on the state and society and sought to build up institutional hegemony.[9]

After 1949 the KMT regime evolved along a rather different path from that of the CCP, although its one-party authoritarian regime conformed to many of the organizational and operational characteristics of classic Leninist parties, with its power centralized in a paramount leader, the party operating in a symbiotic relationship with the state, and the party-state organized in a way that penetrated society.[10] Also, much like the CCP, the KMT was not just a ruling coalition in the normal sense but also a "historic bloc" in the Gramscian sense.[11] It organized the society that it governed, structured the political arena in which it operated, and articulated a worldview grounded in historically specific sociopolitical conditions that lent substance and coherence to its political domination.[12]

The differences were also considerable, however. First, the KMT was closely associated with the West in its ideological inclinations, security alliance, and economic partnership. Second, from early on, it recognized private property rights and the role of the market and to some extent institutionalized the rule of law. Third, it enjoyed the support of a distinctive coalition focused on development and an export-led model of industrialization. Paradoxically, the CCP has deviated from the classic Leninist model ever since China opened up to the West and embarked on market-oriented reform after 1978. With an epic transition from totalitarianism to developmental authoritarianism, the CCP in a sense reconnected itself with the political trajectory of the postwar KMT, albeit at a remove of two decades.

The rapid economic growth of those decades and accompanying social transformation have presented the CCP with a set of political challenges very similar to those that threatened the KMT's hegemonic position in the late 1970s and early 1980s. The KMT responded to these challenges with a number of strategic and institutional adjustments that might have looked incremental or even cosmetic at first but that turned out to be quite consequential. The parallels between the KMT's reform strategies of the 1970s and early 1980s and those undertaken by the CCP's Fourth Generation of leaders under Hu Jintao are striking.

Revamping Regime Legitimacy

The first challenge for both regimes was to build new foundations for their legitimacy in the face of depleted ideologies and discredited revolutionary mandates. The second-generation KMT leadership under Chiang Ching-kuo (CCK) shelved the mission of "recovering the mainland and reunifying China" and concentrated on "building up Taiwan" and achieving "shared affluence" (*junfu*). The leadership adopted this new raison d'être with a sense of urgency, introducing ambitious projects to modernize the island's infrastructure and upgrade Taiwan's industrial structure, and buttressing this with a Chinese-style populism anchored in compassionate, approachable, and public-spirited leadership that exemplified the virtues of unselfishness, frugality, and self-discipline. In a similar vein, China's CCP has attempted to redefine the regime's raison d'être in ways that might resonate with the great majority of the population, as embodied in Jiang Zemin's vision of "a well-off society" (*xiaokang shehui*), Hu Jintao's "harmonious society" (*hexie shehui*), and the idea of China's "peaceful rise" (*heping jueqi*). Hu Jintao also tried to rekindle a similar style of populism by labeling these objectives "the new three principles of the people (*xin sanmin zhuyi*)."[13] Even Wen Jiabao's trademark jacket looks similar to the worn-out one that CCK put on every time he visited villagers and workers.

Refurbishing the Party's Social Foundation

Another challenge for the KMT, as for the CCP today, was how to refurbish the party's social foundation to cope with the new social forces emerging outside its original organizational scope. Its leadership decided to remake the KMT from a vanguard to a catchall party and from a revolutionary to a ruling party. To this end, it vigorously recruited new members, not just from its old constituencies (such as mainlanders, the military and veterans, public-sector employees, teachers, local factions, and farmer and fisherman associations) but also from the expanding social classes that were benefiting from its export-led industrialization strategy (such as the entrepreneurial class, professionals, and the urban middle class at large). At its peak in the mid-1980s, party membership reached almost 18 percent of the entire adult male population. More specifically, CCK tried to replenish older cadres with technocrats, foreign-educated scholars, and native Taiwanese groomed through the party school. Like the KMT's earlier strategic shift, the introduction of the CCP's "Theory of Three Represents" marked a historical decision to transform the party from a vanguard party of the proletariat to a catchall party.[14] With this new vision, enshrined in the PRC constitution in 2004, the CCP cast its lot with the beneficiaries of economic reform.[15] In retrospect, the KMT practiced its own version of the "Three Represents" without labeling it as such.

Safeguarding the Party's Monopoly on Associational Life

Both the KMT and CCP have also had to safeguard their monopoly on organized social life from the encroachment of autonomous social movements and bottom-up civic organizations. By the 1950s, the KMT's party apparatus had filled up virtually all the organizational space in the modern sectors by forcing business and professional associations, labor unions, farmers, state employees, journalists, intellectuals, students, and other targeted groups into state-sponsored corporatist organizations.[16] During the 1960s and 1970s, these corporatist organizations functioned as an arm of both the state bureaucracy and the party extending into the private sector. But as private enterprises became more important to the success of export-led industrialization, the KMT had to formally recognize the economic might of the private sector. Entering the 1980s, existing business associations were upgraded to functional conduits for soliciting policy input and coordinating sectoral strategy. In particular, representatives of three leading national organizations—the Federation of Industry, the Federation of Commerce, and the blue-ribbon National Council of Industry and Commerce—were elevated to the party's top echelon, which included membership in the KMT Central Standing Committee.[17]

At the same time, an important development was taking place outside the existing corporatist structure and martial law framework with the emergence of autonomous labor movements, environmentalist movements, consumer rights groups, and other public interest advocates. The KMT leadership adopted a two-pronged strategy to cope with this burgeoning pluralism: it enacted the Civic Organization Law to license and regulate these voluntary groups; and it upgraded bureaucracies in charge of labor affairs, the environment, and consumer protection to ministry-level agencies and selectively co-opted moderate leaders of social movements into the advisory bodies of the new ministries.[18] As the legal space and mobilizing power of the bottom-up NGOs expanded, the party-state reached less and less into society's associational life.

Again, the CCP finds itself in a parallel situation, wrestling with waves of social protests and autonomous collective actions. Beneath the veneer of rapid economic growth and political stability lie simmering social grievances arising from peasant discontent, massive layoffs in the state-owned sector, government corruption and abuse of power, and environmental degradation. Like the KMT leadership in the early 1980s, today's CCP leaders have shown a great deal of tolerance and flexibility in dealing with popular protests. They have adjusted national fiscal priorities to address the negative consequences of uneven development, upgraded the state's administrative and regulatory capacities to deal with emerging social problems and market failures, and instructed local authorities to handle local incidents with care so as to prevent them from escalating.[19] At the same time, they have put certain segments of society such as underground religious movements, dissident intellectuals, human rights lawyers, and journalists on a tighter leash.

Mainland Chinese authorities are also facing the challenge of an explosion of associational life.[20] The mushrooming of bottom-up NGOs, which typically evade the current regulatory framework owing to difficult registration procedures, has severely rolled back the party-state's pervasive control of organizational space.[21] Nevertheless, with limited success, the communist regime has managed to maintain organic links to some important nonstate sectors by reinvigorating the existing mass organizations that cover the party's targeted constituencies such as workers, youths, women, scientists and engineers, businesspeople, literary and art circles, and so on. Most notable are the intermediary organizations between the state and private sector. Under the prodding of the CCP, business and industrial associations sprang up around responsible government agencies at all levels and were formally assimilated into the hierarchy of state-sanctioned encompassing organizations such as All-China Federation of Industry and Commerce.[22] As a consequence, both private and state-owned enterprises now compete for national policy advantages, often setting the agenda, providing alternative options, and pressing for a favored outcome.[23]

Harnessing the Independent Media

Yet another major issue for the CCP and KMT has been how to contain and harness the demand-driven mass media and alternative sources of information and ideas competing with official organs. During the 1970s and early 1980s, the KMT imposed rigorous censorship on Taiwan's mass media, films, and publications. It froze new licenses for newspapers and restricted the size of existing ones. However, the growing popular demand for independent sources of information, ideas, and critical opinions steadily eroded the party-state's monopoly over the supply of information and ideas. Party-owned newspapers began losing market share to KMT-affiliated but privately owned newspapers, which frequently stepped on the toes of monitoring agencies to gain wider circulation. Independent publishers constantly engaged the law enforcement agencies in hide-and-seek games and found ways to reprint banned books and commentary magazines so as to turn a profit. But the KMT still managed to foster a societal consensus on orderly incremental political change through its direct control over electronic media.

Similarly, the CCP is wrestling with the political impact of the rapid commercialization and internationalization of media industries.[24] Like the KMT, it is adamant about protecting its coveted ownership of electronic media. However, the CCP probably faces a tougher challenge in a race against time and technological innovation, as its policing power has been overwhelmed by the torrential flow of information passing through cyberspace and the explosion of short message service (SMS) via wireless communication.

Political Representation and Participation

Of all the institutional and strategic adjustments the KMT leadership introduced during the 1970s and early 1980s in its response to the political challenges brought about by the island's rapid socioeconomic modernization, none was more consequential than the opening up of national representative bodies for limited popular elections. Under the pretext of preventing a protracted civil war, the KMT had suspended the election of national representative bodies for almost a quarter century and extended the tenure of the incumbent members elected on the mainland in 1948 for life. A series of devastating diplomatic setbacks in the early 1970s compelled the KMT to strengthen its democratic legitimacy at home to compensate for the rapid erosion of its international legitimacy. It therefore opened national representative bodies to limited electoral competition in 1972, then expanded the process in 1980 and again in 1989. Each time a greater percentage of the seats in the Legislative Yuan, as well as the National Assembly, were opened to popular election, known as Supplementary Election.

Initially, this did not seem to be a risky move—after all, the KMT's formula for controlling a limited popular electoral process at the local level had been proven for more than two decades. The KMT had introduced elections for township heads, county/city council and county/city magistrates as early as 1950, and it permitted elections for the Taiwan Provincial Assembly in 1954 to incorporate a diversified native Taiwanese elite into the party-building process and to provide the authoritarian system with a democratic façade. At the grassroots level, the KMT incorporated existing patron-client networks into the party structure. Within each administrative district below the provincial level, the KMT nurtured and kept at least two competing local factions striving for public office and for a share of region-based economic rents in the nontradable goods sector. Local factions and the central party leadership soon developed a mutual dependence. On the one hand, the smooth functioning of irregular campaign practices and the local spoils system depended on the indulgence of the various state regulatory and law enforcement agencies, which were under the influence of the party. On the other hand, the fierce competition among the factions effectively blocked the entrance of opposition candidates into local elections. On top of this, the central leadership could lay claim to overall electoral victories delivered by disparate local factions.[25] Thus for almost three decades the KMT faced a very unorganized and weak political opposition consisting primarily of defiant local factions that had no national political aims and posed little threat to the KMT's dominant position.

In one sense, the gradual opening up of the national representative bodies was merely part of the institutional evolution that had been under way for a quarter century, but it had the unintended consequence of accelerating the demise of authoritarianism. Taiwan's socioeconomic conditions were already ripe for democratic opening, and the introduction of supplementary elections for national representative bodies had given rise to a loose anti-KMT coalition of independent candidates with national political aims, known as *tangwai* (literally, those "outside-the-party"). *Tangwai* candidates used the electoral process to instigate political resocialization and foster the growth of popular aspirations for democratic reform and a separate Taiwanese identity. Emboldened by their electoral success, *tangwai* candidates steadily moved ever closer to forming a quasi party in the late 1970s, eventually founding the DPP in 1986 in open defiance of martial law restrictions.

CCK's decision to tolerate the forming of the DPP, and shortly thereafter to lift martial law and many longtime political bans, marked the point of no return for authoritarianism. From the outset, however, this political liberalization was intended to bring about directed political change. To ensure the predictability of the transition's outcome, the KMT leadership favored a formula of "democratization in installments."[26] Through multistage constitutional reforms, the KMT managed to ensure an orderly sequencing of democratic openings that stretched the transition over almost a decade. In addition, the DPP lacked the political capacity to impose its reform schedule and agenda on the incumbents because the KMT had planted its socioeconomic development program on a broad base, and as the hegemonic party it had already filled up most of the organizational space in society and locked in the support of key constituencies. These prevailing conditions enabled the KMT to engineer a transition from a one-party authoritarian regime to what T. J. Pempel termed "a one-party dominant regime" (best exemplified by the Liberal Democratic Party in Japan), making Taiwan perhaps the only one of the third-wave democracies in which a quasi-Leninist party not only survived an authoritarian breakdown but also capitalized on the crisis to its advantage.[27] Had there not been an eruption over national identity and the resultant intraparty split, the KMT could plausibly have retained its governing position much longer beyond the democratic transition.

Although the delicate political circumstances surrounding the KMT leaders in the late 1970s and early 1980s resemble the situation that Hu Jintao and other top CCP leaders face today, the strategic options available to the two elites are not exactly the same. The KMT regime was severely constrained by three structural vulnerabilities that are absent or much less pressing for the CCP.

First, the KMT was highly vulnerable to the influence of foreign actors, especially the United States, which Taiwan depended on greatly for market access, military security, and international diplomatic support. Second, the postwar authoritarian order, dominated by former mainlanders, rested on a shaky foundation: namely, a precarious claim to sovereignty as the sole legitimate government representing all of China. In an uphill battle, the KMT defended its extra-constitutional arrangements amid a global wave of democratization, insisted on the one-China principle when virtually all major nations had shifted their diplomatic recognition to the PRC as the sole legitimate government of China, and continued to uphold a Chinese identity despite the emergence of a Taiwanese identity. Toward the second half of the 1980s, the KMT found it increasingly difficult to hold off redistributing power from the mainlander elite to native Taiwanese through democratic opening. Third, the KMT was constrained by its own ideological and institutional commitments, which, from the Republic of China's (ROC's) constitution on, embraced democratic norms in principle. Nor did it deny the validity of dissent and open contestation in principle. The KMT had defended the postwar authoritarian arrangements and emergency decrees that superseded many important provisions of the constitution on the grounds that the country was under imminent military threat from the rival communist regime.

By the early 1980s, cross-Strait détente had begun to erode Taiwan's siege mentality and weaken the rationale for maintaining a state of emergency, which made it more difficult and costly for the KMT to suppress popular demands for a return to constitutional "normalcy." Empowered by its accumulated success in engineering electoral dominance and by the cohesion of the political coalition behind its development strategy (which addressed both the growth and equity issues with a high degree of effectiveness), the KMT now found the option of peaceful extrication from authoritarian rule readily available.

The structural situation inherited by Hu Jintao's generation of CCP leaders is in many respects less delicate than what the KMT had to face two decades ago. First of all, the CCP regime is relatively free from the kind of ideological or institutional commitments that constrained the KMT elite. The CCP has committed itself to the development of "socialist democracy," but not Western-style liberal democracy. The CCP's monopoly of power is still protected by the PRC constitution, which implicitly prohibits dissent and public contestation for power. And whereas Chinese nationalism turned out to be a liability for the KMT elite, it remains the CCP's most valuable political asset. Hu Jintao's vision of China's peaceful rise can serve as an important pillar of legitimacy for the communist regime as it addresses the popular yearning for the restoration of China's preeminence on the world stage. Furthermore, among all the transitional societies in the world, China, because of its sheer size and history of anti-imperialist struggle, is more immune to the sway of the United States or the industrialized democracies than most developing countries. Indeed, owing to its size and growing influence, China has the potential to create a more hospitable regional environment for a political regime anchored in developmental authoritarianism. In addition, China is navigating in a different time. The global tidal wave of democracy has receded, and the developing world today has entered a period of what Larry Diamond has dubbed "democratic recession."[28]

Equally significant, the limited electoral pluralism that the CCP has experimented with at the grassroots level has not yet reached a critical point that could set in motion a self-propelling institutional evolution such as Taiwan experienced. True, village elections have become a normal feature of grassroots political life, and they represent an important step forward in China's quest for a more accountable political system, but as Tom Bernstein forcefully argues, the impact of village democracy functioning within an overarching authoritarian environment is limited.[29] If one is looking for a seed of democratization in the existing system, the people's congresses arguably represent a more promising case. The pluralization of economic interests and the deepening of social stratification have already made an impact on the election of deputies to the congresses at the local level and the role they play in setting policy priorities and drafting laws and regulations. In the foreseeable future, however, the CCP will almost certainly continue to exert its supremacy over the local and national congresses. Thus it may take decades for genuine parliamentarianism to emerge.[30]

Taiwan as an Agent of Change

As already mentioned, many Taiwanese social and political actors have served as agents of change on the mainland. Taiwan-based academics, writers, mass media outlets, pop culture icons, and NGOs have all been conducive to China's political liberalization through the transmission and dissemination of information, ideas, and practical knowledge about life in a culturally Chinese democracy.

In particular, many Taiwan-based NGOs involved in a full range of social causes—from Buddhism to the environment, from legal aid to consumer rights, from assistance to battered wives to the preservation of cultural heritage sites—have developed extensive networks with like-minded organizations throughout mainland China. With the spread of satellite television, Taiwan's popular TV anchors and talk show hosts and hostesses such as Lee Au, Sissy Chen, and Shaw-kang Chao have become household names in China, helping mainland audiences achieve a better grasp of political and social events taking place in Taiwan and elsewhere. Taiwan has also become an important source of ideas, information, and practical know-how about developing a *Rechtstaat* (modern law-bound state), which is the prerequisite for liberal constitutionalism. Every aspect of the working of Taiwan's state bureaucracy, from its budgeting and audits to administrative procedures and civil service examinations, has been carefully studied by responsible state cadres in China. Taiwan's law textbooks and legal scholars have been the most important source of overseas ideas during China's recent efforts to overhaul its civic and criminal codes, litigation procedures, and regulatory framework for legal persons. Officials at China's Ministry of Civil Affairs carefully studied Taiwan's election laws and procedures when they drafted and expanded China's own electoral procedures and rules for grassroots democracy. China has also looked to Taiwan in revamping its legal system, favoring the Taiwan model because it is based on German code law rather than Anglo-Saxon common law, which inspired the Hong Kong system, for example.

At the same time, Taiwan's competing political elites could severely complicate the prospect of a democratic future for China. On one hand, Taiwan's democratization could spur democratic aspirations in mainland Chinese if they saw it could lead to a better quality of governance and widespread popular support for democracy on the island. On the other hand, it might throw cold water on pro-democracy forces in China if they thought it imposed high social and economic costs on Taiwan and left a growing number of citizens disaffected and disillusioned. Unfortunately, the second scenario looms large at present. The protracted political chaos, paralysis, and visible deterioration in many aspects of democracy following the 2000 power rotation have made Taiwan's democratic experience less and less appealing to mainland observers. Especially in the eyes of Taiwan's electorate—arguably the final judge of the success of democracy on the island—the gap between the promises of democracy and its real world practice has been widening. According to some recent surveys, Taiwan is the only new East Asian democracy in which the number of people believing in the superiority of democracy is substantially less than the number of people skeptical about it. Equally notable are the sharp decline in the number of democratic believers and the corresponding rise in the number who are either skeptical or indifferent. Between 1998 and 2002, close to 15 percent of the electorate withdrew their unqualified support for democracy. This degree of backsliding is rare among emerging democracies.[31] If these ambivalent attitudes toward democracy persist, or even worsen, Taiwan will in all likelihood be unable to promote the soft power of democracy in the Chinese-speaking world with self-confidence.

Taiwan's political model could also steadily lose its appeal to Chinese citizens if the island becomes more culturally and politically estranged from China. The anti-China nature of Taiwanese nationalism and the ongoing de-Sinicization campaign under the DPP administration have alienated many influential Chinese public intellectuals who might otherwise have been receptive to learning from Taiwan's political experiences. These developments also supply the CCP's propaganda machine with the raw materials it needs to demonize Taiwan's democratization as nothing but a perilous separatist movement. Conversely, Taiwan might be able to maximize its magnetic power over China if it could extricate itself from its current crisis of democratic governance, if it continued to improve the overall quality of its young democracy, and if the island's political leaders were willing to engage China over the long-term prospect of reunification under the principle of one China under democratic rule. To reiterate, the tail can wag the dog, but only if the tail is still attached to the dog.

Last, but not least, as noted at the outset, Taiwan's competing political elites also have the potential to upset the strategic applecart of East Asia and thus reconfigure China's domestic priorities and external environment in a fundamental way. If the DPP leaders push for Taiwan independence too hard, they could ignite a cataclysmic outburst of nationalistic sentiment from below and trigger a major rupture in China's external environment, especially in the country's relationship with the United States. The consequences of a military showdown in the Taiwan Strait would, by any measure, be catastrophic for the two societies and the region as a whole. Without any doubt, it would deal a fatal blow to Taiwan's young democracy, just as it would certainly derail China's economic reforms and wreck the momentum of political liberalization.

This dire projection looks increasingly unlikely as deteriorating economic conditions have dampened the people's appetite for lofty diplomatic objectives and outlandish political designs. As Chen Shui-bian's second term nears its end, Taiwanese nationalism is visibly receding and the political base for a reopening of political dialogue with Beijing and closer cross-Strait economic ties is growing.

Conclusion

My analysis offers many rays of hope for China's further political liberalization and possibly eventual democratization. For one thing, China's rapid socioeconomic transformation has precipitated a cultural shift toward a more open mind to democratic concepts, especially among the younger generation. Before too long, cultural and social conditions in China's urban sector will be ripe for further political opening. Taiwan's experiences have also demonstrated that it is possible for a hegemonic party to engineer a peaceful and gradual transition from one-party authoritarianism to pluralism on the basis of its successful record of economic modernization. Taiwan's model of "democratization in installments" will be of great heuristic value to the next generation of CCP leaders, which will be under mounting pressure to find a viable exit strategy as the popular demand for accountability, representation, and participation continues to rise. In addition, the demise of the KMT regime suggests that developmental authoritarianism, with all its organizational omnipotence and adaptability, eventually becomes the victim of its own success. A highly resilient developmental authoritarian regime can find ways to mitigate the corrosive effect of rapid socioeconomic modernization on its political hegemony, but there is no way to stop the process completely.

Taiwan's transition experience also suggests that a well-entrenched hegemonic party can take its time in moving toward political liberalization. Conceivably, the CCP might enjoy an even longer breathing space because it is navigating in a less restrictive external environment. If the CCP can avoid an irreparable intraparty split (the kind that often comes with a power struggle over succession under authoritarianism), can sustain its growth momentum, and can adequately arrest the trend of growing regional disparity and economic polarization, it might manage to maintain its hegemonic presence in the society for quite a while. To do so, it must find the right mix of coercion and material payoffs, must blend populist leadership and nationalist symbols, rebuild the state's governing capacity, adapt existing representative institutions and consultative mechanisms to new needs, accept eclecticism and pragmatism on socioeconomic issues, selectively co-opt emerging social forces, and reinvigorate its existing mass organizations. Using mainly these recipes, the second-generation KMT leaders stretched Taiwan's political liberalization and authoritarianism's decline over almost two decades (from the early 1970s to late 1980s)—and did so in the midst of rapid socioeconomic change and deteriorating international standing.

Notes

1. Ronald Inglehart, *Modernization and Postmodernization: Cultural, Economic and Political Change in 43 Societies* (Princeton University Press, 1997); Ronald F. Inglehart and Christian Welzel, *Modernization, Cultural Change, and Democracy: The Human Development Sequence* (Cambridge University Press, 2005).

2. For instance, Lucian W. Pye, *Asian Power and Politics* (Harvard Belknap, 1985). For a review of the "Asian values" debate, see Alan Dupont, "Is There an 'Asian Way'?" *Survival* 38, no. 2 (1996): 13–33; Daniel A. Bell and Joanne Bauer, eds. *The East Asian Challenge for Human Rights* (Cambridge University Press, 1999).

3. Samuel P. Huntington, *The Clash of Civilizations and the Remaking of World Order* (New York: Simon and Schuster, 1996).

4. Fu Hu and Yun-han Chu, "Neo-authoritarianism, Polarized Conflict and Populism in a Newly Democratizing Regime: Taiwan's Emerging Mass Politics," *Journal of Contemporary China* 5 (Spring 1996): 23-41.

5. In both localities, all surveys were based on territory-wide stratified samples in accordance with the probability proportional to size (PPS) criterion. Each sample represents all of the adult population above the voting age in a given territory (excluding Tibet in the case of China). The 1993 China survey yielded 3,296 valid cases and the 2002 survey yielded 3,183 cases.

6. Chinese citizens born after 1968 were little affected by the Cultural Revolution, are the best-educated generation that China has ever known, and grew up almost exclusively under the reform era in their adolescent years.

7. Bruce Dickson, *Democratization in China and Taiwan: The Adaptability of Leninist Parties* (Oxford University Press, 1989), chap. 1.

8. The KMT's Leninist legacy was the result of its close cooperation with the Soviet Union in the mid-1920s, after Sun Yat-sen reorganized the party in 1924.

9. Tun-jen Cheng and Lin Gang, "Competitive Elections and the Transformation of the Hegemonic Party: Experience in Taiwan and Recent Development in China," paper presented at the conference on Democratization in Greater China, Stanford University Center for Democracy, Development, and the Rule of Law, October 20–21, 2006.

10. For the quasi-Leninist features of the postwar KMT, see Yun-han Chu, *Crafting Democracy in Taiwan* (Taipei: Institute for National Policy Research, 1992), chap. 2; and Tun-jen Cheng, "Democratizing the Quasi-Leninist Regime in Taiwan," *World Politics* 42 (July 1989): 471–99.

11. In Antonio Gramsci's view, any ruling class that wishes to dominate in modern conditions has to move beyond its own narrow corporate interests to exert intellectual and moral leadership, and to make alliances and compromises with a variety of forces. Gramsci calls this union of social forces a "historic bloc." This bloc forms the basis of consent to a certain social order, which produces and reproduces the hegemony of the dominant class through a nexus of institutions, social relations, and ideas.

12. Yun-han Chu, "Political Parties in Taiwan's Dominant One-Party Democracy," in *Political Parties and Democracy,* edited by Larry Jay Diamond and Richard Gunther (Johns Hopkins University Press, 2001).

13. On March 18, 2003, the day after assuming the presidency, standing before television cameras, Hu Jintao proposed what has come to be known as the "new three principles of the people" (*xin sanmin zhuyi* or *sange weimin*): to use power on the people's behalf (*quan weimin suoyong*), to maintain close ties to the people emotionally (*qing weimin suoji*), and to pursue the interests of the people (*li weimin suomou*).

14. The theory of Three Represents was introduced by Jiang Zemin in his speech at the Sixteenth CCP Party Congress in November 2002. The formal statement of the theory is "The Party must always represent the requirements of the development of China's advanced productive forces, the orientation of the development of China's advanced culture, and the fundamental interests of the overwhelming majority of the people in China." The function of this theory is to legitimize the inclusion of capitalists and private entrepreneurs within the Communist Party.

15. John W. Lewis and Litai Xue, "Social Change and Political Reform in China: Meeting the Challenge of Success," in *The New Chinese Leadership: Challenges and Opportunities after the 16th Party Congress,* edited by Yun-han Chu, Chi-cheng Lo, and Ramon Myers (Cambridge University Press, 2004).

16. These associations were licensed by the state and were based on compulsory membership. They were typically granted exclusive representation and certain regulatory authority.

17. Yun-han Chu, "The Realignment of State-Business Relations in Taiwan's Regime Transition," in *The Changing Government-Business Relations in the Pacific Rim Countries,* edited by Andrew MacIntyre (Cornell University Press, 1994).

18. Yun-han Chu, "Social Protest and Political Democratization in Taiwan," in *Other Voices/Other Visions: Responses to Directed Political and Socio-Economic Change in Taiwan, 1945–1991*, edited by Murray Rubinstein (Armonk, N.Y.: M. E. Sharpe, 1994).

19. Yongnian Zheng, "State Rebuilding, Popular Protest and Collective Action in China," *Japanese Journal of Political Science* 3 (June 2002): 45–70.

20. Shaoguang Wang and Jianyu He, "Associational Revolution in China: Mapping the Landscapes," *Korea Observer* 35 (Autumn 2004): 485–533.

21. Wang Ming, Deng Guosheng, and Gu Linsheng, "China NGO Research: A Case Study," Research Report Series 38 (UN Center for Regional Development, 2001).

22. David L. Wank, "Private Business, Bureaucracy, and Political Alliance in a Chinese City," *Australian Journal of Chinese Affairs* 33 (January 1995): 55–71; Scott Kennedy, *Business of Lobbying in China* (Harvard University Press, 2005), chap. 2.

23. Kennedy, *Business of Lobbying in China*, chap. 3.

24. Stephanie Hemelryk Donald, Yin Hong, and Michael Keane, eds., *Media in China: Consumption, Content and Crisis* (London: Routledge, 2002).

25. The combined mobilizing strength of the KMT party and the local factions had—virtually without exception—delivered more than two-thirds of the popular vote and three-quarters of the seats in all elections before the rise of the opposition in the late 1980s. See Hung-mao Tien and Yun-han Chu, "Building Democracy in Taiwan," in *Contemporary Taiwan*, edited by David Shambaugh (Oxford University Press, 1998).

26. This concept was developed by Masahiro Wakabayashi. See his *Taiwan—Bunretsu kokka to minshuka* (Taiwan: Democratization in a divided country) (University of Tokyo Press, 1992), p. 17.

27. T. J. Pempel, "Introduction," in *Uncommon Democracies: The One-Party Dominant Regimes*, edited by T. J. Pempel (Cornell University Press, 1990); Chu, "Political Parties in Taiwan's One-Party Dominant Democracy."

28. Quoted in Peter Beinart, "Is Freedom Failing?" *Time*, May 10, 2007.

29. Thomas Bernstein, "Village Democracy and Its Limits," *Asien* 99 (April 2006): pp. 29–41.

30. Jean-Pierre Cabestan, "More Power to the People's Congresses?" *Asien* 99 (April 2006): 42–69.

31. Yun-han Chu, "Taiwan's Year of Stress," *Journal of Democracy* 16 (April 2005): 43–57.

Contributors

Richard Baum is professor of political science at the University of California–Los Angeles and director emeritus of the UCLA Center for Chinese Studies. He has written and edited nine books, including *Burying Mao: Chinese Politics in the Age of Deng Xiaoping* (1996) and *Reform and Reaction in Post-Mao China: The Road to Tiananmen* (1991). His latest book, *China Watcher: Confessions of a Peking Tom*, will be published in 2008. Baum is the founder and list manager of Chinapol, an online discussion group for professional China analysts. He has served on the editorial boards of the leading journals in Chinese and East Asian Studies, and is a frequent commentator for CNN, National Public Radio, Voice of America and *BBC World Service*. He has a Ph.D. in political science from the University of California–Berkeley.

Chu Yun-han is a distinguished research fellow at the Institute of Political Science at Academia Sinica and professor of political science at National Taiwan University. He also serves as president of the Chiang Ching-kuo Foundation for International Scholarly Exchange. Chu received his Ph.D. in political science from the University of Minnesota and joined the faculty of National Taiwan University in 1987. His specialties include the politics of Greater China, East Asian political economy, and democratization. He is the coordinator of the Asian Barometer Survey, a regional survey on democracy, governance, and development covering more than sixteen Asian countries. He has authored, coauthored, edited, or coedited eleven books. His recent English-language publications include *The New Chinese Leadership: Challenges and Opportunities after the 16th Party Congress* (2004); *China under Jiang Zemin* (2000); *Consolidating*

323

Third-Wave Democracies (1997); and *Crafting Democracy in Taiwan* (1992). His works have appeared in *World Politics, International Organization, Journal of Politics, China Quarterly, Journal of Democracy, Pacific Affairs,* and *Asian Survey.* In addition to his own research and writing, Chu serves on the editorial boards of *International Studies Quarterly, Pacific Affairs, China Review, Journal of Contemporary China, Journal of East Asian Studies,* and *Journal of Democracy.*

JACQUES DELISLE is the Stephen Cozen Professor of Law at the University of Pennsylvania, a member of the university's Center for East Asian Studies, and director of the Asia Program at the Foreign Policy Research Institute. He received his J.D. and graduate education in political science at Harvard University and holds an A.B. from Princeton University. His writings focus on legal, economic, and political reform in China; legal and political issues in Hong Kong's reversion to Chinese sovereignty; the international status of Taiwan and cross-Strait relations; China's engagement with the international legal and institutional order, including the WTO; U.S. efforts to promote reform in the post-communist world; and uses of U.S. law to address human rights in China. He previously clerked for Supreme Court Justice Stephen Breyer (at the time chief judge of the First Circuit Court of Appeals) and served as attorney-adviser in the Office of Legal Counsel at the U.S. Justice Department, where his work focused on separation of powers and foreign affairs law. He has also served as a consultant to several programs on legal reform in China.

ERICA S. DOWNS is the China Energy Fellow at the John L. Thornton China Center at the Brookings Institution. Previously, she worked as an energy analyst at the Central Intelligence Agency, an analyst at the RAND Corporation, and a lecturer at the Foreign Affairs College in Beijing, China. She earned her M.A. and Ph.D. from Princeton University and holds a B.S. from Georgetown University. Her specialties include Chinese energy policy, China's oil industry and Chinese foreign policy as it relates to the quest for oil. Downs is the author of the online publication "The Brookings Foreign Policy Studies Energy Security Series: China" (2006) and *China's Quest for Energy Security* (2000). Her writings have appeared in *China Quarterly, China Security, Far Eastern Economic Review,* and *International Security.*

JOSEPH FEWSMITH is professor of international relations and political science at Boston University, where he is director of the East Asian Interdisciplinary Studies Program. He also holds a position as a research associate at the John King Fairbank Center for East Asian Studies at Harvard University. Fewsmith received his Ph.D. in political science from the University of Chicago and his

B.A. from Northwestern University. From 2005 to 2006, he was a fellow at the Woodrow Wilson International Center for Scholars. He is the author of *China since Tiananmen: The Politics of Transition* (2001, 2nd ed. forthcoming 2008); *Elite Politics in Contemporary China* (2001); *Dilemmas of Reform in China: Political Conflict and Economic Debate* (1994); and *Party, State, and Local Elites in Republican China: Merchant Organizations and Politics in Shanghai, 1890–1930* (1985). In addition to serving as a regular contributor to the *China Leadership Monitor*, published online by the Hoover Institution at Stanford University, his writings on contemporary politics in China have been published in a number of journals.

JING HUANG formerly held positions at the Brookings Institution, University of Utah, and Stanford University. He earned his B.A. in English from Sichuan University and an M.A. in History from Fudan University, and completed his Ph.D. in Government at Harvard University in 1994. His specialties include Chinese elite politics, U.S.-China relations, Chinese foreign policy and cross-Strait relations, and Chinese civil-military relations. He is the author of *U.S.-China Relations, 1989–1993* (in Chinese, 2003) and *Factionalism in Chinese Communist Politics* (2000), which won the 2002 Masayoshi Ohira Memorial Prize for excellence in research on politics, economics, culture, and technology contributing to the development of the Pacific Basin Community Concept. He has published numerous articles and contributed to books on Chinese politics, China's foreign policy and development strategy, the military and its political role in China, U.S.-China relations, and security issues in the Asia-Pacific region. He is currently writing *Civil-Military Relations in China: A Long March Towards Institutionalization*. He serves as an overseas adviser to the China Foundation for International and Strategic Studies.

CHENG LI is a senior fellow at the John L. Thornton China Center in the Foreign Policy Studies program at the Brookings Institution. He is also the William R. Kenan Professor of Government at Hamilton College. In 1985 he moved from China to the United States, where he earned an M.A. in Asian Studies from the University of California–Berkeley and a Ph.D. in political science from Princeton University. He was a fellow of the Institute of Current World Affairs (1993–95) and a fellow at the Woodrow Wilson International Center for Scholars (2002–03). His specialties include Chinese elite politics, center-local relations, and China's technological development. Among his recent publication are *Bridging Minds across the Pacific: U.S.-China Educational Exchanges* (2005); *China's Leaders: The New Generation* (2001); and *Rediscovering China: Dynamics and Dilemmas of Reform* (1997). His writings have appeared in numerous journals and more than a dozen edited volumes. He serves as a columnist for the quarterly Stanford University journal, *China Leadership Monitor*, and also serves as a director of the National Committee on U.S.-China Relations.

ALICE LYMAN MILLER is a research fellow and general editor of the *China Leadership Monitor* at the Hoover Institution at Stanford University, where she also teaches in the departments of History and Political Science. In addition, Miller serves as a senior lecturer in the Department of National Security Affairs at the U.S. Naval Postgraduate School in Monterey, California. She received her B.A. in Oriental Studies from Princeton University in 1966 and earned a Ph.D. in history from George Washington University in 1974. She is the author of *Science and Dissent in Post-Mao China: The Politics of Knowledge* (1996), as well as a number of articles, and has contributed to several books on contemporary Chinese politics, foreign policy, and history. Her current research projects include a book tentatively titled *The Evolution of Chinese Grand Strategy, 1550–Present*. From 1974 to 1990, she was an analyst of Chinese domestic politics, foreign policy, and Soviet policy in Asia at the Central Intelligence Agency. From 1990 until 2000, she was associate professor and, for most of that period, director of China Studies at the Johns Hopkins University's School of Advanced International Studies in Washington, D.C.

JAMES MULVENON is the acting director of Defense Group, Inc.'s Center for Intelligence Research and Analysis, where he runs a team of more than a dozen Chinese linguist-analysts who perform contract research for the United States government. Mulvenon received his Ph.D. in political science from the University of California–Los Angeles. Previously, he held positions as a political scientist at the RAND Corporation in Washington, D.C., and deputy director of RAND's Center for Asia-Pacific Policy. His current research focuses on Chinese C4ISR, acquisition organizations and policy, strategic weapons doctrines (including computer network attack), nuclear warfare, military leadership and corruption, and the military and civilian implications of the information revolution in China. He has served as the co-organizer of the Center for Naval Analysis's annual conference on the Chinese military and is the coeditor of its latest edited volume, *A Poverty of Riches: New Challenges and Opportunities in PLA Research* (2003). His book, *Soldiers of Fortune* (2001), examined the Chinese military's multibillion-dollar business empire. In addition to his research activities, Mulvenon is a term member on the Council on Foreign Relations, a founding member of the Cyber Conflict Studies Association, and a member of the National Committee on U.S.-China Relations.

ANDREW J. NATHAN is the Class of 1919 Professor of Political Science at Columbia University, where he has taught since 1971. He received his Ph.D. in political science from Harvard. His publications include *Constructing Human Rights in the Age of Globalization* (2003); *China's New Rulers: The Secret Files* (2002); *The Tiananmen Papers* (2001); *China's Transition* (1997); *The Great Wall and the Empty Fortress: China's Search for Security* (1997); *China's Crisis* (1990); *Chinese Democracy* (1985); and *Peking Politics, 1918–1923* (1976), among others, and articles in several journals. Nathan is a member of the editorial boards of the *Journal of Democracy, China Quarterly, The Journal of Contemporary China,* and *China Information.* In addition to his scholarship, Dr. Nathan serves as cochair of the board of Human Rights in China, a member of the board of Freedom House, and a member of the Advisory Committee of Human Rights Watch, Asia, which he chaired from 1995 to 2000. He is also a member of the Council on Foreign Relations, the National Committee on U.S.-China Relations, the Association for Asian Studies, and the American Political Science Association.

BARRY NAUGHTON is the So Kuanlok Professor of Chinese and International Affairs at the Graduate School of International Relations and Pacific Studies at the University of California–San Diego. He earned his Ph.D. in economics at Yale University in 1986. He has published extensively on China's economic transition, industry and trade in China, and China's political economy. Naughton's most recent book, *The Chinese Economy: Transitions and Growth* (2007), is a comprehensive survey of the Chinese economy during the reform era. He served as coeditor of *Holding China Together: Diversity and National Integration in the Post-Deng Era* (2004). His research on economic interactions among China, Taiwan, and Hong Kong, focusing on the electronics industry, led to the edited volume, *The China Circle: Economics and Technology in the PRC, Taiwan and Hong Kong* (1997). His pioneering study of Chinese economic reform, *Growing out of the Plan: Chinese Economic Reform, 1978–1993* (1995) won the Masayoshi Ohira Memorial Prize in 1997 for excellence in research on politics, economics, culture, and technology that contributes to the development of the Pacific Basin Community Concept. He is a columnist for the quarterly Stanford University journal, *China Leadership Monitor.*

MINXIN PEI is a senior associate and director of the China Program at the Carnegie Endowment for International Peace. Pei earned his B.A. at Shanghai International Studies University and received his Ph.D. in political science from Harvard University in 1991. He has taught at Davidson College, Harvard University, the University of Pittsburgh, and most recently in the Department of

Politics at Princeton University from 1992 to 1998. His main interests are U.S.-China relations, the development of democratic political systems, and Chinese politics. He is the author of *China's Trapped Transition: The Limits of Developmental Autocracy* (2006) and *From Reform to Revolution: The Demise of Communism in China and the Soviet Union* (1994). Pei's scholarly and public policy writings have been published widely in a number of journals and edited volumes. His op-eds have appeared in the general press, including *Financial Times*, *New York Times*, *Washington Post*, and *Christian Science Monitor*, and he has testified before the Senate Foreign Relations Committee on the subject of legal reform in China and other issues.

DAVID SHAMBAUGH is professor of political science and international affairs, founding director of the China Policy Program in the Elliott School of International Affairs at George Washington University, and a nonresident senior fellow in the Foreign Policy Studies program at the Brookings Institution. He received his B.A. from George Washington University, his M.A. from the Johns Hopkins University School of Advanced International Studies, and his Ph.D. from the University of Michigan. He previously served as director of the Sigur Center for Asian Studies in the Elliott School from 1996 to 1998. Before joining the faculty at George Washington University, he was Reader in Chinese Politics at the University of London's School of Oriental and African Studies from 1986 to 1996. He served as editor of *China Quarterly* from 1991 to 1996. From 2002 to 2003, he was a fellow at the Woodrow Wilson International Center for Scholars. His recent books include *Power Shift: China & Asia's New Dynamics* (2006); *Modernizing China's Military* (2002); and *China's Communist Party: Atrophy & Adaptation* (2008). His nearly 200 articles, chapters, and editorials have appeared in edited books, scholarly and policy journals, and newspapers.

DOROTHY J. SOLINGER is professor of political science at the University of California–Irvine and senior adjunct research scholar at the Weatherhead East Asian Institute at Columbia University. She was codirector of the Center for Asian Studies at University of California–Irvine from 2004 to 2006. She earned her B.A. at the University of Chicago and her Ph.D. at Stanford University, both in political science. She was associate director of Asian Studies and taught political science at the University of Pittsburgh from 1975 to 1984, and taught (by invitation) at the University of Michigan and Stanford University. Her book *Contesting Citizenship in Urban China: Peasant Migrants, the State and the Logic of the Market* (1999) won the 2001 Joseph R. Levenson Award of the Association for Asian Studies for the best book on twentieth-century China published in 1999. Among her other books are *From Lathes to Looms: China's Industrial Policy in Comparative Perspective, 1979–1982* (1991) and *Chinese Business under Socialism* (1984), and she has edited several volumes and contributed to many books on China. She has received numerous fellowships, most recently one from the Smith Richardson Foundation.

YU KEPING is professor at and director of the China Center for Comparative Politics and Economics (CCCPE), and also professor and director, Center for Chinese Government Innovations, at Beijing University. He currently serves as deputy director of the Bureau of Translation of the CCP Central Committee. Yu also serves as one of the principal experts of the Project on Marxism of the Central Committee of the Chinese Communist Party and the director of the Chinese Government Innovations Awards Program. His major fields of expertise include political philosophy, comparative politics, globalization, civil society, governance, and politics in China. Some of his published works include *The Institutional Environment of Civil Society in China* (2006); *Chinese Rural Governance in the Past and Present* (2004); *Globalization and Sovereignty* (2004); *Politics and Political Science* (2003); *Incremental Democracy and Good Governance in China* (2003); *Globalization and China's Political Development* (2003); *The Emergence of Civil Society and Its Significance for Governance* (2002); *Politics of Public Good or Politics of Rights* (1999); and *China's Contemporary Political System* (1998). Yu has spent time as a visiting scholar at Duke University and the Free University of Berlin.

Index

Administrative Litigation Law *(1990)*, 174
Africa, 188
Aging, aged and, 16–17, 253–55
All-China Federation of Trade Unions, 50, 175
Angang Constitution, 34
Anti, Michael, 172
Anti-Rightist Campaign, 196
Anti-satellite weapons (ASATs), 267, 270–76
Asia, 293, 294
Asian Development Bank, 257
Authoritarianism, 27, 34, 157, 198–99

Bachelors, 254–55
Bai Chunli, 105
Bank of China, 240
Banyuetan (Semi-Monthly), 236
BBC (British Broadcasting Company), 171
Beijing, 189, 245, 269, 271, 284
Beijing Daily, 3
Beijing Evening News, 163

Beijing Youth Daily, 163
Bingdian, 177
Blue Book of Social Development, 257
Bolivia, 295
"Bourgeois liberalization," 81
Bo Xilai, 31, 100, 110
Brandt, Willy, 285
Brezhnev, Leonid, 76
British Broadcasting Company. *See* BBC
Budget, redistributive, 145–47
"Building Harmonious Society Crucial for China's Progress," 185
Bulgaria, 285, 286
Bureaucrats, selection of, 6
Bureau of Civil Organizations, 49
"Burgher's society" (shimin shehui), 48
Bush, George W., 270–71
Business elite, 14

Caijing, 163, 177, 240–41
Cao Gangchuan, 69, 71, 105
Cao Jianming, 101–02, 106

CASS. *See* Chinese Academy of Social Sciences

Castro, Fidel, 291

CCDI. *See* Central Commission for Discipline Inspection

CCP. *See* Chinese Communist Party

CCP Central Committee, 29, 56, 62–64, 66, 99; on private property, 47; Translation Bureau, 3, 6–7

CCYL. *See* Chinese Communist Youth League

CDIC. *See* Central Discipline Inspection Committee

Cell phones, 167–68, 172

Central Asia, 192, 277

Central China Development Office, 149

Central Commission for Discipline Inspection (CCDI), 99

Central Cultural Revolution Group, 66

Central Discipline Inspection Committee (CDIC), 63, 229, 245–46

Central Military Commission (CMC), 63, 80, 85

Central Organization Department, 245–46

Central Party School, 3–4, 6, 105, 112, 236

Central Propaganda Department, 169, 170, 176

Chambers of commerce/industry associations, 218–21

Chavez, Hugo, 295

Chen Liangyu, 71, 90, 156, 192, 229

Chen Shui-bian, 6, 319

Chen Tonghai, 136

Chen Yun, 63, 66–67, 284

Chen Zhili, 106

Chiang Ching-kuo, 310–11

Chi Haotian, 69

Chile, 295

China Daily, 256

China Economic Times, 177

China Human Development Report *(2005),* 257

China Mobile, 172

China National Offshore Oil Corporation (CNOOC), 122–23, 130, 188; as internationally listed subsidiaries, 125–26; profits of, 126; senior management of, 126–27, 135–36

China National Petroleum Corporation (CNPC), 122–23; as internationally listed subsidiaries, 125–26; operations of, 130–32; profits of, 126; senior management of, 126–27, 135–36

China Petrochemical Corporation (Sinopec), 122–24, 130; as internationally listed subsidiaries, 125–26; profits of, 126; senior management of, 126–27, 135–36

"China: Political Development and Political Stability in the Reform Era," 33

"China's Ban on Bad News," 161

China Statistical Yearbook, 257

China Youth Daily, 177

Chinese Academy of Social Sciences (CASS), 6–7, 34, 257, 284, 285–86

Chinese Communist Party (CCP), 1, 99; age/term limits of, 85–87; cadre promotion/retirement system within, 89; central revenues of, 213; corruption and, 229–47; on democratization, 53–57; elite politics of, 61–62, 75–78, 81, 84, 196; on governance, 29–30; institutionalization of, 85–91; internal reforms of, 283–97; International Department, 288–89, 296; leadership of, 44, 61, 63–66, 132–36; leadership transition within, 80–84; Mao Zedong and, 44, 63–66; members of, 112; "New Democracy" (xin minzhuzhuyi), 4; Organization Department, 88, 123; "people-centered" principle and, 45; political power of, 4–5, 212–25; political reforms and, 3, 6, 10, 37; on rule of law, 46–47, 55–56; Taiwan and, 302–20; Three Objectives strategy of, 48; Two Objectives strategy of, 48; as ultimate authority, 10–11, 26–27, 157. *See also* CCP Central Committee

Chinese Communist Youth League (CCYL), 50, 108

Chinese Lessons: Five Classmates and the Story of the New China (Pomfret), 251

Chinese Ministry of Public Affairs, 11
Chinese People's Political Consultative Conference (CPPCC), 62, 85
Chinese Republican Revolution, 181
Christianity, 11
Chun Doo Hwan, 180
Civic institutions/organizations, 10–11, 50
"Civilian-run non-enterprise units" (CRNEUs), 50
Civil liberties, 10–11
Civil-military relations, 17, 267–77
Civil society (gongmin shehui), 15; elements of, 48–49; emergence of, 50; "rights defense" movement and, 174–76
CMC. *See* Central Military Commission
CNOOC. *See* China National Offshore Oil Corporation
CNPC. *See* China National Petroleum Corporation
Collective decisionmaking, 64–66, 92, 124
Collective leadership: Deng Xiaoping on, 66–71; dynamics of elite/leadership politics and, 61–62, 75–78, 81, 84, 196; institutionalization of, 64–66; long-term prospects for, 75–78; system of, 64–66
College entrance examinations, 102–03
Collusion, 243–44
"Color revolutions," 218, 283, 292
Communism, 17, 76–77, 283–97
Communist Party League, 31
Company Law *(2005)*, 186–87
"Conditional compliance," concept of, 17, 268–70
Confucianism, 304
Constitution (xianfa), 10–11
Constitutionalism (xianzheng), 10, 199–201
Contract Law *(1999)*, 186–87, 189
Cooperative Health Care, 145
Corruption, 16; CCP and, 229–47; in China, 229–47; collusive, 243–44; costs of, 237–38; democracy and, 243–47; enforcement record of, 230–36; financial sector and, 240–41; high-risk sectors of, 238–41; infrastructural projects and, 238–39; insurance industry and, 240; in

key institutions, 242–47; land acquisition/leases and, 239–40; magnitude/scope of, 236–38; maiguan-maiguan (buying/selling of government appointments) and, 241, 242–43, 246; measures, anti-, 245–46; pharmaceutical industry and, 241; across sectors, 241
CPPCC. *See* Chinese People's Political Consultative Conference
CRNEUs. *See* "Civilian-run non-enterprise units"
Cuba, 287, 291–92
Cuban Communist Party, 291–92
Cui Jian, 177
Cui Zhiyuan, 34
Cultural Revolution, 14, 46, 200, 243; decade during, 61, 100–01; repression during, 55
Cultural/social conditions, 35
Czechoslovakia, 285

Dahl, Robert, 8
Daqing oil field, 121, 124, 134, 136
Darfur crisis, 131–32
Dazhai model, 34
Decision of the CPC Central Committee on Enhancing the Party's Ruling Capacity, 287
Democracy: as "adventure of political idea," 5; as competitive political system, 7–8; corruption and, 243–47; definitions of, 7, 26–27; Hu Jintao on, 28–29, 35; ideological innovation/political change associated with, 50–53, 56–57; implementation of, 29–30; incremental, 3, 44, 53–56; "inner-party," 107–11, 218; institutions and, 7–8; intellectuals on, 32–36, 40–41; liberals' concerns/views regarding, 36–41; methods and procedures in, 7; modernity and, 34, 35; new political ideas in, 44–49, 56–57; "new wave" of discourse in, 2–5; orderly, 55; purpose and source of, 7; rejection of, 33; socialist, 28–29, 316; universalism and characteristics of, 5–12; Wen Jiabao on, 25, 27–28, 35

"Democracy Is a Good Thing," 29–30, 113
"Democracy wave" debates, 3
Democratic consultation meetings, 222–23
Democratic People's Republic of Korea
　　(DPRK), 288–90
Democratization, 153–55, 319; CCP on,
　　53–57; by installment, 18; legalization
　　without, 15–16, 185–204; rule of law
　　and, 55–56, 57
Demographics, 16–17
Dengism, 34
Deng Xiaoping, 37–38, 55, 80, 105, 190,
　　192, 268; agenda of institutionalization,
　　62–66, 80; on collective leadership,
　　66–71; on "emancipating the mind,"
　　44–45; era, 61, 165–66; legacy of,
　　85–91, 212; on Second Generation, 68;
　　successor to, 80, 84, 85–92
Department of Social Associations. *See*
　　Bureau of Civil Organizations
Diamond, Larry, 317
Dissidents, Chinese, 26
DPRK. *See* Democratic People's Republic of
　　Korea
Du Qinglin, 100

East Asia, 294, 318
Eastern Europe, 283–87, 296–97
Economic Contract Law *(1981),* 186
Education, 259–60
Eighteenth CCP Congress, 74, 92
Eighth Central Committee's Fifth Plenum,
　　64
Eighth Party Congress, 64–65
Elections: direct, 9, 26–27, 51; indirect, 9,
　　26–27; public, 222–23; village, 10,
　　26–27, 51, 198
Eleventh Central Committee: Fifth Plenum
　　of, 66; Third Plenum of, 62, 63, 66–67
Eleventh Five Year Plan, 147–48, 150
Elite democracy, future leadership transition
　　toward, 92–93
Elite politics: of CCP, 61–62, 75–78, 81,
　　84, 196; division of labor among, 90,
　　110–11; institutionalization and dynam-

ics of, 61–62, 75–78, 81, 84; NOCs
　　and, 135–36
"Emancipating the Mind, Seeking Truth
　　from Facts and Unite as One in Looking
　　to the Future," 44
Energy Leading Group, 129
Enterprise Income Taxation Law, 187
Environment/environmental policies, 147,
　　150
"Era, Mission, and Readiness," 102
Ethiopia, 131
Europe, 283
Exceptionalism, 34–35

Falun Gong, 11, 172, 190
Federation of Commerce, 260, 312
Federation of Industry, 260, 312
Fei Guo, 256
Feng Jianshen, 106
Fewsmith, Joseph, 293
Fifteenth Central Committee, 69, 73, 132
Fifteenth National Congress, 47
Fifteenth Party Congress, 86, 89
Fifth Generation, 277; adolescent experi-
　　ences of, 100–02; bipartisanship and,
　　107–08, 114–15; defining characteristics
　　of, 99–107; as diverse and famous "Class
　　of *1982*," 102–03; ideas of, 30–32;
　　"inner-party democracy" and, 107–11,
　　218; as lawyers and technocrats, 104,
　　106–07; leaders, 14, 26, 70; postgradu-
　　ate degrees/study fields of, 103–05; tuan-
　　pai leaders and, 109–11; upcoming,
　　98–99; Western educational experience
　　of, 105–06. *See also* Neoconservatism
Fourteenth CCP Congress, 68, 82–83
Fourteenth Central Committee Politburo,
　　73
Fourth Generation, 82, 89, 103, 105–06,
　　115, 310
Fu Chengyu, 122
Fuyang Intermediate Court, 242

Gandhi family, 294
Gang of Four, 200

Gao Yangwen, 133

GDP. *See* Gross domestic product

George Soros Foundation, 285

German Democratic Republic, 286

Germany, 295

Gerontocracy, 83

Globalization, 35, 122, 135

Gong Xiangrui, 37

Google, 171

Gorbachev, Mikhail, 76–77, 284, 285–86

Government(s), 3, 37; central, 16; cooperative state, 33–34, 39; current policy shift in, 149–56; GDP of, 145–47, 252; innovation of, 218–23; left tilt in economic policy within, 142–57; local, 16, 216–18; service-oriented, 52

Great Britain, 11, 285, 295

Great Firewall of China, 161

Greenberg, Maurice R., 4

Gross domestic product (GDP), 162, 237–38; of China, 145–47, 252; green, 150

Guangming Daily, 163

Gu Mu, 133

Guo Boxiong, 69

Habermas, Jürgen, 11

Hadley, Steven, 271

Hainan Province, 135, 136

Han Changfu, 109

Han Fei, 309

Han Guizhi, 242, 243

Han Jianlin, 242

Han Zheng, 99

Harmonious society (hexie shehui), 252; class reconciliation/struggle and, 49; Hu Jintao on, 31, 109, 143, 185

He Guoqiang, 31, 132

He Jiadong, 36

Helsinki Process, 285

He Qinglian, 244

Heshang (River Elegy), 170

He Weifang, 36, 200

Hong Kong, 32, 74, 190; stock exchange, 122–23, 124

Hou Wujie, 244

Hua Guofeng, 81, 83

Hu Angang, 3

Huanqiao ribao (Global Times), 163

Hu Jintao, 3–4, 10, 45, 153, 156, 192–93, 268–69, 271, 283, 292; on democracy in China, 28–29, 35; economic policies of, 15, 142; on harmonious society, 31, 109, 143, 185; leadership of, 61–64, 71, 73–75, 92, 108–09, 114; "legalization without democratization" under, 15–16, 185–204; successor to, 75, 80–84; Tuanpai leaders and, 108–09, 111–14

Hu Jiwei, 36

Human rights (renquan), 1–2, 46, 190

Hungary, 285, 286

Huntington, Samuel, 304

Hu Yaobang, 66–67, 81, 82

ICBMs. *See* Intercontinental ballistic missiles

Incomes, 213, 214, 258–61

"Incremental democracy" (jianjin minzhu), 3, 44, 53–56

India, 5, 6

Indonesia, 294

Industrial policies, 147–49, 151

Informatization, 174

Institute of Soviet and East European Studies, 284

Institutionalization: of CCP, 85–91; of collective leadership, 64–66; Deng Xiaoping's agenda of, 62–66, 80; dynamics of elite/leadership politics and, 61–62, 75–78, 81, 84, 196; formal process of, 86; long-term prospects for, 75–78; during Mao era, 86–87; of policymaking process, 94; political, 7–8, 14, 89–91, 94; of political participation, 94; of political process and Jiang Zemin, 85–91; of political succession, 80–95; in post-Mao politics, 62; of power, 94

Intercontinental ballistic missiles (ICBMs), 267, 269–70

International Covenant on Civil and Political Rights, 190

International Covenant on Economic, Social and Cultural Rights, 190
Internet, 4, 100, 169; control of, 171–73; growth of, 166–67; users of, 163–64, 167, 172
Internet Affairs Bureau of the State Council Information Office, 171

Japan, 190, 276, 294, 315
Jiang Daming, 102
Jiang Jianqing, 101, 106
Jiang Jiemin, 122, 134, 136
Jiang Qing, 66
Jiang Zemin, 4, 15, 63–64, 108, 142–43, 153–54, 156, 213, 268–69; leadership of, 69, 73–74, 85–94, 114, 188; retirement of, 80; succession of, 80–84, 93
Jiaodian fangian (Focus Report), 165–66
Jiao Guobiao, 169
Jia Qinglin, 75
Joffe, Ellis, 17
John L. Thornton China Center, 12
Judges, 189–90, 195
Judicial systems, 3; independence of, 10, 27; reforms and, 9–10; "supervision" (jiandu) within, 9

Kang Xiaoguang, 33
Khilnani, Sunil, 5
Khrushchev, Nikita, 287
Kickbacks, 238–39, 241
Kinetic kill vehicle (KKV), 270
KKV. *See* Kinetic kill vehicle
KMT. *See* Taiwan's Koumintang Party

Labor: elite politics division of, 90, 110–11; rights, 1–2
Lan Chengzhang, 177
Latin America, 277, 294, 295
Law(s), 106–07, 318; administrative, 10, 192–93, 194; autonomous legality/party-state and, 191–93; civil, 194; criminal, 192, 194; demand/supply of, 193–97; democratic institutions and, 7–8; economic, 186–87, 192–94; establishment

of, 10; implementation/institutions of, 188–90; letter of, 175; organs of, 29; political, 190–91; PRC and international norms/reforms, 186–91; provincial, 10; regulations and, 236–37; respect for, 8; rise of, 15–16; rule the country by, 190. *See also* Rule of law
Law on the Organization of Village Committees, 51
Lawyers, 10, 106–07, 189–90, 195
Lee Teng-hui, 294
Legality, 196; constitutionalism and, 199–201; democracy and, 197–99, 202–04; populism and, 201–02
"Legalization without democratization," 15–16, 185–204
Leninism, 180–81, 291, 309
Lianzheng zhoukan (Government Integrity Weekly), 241
Liberalization: Bourgeois, 81; media, 161, 179–81
Liberals: concerns/views of, 36–41; critiques of, 34
Li Changchun, 155
Li Datong, 169
Li Hongzhong, 102, 106
Li Huijian, 200
Li Junru, 92, 213
Li Keqiang, 31, 74–75, 99, 101–02, 104, 109
Lin Biao, 82
Ling Jihua, 99
Ling Zhijun, 1
Lin Hujia, 133
Li Peng, 130
Li Rongrong, 155
Li Rui, 36–37
Liu Jingbao, 240
Liu Shaoqi, 49, 65, 82
Liu Yandong, 100
Liu Yunshan, 73
Liu Zhijun, 100
Li Wen, 293
Li Xinde, 172
Li Yizhong, 124, 132

Li Yuanchao, 31–32, 74–75, 99; as Fifth Generation leader, 101, 104, 106, 109, 113–14
Li Yuchang, 102
Local autonomy, 51
Localism, 88–89
"Lost Generation," 98–99, 100. *See also* Fifth Generation
Lou Jiwei, 99, 102, 110, 155
Lucheng District Shoe Industry Association, 219
Luo Gan, 29, 71, 105
Lu Zhangong, 101–02

Ma De, 242, 243, 244
Ma Fucai, 124, 129, 134
Maiguan-maiguan (buying/selling of government appointments), 241, 242–43, 246
Ma Kai, 100, 102, 110
Malaysia, 293
Males/men, 255
Maoism, 34
Mao Xianglin, 291
Mao Zedong, 29, 36, 50, 142, 170, 268; CCP and, 44, 63–66; experiments/models under, 34–35; "Great Democracy" (da minzhu) of, 4; institutionalization during era of, 86–87; legacy of, 81, 82, 212; politics of, 62–64, 80; totalitarian regime of, 2, 61
Marketization, 122, 174
Marxism, 291; Chinese, 35–36; theories of, 46
Mass disturbances, 175
Ma Ying-Jeou, 113
Media: broadcast, 165–66, 170–71; commercialization, 15, 164–65; control, 168, 173–76; decommercialization, 164; freedom of, 10–11; independent, 15, 313; liberalization, 161, 179–81; mass, 4, 162–65, 179–82; print, 162–65, 169, 179–82; radio as, 165–66; role of, 176–77; state's regulatory apparatus of, 168–73; telecommunications and, 11; television as, 165–66

Medium-range ballistic missile (MRBM), 270
Meng Jianzhu, 100
Meritocracy, 6
Mexico, 295
Microsoft, 171
Middle class, 2, 258–61
Middle East, 277
Migrants, 2, 16–17, 255–57
Military, 92–93; -civil relations, 17, 267–77
Ministry of Energy (MOE), 128–29
Ministry of Land Resources, 239
Ministry of Petroleum (MOP), 123, 128
Min Weifang, 101, 102, 105
MOE. *See* Ministry of Energy
Mohamad, Mahathir, 293
MOP. *See* Ministry of Petroleum
Movement to Emancipate the Niger Delta, 131
MRBM. *See* Medium-range ballistic missile
"Multiparty cooperation" (duodang hezuo), 29

NAFTA. *See* North American Free Trade Association
Nathan, Andrew, 283
National Audit Agency, 236–37
National Bureau of Statistics (NBS), 258
National Committee of the Chinese People's Political Consultative Conference, 260
National Council of Industry and Commerce, 312
National Development and Reform Commission (NDRC), 124, 130, 148, 149
National Endowment for Democracy (NED), 285
National Inspector General of Land, 149
Nationalism, 4
National Leading Group on Governmental Transparency, 51
National oil companies (NOCs), 14, 137; elite politics and, 135–36; energy bureaucracy and, 128–29; growing independence and power of, 125–29; impact on China's leadership by, 132–36; impact

on national policies/projects by, 129–32; investment approval system/party-state control of, 124–25; nomenklatura system and, 123–24; oil pricing by, 129–30; party-states and, 122–25; PRC and, 121–22; profits of, 126; senior management of, 126–27. *See also* "Petroleum faction"

National People's Congress (NPC), 3, 169, 258; chairmanships of, 85–86; Electoral Law of, 51; Eleventh, 14, 74; human rights and, 46; sessions of, 62; Standing Committee, 50, 51, 52

NBS. *See* National Bureau of Statistics

NDRC. *See* National Development and Reform Commission

NED. *See* National Endowment for Democracy

Negotiations, 55

Neoconservatism, 14, 32–33, 293. *See also* New Left

New Left, 32–33. *See also* Neoconservatism

News Reporter, 177

"New Thinking," 286

New York stock exchange, 122–23, 124

New York Times, 170, 171, 178, 271

NGOs. *See* Nongovernmental organizations

Nigeria, 131

Ninth Congress *(1969),* 66

NOCs. *See* National oil companies

Nomenklatura system, 123–24

Nongovernmental organizations (NGOs), 292, 302; Chinese, 10–11, 37; development/roles of, 218, 219, 246; environmental, 176

"Nongovernmental society" (minjian shehui), 48

North American Free Trade Association (NAFTA), 295

Northeast Revitalization Plan, 149

North Korea, 287, 288–90, 292

NPC. *See* National People's Congress

Ogaden National Liberation Front, 131

"On the Reform of the System of Party and System Leadership," 61, 80

Ostpolitik strategy, 285

Pan Wei, 112–13, 204

Pareto optimality, 54–55

Partido Revolucionario Institucional (PRI), 295

Party-state(s): autonomous legality/law and, 191–93; NOCs and, 122–25; non-communist, 293–97

Peasants, 51, 192–93, 222

Pei Minxin, 154

Pempel, T. J., 315

"People-centered" principle (yi ren wei ben), 45

People's Action Party, 293

People's Daily, 28, 37, 109, 163, 168, 172, 178

People's Liberation Party (PLA), 267–70; authority/control of, 84, 87–89, 93; General Armaments Department, 271; as political institution, 88

People's Republic of China (PRC), 29, 162; bipartisanship in, 107–08, 114–15; constitution of, 63; establishment of, 45; international norms/law/reforms in, 186–91; national legal system of, 10, 50–51, 106–07; oil companies and, 121–37; political power of, 4–5; political succession within, 14, 80–95

People's University, 33

Peru, 295

PetroChina, 124, 126, 131

PetroKazakhstan, 125

"Petroleum faction," 121, 133–36

Philippines, 294

PLA. *See* People's Liberation Party

Pluralization, 37, 39; under monolithic leadership, 37; of social interests, 29

Poland, 285

Policymaking, 90

Politburo, 37–38

Politburo Standing Committee, 29, 61, 63, 276; authority of, 67–68; creation of, 64; members of, 69–75, 99–100; organization of, 65–71; provincial party secretaries of, 68; Secretariat of, 61, 74

Political choices, 4–5, 7–8
Political civilization (zhengzhi wenming), 48
Political development, 1–2, 5–13, 54, 86
Political leaders, 3–4, 10–13, 27–30
Political stability, 33–34, 55
Political systems, 152–57
Political trajectory, 25–40
Political transparency, 51–52
Pomfret, John, 102, 251
Population, 2, 10, 51, 253
Populism, 201–02
Poverty, urban, 257–61
PRC. *See* People's Republic of China
Press Freedom Index *(2006),* 161
PRI. *See* Partido Revolucionario Institucional
Private entrepreneurs/firms, 2, 112, 258–61
Private property (siyou caichan), 47
Production/public ownership, 47
Property Law *(2007),* 47, 52–53, 187, 192–93, 200
Provinces, 51
Public attitudes, 214–16
Public health, 1–2
Public recommendations, 222–23
Public Security Bureau, 171
Public service, 51
Pye, Lucien, 304

Qiao Shi, 89
Qin Hui, 36

"The Reasons for the Changes in Eastern Europe and Their Lessons," 285
Redistribution/pro-rural shift, 144–45, 151–52
Redistributive budget, 145–47
"Reform and opening" policy, 1
Religious freedom, 1–2, 11
Renmin wang (People's Net), 163
Reporters without Borders, 161
"Resolution on Enhancing the Governing Capacity of the CCP," 29, 56
Rigby, T. H., 76
"Rightists," 196

Rights-protection (weiquan) activists, 26
The Rise of Great Powers, 113
Romania, 285, 286
Rule by law (yifa zhiguo), 46
Rule of law (fa zhi), 8, 10, 15–16; CCP on, 46–47; concept of, 46–47, 175; deepening of, 50–51; democratization and, 55–56, 57; development of, 55–56
Rural sector, 252
Rural-to-urban migration, 2

Sanlian shenghuo zhoukan (Sanlian Life Weekly), 177
SAPP. *See* State Administration of Press and Publication
SARFT. *See* State Administration of Radio, Film, and Television
SARS (Severe Acute Respiratory Syndrome), 52, 173–74, 177, 197
SASAC. *See* State-Owned Asset Supervision and Administration Commission
Schattschneider, E. E., 7–8
Schumpeter, Joseph, 7
SCO. *See* Shanghai Cooperation Organization
SDPC. *See* State Development Planning Commission
Second Generation, 68
Securities Law, 186–87
SEO. *See* State Energy Office
Seventeenth Central Committee's First Plenum, 61
Seventeenth Party Congress *(2007),* 1, 61, 155–56; civil-military relations after, 17, 267–77; leaders of, 14, 26, 71–75; legalization under, 185, 198, 202–04
Severe Acute Respiratory Syndrome. *See* SARS
Sex ratio imbalances, 254–55
Shambaugh, David, 3
Shang Fulin, 103
Shanghai, 189, 193
Shanghai Cooperation Organization (SCO), 292
"Shanghai faction," 90, 91

Sheng Dewen, 36
Sheng Huaren, 132
Shengli oil field, 124
Shengli Petroleum Administration, 134
Shen Yueyue, 109
Short message service (SMS), 161, 167–68, 172, 174
Singapore, 293
Sinopec. *See* China Petrochemical Corporation
Sixteenth Central Committee, 132; Fourth Plenum of, 29, 56, 287; Politburo, 70, 71, 104–05
Sixteenth National Congress of the Chinese Communist Party, 36, 48, 49, 63, 71, 80, 86, 89, 124, 134, 135, 260
SMS. *See* Short message service
Social/cultural conditions, 35
Social future, 145, 251–61
Social interests, pluralization of, 29
SOEs. *See* State-owned enterprises
Solidarity, 285
Song Xiuyan, 101, 109
Song Zhenming, 133
Southern Metropolis, 178
Southern Metropolitan Daily, 163
Southern Weekend, 163, 178
South Korea, 180, 294
Soviet Communist Party, 76–77
Soviet Union, 76–77, 283–87, 296–97
Stalin, Joseph V., 76
State Administration of Press and Publication (SAPP), 169, 170
State Administration of Radio, Film, and Television (SARFT), 165, 170
State Asset Supervision and Administration Commission (SASAC), 123, 148
State Audit Agency, 240
State Council, 50; on administrative examination/approval system, 52; Development Research Center, 236; Executive Committee, 69; Regulations on Open Government Information, 51; white paper *(2005),* 30
State Development Planning Commission (SDPC), 129

State Energy Office (SEO), 129
State-owned enterprises (SOEs), 14, 147, 152, 240–41, 245
State Planning Commission, 121, 128–29, 134, 148
Straits Times, 170
Sudan, 131–32, 188
Suharto family, 294
"Sunan model," 218
Sun Jingwen, 133
Sun Yat-sen, 181
Supergirl's Voice, 165–66, 167
Supreme People's Court, 195
Supreme People's Procuratorate, 238
Su Shulin, 122, 132, 136
Swaine, Michael, 268
Sweden, 285
"Sweep Away Pornography and Strike Down Illegal Publications," 172
Syria, 295

Taiwan, 6, 113, 137, 292, 294; as agent of change, 317–20; CCP and, 302–20; "democratization by installment" and, 18; political development within, 17–18, 180; population of, 305–09
Taiwan Provincial Assembly, 314
Taiwan's Koumintang Party (KMT), 137, 294; evolution of, 309–10; as monopoly, 311–13; political fortunes of, 302–03; political participation/representation by, 314–17; social foundation of, 311
Taiwan's Nationalist Party, 113
Takung Pao, 3
Tang Ke, 133
Tax reforms, 187, 213
Telecommunications, 11
Tenth National People's Congress, 47
Thailand, 294
Third Generation, 68, 70, 88, 115
Thirteenth Central Committee's First Plenum, 67
Thirteenth National Congress, 52–53
Thirteenth Party Congress, 37–38, 67
Thornton, John, 27–28

"Three People's Principles" (sanminzhuyi), 4
"Three Represents" theory, 213, 311
Tiananmen crisis, 7, 17, 70, 81–82, 188, 190, 219, 243, 276
Townships, 34
Tsou Tang, 34
Tuanpai leaders: Fifth Generation and, 109–11; Hu Jintao and, 108–09, 111–14
Twelfth Central Committee, 67, 69
Twelfth Party Congress, 66
21st Century Economic Herald, 163

UMNO. *See* United Malays National Organization
Underclass, new, 257–61
Unemployment, 257–61
Unicom, 172
Unions, 285
United Malays National Organization (UMNO), 293
United Nations Convention Against Torture, 190
United Nations Human Rights Council, 190
United States (U.S.), 5–6, 38, 61, 276, 292, 315–16
Universalism: characteristics of Chinese democracy and, 5–12; "people-centered" principle, humanism and, 45; Wen Jiabao on, 9–10
Unocal, 125, 188
Urbanization, 16–17, 255–57
Urban land, 149, 150
Urban poverty, 257–61
U.S. *See* United States
U.S. National Democratic Institute, 285

VCP. *See* Vietnamese Communist Party
Velvet Revolution, 285
Venezuela, 295
Vietnam, 287, 290
Vietnamese Communist Party (VCP), 37, 290
Village: elections, 10, 26–27, 51, 198; enterprises, 34

Wang Anshun, 132, 136
Wang Hui, 34
Wang Huning, 99, 106
Wang Jun, 101
Wang Juntao, 32, 102
Wang Keqin, 177
Wang Min, 104, 105
Wang Qishan, 31, 100, 102, 110
Wang Ruoshui, 161, 179
Wang Tianpu, 136
Wang Xuebing, 240
Wang Yang, 99, 109
Wang Zhaoyao, 244
Wang Zhen, 284
Washington Post, 3, 102
Wei Liucheng, 132, 135–36
Wen Jiabao, 3–4, 31, 108, 153, 204, 322; on democracy in China, 25, 27–28, 35; economic policies of, 15, 142–43; on universalism, 9–10
Wenling, 221
Wenzhou, 218–20
West-East Pipeline, 129, 130–31
Western Development Plan, 149
Women, 255, 256, 259
Women's Federation, 50
World Bank's Development Report, 257
World Trade Organization (WTO), 149, 187–88, 295
WTO. *See* World Trade Organization
Wu Aiying, 99, 101, 109
Wu Bao'an, 242
Wu Guanzheng, 71
Wuhan's Intermediate Court, 242
Wu Yi, 132
Wu Zhenghan, 242

Xibaipo, 142
Xie Tao, 112–13
Xi Jinping, 31, 91, 99, 101, 104, 110, 156
Xi Linhua, 136
Xinhua News Agency, 163, 168, 169–70, 175, 176–77
Xi Zhongxun, 31
Xu Dingming, 129

Xu Guojian, 242, 243
Xu Kuangdi, 106
Xu Xiaogang, 244

Yahoo, 171
Yang Baibing, 85, 87
Yang Jiechi, 100, 106
Yang Shangkun, 85, 87
Yan Xuetong, 113
Ye Jianying, 67
"Youth League faction," 90
Youth Weekend, 178
Yuan Chunqing, 104, 109
Yu Keping, 8–9, 29–30, 113, 204
Yu Qiuli, 121, 133–34

Zeng Peiyan, 71, 155
Zeng Qinghong, 75, 108, 132, 134
Zhai Huqu, 105
Zhang Baoshun, 101, 109

Zhang Chunxian, 99
Zhang Dejiang, 105
Zhang Engzhao, 240
Zhang Gaoli, 132, 136
Zhang Lichang, 71
Zhang Nianchi, 113
Zhang Qingli, 109
Zhang Wannian, 69
Zhang Yi, 253
Zhang Zhen, 133
Zhao Leji, 99
Zhao Ziyang, 37–39, 67, 81, 82
Zhejiang Province, 218–20, 221
Zhou Enlai, 66
Zhou Ruijin, 37, 113, 178
Zhou Xiaochuan, 100, 110, 155
Zhou Yongkang, 32, 132, 136
Zhu De, 66
Zhu Houze, 36
Zhu Rongji, 88–89, 130–31, 143